Star Wars Meets the Eras of Feminism

Star Wars Meets the Eras of Feminism
of Feminism

Weighing All the Galaxy's Women Great and Small

Valerie Estelle Frankel

LEXINGTON BOOKS
Lanham • Boulder • New York • London

Published by Lexington Books
An imprint of The Rowman & Littlefield Publishing Group, Inc.
4501 Forbes Boulevard, Suite 200, Lanham, Maryland 20706
www.rowman.com

6 Tinworth Street, London SE11 5AL, United Kingdom

British Library Cataloguing in Publication Information Available

Library of Congress Cataloging-in-Publication Data Available

ISBN 978-1-4985-8386-2 (cloth)
ISBN 978-1-4985-8387-9 (electronic)
ISBN 978-1-4985-8388-6 (pbk.)

Contents

Introduction   vii

1: The Original Trilogy Meets Seventies Feminism

1   The Mighty Token Female   3

II: The Girl Power Prequel Era

2   Warrior Queen Turned Romance Heroine   43

3   Introducing the Legends: Mara, Jaina, and the New Jedi Order   109

4   The Butt-Kicking Teen: Ahsoka   119

III: The Fourth Wave Hits the Sequel Era

5   Rey, Maz, Rose, Leia, Holdo, and Phasma   161

6   Redefining Cartoons: *Star Wars Rebels*   227

7   From Picture Books to *Forces of Destiny*: Multimedia for Younger Fans   255

8   Rewriting the Galaxy with *Rogue One*   271

9   Balanced Genders: Disney's Original Era Comics   283

10   Back to the Binary *Solo* Western   295

Conclusion: The Lasting Legacy   325

Works Cited   327

Index   341

About the Author   353

Introduction

Star Wars is one of the most popular franchises of all time, setting the standard for science fiction films. It also raised the bar for action women, as blaster-toting Princess Leia destroyed barriers as one of the very first to defend herself and her teammates on the big screen. With this, she carried science fiction into the feminist era, proving that she could hold her own, and more importantly, that audiences would adore her for it. She was mouthy, funny, authoritative, smart—a dazzling role model. Ignominiously, however, she ended her trilogy with the gold bikini, with actress Carrie Fisher unsuspecting that this would spark multiple generations' teenage lust and objectification. Further, there were basically no other women in the trilogy—Luke's clichéd peacemaker aunt makes breakfast, and Mon Mothma, a stand-in leader with almost no screen-time, provides a figurehead in the third film. Toss in a couple Ewok moms and a sacrificed alien dancing girl, and the list is basically complete.

Princess Leia's story reveals much about the movie-making filmscape of the time and emphasizes even more about the nature of her audience. In fact, the alternating toughness and sexualization exemplified her audience's worry over the recent feminist strides and their subsequent backlash into postfeminism. This examination of culture is fascinating as a glimpse into the female role models science fiction provides . . . especially as new eras followed Leia's.

For every period of *Star Wars*, there are correspondences with the culture of the time. By now, there are many metrics for evaluating these characters, all with plenty of buzzwords—representation, diversity, tokenism, the Bechdel Test, the Smurfette Principle. All are imperfect but provide useful lenses through which to examine the role models the films and shows are presenting. Meanwhile, dress and gaze reveal a great deal beyond individual agency, emphasizing whether the franchise is presenting warriors or models.

1999 marked *Star Wars'* long-anticipated return with the prequel series. This galaxy offered more women and people of color. However, the new heroine, Queen Padmé Amidala, spent her time in such intricate outfits that she could barely move. In fact, she harnessed these as her superpower, switching with a decoy so she could don a simple wool tunic and go out on desert adventures. Nonetheless, as a distressed queen needing rescue by the Jedi heroes and as a teen elected for her innocent *lack* of experience, she's more damsel than heroine. Still, the blame shouldn't all go to filmmakers. Like Leia, Padmé fit well into her era. The nineties' version of feminism stressed girl power—heroines whose strength was undercut by frills and bows as well as a juvenile or campy look. They were supergirls—mighty but frivolous and eager for passion. As Padmé's own romance overshadows her plot, she soon tumbles into this trope. By her third film, she's so caught in her tragic romance that it kills her, even as she begins living another critical work of the era—*Reviving Ophelia.*

"Did you know that 96 percent of the *Star Wars* universe is controlled by white men? Yes, this is true. In the forty-one years since *Star Wars* first hit the big screen, between the writers, directors, and executive producers spanning three different trilogies—and now various one-off stand-alone stories—just about every single person calling the shots has been a white man" (Paige 2018). Sometimes, as with Rey and Rose, the characters appear believable. Other times, with drippy Padmé or the fridged caricatures of *Solo,* there's more of a problem.

The sequel era of 2015 created a new kind of heroine with Rey and Jyn: both are respected fighters, equal partners with the men, who are never sexualized or stripped. Both defeat the male villains and save the day, emphasizing their competence—though Rey was in fact so skilled that she drew comments of being *too* superpowered. Embracing the culture of the twenty-first century, her film responded to online criticism and cast more women—not just older Leia, but mentor Maz Kanata, chrometrooper Phasma, and a plethora of background characters of all races and ages. *The Last Jedi* built on this with new central heroine Rose Tico and a friend for General Leia in Admiral Holdo. The new era insisted on respect for women with its new competent professionals leading the charge. Further, like *Rogue One, Last Jedi* emphasized an end to the chosen one story (which privileged a single hero, most often white, young, and male) and emphasized that a galaxy of the underprivileged were now welcome to join the Resistance. Clearly the sequels, corresponding to an emerging fourth wave of global and internet-based feminism, were striking down glass ceilings in space. At the time of writing, filmmaking has found a new level of diversity and representation with nonsexualized, multiracial, and—above all—competent girls and women starring in *Wonder Woman, Black Panther, Mad Max: Fury Road, Frozen, Moana, A Wrinkle in Time, Ghostbusters,* and so many other celebrated films.

Of course, examining only the films leaves out a great deal. Two television shows—*Star Wars: The Clone Wars* (2008–2015) and *Star Wars: Rebels* (2010–2018) have spanned the second and third movie eras with their own takes on third- and fourth-wave feminism. In fact, the former show stars the franchise's first female Jedi protagonist—and a minority alien to boot. Ahsoka charmed boys and girls with her irrepressible energy and cleverness . . . though in girl power fashion, she spent years in a tube top. *Rebels* moved forward for a new generation—it offered two women, splitting the representation and giving the Bechdel test a shove forward. Hera is the respected captain and leader of their band. Still, she most often remains on the ship, leaving the younger heroes to go in shooting. Among these is Sabine, a punk-artist whose favorite act of defiance is graffitiing imperial property, and often the imperials themselves. As a Mandalorian, she generally wears her full armor and helmet—desexualizing herself even as she personalizes it all with her painting. In contrast with Ahsoka and Anakin's master-and-padawan relationship, the team of *Rebels* trade authority back and forth, each stepping up to contribute for a more egalitarian model.

Beginning in 2017, the children's spinoff *Star Wars: Forces of Destiny* offered a new model with girl-featured stories. The heroines rescue themselves and others while displaying courage and friendship. It's a transmedia brand, with action figures, short YouTube cartoons, and books for different ages. Clearly, Disney is making an effort to move beyond the strict gender segregation of action heroes for boys and princesses for girls. Still, while the *Star Wars* picture books for the youngest children offer some agency in their role models, there are even more static figures and damsels awaiting rescue.

For decades, the novels, computer games, comics, and so forth expanded the universe. They offered many multifaceted women like Luke's love Mara Jade and Leia and Han's Jedi-mechanic daughter Jaina. Though this universe was de-canonized by Disney and referred to as *Star Wars: Legends*, the books are still available, and much of their extensive worldbuilding was used in the prequel era and beyond. Still, only a little of this is included, in order to focus on the films as central. Likewise, small tidbits from the new canon novels, which tie in even more closely to the films, are included mainly for reference and backstory, along with cast interviews, film guides, and other secondary sources.

This book mainly examines female portrayal in the three eras, compared to trends of the time, and explores how well they're presented. For filmmakers, feminists, and eager fans, it's a question emerging alongside the new era of storytelling, addressing where it's headed and how much further there is to go.

1

The Original Trilogy
Meets Seventies Feminism

ONE

The Mighty Token Female

LEIA, WARRIOR PRINCESS

"Without Carrie Fisher's Leia, there may have never been a Xena, an Elsa, or a Daenerys Targaryen. Luckily none of those princesses—or the many to come—have had to wait for a man to come along to save them. They know they can save themselves" (Dockterman 2017b, 38). Before the release of Episode IV in 1977, women, let alone strong women, were rare in science fiction. However, Princess Leia became instantly beloved for her toughness, proving that women had a part in outer space adventures. Now many regard her as one of the best female characters ever created (Game of Nerds 2015). Laura Dern, who starred in Episode VIII, notes, "For us growing up it was like, 'Oh! Women can be sensual and complicated and tough and fiery, and be a badass, and be a superhero'" (Yamato 2017). Fan Diana Dominguez (2007) writes of the original film:

> Leia's impact cannot be dismissed. Teenagers like me in the late 1970s were the first group of girls on the verge of womanhood who could hear their parents say, "you can be anything you want," and have it be true. The problem was we had few visible role models to follow into that wide "anything" world. Our mothers may have been the pioneers of the contemporary women's movement, burning bras, taking birth control pills, and breaking all-male barriers down, but we were the first generation to have to fulfill the promise of "business as usual." We were no longer "door-busters," but we weren't really status quo yet. Lucas's portrayal of Leia as a no-nonsense, outspoken, unquestioned leader, who happens to be female, a princess, and unpunished for pushing the traditional boundaries of gender, shattered, for me at least, the unspoken assumption of what waited in my future. (129)

Leia arrived during an era of change, as the first female Air Force pilots graduated in 1977. The seventies were packed with feminist marches and protests, creating an era most call the Second Wave (following the nineteenth and early twentieth centuries First Wavers' campaign for the vote). Martha Rampton explains in "Four Waves of Feminism" how the era began with protests against the demeaning "cattle parade" as the women called the Miss America pageants in 1968 and 1969: "The radical New York group called the Redstockings staged a counter pageant in which they crowned a sheep as Miss America and threw 'oppressive' feminine artifacts such as bras, girdles, high-heels, makeup and false eyelashes into the trashcan." On August 26, 1970, 20,000 women marched through the streets on New York, demanding equality. That year, only 5 to 10 percent of medical and law school students were female (Gourley 2008, 7). As protests swelled, representation and opportunities began changing.

Further, the seventies emphasized the perils of the evil warmongering empire: "The backdrop to all of this is political drama like nothing seen before in this country: Watergate, and President Nixon's resignation under threat of impeachment in 1974. There's no rejoicing when the Vietnam War ends the following year and American veterans return home. This was the longest war in American history and it was a widely opposed war, and a lost war. A cloud hangs over Bicentennial celebrations in 1976. The Generation Xers have inherited a new world" (Sherman 2014, 188). Civil rights had integrated the races, emphasizing that protest could change the world. Inspired by the anti-war and civil rights movements, the New Left demanded equality in the workplace, along with reproductive rights and the long-sought Equal Rights Amendment.

As freedom and individualism were celebrated, feminism took its place among them. "The 1970s bring greater freedom of choice, and the trend trickles down to young girls, who see it modeled around them. More mothers raising kids are in college or working, divorce is on the rise, and there are more single mothers and more expanded families, with stepparents and half-siblings" (Sherman 2014, 188). Women no longer were prizes to be won but could hold careers and save themselves. A new generation of storytelling reflected this. 1973 launched *Ms. Magazine.* Its founder, Gloria Steinem, described it as "a how-to magazine for the liberated female human being—not how to make jelly but how to seize control of your life" (Gourley 2008, 23). In 1976, *Charlie's Angels* and *Laverne and Shirley* premiered on TV, to the delight of fans. Wonder Woman already ruled the small screen beside the Bionic Woman, Isis, Maude Findlay, and Mary Tyler Moore.

Still, 1977's Princess Leia was the one who broke the film barrier and almost immediately sparked a groundbreaking upswing in strong female leads. Only two years later, Ellen Ripley battled through a starship on the *Alien* series, guns blazing. In 1984's *The Terminator*, Linda Hamilton as

Sarah Connor joined her. "In this gender-charged atmosphere, Princess Leia—the only prominent female character of *A New Hope*—served as a reflection and role model for a generation of US women looking to break down the remaining gender barriers," comments Valerie Bodden in *How to Analyze the Films of George Lucas* (2012, 29).

The seventies rejected makeup, elaborately coiffed hair, and girdles. Following this revolution, Leia maintains the hair to some extent but also wears a simple gown and tough boots—not to mention the jarring black blaster. As such, she appears fully prepared for action, unlike the heroines of the sixties' *Star Trek*, laying out the captain's uniforms in their beehive-hairdos and miniskirts or screaming to be saved. "*Star Wars* has always pushed at the boundaries of its culture. Princess Leia was mainstream filmmaking's first self-rescuing princess, and the films were unstinting in depicting her importance to the military strategy of the Rebellion, reflecting an incipient 70s feminism" (Hillman 2017). George Lucas adds, "I felt that I needed to have a woman in the script. The interesting thing is she does get in jeopardy, but she is very capable of taking care of herself" (Bouzereau 1997, 14). Leia stands out as the planner and decision maker of the trilogy. Instantly she must not only take charge but rescue the men.

Further, her role as a snarky, funny princess was especially unusual. As Laura Dern adds of Carrie Fisher, "To witness her performance you see the wisdom she held at this point in her life, her art, her irreverence, her unbelievable sense of comedy" (Yamato 2017). Her actress was cast because she had great chemistry with Harrison Ford. Moreover, as Lucas considered contrasting trios—one Ford, Hamill and Fisher; the other, Christopher Walken, Will Seltzer, and Terri Nunn, he considered the latter "a little more serious, a little more realistic," while the trio he finally chose were "a little more fun, a little more goofy" (Jones 2016, 203).

As the character came into focus, her strength dominated the story. Leia kicked off the plot by hiding the plans in R2-D2 and sending him to Tatooine even as the enemy captured her. The original film novelization from 1976 (ghostwritten by Alan Dean Foster) emphasizes the moxie Leia shows from her first moments, through the eyes of a Stormtrooper:

> Once his attention turned from the girl to his communicator her shivering vanished with startling speed. The energy pistol she had held out of sight behind her came up and around as she burst from her hiding place. The trooper who had been unlucky enough to find her fell first, his head a mass of melted bone and metal. The same fate met the second armored form coming up fast behind him. Then a bright green energy pole touched the woman's side and she slumped instantly to the deck, the pistol still locked in her small palm. (Lucas [1976] 1995, 15)

"Leia almost immediately is captured by the Empire, but when confronted by her captors, she shows an incredible fearlessness, a very uncharacteristic trait of your typical damsel-in-distress," John Paul Pianka (2013, 37) comments in his thesis *The Power of the Force: Race, Gender, and Colonialism in the Star Wars Universe.* "Immediately, we know she is hunted, she is beautiful, and she is brave. She is clearly a fighter as she draws a weapon, but she is also a tactician, as she allows herself to be captured so that her droid can escape. It is a selfless, heroic moment," adds critic Trisha Barr (2018, 67). The low angle shot shows the scene from her perspective, making her the audience-identification figure on a ship of arrogant villains. It also emphasizes how Vader looms over her, making him look bigger in the frame. Despite his power here, she addresses him with cool arrogance, quipping, "Lord Vader, I should have known. Only you could be so bold. The Imperial Senate will not sit for this, when they hear you've attacked a diplomatic . . ." On the audio commentary for *A New Hope*, Lucas says Princess Leia is young, but "instead of being kind of an idealistic young farm boy from the nether lands of the galaxy [she's] very sophisticated, an urbanized ruler, a senator . . . She rules people and she's in charge."

With her verbal jab, she introduces and invokes the power of her position (presumably partly earned and partly inherited from her viceroy and senator father) to protect herself, while also claiming protection from the massive patriarchal government, shielding herself from the brutal men by summoning a higher level of the patriarchy. This makes a clever strike though also emphasizes her lack of power, as she must summon the Senate to fight for her. She stands there, smaller than all the men, watched by an American audience represented at the time by one female senator, fourteen women in the House of Representatives, and no women on the Supreme Court or in the Oval Office. Thus, the Senate becomes an image of mostly men, invoked by the young princess to save herself. How many women, fighting in court for more rights, must have likewise invoked the decisions of the patriarchy as the only way to advance their cause?

However, Vader retorts that the Senate is dissolved and with it the illusion of democracy in the galaxy. The Emperor and his subordinate Vader have full reign to torture a woman, even the privileged senator and princess who had considered herself beyond the reach of men's brutality only moments before. Vader identifies Leia as a Rebel and demands the Death Star plans. Even as she stoutly continues denying her involvement, his guards drag her away. After comes a torture scene, though one carefully left off-camera. While *Empire* has no problem visibly and audibly torturing Han later on, the first film draws the line at so hurting a woman.

Jeanne Cavelos (2006, 311) points out in her essay on gender in the franchise how Leia is tortured by Vader, a horrific act weakened by being cut. "We are shown a needle and are told her resistance is 'considerable,' but we don't see her resistance. Heaven forbid we see a woman in pain! But 'sparing' us from that removes the heroism from Leia's captivity and makes her simply an object to be rescued." While Leia was scheduled to be tortured, "it would take Lucas one more draft to develop a distaste for putting a bruised and battered woman in his movie" (Taylor 121).

Still, the torture scene is portrayed in detail in the 1981 radio adaptation. Starring Mark Hamill and Anthony Daniels, it was consumed by a mainstream audience—increasing NPR's regular audience by 40 percent, setting records at the time. It expanded the film into thirteen half-hour episodes, allowing viewers to spend more time with the characters. In the torture scene, Vader invades her quarters. As she cries, "Vader keep that thing away from me" and "Let go, you stop that," and then breaks into agonized moans for a few seconds, the torture commences. Vader drugs her into a hypnotic state, and cajoles her, insisting he's a fellow Rebel who needs her help. Ironically, as he tricks her, he gets in the line "Your father orders you to tell us."

When this fails, he inflicts a universe of pain, and she begins sobbing, "help me" and "please make it stop," as he hypnotizes her to thinking her skin is on fire and that she's dying—a special effect that arguably works better on radio. Ann Sachs (radio Leia) still gets the shivers when she recalls taping that scene. "It was really scary," she says. "I'll never forget after it was finished, [Brock Peters, Darth Vader] came out to the green-room and he gave me a big hug. And I kind of clammed up as he hugged me and he said, 'Oh, you poor dear. I am so sorry'" (*NPR*). After this, he brings her once more to the peaceful state and calls for a medic to attend her. The scene is visceral in its horror, but also surprisingly emphasizes Vader's gentleness. This works for Vader's eventual revelation of their relationship, but also emphasizes her role as "the girl."

Likewise, the Expanded Universe of novelizations, comics, and other tie-ins offers a bit more depth. The novel *Death Star*, a reimagining of the story, sees prisoner-Leia through the eyes of a doctor called in to heal her as "the princess lay on the cell's platform in no small amount of distress" (Reaves and Perry 2007, 279). Unfortunately, he instantly objectifies her. He's shocked by her incongruous beauty on the soulless Death Star, and instantly sympathizes as he sees Vader is hurting her. Even as he saves the wounded young woman, the book presents cascading images of her beautiful, injured, and passive. Even in the midst of this, Leia jokes with him, offering a little attitude to break the stereotype.

In the same novel, Vader thinks admiringly that truth drugs, electrical shocks, and other tortures have had surprisingly little effect on Leia. "She was physically weakened and in considerable pain, but her mind remained shielded. She had revealed nothing. Most unusual for anyone except a Jedi to have such control" (Reaves and Perry 2007, 278). This actually removes agency from her, giving credit to her innate powers, not her determination or training. In fact, through the trilogy, her not using the Force—a magical catch-all that saves the teenage Luke over and over—emphasizes her abilities as an ordinary person, not magical girl. Her powers as authority figure, brave rebel, subversive trickster are all ones she has earned.

On being confronted with Governor Tarkin after the torture session, Leia is sassy and rude, greeting him with "Governor Tarkin, I should have expected to find you holding Vader's leash. I recognized your foul stench when I was brought on board." When she hears she's to be executed, she's unafraid and goes on to add, "I'm surprised you had the courage to take the responsibility yourself!" Her bravado in the face of a crowd of Imperials, including the looming Darth Vader, is fun and assertive—it's implied that if she is to be executed, she will go down defying her captors to the last. This strength stole the viewing audience's hearts—especially the girls who'd longed for an assertive role model.

As she's hauled before the Empire's top commanders, tortured and completely at their mercy, she gives up a useless planet rather than the one hiding her friends. Thus, Leia successfully tricks the patriarchy—both Vader and Tarkin. However, this is a short-lived defiance, as the men hold all the power: "Because *Star Wars* white women master neither technology nor the Force, they resort to passive resistance against dark masculinity," critic Gabriel S. Estrada (2007) explains. Increasing the brutality, Tarkin sentences her peaceful homeworld to destruction. Vader even holds her against his hard black armor, keeping her motionless and making her watch as Alderaan explodes. All this emphasizes her helplessness—she can defy the Empire but cannot save her planet or even herself. Fulfilling their roles as the brutal males who care nothing for spunky, clever defiance, the men then choose to punish her with execution.

After this, she practically *is* executed, since she vanishes from the story until the more active character Luke comes to find her. As the men assemble a rescue team, her recording, not herself, is their call to action. The cry of "Help me, Obi-Wan Kenobi, you're my only hope" is personal, even pathetic in its desperation. Obi-Wan, seeing it, is called to duty, while Luke is mesmerized by the princess's beauty.

Feminist film theory is a product of the Second Wave. With the slogan "the personal is the political," critics revealed the hidden power structures in books, television and movies along with reproduction, language use, fashion, and appearance, all previously accepted as a matter of course. In particular, Laura Mulvey (1975), author of the groundbreaking essay "Visual and Other Pleasures," criticizes many films for their objectified women. As she explains, "In a world ordered by sexual imbalance, pleasure in looking has been split between active/male and passive/female. . . . In their traditional exhibitionist role women are simultaneously looked at and displayed, with their appearance coded for strong visual and erotic impact so that they can be said to connote to-be-looked-at-ness." Even when the women aren't sexualized, male characters stare admiringly, taking the more dynamic role between them. Exemplifying this trope, the holo-message, gazed at by Luke, inspires him to action but also emphasizes a woman's passivity—the actual Leia is not even participating in events.

As Mulvey criticizes, cameras zoom in on men's movements but women's body parts, ogling them with a heterosexual male viewpoint. Estrada (2007) quips that Leia's "intense stare also draws attention away from her clingy wet attire that testifies that she wears no bra." Fisher (2016, 15) also describes her "no-underwear-in-space look." Soaked from the trash compactor, it's especially evident. Of course, one can argue that she isn't confined by the pre-bra-burning trappings of conventional women on earth, but this moment appears instead have been made for fan service.

Further, Fisher (2016, 42) recalls, "I had so much lip gloss on you might have slid off and broken your own lips if you tried to kiss me." She adds, "I got [the part] with the proviso that I went to a fat farm and that I lose ten pounds" (Jones 2016, 204). This contradiction of giving her a fun, assertive personality yet also objectifying her as attractive heroine (and demanding she become more attractive) exemplifies Leia's contradiction—glamorized but also prim. While she has bright red lips and dark eyeliner, her hairstyle is more striking than alluring, in dark brown instead of a fairytale princess's blonde.

Visually, this links her with another competent blaster-wielding princess, Dale Arden from the *Flash Gordon* comics and serials. Lucas pitched *Star Wars* only when he couldn't get the rights to *Flash*. "Every true believer on the set of *Star Wars* remembered it fondly" (Taylor 2014, 24). The screen wipes and roll-up credits are a direct homage. "Loving them that much when they were so awful," Lucas said after *Empire*. "I began to wonder what would happen if they were done really well" (qtd. in Taylor 2014, 24). Lucas also adored Tommy Tomorrow of Action Comics, with "sassy female character Joan Gordy" (Taylor 21). Lucas of course was setting out to make a story in this model, and present Leia as the sassy, smart girl next door. (The comics heroine often has black mid-length hair, but it's occasionally longer and brown. A slave girl outfit even makes an appearance. Coming full circle in story influence, brunette Melody Anderson's Dale from the 1980 film in elaborate gowns and headdresses looks even more similar to action-princess Leia.)

Carrie Fisher comments, "I spent the first film in a white turtlenecked dress meant to emphasize my purity" (Biggar 2005, 113). The hood gives her robe a monk or nunlike feel and the cut with high neck is very conservative. Fisher (2016, 34) recalls, "My life had started all right. Here I was crossing its threshold in a long white virginal robe with the hair of a seventeenth-century Dutch school matron." In her concealing white gown, Leia is more child or priestess than alluring teen. "When we first meet Leia, she is introduced as a senator from Alderaan, wearing a gown that exposes no skin whatsoever, and sporting a high—and—tight hairstyle. In other words, she is immediately perceived by the audience as an authority figure and is in no way over-sexualized," adds Pianka (2013, 37). The fabric is a bit luxurious—crepe de chine, a thin, lightweight silk. However, aside from this and the elaborate hairstyle, it's quite simple. Leia mentions in the comic *Union* that this look came from "Imperial chic" in which all fashions "come in severe and gray." As she adds, elegance only appeared "in the upper echelons of society. In the stratas that had insulated itself from reality" (Stackpole and Teranishi 2000). Whether or not this was the film's intent, Leia is a simple working princess and senator.

The "cinnamon buns" hairstyle is elaborate and unusual, but not styled for maximum attraction. Dominguez (2017, 116) describes it as "modeled on the traditional hairstyle of the Hopi Indian Corn Maiden, who symbolizes both fertility and wisdom and which was worn by Pancho Villa's *soldaderas* (female warriors) during the Mexican Revolution of the early 1900s." Looking at the story through a Native American lens, Estrada (2007) agrees: "Subliminally, audiences may register the strong Hopi woman's presence as a potential Clan Mother of political and religious weight symbolized by her hair and costume."

However, Luke's gaping stare and the suggestion that her beauty and form have summoned him to the Rebellion emphasize how much he is the hero and she, simply the message. She spends most of the film locked in her cell, with her hologram letter her only way of impacting the world. The fact that the heroes, without having met her, rally to save her emphasizes her power as archetype, not person. As Mulvey adds of the objectified heroine, "What counts is what the heroine provokes, or rather what she represents. She is the one, or rather the love or fear she inspires in the hero, or else the concern he feels for her, or who makes him act the way he does. In herself the woman has not the slightest importance."

"At its core, the first *Star Wars* film is a classic tale about a hero rescuing a princess from an evildoer's 'castle.' In that sense, the film immediately portrays women on a lower plane than men; they require rescuing since they cannot rescue themselves" (Pianka 2013, 37). When Luke rescues her, after an hour and fifteen minutes of mostly *his* adventures, she's passively draped on her prison cell bed, Sleeping Beauty awaiting her prince. Still, she subverts the moment by awaking on her own and then not only sizing up Luke skeptically but objectifying *him* with her famous line "Aren't you a little short for a Stormtrooper?" With this, she makes it clear that she'll keep fighting the fairytale tropes. Nonetheless, they continue. From the moment Luke heroically breaks her out, they're following a conventional plot (escape and take the princess to safety with her people) where the men are rewarded with wealth (Han) and with a cause

(Luke) before the princess and all her people are placed in even greater jeopardy. Then the men save them again.

A woman, according to emerging seventies feminism, didn't exist to please men. However, Leia spends much of her time in the original film in such a role. She's the alluring damsel in distress for Luke, helpless yet spirited victim for Vader, and sparring partner for Han. She only exists to move the men's plot along—as the object they all fight over, then once more the face of the victim as the Death Star prepares to blow up the Rebel Base. While her character is assertive and delightful, her role in the story is disappointingly traditional. "Two generations of girls watching these films had to make a choice between identifying with beautiful, accomplished royalty who were being framed as objects of perfection, or with scrappy guys who were allowed to be witty, earnest, and heroic," critic Leah Schnelbach (2017) writes, considering how the roles have changed.

Still, within the plot, mouthy seventies feminist Leia insists on taking charge, giving the orders even as she criticizes their efforts. "This is some rescue. When you came in here, didn't you have a plan for getting out?" she demands. Her large black blaster undermines the dress and hair as she shoots guns and stands up to the men, in an era where both were unusual onscreen. As Fisher revealed in her memoir, Leia had been intended to be hanging upside down, to be rescued by Han and Chewie "and Chewie would carry me, slung over his shoulder through thigh deep water as we made it out of (interplanetary) harm's way," Fisher comments (2016, 29). However, Peter Mayhew's condition made him unable to lift weight, so this concept was fortunately scrapped.

While her clothing is identified with her role as senator, she emerges from her cell fighting and dodging in it, emphasizing its flexibility. It's also less-than-pristine. As the costume guide reveals, "Her entire costume was broken down [deliberately aged] before filming began to imply that she was a woman of action, rather than politics" (Alinger 2014, 14). Further, it's split up the side so she can run, but only displays her fully-covered leg. Knee-high white boots echo Luke's, suggesting action.

The comic based on Lucas's original script has Leia dressed in a jumpsuit and leather vest. Despite this tough apparel, she's more girlish than film-Leia, never shooting villains with a blaster. Instead, she sings songs in the hovercraft with her younger siblings. Covering much of Episode V's territory, she flirts with "Annikin Skywalker"—a composite of Luke and Han with a blond topknot—and directly tells him that she loves him. When she insists on packing her belongings and taking her servants while fleeing danger (echoing the spoiled princess of *Spaceballs*), he actually punches her out and carries her off for her own good. In Lucas's original concept, he's more manly and she, more frivolous and sweet. This time, the trash compactor is his idea, while she complains and gets grossed out. Her mother accompanies her, taking part of the agency but giving the galaxy two significant females. In addition to destroying the deadly threat, there's a quest to take the young student and place her on the throne after her father's death. Thus, everything except the outfit and coronation make this proto-version weaker—a spoiled schoolgirl-princess and nursemaid instead of warrior and rebel senator. When compared with this earlier treatment, the film version is strikingly empowering—showing a deliberate break from the classic damsel role.

Luke is stuck in his own traditional pattern as hero—from the rope swing over the chasm to the fact that his macho trigger-happy firing has destroyed the bridge they need. In the chute, Han is likewise the one firing his weapon without thinking through the consequences, while Leia tries the more practical wall-bracing choice and the overlooked droids actually save them. Lucas adds, "She is a leader, and even though she gets captured, the guys are the ones who are fumbling around and bring in trouble . . . I mean, they can't even rescue her!" (Bouzereau 1997, 14). Leia's actions always come from outside the box. Further disrupting her damsel image, she not only gives orders and blasts the wall open but unhesitatingly dives into garbage. "Somebody has to save our skins. Into the garbage chute, flyboy," she tells the surprisingly prissy Han and Chewie in a fun gender role reversal. Clearly, the white-gowned princess doesn't mind getting her hands (and the rest of her) dirty. In the audio commentary, Lucas says Leia is "very, very strong even though she's very young . . . She's pretty much in control of things."

Downward camera angles emphasize that Leia is shorter than Han as well as Vader and Chewie. This arguably disempowers Leia's gaze, or perhaps emphasizes how she knows she must argue harder to be heard, again connecting with the female audience of the time. "The stare, high neckline, and shoulder cropping of the image indicate that Leia is commanding Han to focus on her intelligence, not her cleavage" (Estrada 2007). With crisp commands, she asserts, "I don't know who you are, or where you came from, but from now on you do as I tell you—okay?" Without waiting for an answer, she pushes past her male helpers. As he blusters that he only takes orders from himself, she gets in a zinger with "It's a wonder you're still alive." Even in her white dress, she commands the show. Dominguez (2007, 116) concludes that this makes her a standout protagonist: "Leia is a hero without losing her gendered status; she does not have to play the cute, helpless sex kitten or become sexless and androgynous to get what she wants. She can be strong, sassy, outspoken, bossy, and bitchy, and still be respected and seen as feminine."

"Wonderful girl! Either I'm going to kill her or I'm beginning to like her," Han bursts. This line invokes the men of the time's mingled admiration, frustration, and confusion at the emerging tough heroine. "Princess Leia breaks barriers for white women by acting as a spy, a tactical leader, and a gun-wielding Rebel as she consistently defies Han Solo's misogynistic comments," Estrada (2007) adds. After the garbage chute adventure, Han complains, "If we can just avoid any more female advice, we ought to be able to get out of here." Here his word choice marks him as the caveman the empowered princess is defying. She takes his bluntness in stride. "Although his emphasis on her advice being 'female'—and by implication, inferior—reflects the attitude of many males in the workplace of the late 1970s, who were dealing with females in their profession for the first time, Leia is not intimidated" (Bodden 2012, 30).

Of course, even fighting for her own rights, she ignores those of others. First and second-wave feminisms often were more concerned with raising up white women than noticing the plights of minorities, including those oppressed across the globe. Leia is battling tyranny but is also dismissive of Chewbacca—the minority whose people were enslaved by the Empire. As she demands that someone "Get the walking carpet out of my way," she's humorously abrasive but clearly not fully considering the dynamics of her privilege in response to his.

After Obi-Wan sacrifices himself to clear the way for their escape (a moment that certainly symbolizes the old-guard British patriarchy stepping aside for a new generation of heroes, male, female, and alien), Captain Han flies them away. Onboard, Leia directs from the cockpit while the men fire the guns, showing the woman taking the communications role while men fight. This scene, echoing classic war films, is thus more traditionally gendered. Leia also takes a moment to comfort Luke with a blanket after the loss of his mentor. It's a sweet scene but emphasizes that the story is fundamentally all about him. Leia, who was tortured and condemned to death, as well as watching the genocide of her family and entire world, doesn't merit even a sympathetic word. In a *Robot Chicken* spoof of this scene, Leia (played here by a guest-starring Carrie Fisher), retorts, "Oh, did the eighty-year-old man you met yesterday just die? Sorry if I didn't notice. I was just busy thinking about my entire family and the other two billion people from Alderaan who were just vaporized into dust about three hours ago." Fisher even sounds like she's been wanting to say this for a while.

These moments mark her as the token girl on their otherwise all-male team. Having her there is a blow for equality but leaving her basically the only woman in the galaxy for all three films is particularly problematic. As Katha Pollitt writes in her famous 1991 essay, "The Smurfette Principle":

> Contemporary shows are either essentially all-male, like "Garfield," or are organized on what I call the Smurfette principle: a group of male buddies will be accented by a lone female, stereotypically defined. . . . Thus, Kanga, the only female in "Winnie-the-Pooh," is a mother. Piggy, of "Muppet Babies," is a pint-size version of Miss Piggy, the camp glamour queen of the Muppet movies. April, of the wildly popular "Teen-Age Mutant Ninja Turtles," functions as a girl Friday to a quartet of male superheroes. The message is clear. Boys are the norm, girls

the variation; boys are central, girls peripheral; boys are individuals, girls types. Boys define the group, its story and its code of values. Girls exist only in relation to boys.

Of course, this sends a painful message to young viewers. As Pollitt goes on to explain, "Little girls learn to split their consciousness, filtering their dreams and ambitions through boy characters while admiring the clothes of the princess. The more privileged and daring can dream of becoming exceptional women in a man's world—Smurfettes." Their only options, as they're taught, are to be sisterly comforters or rare action heroes in an all-boys club, not to take joy in empowered, feminine sisterhood. As Pollitt concludes sadly, "Boys, who are rarely confronted with stories in which males play only minor roles, learn a simpler lesson: girls just don't matter much." A team of two white men, one alien, and one woman (and no actors of color) places Leia on a level with Chewbacca, the alien misfit. The droids have double the representation.

After, Leia gives them directions to her rebel base where the men can fulfill her mission and deliver the Death Star plans to her people. Offering her more agency in the film's audio commentary, Lucas says he considers Episode IV to be Leia's story. "The boys just kind of tag along on her adventure." Even while being rescued by the men, she returns to her own place of power, where she issues orders to the pilots. Expanded Universe materials suggest she also has contributed substantially to building the base: "Princess Leia's influence, royal connections, and diplomatic abilities obtained much of the vital communication and scanning equipment in the Rebel command center," the licensed *Visual Dictionary* asserts (Reynolds 1998, 12). Further, the *Force Unleashed* series of video games, novels, and comic books show Leia as one of the founding members of the Rebel Alliance. Its emphasis on her team-up with her father Bail Organa (played by Hispanic actor Jimmy Smits), and female mentor Mon Mothma subverts the original film's all-white, mostly male hero team with the behind-the-scenes diverse heroism that enabled their success, much as *Rogue One* does later.

Still, in an odd plothole that subverts Leia's competence, on cleverly realizing they're being tracked, she still leads the Death Star to the hidden base she's been protecting so desperately. There, Luke and Han save Leia a second time when they stop the Death Star from blowing up Yavin. She stands helplessly, watching the Death Star advance on her, unable to order an evacuation or defend their team in any way. Instead, she is once more the princess about to be devoured by the monster, awaiting the young hero's rescue. "She remains on the sidelines during Episode IV's big battle. She is a mere onlooker as males pilot the fighters and males direct the battle. She's the cheerleader, there to witness the glory of the males and pay tribute to it," Cavelos (2006, 308) complains.

The film ends with Leia as conventional princess once more, bestowing rewards on the heroes who have saved her. Cavelos (2006, 308) adds, "Though she delivered the plans that led to the victory, she receives no medal herself. She is neither a leader nor a valued participant." With this ending, the film does not challenge race or gender norms—after Luke and Han rise from farmboy and smuggler to military heroes, the princess, Chewie, and the droids receive no corresponding military positions. After Leia's fieriness, this return to "classic family entertainment" is quite conventional as it reassures viewers with the classic safe tropes.

At the awards ceremony, Leia's simple white gown leaves her archetypal princess yet again. John Mollo, costume designer from episodes IV and V, says of Leia's presentation gown. "We didn't want anything very regal or complicated or heavily bejeweled or aggressively ethnic—just a smarter version of what she was wearing before" (Biggar 2005, 53). In the context of the elaborate costumes the prequel films will give Leia's mother, her elaborate hairstyles over simple gowns suggest a nod back to the previous generation's opulence—unlike the heavy robes and elaborate headdresses, a detailed hairdo costs nothing and recalls a time of luxury, even as the Rebels face endless hardship and make do with simple clothing. White can symbolize transcendent perfection in the heroes' journey toward divine achievement—as it does here for the men's ceremony (Cooper 1978, 41).

With this celebration, the film ends on a high note and begins a new era of feminist fandom. "Leia's contributions," Merlock and Jackson (2012, 85) proclaim, "not just to the destruction of the Empire but also to the establishment of a new kind of female role model and to the possibility of feminine potential cinema and popular culture—merit a degree of appreciation." So they do.

A SOFTER SEQUEL, OR LEIA FINDS LOVE

"Whereas the first wave of feminism was generally propelled by middle class, Western, cisgender, white women, the second phase drew in women of color and developing nations, seeking sisterhood and solidarity, claiming 'Women's struggle is class struggle'" (Rampton 2015). As racial diversity took its place in the Second Wave, it also found a spot in *Star Wars*. The sequel famously brought in a single Black character (along with a few more working on Bespin), but basically no more females, as a single (white) rebel technician has a single line. Meanwhile, the two Black characters on Bespin remind viewers how none exist among the Rebels. "Interestingly, while significantly raising the Black presence in the *Star Wars* universe, *Empire* still manages to promote the idea that while humans are everywhere in the galaxy, the vast majority of them are white," explains Kevin J. Wetmore, Jr. (2005) in *The Empire Triumphant: Race, Re-*

ligion and Rebellion in the Star Wars Films. Clearly, even with a history of seventies feminism heralding intersectionality, *Star Wars* wasn't ready to pull it off.

The crawl relates that freedom fighters have been "led by Luke Skywalker." Luke is a commander now and Han a general. Leia, however, has not risen in status, but only helps at the base. The film begins with Luke being lost in the snows of Hoth and Han heroically riding out to save him. Though Leia cares about both, her plotline involves staying inside, sadly awaiting their return. This is hardly an empowering moment. When Luke is saved, she raises the stakes in the love triangle by kissing Luke (certainly a cringe-worthy moment thanks to later revelations). Worse, this is a ploy to make Han jealous and gain the upper hand in their romantic squabbles—an immature, problematic move. She's still the prize of the story and she knows it.

At the same time, Leia has gotten tougher, abandoning her princess identity. On Hoth, she wears a distressed military snowsuit and knee-high boots. Her braid, wrapped around her head, is less showy and more practical than the last film's hairstyles. Leia shares command with General Rieeken through the Battle of Hoth, coordinating the troops and then organizing the evacuation. "She leads troops on Hoth, like Washington across the Delaware. She proves to be a talented welder, patching up Rebel starships in her downtime" (Dockterman 2017b, 36). Selflessly, she's the last one out, an act that almost gets her stranded. Of course, this requires Han to rescue her again, leaving her strength in the story quite ambiguous: Han drags her toward her transport, and when a cave-in blocks them, Han informs the transport that he will save Leia. "She is not making the decisions or even influencing them. She is simply a problem to be handled" (Cavelos 2006, 309).

On the surface, this film has a conventionally gendered plot like the last one—Leia's arc involves waiting helplessly for Han to rescue Luke then herself on Hoth, falling in love with him on the Millennium Falcon, being fought over by Han and Lando on Bespin as she's held as a pawn to bring Luke there, and finally sobbing as her lover is stolen away and she stands helpless. In contrast with Han's big sacrifice and Lando's redemption arc Leia only learned "how to tremble in Han's arms, how to 'use a good kiss' how to tell a man you love him" (Taylor 2014, 247). Fisher was frustrated with her character's lack of nuance. "I know Leia's favorite color is white," she said but that was about it. "She is more of a caricature, somewhat one-dimensional" (Taylor 2014, 247).

"You stuck-up, half-witted, scruffy-looking nerf herder" is apparently fans' favorite line, according to Fisher (2016, 227). However, the romance, too, has its problematic side. Pianka describes in a close viewing how "Han confronts Leia, backing her into a corner and questioning her about her true feelings" (2013, 41). As he does so, he takes hold of her hands, preventing her escape. Leia appears less independent and more frigid as

Han proclaims, "You could *use* a good kiss." His commands appear to be breaking through her leadership, which the movie implies is a tough mask over the women who secretly longs for romance. When he plants one on her she's happy to be "mastered" by the strong, virile man. "The implications of this scene are incredibly disturbing. For one, it teaches men that intimidation is a viable way into a woman's heart. For another, it teaches women that men who act this way must truly be in love with them, and that this love justifies borderline violent behavior" (Pianka 2013, 41).

In their Millennium Falcon adventures, Leia is actually frightened of vermin and requires Han to kill them for her. While she appears disgusted by the batlike Mynocks, Han tells her, "Go on inside. We'll clean them off if there are any more." Onboard the ship, Threepio prissily shows a similar disgust, emphasizing how Leia reflects the constantly victimized droid, not tougher, more heroic Han and Chewie. "Ohhh! Go away! Go away! Beastly little thing. Shoo! Shoo!" Threepio humorously fusses.

Further, Leia lets Han not only make plans onboard the ship but fail to share them with her, emphasizing his quick-witted heroism, but sidelining her. He can only offer jaunty, heroic comebacks like "No time to discuss this in committee" and "Sit down, sweetheart. We're taking off!" As the hero of their adventures, he realizes they've been exploring a creature's mouth, just as he is the one to plan their near-suicidally brave jaunt through an asteroid field, charge at an Imperial ship, and ruse of floating off in the garbage. Meanwhile, Leia protests, complains, and fails to solve any of their problems. The snarky insults of the previous film have become negative and unhelpful. When Imperial forces close in on the Millennium Falcon, Leia says, "This bucket of bolts is never going to get us past that blockade," fatalistically criticizing instead of offering a suggestion. She has no ideas here, and can't even work out Han's plan, leaving him to snatch up the heroic role.

After this, Leia rewards him with a kiss and the lines, "You do have your moments. Not many, but you have them." The hero has saved the day as well as the princess. However, as with the first film, her actions subvert the larger plot. When she falls for Han, she's wearing a clumsy androgynous quilted outfit with tightly braided up hair. Her lines are understated ("My hands are dirty") instead of flowery. Further, she's busy welding with goggles, working with Han as equal partners to fix the ship and elude the Empire, not flirting and picnicking in a meadow like Anakin and Padmé. They also have an amused audience in Chewie, and an awkward one in Threepio.

On Bespin, Lando swaggers and flirts heavily, repeating the dynamic from Luke's recovery room that two men must compete for the story's solitary woman. His opening line to Leia, "Hello. What have we here?" is worded to treat her as a possession, a "what." He bows and kisses her hand, prompting Han to immediately grab her hand for himself and steer her away. "Good white and nonwhite male characters only gain more power once the squeaky white purity of protagonist women is sullied by their female desires for men," Estrada (2007) notes satirically.

Further, Leia is surprisingly happy to play tourist on Cloud City. While she allows the men to coordinate the repairs, she "changes clothes, fixes her hair, frets about the missing Threepio and paces back and forth in her room in the clouds, like an ill-tempered Rapunzel," as Cavelos (2006, 307) puts it. When Leia senses something amiss, Han treats her more as his girlfriend than his leader—he condescendingly kisses her forehead and tells her to "relax," he'll handle it. Because he shows disrespect, the audience begins to share it.

On Bespin, Leia discards the white for a less innocent red tunic dress and matching pants. Both are modestly cut, suggesting the princess is on vacation rather than dressing to please the men. The outfit is more civilian than princess (and certainly nothing like the royal ensembles of the prequels). Costume designer John Mollo says, "In a film like this, you can go in any direction, provided it works in the end. After much discussion, we decided Leia's dinner dress should have a slightly Indian look. We wanted it sort of soft and simple" (Alinger 2014, 110). Several times, Leia insists she doesn't trust Lando, and the crimson can be seen as bolstering her strength and courage. Over it all, her white cloak becomes a kind of camouflage, both veiling her and reassuring the men she's still the princess even as she toughens underneath. Notably, Leia pulls in the cloak as soon as Lando enters and looks her up and down.

On Bespin, her double-looped braids are fancy yet practical—and the most rebellious part of the look. "For Leia's hair, George Lucas was inspired by the hairstyles of rebel Mexican women fighting in the Mexican War of Independence in the early 1900s" (Bray et al. 2015, 45). This salutes the first wave feminists, who battled beside their men to win freedom for their country, and in the process proved that they were equal to any soldier.

While she's clearly styled her own hair, it's possible Lando has presented Leia with the dress, imposing a more feminine style on her. If so, it suggests he's offering her luxury and romance, indicated by the decorations and deep red color. It's a conventional dress-up scene, though the pants and cloak make it less exploitative, as does the modest cut. Still, it's a moment of refinement the men don't bother with themselves, which gives them the opportunity to admire her. (As Han says in a deleted scene, she looks beautiful in her "girl clothes.") When Lando sees Leia, he offers her the rather smarmy and superficial line, "You look absolutely beautiful. You truly belong here with us among the clouds." She responds with cool thanks, accepting his arm and dinner invitation but not trusting him.

Vader bursts in, and Han blasts back at him while the quieter Leia does not. While Han shoots repeatedly at Vader, and Vader threatens him with death—and then near-fatally freezes him in carbonite—Leia and Chewie are more like pawns. The weak administrator Lando argues with Vader for their lives and is crushed when he loses. In the larger picture, all are held as hostages to lure Luke to Bespin. All this emphasizes Leia's role as princess needing rescue once again. Moreover, the torture is specifically gendered, giving Han the chance for suffering and heroism, but not Leia. In the carbon-freezing chamber, Han makes the ultimate noble sacrifice. There, the pair share an epic kiss and exchange vows of love (though taciturnly in Han's case). After Han is frozen, Leia strikes out, emphasizing her warrior strength as soon as her man is out of the picture: "Leia exhibits the kind of determined, single-minded behavior one would expect from a traditional action hero like Sylvester Stallone or Arnold Schwarzenegger: she stands at the doorway and shoots her blaster, face stoic, ignoring the possible danger to herself" (Dominguez 2017, 117). Instead of succumbing to tears, she takes a quick moment to emphasize her Rebel status. However, she only becomes hero in *Empire* with the stronger Han unavailable.

Soon enough, Luke takes over the story, dueling with Vader as Leia, Lando, and Chewie escape. In this scene, Leia senses a suffering Luke and directs the ship to find him, using her feminine-coded sensitivity and love for him—with a skill that goes unexplained until the following film. Nonetheless, it's her first step into the world of the Force. "Leia takes control of the situation without pause. She does not stop to question her instincts or to weigh up the odds . . . the Force is perhaps her own salvation as much as it is Luke's" since his survival offers her hope in the midst of her despair (Barr 2018, 71). It's a heroic moment, but one Luke mostly directs. The story ends as Luke gives Leia a comforting hug and they both gaze off into space where the more active Lando is chasing off to rescue the heroic Han. Leia, back in her Episode IV dress, is implied to be the young teen again, statically awaiting the deeds of others.

Leia's plot is almost wholly romantic, but it doesn't lack agency. During the feminist movement, women sought control over their bodies. "The personal is political," they insisted. Leia only does this metaphorically, in a PG-rated story without sex or pregnancy to consider, but she makes the choices about her romance with Han in this film. If as the creators noted, a kiss was equal to a sex scene, Leia fully initiates Luke's kiss (to his surprise) and flirts with Han, welcoming his kiss on the Falcon. As he's about to be frozen in carbonite, she chooses to kiss him again, and then brings their romance to a deeper level as she tells him "I love you." When she removes her mask and kisses him in *Jedi*, it's clear that she's taking the reins in their relationship.

Leia's seriousness and devotion to duty are the biggest obstacle: "A beautiful and pensive young woman, she understands only too well her crucial position at a fateful time for the galaxy, and she hides her personal feelings behind stern discipline and dedication to her cause," specifies *The Star Wars Visual Dictionary* (Reynolds 1998, 12). While she doesn't mention this onscreen, a princess is traditionally supposed to make an alliance-marriage with other royalty, not run off with a scoundrel. Indeed, the novels and comics address this as one of each actually has the duty-bound princess agree to an alliance marriage, choosing the good of her people over her feelings for Han.

A further level of complex psychology the princess must be experiencing is her mingled freedom, duty, and guilt over the fact that her parents, advisors, and entire planet have been wiped out. This too goes basically unprocessed onscreen but has given the princess the chance to choose for herself with none of these barriers stopping her. This she finally does, declaring her love for the man who has not yet committed to the Rebellion, who has no home or loyalty besides to ship and friends, who says and does whatever he wishes. To the duty-raised princess, he represents freedom indeed. Thus her dream is specifically not one of Prince Charming from Snow White's era, but of adventuring with a rascal. Ironically, to rescue her smuggler-love, she would have to turn slave.

THE INFAMOUS GOLD BIKINI

"For a generation of women and girls, Princess Leia was groundbreaking in her power. That she is often best remembered for the slave bikini scene in *Return of the Jedi* is unfortunate, as it reduces a character who was ahead of her time to a poster on a 14-year-old's wall" (Keegan 2015). The first film gives Leia two simply cut white gowns. The next puts her in a cold-weather jumpsuit and Rebel combat suit (both very utilitarian), with Lando (one assumes) providing her with more feminine clothing. *Jedi* has her begin in the androgynous Boushh cover and then wear camouflage gear, the latter practical and identical to the men's. However, Jabba and then the Ewoks dress her in far more feminine outfits.

"Carrie Fisher had asked Lucas for some sort of edge to the character, perhaps a drinking problem; something, at least, to suggest the suffering the princess had been through, the genocide of her entire planet. She got a slave bikini" (Taylor 2014, 267). Disguised as the Ubese tracker, Boushh, Leia is completely sexless. Her clothing is brown and concealing, with a facemask and voice disguiser. A second wave feminist in this garb, Leia also maintains second-wave ideals. Her desire to make reproductive choices for herself is seen in her rescue of Han—if she was not interested, she could leave him in the carbonite indefinitely.

Wrapped up without a trace of skin showing, Leia infiltrates Jabba's palace to rescue her man. Posing as a "ruthless" bounty hunter, she pulls out a thermal detonator and plays chicken with the great Jabba, beating him at last. Of course, she's staged the moment so she can sneak unescorted through Jabba's palace and unfreeze Han. In a dramatic, romantic reveal, she doffs her helmet and kisses him. However, the moment is undercut by Jabba's laughter. He drags her close, menacing her with a phallic tongue as she looks revolted.

Next, the captured princess is forced to don scanty clothing and lounge beside Jabba. She thus becomes a nearly naked damsel displayed centrally as a goad for her friends and awaiting rescue. Pornography is "the graphic sexually explicit subordination of women though pictures or words that also includes women dehumanized as sexual objects, things, or commodities; enjoying pain or humiliation or rape; being tied up, cut up, mutilated, bruised, or physically hurt; in postures of sexual submission or servility or display," Catherine MacKinnon writes in *Feminism Unmodified* (1987, 176). This all appears in Leia's slave girl outfit as she's denigrated to a possession and a tool for others' sexual purposes. With this, objectification constitutes a serious harm to a person's humanity. Symbolically, she is no longer a person and need not be treated as one. Of course, since Leia is practically the galaxy's only female, this definition extends from her to all women.

There are also the possibilities that may have happened offscreen. "The film is vague about whether or not she has been raped or forced to engage in sexual acts with Jabba, but from here on out, Leia's image as 'Slave Leia' has gone down in pop culture as well as sexual fetish history and continues to be a popular cosplay for nerd gals and others" (Rodriguez 2014). While some find the bikini look empowering or sexy, many criticize them as a disturbing invitation. Pornography, according to MacKinnon, makes women's sexuality into "something any man who wants to can buy and hold in his hands . . . She becomes something to be used by him, specifically, an object of his sexual use" (1987, 138). As she insists, "All pornography is made under conditions of inequality based on sex" (2000, 103).

"The room itself—indeed, his whole enterprise—is like that of a Mafia don removed to some 'oriental' setting, with harems, dancers, prostitutes, and a constant mixture of business, corruption, pleasure, sexual exploitation, violence, pain, and death," the book *Star Wars and History* explains. Thus, it evokes a generic exoticism: "It could be a fort on the African coast, set up for slave trading; a decadent pasha's palace in some far-off corner of the Ottoman Empire; or a similarly exotic palace, somewhere between Timbuktu and the Taj Mahal" (Reagin and Liedl 2013, 248). With this, tropes of the foreigner sexually exploiting the underdressed white woman (a princess even) appear, feeding into old stereotypes while encouraging the traditional hero to save her.

This trope also appeared in *Flash Gordon* comics, complete with a similar-looking slave-girl outfit, as Ming the Merciless and Prince Vultan menaced spunky Dale Arden. Red Sonja, the sword-and-sorcery babe famed for her own chainmail bikini, not-so-coincidentally dates back to the same thirties pulp adventures but found a new popularity in her 1985 film. Around the same time, Starfire, DC's Teen Titans' alien ex-slavegirl superhero, dressed similarly. Over at Marvel, Chris Claremont's comics saw the otherwise very powerful X-Men (and more often X-Women) like-wise stripped by villains and mutant captors, Bad girl comics were begin-ning, with their warrior heroines dressed in chainmail bikinis or fetish gear. Thus Princess Leia found her costume moving with the times.

"She absolutely loathed and despised the bikini costume," says ward-robe assistant Janet Lucas-Wakely. "She looked great in it, but it was not her scene at all. She was quite happy in her princess dress and she was quite happy in her fighting gear, but she was not comfortable in the bikini" (Alinger 2014, 141). Indeed, it's a degrading scene. Fisher notes, "Let's not forget that these movies are basically boys' fantasies. So the other way they made her more female in this one was to have her take off her clothes" (Dockterman 2017b, 36). MacKinnon adds that pornography is responsible for both men's and women's conception of women as ob-jects available for men's consumption: "Pornography defines women by how we look according to how we can be sexually used. . . . Pornography *participates* in its audience's eroticism through creating an accessible sexu-al object, the possession and consumption of which *is* male sexuality, as socially constructed; to be consumed and possessed as which, *is* female sexuality, as socially constructed" (1987, 173).

Such an outfit in the time of such feminist outcry is depressing, but not all that surprising. In fact, several strains of postfeminism were emerging at the time, some of which considered the struggle for equal rights over and encouraged women to return to the home. Others struck back at the image of unfashionable, frumpy women, urging postfeminists to reclaim sexualized images and even pornography. "In the late 1970s and early 1980s, women who followed the leading anti-pornographers Andrea Dworkin and Catherine MacKinnon clashed violently with those feminists opposed to censorship, who saw the anti-pornography cam-paigners as authoritarian, right-wing, and denying women the pleasure provided by a full exploration of their sexuality" (Gibson 2014, 202). Even as women expressed anger at being objectified, some preferred dressing to imitate the sexualized women of advertisements over the invisible professionals in business suits.

Fisher (2016, 228) adds in her autobiography, "I wish I'd understood the kind of contract I signed by wearing something like that, insinuating I would and will always remain somewhere in the erotic ballpark appear-ance-wise." After all this, Fisher advised Daisy Ridley not to let anyone pressure her into her own gold bikini scene (Dockterman 2017b, 36). Fish-er also told Ridley that dating was difficult, adding, "I never wanted to give anyone the anecdote 'I slept with Princess Leia'" (Grossman 2017, 56). She describes with confused ambivalence the honor of being so many boys' first crush and the squickiness of that honor. Fisher adds, "I think boys may have been attracted to my accessibility. Even if I did have some princess qualities, I wasn't conventionally beautiful and sexy, and as such was less likely to put them down or think that I was too good for them" (2016, 192). Even in the midst of this, Fisher apparently tried inserting snark in the scenes—after the men left her as Jabba's prisoner in the bikini, she shouted after them, "Don't worry about me! I'll be fine! Seriously!" (Dockterman 2017b, 36).

Further, the novel makes this moment all about Luke. "He could feel her pain immediately from across the room—but he said nothing, didn't even look at her, shut her anguish completely out of his mind. For he needed to focus his attention entirely on Jabba" (Kahn [1983] 1995, 373). In the film, when Han asks, she responds with a simple "I'm here," so as not to distract or worry the men with her servitude.

Though Luke looks away in the novel, and Han can't see her, this is definitely a moment that invites the audience to stare. Giant Jabba sits front and center with Leia draped out before him, skin mostly bared, golden metal gleaming to attract the eye. "Woman, then, stands in patriarchal culture as a signifier for the male other, bound by a symbolic order in which man can live out his fantasies and obsessions through linguistic command by imposing them on the silent image of a woman still tied to her place as the bearer of meaning, not maker of meaning," Mulvey writes. Leia is not making choices here, but, like the other slave girls, is one of Jabba's many conquests, presented for the straight male viewer's enjoyment. Of course, Jabba too gazes at her, and demeans her by inflicting the outfit in the first place. This reinforces their roles of owner and slave, not only for the two characters, but for all who visit Jabba's palace. As Bill Spangler (2006, 332) comments in "Fighting Princesses and Other Distressing Damsels": "It's been suggested that Jabba wouldn't have chosen those clothes for Leia, since he probably wouldn't have found her physically attractive. It's not difficult, though, to come up with other reasons why Jabba might've made this choice. That outfit would've kept most women feeling vulnerable and off-guard. It's also an effective way for the gangster to display his new prize to the other members of his entourage." *The Clone Wars* novelization explains "the Hutts' need to flaunt Twi'lek dancers and other glamorous humanoids, so radically, physically *different* that no Hutt could possibly have found them attractive." As it insists, "They collected them because humanoids coveted them, and so it sent the message clearly: *I possess everything you lust after, so I have power over you*" (Traviss 2008, 11).

Jabba's giant body suggests physical power and also corpulent greed. *The New Essential Guide to Alien Species* explains, "Hutt culture is essentially egocentric. They consider themselves the center of the galaxy and on the worlds they control are likened unto gods. A Hutt's success in life is comparable only to its ego, and a Hutt's ego can be tremendous" (Lewis and Keier 2013, 83). Clearly, the entire palace is a boy's club, with powerful men and subjugated, underdressed women. His slave girls wear little clothing or form-fitting bodysuits. Each is a different type of alien, stressing the exotic. "Only the most notorious smugglers and bounty hunters are allowed to consort openly in the throne room—those who have proved themselves adept at murder, mayhem, or crimes of high standing" (Luceno 2003, 37). Thus, Leia's blow against him is one against the patriarchy.

Fisher wraps up her story by noting, "The women forgive me for being in the metal bikini because they know I'm not in it voluntarily, and they let the men like it . . . because they know that I represent something else and not just that sex thing. Capable, reliable, equal to if not better than a man" (2016, 230). She calls killing Jabba "my favorite moment in my own personal film history" and adds that she recommends everyone "find an equivalent of killing a giant space slug in your head and celebrate that" (Fisher 2016, 39). As she does so, the glee shows on Fisher's face. Clearly all of Jabba's slaves need a liberator—though Leia isn't shown freeing them directly, it's suggested that her killing of Jabba does the task. She also strikes a subtle blow against the trope of pornography: MacKinnon notes that degraded women are presented as enjoying how they are being violated: "In pornography, women desire disposition and cruelty. Men . . . create scenes in which women desperately want to be bound, battered, tortured, humiliated, and killed. Or merely taken and used. Women are there to be violated and possessed, men to violate and possess us" (1987, 148). However, Leia violently murders Jabba, liberating herself and making her opinion of his sexual servitude clear. She takes the power back by strangling him with the very chain with which he trapped her. "The powerless and sexually enslaved female uses the very elements of that enslavement to kill a captor that understood too late that he dangerously underestimated his prey," Dominguez concludes (2007, 117).

Of course, compared to blowing up a Death Star or dueling Darth Vader, this is a small triumph: a lazy, literally sluggish crime boss who likely hasn't moved under his own power in years. He's the Great and Powerful Oz—more like the façade of power waiting for the young woman to reveal him as a useless fraud. Cavelos protests, "If George Lucas had cared as much for Leia's character, he would have given Jabba a gun or toxic slime so he could pose more of an immediate threat" (2006, 311). Further, Leia has no emotional arc, either feeling guilt at the murder or triumph at avenging Han's suffering. This triumph doesn't even help their cause, as Luke blows up the entire barge just after. In fact, she awaits Luke's signal before she acts, further weakening her character.

Finally, Luke swings her away, literally rescuing her and connecting back visually to their rope swing of the first film. In both, he is doing the saving and she clings to her powerful hero . . . this time wearing far less.

Wetmore claims, "She might be considered a strong female character, but the image of her in the slave girl costume on Jabba's barge, being grabbed by Luke . . . and carried by him as he swings himself and her over to the rescue ship summarizes her position in the trilogy: she is an object to be rescued." It's a romanticized, traditionally gendered end to the visually exploitative arc.

The massive legacy of the film certainly came as a surprise. "Given that there had never actually been a film that had been that big of a hit before, who could possibly have assumed that there now would be?" Fisher notes (2016, 201). From 1995 through 2012, there were forty-four Leia action figures (in contrast with fifty-seven Vaders and eighty-nine Lukes) (Taylor 2014, 206). With this, the gold bikini found its place in history. Its legacy continues, not just among cosplayers and jokes on sitcoms. Apparently the only available toy or figurine of Princess Leia available even as late as 2015 stuck her in the "Slave Outfit" from Jedi (though seventies and eighties action figures had put her in the other film outfits). "Bikini? Check. Loin cloth? Check. Chain around the neck? Check. And in case you were wondering if it was actually geared towards children, it's listed for kids ages 4+" (Aran 2014). Critic Isha Aran continues: "That's right little girls, if you want to play with a doll of one of the most iconic sci-fi heroines, you're going to have to play with most sexualized scantily-clad version of her." One set of blueprints for a slave Leia figure were covered in gender-specific notes to the design team: "Eyes should be more sultry. More petite overall. Smaller breasts. Outer parts of nostrils not so tall. Please sculpt some underpants!" (Taylor 2014, 206).

Of course, this toy line teaches children that in a cast of strong action heroes, the girl is the one objectified in the bikini and enslaved by a giant slug. For MacKinnon (2000, 108) if representation *is* reality "then pornography is not less an act than the rape and torture it represents." Even with plastic weapons, her outfit and designation of "Slave Leia" mark her as a victim. The bikini appeared in toys, Lego, trading cards, comics, and more even after Disney acquired the franchise. Many were appalled that Disney had such a lineup of superhero and *Star Wars* toys for boys and princesses for girls, furthering a strict binary gender dynamic. However, they soon fixed the mistake with *Forces of Destiny*, a girl-power friendly cartoon with books, comics, and fully-clothed action figures for girls.

LEIA MEETS THE EWOKS

"The only way they knew to make the character strong was to make her angry," Fisher said in a *Rolling Stone* interview just before *Jedi*. "In *Return of the Jedi*, she gets to be more feminine, more supportive, more affectionate" (Dockterman 2017b, 36). Indeed, the sarcastic, confrontational princess softens through the trilogy. While she has a position of authority in the first two, in the third, she has no particular role assigned on Endor. In an early draft, Leia commands the team on Endor. "By the time Kasdan wrote his draft, she was just one member of Han's mission to the moon" (Taylor 2014, 267). Lando and Han, the generals, divide the war between them, while Leia goes along as part of Han's strike force. On a subtle level, she's lost status in the Rebellion.

She goes down to Endor dressed rather like Han with light blue pants, black boots, tan shirt and grey vest, all under the Rebels' camouflage cape and helmet. Visually, she's a soldier and respected member of the team. Further, the Endor mission shows her as a woman on the front lines of combat, a political statement for the eighties. "Leia is right to be worried about what fate they face as resistance fighters: our history and her own galaxy's past show that women were not spared when they took part in the irregular warfare of the resistance fighter. Yet the Empire should be worried too because it faces a resistance made all the stronger by the women who lead and support the Rebel forces," Reagin and Liedl explain in *Star Wars and History* (2013, 42).

However, Pianka points out that the speeder bike chase "exemplifies yet another stereotype about women: they can't drive." As he points out, her fighting skills have diminished as well: "In a scene where, moments earlier, Luke kills two Stormtroopers by showcasing his extraordinary piloting skills, Leia ends up in trouble once again when she proves unable to finish off even one" (Pianka 2013, 42). She killed more Stormtroopers in *A New Hope* than any of the male main characters but has clearly diminished. She tops all this off by getting knocked out and left to be rescued.

When she wakes, Leia meets up with Wicket the Ewok, whose trust she wins with food, once again stressing her feminine empathy over warrior skills. "On a straightforward level, it's a heartwarming scene that makes good on Leia's earliest claims to be a diplomat. On a broader scale, it's indicative of how Leia's sometimes snarky attitude is merely a shield for a deep humanity" (Barr 2018, 71). In fact, Wicket must warn her of danger, and then leads her back to his village. Ewoks have a "sixth sense" for threats, explains *The New Essential Guide to Alien Species* (Lewis and Keier 2013, 56). She appears to be an honored guest, not a hostage, but it's hard to tell. "They protect her and ignore her. Essentially, the Ewoks relegate Leia to a traditional female role, removing her agency. Leia is rescued by her friends yet again," Rodriguez notes. Even her intervention for their lives is the princess's traditional role. She isn't seen trying to rejoin her friends or asking the Ewoks about the shield generator. Unlike Luke, she appears, puzzlingly, to just be taking a break from the conflict.

The Ewoks dress her in a brown dress—suggesting a link with the forest and its dwellers but also making her soft and feminine as Leia literally lets her hair down. The Endor dress is a leatherlike lace-up tunic.

This is "her most casual—representative of the peaceful theme of the saga's conclusion" (Alinger 2014, 192). They dress in leather, bones, and feathers. Their mud-and-thatch villages link symbiotically with the forest thanks to the rope ladders and swinging vines that help them reach their homes in the trees. The Ewoks accept her, unlike the men, whom they consider killing and eating. On a subtle level this seems to be nodding to eco-feminism, the seventies joining of the feminist agenda with a pro-nature philosophy and desire for conservationism.

> One of the strains of this complex and diverse "wave" was the develop-ment of women-only spaces and the notion that women working to-gether create a special dynamic that is not possible in mixed-groups, which would ultimately work for the betterment of the entire planet. Women, due whether to their long "subjugation" or to their biology, were thought by some to be more humane, collaborative, inclusive, peaceful, nurturing, democratic, and holistic in their approach to prob-lem solving than men. The term eco-feminism was coined to capture the sense that because of their biological connection to earth and lunar cycles, women were natural advocates of environmentalism. (Rampton 2015)

The pro-environment message is nice, but once again, Leia is more archetypal damsel than well-rounded person. Bonding with the Ewoks on Endor, Leia appears to match the furry people's love of the forest, and she fights to defend it with all her power. However, she's Smurfette once again. Though the Ewoks may symbolize underprivileged races (or even genders), they are mostly male characters. "Their culture is gender-based, with the males serving as hunters, warriors, chieftains, and shamans, and the females acting as gatherers and domestics" (Lewis and Keier 2013, 57). Here, the metaphor of the female eco-warrior falls short as the great symbiotes with nature—Yoda, the Ewoks, and Chewie—are all male.

At last, Luke tells Leia that they are siblings, and that she is the last potential Jedi and savior after him. "If I don't make it back, you're the only hope for the Alliance." At the time, this was a momentous surprise, and not altogether a good one. While fans had enjoyed Luke and Leia's kiss "for luck" and her big smooch in the medical bay, both were now tainted. "Now it turned out that any fan rooting for Luke and Leia to get together had in fact been rooting for incest. The decision may have defini-tively settled the question of who Leia would end up with, Luke or Han, but it left a bad taste in its wake" (Taylor 2014, 263). Taylor believes this was an attempt to tie up Yoda's throwaway mystery line from the previ-ous film of "There is another," though many speak of the mythological significance of twins and see Leia's Force sensitivity in the previous film.

Whatever the reason, acknowledging Leia as an equal with Luke's same power is excellent, but no one remains to train her. Further, Luke is specifically leaving her in safety while *he* goes off to confront and save

their father or die trying. Leia, with just as heroic a birth and more combat experience, must remain hidden in safety. In the novel, when Luke
discovers Leia is his sister, he protests, "But you can't let her get involved
now, Ben . . . Vader will destroy her" (Kahn [1983] 1995, 404). In turn, Ben
agrees that Luke should keep Leia's identity secret to keep her out of the
battle—both as the last hope and as the untrained innocent.

This moment also lacks character development, as Cavelos observes:
"Being told that Vader—the archenemy who has pursued her through
the trilogy, tortured her twice, killed countless Rebels, frozen her love,
tormented and cut off the hand of her other love, and repressed countless
planets—is her father ought to trigger the biggest outburst from Leia
we've ever seen. It ought to be the climax of an internal conflict that's
been building in her throughout" (2006, 313). Of course, it isn't—her only
emotional arc is her romance, which doesn't affect the larger plot. Luke is
given a vast internal struggle with being Vader's son, while Han struggles with joining the Rebellion. Leia debates falling in love but has no
soul-crisis over her father.

Several novels remedy this, as Leia spars verbally with Anakin's
ghost, or describes the torment she felt upon realizing that her torturer,
murderer of Alderaan, was her birth father. In the new canon novel
Bloodline, she reveals more of the pain she underwent as she protests: "He
tortured me until I screamed and shook and thought I would just die
from the pain. Alone. Did you bother to ask yourself how it might feel, to
realize the person who'd done all that was your father? Can you imagine
how terrible it is to realize all you'll ever know of your birth father is how
much he enjoyed making you suffer? That's what I have to live with"
(Gray 2016, 256).

In the 2016 comic *Vader Down*, set after *A New Hope*, Leia faces Vader
and tells him, "You'll pay for everything you've done . . . You can kill me
but you can't kill what I stand for . . . and you won't stop justice" (Aaron
and Gillen 2016). In fact, she is prepared to blow herself up to stop Vader
and take her revenge for her people. More chillingly, she leaves Luke
behind in her single-minded pursuit. However, in a small character arc,
she hears Threepio's frantic distress call and for a moment, pictures all
her friends lying dead at her feet. Even with a possible shot at Vader
available, she abandons it and goes to save her team.

Leia and Han go off to battle beside the Ewoks, like the forces of
nature personified. Still, Leia's fighting power is significantly less than
her male counterpart's. When they assault the shield generator, Leia is
the first of the team to retreat to the bunker door. Han shoots masses of
Stormtroopers while she stands there, blaster drooping. Later, she
shrinks behind him as he covers them both. When she finally does shoot
a Stormtrooper, Han praises her, overdoing it as he's shot half an army
by this point. She's also wounded in the firefight.

She does rally a bit—Han finally tells her he loves her when they're trapped, but she reveals she has a blaster—a delightfully tough moment. She replies with his "I know" before shooting two Stormtroopers. However, Han, the leader, is the one to get the idea to blow up the bunker, and then lead his men in doing so. Meanwhile, Leia is presumably huddled up nursing her injury. The story shifts to Lando's team and Luke as they each defeat the Empire. Apparently, co-writer Lawrence Edward Kasdan thought it would be an interesting plot twist to have Vader kill Luke and Leia accept the Skywalker mantle as the real chosen one. However, Lucas declined (Bouzereau 1997, 314).

With Luke's survival, Leia remains the galaxy's alternate hope, but one no longer needed. The film only returns to Leia and Han as they celebrate the Death Star's destruction and Leia and Han resolve their romance with Leia choosing him (or rather, having her other love interest conveniently turned sibling so there is no choice to make). She can sense Luke, suggesting at least a glimmer of potential Force power developing, now that she's learned to listen.

Though Leia doesn't train with Obi-Wan and Yoda, the Legends Universe has Luke pass on what he learned. The post-Disney one has some of this too, as Luke apparently explained Obi-Wan's death to Leia with the words "We're not just flesh and bone. Not just stuff. We're more. We're luminous" (Soule and Unzueta 2017).

They all celebrate together, with Leia back in the brown dress. It's a festive moment, but also a softening, as she, the princess, is the one who must change into party clothes. Though she shares the power, there's no indication she can see the Force ghosts as Luke can. She doesn't even join him at their father's pyre, leaving Vader's redemption and all the associated emotions solely in the province of the hero.

A SINGLE-GENDER GALAXY: OTHER ORIGINAL TRILOGY WOMEN

Basically no women other than Carrie Fisher speak in the original movies. Wade and Riesman (2015), who made a video of them all, counted three, with 63 seconds of total dialogue out of 386 minutes of film. Since none ever speak to each other, and only Aunt Beru is named onscreen, the Bechdel Test lies in shambles. Further, Dr. Rebecca Harrison (2018), a professor of film and television studies at the University of Glasgow, edited down the nine major films through *Last Jedi* to leave behind only scenes with women present. Harrison puts the screentime (not dialogue, just presence) for any women including Leia herself at 15 percent *A New Hope* (lowest of the films—and clearly a product of Leia, basically the only woman, spending much of the action locked away on the Death Star), 23 percent *Return of the Jedi*, and 22 percent *Empire Strikes Back*. Even the powerful princess, who so defines the films, appears in only about a fifth of the trilogy.

As for the other women, Aunt Beru (Shelagh Fraser) has the first human line on Tatooine, though she's mediating between Luke and his uncle—her only role in the film. All of her few lines do this and nothing else. After introducing Luke, she insists to her husband that he's not a farmer and describes how he takes after his father, how he isn't around because he has "some things to do before he started today," etc. The novelization adds, "Beru was not a brilliant woman, but she possessed an instinctive understanding of her important position in this household. She functioned like the dampening rods in a nuclear reactor. As long as she was present, Owen and Luke would continue to generate a lot of heat, but if she was out of their presence for too long—*boom!*" (Lucas [1976] 1995, 48). She also has no stand-out personality traits but is just the clichéd mom, making dinner and reminding her husband of their child's feelings.

The beloved 1981 radio play adaptation expands this conversation. Owen pushes Luke harder, even insisting, "You pull your weight today or there'll be trouble!" Beru chides him with "Owen!" and continues trying to mollify him as he tells Luke to do his share and show gratitude for his adoption. At this, Beru cries "Owen Lars!" angrily. After Luke leaves, she lets fly: "Honestly, Owen, I don't know what gets into you at times. Luke's never asked us for a thing. He works as hard as any farm-hand. He could've gone off on his own long ago and you know that. . . . You can't begrudge him his dreams! A person has to have their dreams." She then begins complaining about their isolation and poverty, empha-sizing her own life of painful selfless sacrifice and how miserable it's made her. Here, both lose some positive qualities, clarifying why Luke is so desperate to leave.

Of course, she's killed like the dead mothers of Disney, to propel the hero on his path. Meg Cabot's lighthearted monologue in *From a Certain Point of View* allows Beru to share her perspective—an awareness that adopting Luke could get her and Owen killed, yet her determination to do it anyway. She offers the self-effacing, "It wasn't because *I* wanted Luke to go. It's because that's what Luke wanted. And I wanted Luke to have whatever he wanted" (2017, 90) but then reflects that sending Luke off to school might have saved their lives. Through the story, she's quite self-aware of her choices and priorities yet bravely accepts the death that follows them.

A cut scene in the original film has Luke hanging around with his friends as he discusses the nearby space battles. One companion, Camie (Koo Stark), is female, with long brown hair and a white tunic like his. In the novelization, Luke is open to her as a love interest among his very small circle of acquaintances. Of course, cutting her scene (much as it didn't move the film along much) significantly reduces the female characters that appear.

The radio play, which spends an entire half-hour episode on Luke with his friends, gives Camie a bit more personality, though not to her credit. As the substitute mother/babysitter, she also gets fed up with the guys' macho posturing at Beggar's Canyon and tells them "I want this to stop right now!" Still, she leaves Luke for someone Biggs considers weak and provincial. Biggs, returning from the Academy on a visit, tells Luke, "Camie is dumb enough to think she's made the prize catch hereabouts" in contrast with Luke, whom Biggs insists will someday get off Tatooine. As Camie chats with her friends, she flirts that Biggs looks "fabulous in his uniform" but offers little that's more personality-establishing. In their group, she's the girl, admiring and available.

In canon, Camie returns in a surprising cameo. The novelization of *The Last Jedi* jarringly begins with Luke and Camie married in a peaceful, loving, though childless existence (5–10). He never found Obi-Wan in the desert, and instead turned the droids to the Imperials and lived out his days as a moisture farmer like his Uncle Owen. Camie, the voice of normalcy and domesticity like Beru, complains that he often looks as if he "got cheated" or was "meant to be far from here" (Fry 2018, 9). However, Luke insists he's happy, only to wake from this dream sequence and realize a change is coming on his isolated island. Camie was never meant to be his destiny but is a talisman of the ordinary life he rejected.

A final female significant in *A New Hope*, though she doesn't appear, is Leia's mother (played by Rebecca Jackson Mendoza in a single wordless scene of *Revenge of the Sith*, in which she cradles baby Leia). A more central Queen Breha appeared in George Lucas's 1974 rough draft of the film, in which she assisted her daughter to the throne. She was the wise counterpart for the spoiled young princess, an impetus for her to learn and grow. This version aside, all the extended universe material (classic and reboot both) agrees that Leia's parents were together on Alderaan during its destruction. Echoing Beru, Queen Breha cannot have children and lovingly adopts Padmé's child. After this, she runs interference between Leia and her father, though she also plays a strong role in the Rebellion. While her husband and daughter travel the galaxy as senators, Breha holds matters together at home, covering their sedition—a quieter job but one that involves both ruling a planet and working with the Rebellion.

Claudia Gray's novel *Leia, Princess of Alderaan*, shows the princess interacting with her mother, a brave woman who leads the Rebels into entering combat. It is Breha, not Bail, who sends Leia on her first real mission—to rescue Bail together with the fleet. In her own plot arc, Leia must choose and complete three challenges to become crown princess, and she chooses to climb the hazardous Appenza Peak like her mother did in her own royal challenge. Leia ends the novel climbing it beside her mother . . . though Breha lost her heart and lungs—and the ability to safely have children—when she fell on her descent. On the mountain, Breha tells Leia, "We look at our challenges—at our lessons—as things we master in order to achieve our goals. But the most important lessons in life sometimes have to do with what happens when we fail" (Gray 2017, 404). She poignantly tells Leia she's learning the most important lesson—how to fall.

Rogue One features Senator Bail Organa but the short story in *From a Certain Point of View* has him returning home to confide all the latest bad news to his wife, Breha. In the rare story from *her* point of view, Bail tells Breha that Leia's ship has been destroyed, and Breha coordinates a determined search in their last remaining days. The Death Star arrives, and Breha sadly thinks to herself that the destruction of their beautiful, peaceful planet is "the perfect symbol to destroy. The perfect message to send" (Roux 2017, 245). As the couple hold each other, her and Bail's final words are that their daughter still lives, with Breha touchingly finishing, "I know." Like Luke's relatives, Leia's foster parents provide an extra stake for the heroine and impetus to complete her mission. She continues thinking of them through the extended universe, determined to never again lose so many civilians.

The Empire Strikes Back has just one female speaking role other than Leia. a Rebel desk-watcher at the Hoth base. Brigitte Kahn as Toryn Farr says, "Stand by, Ion Control. Fire," and nothing else.

"The other women present in the films serve as background or to present an exotic (and perhaps once or twice, erotic) presence" (Wetmore 2005). In *Jedi*, the memorable women appear among Jabba's slaves. The six-breasted woman is an Askajian, corpulent because her body is storing massive amounts of water. She wears a grass skirt, leather multi-bra and elaborate, but not particularly attractive, headdress. According to *The New Essential Guide to Alien Species*, her rather primitive tribal people are led by males, while dancers are their spiritual leaders, devoted to the Moon Lady (Lewis and Keier 2013, 193). Thus, her coding beyond the large, many-breasted feature is maternal, spiritual, and primitive—classically feminine traits. The background short story collection *Tales from Jabba's Palace* has Jabba forcing her to retain the water weight and wear ugly face patches to resemble his mother. This domination over her body is particularly high-handed. Like the audience, the men of Jabba's palace find her humorous. As she explains, "They called me gross and ridiculous and . . . fat. Even Jabba laughed at me. But he did not laugh because I was ugly, he laughed because he knew it hurt me to hear them" (1996, 396–97). Her plea for tolerance hauntingly addresses the audience as she cries, "I am the way I was born. Why do beings have to judge each other? Why do they have to stare and sneer and say cruel things?" Jabba also brutally holds her children hostage. As he controls her weight and threatens her babies, they're both stuck in very conventional gender roles. A.C.

Crispin's short story, however, gives her a happy ending. She escapes the palace with another of Jabba's servants, relying on her water retention and then bodily carrying him through the desert after they lose their speeder. After each heroically sacrifices for the other, they reclaim her children and fly off together, a happy family.

Sy Snootles (the lead singer of Jabba's band from the 1997 Special Edition), is clearly female—though a CGI character. Snootles resembles a frog, with a pudgy green mottled body, snail-like eyes on stalks and tusks well as pursed, lipsticked lips and exaggerated black eyelashes. She's thus grotesque, even as she dresses in a grass skirt and bangles and a feathered hat. This costume, along with her protruding eyes and lips, suggests exaggerated femininity. She's a Pa'lowick, a species with a long religious and oral-based tradition of song (Lewis and Keier 2013, 131). In the short stories, she's a Prima Donna type (a feminine cliché) insisting, "You *know* how frail I am, Evar. This desert air just isn't good for my lips. Let alone my throat. Let alone my lungs" (Betancourt 1996, 197). She's disgusted by her room and orders around the droids. In a farcical plot, sixteen different people bribe her to spy and, disloyal as she is, she accepts them all. She shrugs off Jabba's murder and leads the team off to get a better contract. Unlike the other entertainers in the palace, she and Oola are named in the credits and speak, though in an alien language.

Oola the green Twi'lek slave girl dresses only in black mesh with a slave collar, emphasizing her servitude and exploitation. "Oola was once kidnapped from a primitive clan by Jabba's majordomo Bib Fortuna and trained by other Twi'lek girls in the art of seductive dance. Although Jabba finds her highly desirable, Oola refuses to give in to him," *The Star Wars Visual Dictionary* explains (Reynolds 1998, 44). Oola "is an ornament of his power, a diversion, and entertainer, and when he wishes, a vehicle for his sexual pleasure. Stripped of her dancer's costume, she is dressed in flimsy netting, barely clothed, and on display for all. She is eye candy for all those who have an audience in Jabba's throne room" (Reagin and Liedl 2013, 248).

She is a slave, pointlessly sacrificed, who dies as a slave, fighting her master though she knows she won't survive it. "Her resistance—pointless, senseless, and without any chance of success—is motivated by fear, anger, and a sense of hopelessness. Life as Jabba's slave, chained to his throne, to be his plaything, is not worth living. It is better to die resisting bondage than to be slowly destroyed and then die" (Reagin and Liedl 2013, 248). She is a symbol of Jabba's cruelty, not a person. She cringes, struggles, and begs as Jabba keeps her literally chained to his throne but he finally tires of her and feeds her to his rancor. "Jabba's dancers, such as Oola, and the nameless others exist to provide background in Jabba's palace. Oola exists to resist Jabba's advances and thus serve as a victim for the Rancor, alerting the audience to the threat and making Luke seem all the more heroic for defeating the monster," Wetmore explains.

In her short story, she suffers somewhat from Stockholm Syndrome, preferring luxury under Jabba to freedom on Tatooine. Her rather feeble wish is to "dance the perfect dance. Once" (Tyers 1996, 99). She has no other dreams or goals outside her existence in slavery. This, the story suggests, is why she tugs on her chain, denying Jabba and getting killed. Whatever her motives, her entire culture is introduced through this one slave. This becomes important later, as echoes of her are reflected in Jedi Master Aayla Secura in the prequels and several Twi'lek characters in the Legends novels, all of whom go sexily underdressed.

Just as the Wookiees, Ewoks, and droids are coded as the various ethnicities of the galaxy, the space monsters are coded as female. This is nothing new in film: "The archaic mother constructed as a negative force is represented in her phantasmagoric aspects in many horror texts, particularly the sci-fi horror film. We see her as the gaping, cannibalistic bird's mouth in *The Giant Claw*; the terrifying spider of *The Incredible Shrinking Man*; the toothed vagina/womb of *Jaws*; and the fleshy, pulsating, womb of *The Thing* and *The Poltergeist*" (Creed 1999, 261). The space worm that tries to devour them is a passive orifice, while the Sarlaac on Tatooine is recognizable to mythologists as the "vagina dentata" that will devour a man when he's vulnerable during sex—a primal fear the world over. (Humorously, in the *Family Guy* parody, these characters are both played by the unwanted daughter Meg, as is the garbage creature.) "What is common to all of these images of horror is the voracious maw, the mysterious black hole which signifies female genitalia as a monstrous sign which threatens to give birth to equally horrific offspring as well as threatening to incorporate everything in its path. This is the generative archaic mother, constructed within patriarchal ideology as the primeval 'black hole'" (Creed 1999, 261). *The New Essential Guide to Alien Species* comments, "The female Sarlacc is the true danger. Growing to enormous sizes, it is the dominant of the two sexes. Male Sarlaccs are much smaller, and parasitic, attaching themselves to their mates to feed off them" (Lewis and Keier 2013, 145). Female monsters suggest that females are evil creatures awaiting male culture heroes to defeat them, and thus a painful repeated image.

According to *The New Essential Guide to Alien Species*, the garbage creature is a seven-tentacled dianoga, all stomach and digestive system "along with a huge, toothy mouth that can swallow items far larger than the dianoga itself by stretching around them, similar to a snake" (Lewis and Keier 2013, 45). This creature too is a passive devourer and thus an image of horror as it nearly swallows Luke. "The archaic mother is present in all horror films as the blackness of extinction, death. The desires and fears invoked by the image of the archaic mother, as a force that threatens to re-incorporate what it once gave birth to, are always there in the horror text all pervasive, all-encompassing because of the constant presence of death" (Creed 1999, 261). The dianoga is shy and peaceful but also incredibly fecund, able to procreate without a mate (Lewis and Keier 2013, 45). All this is particular feminine coding. It even wraps Luke in a strangling hug.

Nnedi Okorafor's "The Baptist" in *From a Certain Point of View* follows the creature, called Omi, as it's kidnapped from its home swamp and carted off by Imperials. She's aggressive and very female as a male of her species propositions her and she fights him. "To her, the battle had been like an argument that she controlled and eventually won" (2017, 321). She has a poignant emotional story as she battles Stormtroopers and kills two. Then she's taken to the Death Star trash compactor where she grows and learns. When the heroes enter, she regards Leia with respect as "the female would beat savage and cunning" (2017, 329). She also senses Luke's Force connection and symbolically baptizes him in the life-giving water, a feminine blessing for his struggle ahead.

That's nearly it for the galaxy: In *Jedi* there are female Ewoks, though they don't particularly stand out. Even the central slave girls' names go unmentioned in the film, as does Rebellion Leader Mon Mothma's.

MON MOTHMA: BACKGROUND LEADER IN THREE ERAS

Jedi introduces the control center of the Rebellion—and with it female leader Mon Mothma (played by Caroline Blakiston). The script describes her as "a stern but beautiful woman." Her white robe is shapeless, more poncho than gown, with a brown dress underneath. Besides this, she wears the Chandrilan medal of freedom and a livery collar of silver chain, in colors that make her appear serene and futuristic (Hidalgo 2016, 41). The colors echo the Rebels' simplicity and earth tones. In fact, early designs gave her a nun's wimple-like hood, which would have emphasized her mentoring role and linked her outfit with Leia's (Alinger 2014, 157). Of course, it also would have helped her fade into the background. Instead, her striking red hair is bobbed, leaving her more prominent but also androgynous as a fitting Second Wave leader. Onscreen, Mon Mothma is accepted without a word as the Rebellion's military leader—a nod toward equality. Still, this appears a very token nod indeed, as "Many Bothans died to bring us this information" is nearly her only line.

She's given more of an arc in the later *Clone Wars* show: As senator of Chandrila, she's an outspoken opponent of the war with the Separatists and stands against increased power for Chancellor Palpatine. Still, Mothma (Kath Soucie) and Padmé are shown fighting a losing battle, with Anakin and Ahsoka's heroics given center stage. Many of her appearances are little more than cameos. Despite this, she serves as an inspiration for the others. In her own novel, young Leia is struck by Mon Mothma's poise. "Only this woman looked completely ready to accept whatever came. She wasn't afraid, and it was difficult to feel afraid when with her" (Gray 2017, 227). As the senators plan, Mon Mothma insists, "There comes a time when refusing to stop violence can no longer be called nonviolence. We cease to become objectors and become bystanders" (Gray 2017, 211).

The novelization of *Return of the Jedi* adds that she stayed a senator to the end "organizing dissent, stabilizing the increasing ineffectual government" (Kahn [1983] 1995, 408). As both the novels and now *Rogue One* establish, she becomes the last surviving leader of the resistance behind the scenes of the first two films after Bail perishes. "Mon Mothma went underground. She joined her political cells with the thousands of guerillas and insurgents the Empire's cruel dictatorship had spawned. Thousands more joined this Rebel Alliance. Mon Mothma became the acknowledged leader of all the galaxy's creatures who had been left homeless by the Empire. Homeless but not without hope" (Kahn [1983] 1995, 408).

Women's liberation was led historically by white middle-class women, just as the Rebellion of the original films is led by Leia and Mon Mothma (pale, privileged human senators), and basically no other women. Many believed the feminist leaders were oblivious to the racism of the time—the alien women of *Star Wars*, if any have positions in the Rebellion, likely feel the same. An important part of feminism was consciousness-raising—gatherings that revealed to women that they weren't alone in feeling frustrated. Leia does not free or inspire any oppressed women onscreen, abandoning this aspect of the cause. Mothma may be feared to follow her path, grieving for the Bothans but not including them on an equal level.

The expanded universe offers a bit more about her, though less than most characters. In all books, even those with scenes from her point of view, she's a rather colorless leader, devoted to protecting the galaxy from the Empire's rise. "The Republic was deeply flawed. But to replace it with tyranny is worse," Mothma quietly asserts in her notes in *The Imperial Handbook*, taken from the Emperor's possessions after his death and annotated by the Rebellion. Throughout it, she calls out the Empire's attempts to rewrite history, coolly attesting to events she witnessed firsthand. After Palpatine's explanation of the extermination of the Jedi, she objects, "No, I was there. Palpatine may think he can rewrite his own history, but he cannot erase my memories" (Wallace 2015, 99).

In the Legends novels, she has a major arc as she creates the New Republic and rules it as Chief of State, finally passing the title on to Leia. In the new canon, she becomes chancellor but perishes before *The Force Awakens* and leaves instability behind. Leia thinks, "Mon Mothma had remained hugely influential even after her term as chancellor . . . more so than Leia had realized before Mon Mothma's illness. Without someone able to bridge philosophical gaps and create consensus, the political process they'd forged for the New Republic was showing its weakness" (Gray 2016, 7).

The 2017 prequel novel *Leia, Princess of Alderaan* has Mon Mothma working with young Leia's parents to help form the Rebellion. Though the older woman keeps secrets, she's also happy to advise Leia in a friendly, nurturing fashion. She tells Leia that they must learn to carefully use loopholes to outwit the Empire's brutality and save innocents, even as she frets that she can't tell Leia about the Rebellion. She doubts her secret alliance can actually manage to keep smart, observant Leia safe, but refuses to lie to her parents about Leia's activities. "Mon Mothma's always fun—at least, I think so," enthuses the author Claudia Gray. "To me, it seems clear that anybody who could put together and (maybe more significantly) hold together a Rebel Alliance would have the ability to size people up clearly, to connect with a lot of different attitudes and personalities, and a fundamentally pragmatic approach to most things" (Floyd 2017). Notably, Mon Mothma acts as mentor, refusing to dismiss Leia as too young or too sheltered.

She most often appears as Leia's guide and then Leia's boss in the Legends novels as she assigns missions to the younger woman. For this reason, like Yoda and Obi-Wan, she is sidelined in the novels in favor of her student. Still, she provides a strong, trustworthy presence and much-needed mentorship for the princess with no female companions in the films.

In the young adult novel *Moving Target*, in a scene that takes place just after *Empire*, Mothma startles Leia by saying she had been planning to propose a mission to rescue Han. However, she tests Leia's loyalties, asking if she'd want to go on such a mission and thus abandon her priorities. Once again, she straddles motherly mentor and dictating commander. When Leia asserts her commitment to rebellion, Mothma surprises her again by asking what she owes herself and encourages her not to let the Empire take her chance at happiness (Castellucci and Fry 2015, 66).

In a brief flash during the novel, she also shows depth with her own struggle outside of mentoring Leia. She tells the younger woman, "For decades, many on Chandrila have begged me to stop opposing the Empire—because of the danger to my homeworld . . . If what Palpatine desires comes to pass—if his new Death Star is built and his invasion fleets fly—will Chandrila's fate be because of my actions?" (Castellucci and Fry 2015, 68). Every moment of her defiance could cost not just her life but her world—Alderaan's example and then the second Death Star of *Jedi* thus poignantly affects her, though her few words of the film don't address this. Like Leia, Mon Mothma has seen her planet conquered, subverted to the Empire's will. *The Imperial Handbook* details the "Pacification of Salline," the port city of Chandrila. "The governing council of Salline had protested the seizure of its citizens by the ISB secret police.

The Imperial governor branded them traitors. This was the result," Moth-ma writes sadly in her notes. (Wallace 2015, 94). The AT-ATs and AT-STs blow up buildings, killing civilians to take out the rebels.

The character is interesting as she's a leader in all three eras of *Star Wars*. In cut scenes from *Revenge of the Sith*, Mothma (now played by Genevieve O'Reilly) comes to political prominence when, alongside Bail Organa and Padmé, she argues for peace with the Separatists and resists Palpatine's increasing emergency powers. She conspires with her friends to end Palpatine's rise to power (though, again, with few lines) by pre-senting the Delegation of the 2000—a mass insistence that Palpatine give up his emergency powers. In *The Imperial Handbook*, Tarkin writes that the Rebellion began from this moment: "The Emperor issued arrest warrants for the majority of those who had signed the Delegation of the 2000. Organa and Mon Mothma held onto their political careers through out-ward obedience. Behind the scenes, they masterminded the unification of disparate bands of insurgents into what they termed the Rebel Alliance" (Wallace 2015, 140).

Like Padmé's, Mothma's gowns here dominate the scenes—even her simple white gown of *Revenge* is made from elaborate fabrics to blend her more modest appearance in *Jedi* with the elaborate fabrics of a senator—pin-tucked silk and felted wool with white-on-white patterns. This sug-gests a luxury in peace contrasted with austerity in the age of the Empire.

As Disney and new sequels brought a new expanded world canon, the novels, *Rebels*, and *Rogue One* all helped to fill in Mon Mothma's story between *Revenge* and *Jedi*. The children's show *Star Wars: Rebels* sees her step out of the shadows at last. In "Secret Cargo," Mon Mothma gives a speech condemning the Ghorman Massacre and resigns from the Imperi-al Senate. After this, she flees Chandrila and meets up with the crew of the Ghost, one of many Rebel cells. She tells them she plans to build an alliance, with a first meeting on Dantooine. When she finally reaches the planet, she gives an impassioned speech before Senator Organa, General Jan Dodonna, and members of several cells:

> This is Senator Mon Mothma, I have been called a traitor for speaking out against a corrupt Galactic Senate. A Senate manipulated by the sinister tactics of the Emperor. For too long I have watched the heavy hand of the Empire strangle our liberties, stifling our freedoms in the name of ensuring our safety. No longer! Despite Imperial threats, de-spite the Emperor himself, I have no fear as I take new action. For I am not alone. Beginning today we stand together as allies. I hereby resign from the Senate to fight for you, not from the distant hall of politics but from the front lines. We will not rest until we bring an end to the Empire, until we restore our Republic! Are you with me?

The Rebel fleet arrives, and the Alliance is formed. In a further tie-in to modern movements, Mothma calls forth the Rebellion using the all-encompassing Holo-net, a clear internet metaphor. As Winifred Woodhull notes in her essay on global feminisms, "This new public sphere is said to be capable of fostering innovative forms of political activism despite its genesis by the very communication technologies and migratory flows that make possible state-of-the-art modes of domination" (2007, 161). Further, *Rebels*, with some of the strongest heroines in the franchise, unsurprisingly propels Mothma forward, giving her this moment of true leadership.

Rogue One (the 2016 film set concurrently with *A New Hope*) gives Mon Mothma a large role as Rebellion leader as well as mentor to another young girl—Jyn. In her initial scene, she largely provides exposition, directing the younger woman's mission. Halfway through the film, when Jyn returns, Mon Mothma tries to persuade her fellow rebels to fight and helps her get the Council's attention.

However, she fails. "I'm sorry, Jyn. Without the full support of the council, the odds are too great," she tells the younger woman defeatedly. "When her idea to get the Death Star plans is voted down, Mon Mothma can't go against the free vote, but she looks the other way while Jyn leaves, and she does mobilize back-up once it's clear the Rogue One group have infiltrated the Scarif base" (Schnelbach 2017). Nonetheless, it's the pilots who defy orders to abandon their leader in favor of Jyn—a visual vote of no confidence in Mon Mothma. After this, she has a few lines directing messages to be sent but the battle is far out of her hands as she waits at home for news. This weakness emphasizes her roots in the earlier eras, leaving her less able to break out of her role than General Leia in the films released nearly concurrently.

Once again, there are a few glimmers of the woman's larger conflict, especially in Expanded Universe materials. Mon Mothma writes in the *Rogue One Rebel Dossier*, "I understand that for our rebel movement to survive, brave men and women must do terrible things that we'd rather not talk about. But what happens to those men and women afterward? Are we doing enough to help them live with what they've had to do?" (Fry 2016). As she insists they must encourage and comfort their operatives . . . and also monitor when they've become hardened to their jobs, she straddles the line between commander and mother.

In the same book, Advisor Hostis Ij tells Mon Mothma, "With respect, ma'am, the Senate could not protect you. Yours was the most passionate voice to speak up against Palpatine, and you had to flee for your life or face imprisonment and execution" (Fry 2016). This emphasizes her courage but also the naiveté of relying on her position. Later, she insists they must get proof of the Death Star's existence and present it to the Senate so they will revolt against Palpatine. Of course, he dissolves the Senate, emphasizing their lack of power in his regime.

Alexander Freed's 2017 short story "Contingency Plan" reveals what Mon Mothma was doing just after *Rogue One*, during the events of *A New Hope*. She is evacuated, to restart the Rebellion on her own if they lose at Yavin. The story follows her point of view, emphasizing the senator's terrible guilt at sending children out to die and her knowledge of the Rebellion's futility now that the Empire's superweapon has been re-vealed. "It's one thing to endanger oneself for a cause, after all; another to endanger one's entire home planet" (426). As she flees to Coruscant to band together with the Senate and express their outrage over Alderaan—or so she claims—she anticipates the surviving Rebels scattering and yet being hunted down. Even if the galaxy supports the Rebellion and its ranks surge with new membership, the Death Star will come and destroy all their beautiful homeworlds. Her final picture of the future has her surrendering to the Empire—this time no other planets will die. The Re-bellion will end. "Mon Mothma is responsible for her own failures. How can she believe she has the right to start the cycle over again—to rebuild the same Rebellion that was defeated once already?" (430). This, it ap-pears, is her true plan, to capitulate and save lives. All these contingen-cies and more flash through her mind, until her aide tells her the wonder-ful news—that the Death Star itself is destroyed. The Rebellion is saved . . . though once more, not by her actions.

II

The Girl Power Prequel Era

TWO

Warrior Queen Turned Romance Heroine

PADMÉ/AMIDALA: SWITCHING ROLES IN *PHANTOM MENACE*

"*Star Wars* was a Seventies trip on feminine power, with Luke getting in touch with the Force by learning to submit to Princess Leia in all her girliness. But in *Phantom Menace,* the Force is girliness, which is why Amidala has it and the Jedi dudes don't" (Sheffield 1999). Though Padmé is Leia's mother in the franchise, her appearance a generation later, in a white jumpsuit and elaborate hairstyles (often including the double buns), emphasizes her role as heir to Leia's female legacy. Burning with capability and attracting the fannish gaze, she became a new role model for a far different era. *Star Wars* critic Mara Wood (2016, 70) comments, "Padmé is the primary female character in the *Star Wars* prequels. She is the 'Leia' of the millennial generation, a character meant to satisfy the changing societal norms of third wave feminism." This was an era of contradictions, seen in the variously empowered and weakened character.

Third wave feminism followed seventies feminism and indeed post-feminism, in which eighties women returned to the home. Nineties third wavers were born into a world of equal opportunities and taught they could do anything boys could. "An oversimplified timeline might say that the first wave won the right to vote; the second wave won the right to enter the professional workforce; and the third wave combines previous efforts, modified by a woman's right to choose what works best for her—either 'traditional' female roles, 'nontraditional' roles, or a combination of the two," explains Kristen Rowe-Finkbeiner in *The F-word: Feminism in Jeopardy* (2004, 8–10). Following this pattern through her three-film arc, Padmé wants a career and a family. Before these, however, Episode I centers on the third wave concept of "girl power."

Anita Harris explains in *Future Girl: Young Women in the Twenty-First Century* (2004, 16–17): "Originally, girlpower or *grrrlpower* was the catchword of an underground young radical feminist movement that advocated for the improvement of girls' lives. Emerging in the early 1990s as a blend of punk and feminist politics, it became the first powerful youth movement or political subculture to be organized entirely around young women's concerns." Through the nineties, bands like the Spice Girls and films like *Clueless* or *Batman and Robin* (both starring glamorous, fashionable, capable Alicia Silverstone) all introduced strong yet attractive young women. This became a movement in itself, promoting commercialism and even frivolity. Second-wave feminists tended to reject the feminine, as they saw frills and pink as part of the patriarchy's effort to infantilize them. Third-wave feminists, however, reclaimed the bows and tutus as a source of strength and glamour. "They were feminists and they were feminine. They were material girls who wanted to have fun, but they were guerrilla girls too," explains Catherine Gourley in *Ms. and the Material Girls* (2008, 131).

"Well, the revolution is here, and it has bright-red toenails. And it shops. And it carries diaper bags," reported *Sports Illustrated* in July 1999 (Gourley 2008, 131). American Brandi Chastain had won the Women's Cup Finals and celebrated it by ripping off her top to reveal a sports bra. Ninety thousand fans had watched her win, emphasizing that women did indeed have a place in sports. "Suddenly girl power was a good thing—strong, confident, and as *Sports Illustrated* pointed out, feminine too" (Gourley 2008, 131). Girlie feminists insisted they weren't brainwashed by the patriarchy but were following their own path to self-expression.

Certainly, Queen Amidala epitomizes girl power, as she's literally a fourteen-year-old. The novelization adds, "New to the throne, she had only been queen a few months before the blockade had begun. She was young, but it was rumored she was prodigiously talented and extremely well trained" (T. Brooks 1999, 28). With this, she's a child prodigy doing an adult job. This was a typical pattern in the girl-power era of the nineties and 2000s—*Xena, Warrior Princess*, *Buffy the Vampire Slayer*, and the *Powerpuff Girls* were all diminutized down to their goofy and younger-sounding names to make them less threatening to the traditional gender dichotomy.

In fact, Queen Amidala's sweet innocence is part of her backstory: *Star Wars Absolutely Everything You Need to Know* explains, "Naboo's people vote for their monarchs. Often they elect young women as queens, believing they possess a childlike wisdom that is more pure than that of an adult!" (Bray et al. 2015, 152). Another extended universe book by Lucasfilm Story Group head Pablo Hidalgo adds, "The notion of electing so young a monarch underscored the emphasis that the Naboo people placed on educating children and their desire to keep cynical manipulators of the type tempered by decades in politics out of their local government" (2016a, 21). Choosing a queen who's pure and innocent links with ideals of the nineteenth century, that women should be given power because of their innate morality and goodness. Queen Amidala is not elected as a person, but as a symbol and a childish blank slate.

While Twi'lek and a few other species are shown being sexist as a matter of course, the appointing of child queens is the most sexist behavior seen in the *Star Wars* universe among humans. Even as the films and especially extended universe stories suggest men and women can all be engineers, pilots, rebels, or rulers, *Phantom Menace* shows the people appointing a young girl to rule them because of her innocence. Royal tradition then garbs her in heavily gendered, excessively elaborate apparel. Her successors follow the same pattern, suggesting a built-in sexism that might last centuries, as it did on earth.

She tells Anakin in a cut scene from *Attack of the Clones:* "I wasn't the youngest Queen ever elected. But now that I think back on it, I'm not sure I was old enough. I'm not sure I was ready." These words have her joining the Emperor, Trade Federation, and everyone else in calling the young woman unfit for the job. In this moment, she suggests she's a child doing a grown woman's job, so she deserves sympathy and aid from the men, to reward her hard work and good intentions. This makes her non-threatening, thus comforting viewers threatened by a strong woman. Nineties-style, she's strong but not *too* strong. Third wave feminism "railed against the emerging 'Men's Movement,' which not only suggested that feminism had gone too far and was no longer needed, but that women who were feminists were 'ball-breakers' who were out to get men" (Phillips and Cree 2014). Presenting softer, girlish heroines whose strength was often subverted emphasized that these women were no threat. With this, men could admire, date and marry them without, as girls feared, being repelled by the strength of feminism.

"This kind of girl power constructs the current generation of young women as a unique category of girls who are self-assured, living lives lightly inflected but by no means driven by feminism, influenced by the philosophy of DIY, and assuming they can have (or at least buy) it all" (Harris 2004, 17). Girl power became synonymous with purchasing power. Certainly, Amidala is a queen with all the gowns a character can possibly wear in a single film. However, the heroine gives up much of her assertiveness to the physically dominating costumes she wears. There's even a *Star Wars* wiki page dedicated to her extensive wardrobe.

"Much of her Naboo state attire is even offensive with its appropriation of Asian cultural aesthetic" (Rodriguez 2014). The Mongolian and Imperial court-inspired gowns, all intended to be "exotic," are problematic for some of the audience. Since the queen is not Asian and is not suggested to have chosen or altered these traditional gowns for herself, she is playing a part, with the exotic imagery imposed from outside. They're also a sign of their era—the girl power consumer culture often sought out fashions from around the world, obsessed as it was by acquiring the new and different.

This isn't the only way in which she plays a part. Iain McCaig, the concept artist, comments, "We were told that Queen Amidala was to be in disguise: that you could sneak out the back of her costumes and you wouldn't know she was gone, which is why she is wearing clothing up to her chin and white facepaint, like you find on geishas, Mongolians, or Elizabeth I of England" (Biggar 2005, 41). This unnatural appearance characterized much of historical royalty. "In the fifteenth century, European queens and noblewomen wore tortuous court fashions: headdresses of wire mesh molded into unnatural shapes and stiffened gowns lined with fur made them seem almost inhuman" (Reagin and Liedl 2013, 170). As the *Phantom Menace* junior novel, written by celebrated children's book author Patricia C. Wrede explains, "The elaborate royal costumes and formal face paint were as much a part of her new position as the decisions she was called upon to make every day" (14). She thinks that her immaculate appearance will help offset her youth.

Indeed, she manages politics through her particularly girly superpower, especially focusing on the power of illusion and dress-up. Critic Rob Sheffield of *Rolling Stone* snarks, "You can't tell whether you're seeing the real queen or the handmaiden Padmé pretending to be the queen, and you never really care, because they're the same suburban girl just playing dress-up. (Also, they have about two-thirds of a facial expression between them.) The queen's authority is all in her makeup, especially that lipstick job—maybe she's born with it, maybe it's the Force!"

Third-wave critic Sarah Projansky describes *Time* and *Newsweek* magazine covers in the early nineties with an anonymous girl (unmentioned by name in the article within) standing for society's problems—divorce or learning disabilities, for example (2007, 50–52). Politicians likewise would introduce causes to save young, vulnerable unspecified women. With this, they became invisible, undefined. Her superpower is not just a fictional construct but a reflection of her time. Filmmaker Mike Stoklasa in an Episode I review asks fans to describe characters from the story. While Han Solo has lots of personality, for Padmé, "The fans cannot come up with a single description that doesn't mention her makeup, clothes, or royal position" (Taylor 2014, 361).

Famed feminist Judith Butler (1990, 45) argues that all women play a part, encouraged by culture: "Gender is the repeated stylization of the body, a set of repeated acts within a highly rigid regulatory frame that congeal over time to produce the appearance of substance, of a natural sort of being." In fact, third wavers often considered gender a performance, and would wear pretty dresses and elaborate hairdos ironically or deliberately in order to hide behind them. Womanliness is a mask which can be worn or removed as the woman deliberately uses her own body as a disguise. In Amidala's costume, hair, and face paint, gender looks quite unnatural, emphasizing how much being a queen of Naboo is an artificial role. At the same time, it underscores the artificiality of femininity—to be the new damsel of *Star Wars*, Padmé's actress is playing a role that's just as false.

Originally Lucas had planned three costumes for Queen Amidala. However, this soon expanded to eight as well as four more for Padmé the handmaiden. This had several effects: certainly, it stressed her formal, ceremonial duties. Lucas adds, "Somebody of that stature would automatically be changing her costumes to fit the occasion. She travels. She goes to the Senate. She has sort of official functions and not-official functions, and each one of those demands a different type of costume" (Lucas et al. 1999a). Her first costume, the widely-publicized crimson dress, is the color of royal authority and power. "Red is the color of life—of blood, fire, passion, and war" (Bruce-Mitford 1996, 107). In it, she shows off her power and courage. The escoffiate headpiece provides gold face frames, while gold embroidery, fur-trimmed sleeves, and lit jewels around the base add to the trappings of majesty.

The film guide explains, "Amidala's stylized white makeup draws upon Naboo's ancient royal customs. The red 'scar of remembrance' marks Naboo's time of suffering, before the Great Time of Peace" (Reynolds and Fry 2012, 41). It emphasizes a costume passed down from generation to generation, one replacement queen after another. "She's an Elizabethan vampire doll in Virgin Mary drag, living large in an Epcot Center palace obviously built to match her clothes. She looks like the Cure's Robert Smith trick-or-treating as Liz Taylor's Cleopatra, attended by her posse of smashingly accessorized harem girls; and you just know all the ladies' rooms on Naboo have air conditioning and back issues of *Vogue*," Sheffield (1999) explains. Of course, this aids in allowing the queen and decoy to impersonate each other—if the clothes make the queen, they're a useful disguise. The lack of eye makeup (which differentiates this look from a geisha's) also helps the heroine de-emphasize her individuality.

Cultural theorist Susan Hopkins argues, "Girlpower is a provocative mix of youth, vitality, sexuality, and self-determination. The story on offer here is one of power through and control over one's own identity invention and re-invention" (quoted in Harris 2004, 17). Indeed, the queen's imposing face paint hearkens back to ancient traditions worldwide. Masks often symbolized a person borrowing the face of the god—manifesting supreme power and often spiritual light. Masked, Amidala is no longer a teenager but the embodiment of Naboo and all spiritual authority. Masks conceal emotion—and some, like the face of Medusa—terrify with the sternness of female fury. In modern times, masks suggest concealment of the ego. "They symbolize the inner characteristics which may normally be hidden by the outward personality" (Cooper 1978, 104). These are the buried power yet to develop in the young queen, assumed as a persona when she gives public addresses. Clearly the uncertain teenager takes courage and poise from all her face paint and costume represent—the royal tradition and authority. On a practical level, it gives her an easier time swapping places with her double, confusing her foes as well as the viewing audience. Masks indicate "protection; concealment; transformation; non-being" (Cooper 1978, 104). In some cultures, tricksters wear masks, using them to beguile the enemy. Once again, Amidala is presented as filled with secrets and hidden undercurrents, taking power from nontraditional abilities and subversion of expectations. She unleashes this power against the underhanded Trade Federation, and against her allies as well.

Amidala first appears on the Trade Federation's screen (another level of distance and disguise), motionless except for her lips. "You will not be pleased when you hear what I have to say, Viceroy . . . Your trade boycott of our planet has ended," she says firmly. She reminds him the Senate's ambassadors will quickly end their stand-off. As she threatens from a position of strength, she nonetheless appears robotic. Butler (1990, 71) comments, "The woman in masquerade wishes for masculinity in order to engage in public discourse with men." To compensate for her youth, the queen wears extremely formal, regal robes that are far larger than she is. Certainly, under this charade, Queen Amidala resists the Trade Federation, her political antagonists (and notably played by all men). "She is forceful, commanding, and calm. She speaks to the Trade Federation as their equal, not as a child. Her team of advisors respects her decisions; there are no remarks made about her course of action or of her age or experience," Mara Wood notes (2016, 70).

Still, she only argues to a stalemate. Further, her righteousness is undercut when the Trade Federation leaders dismiss her assertion that the Senate has taken her side. Viceroy Nute tells her, "I know nothing of any ambassadors . . . you must be mistaken." Surprised at his reaction, she studies him carefully and blusters that the Federation has gone too far. Unsettled by the bold-faced lies, Amidala has no idea how to keep fighting, and she backs down. She ends the conversation with the flimsy "We will see." Though their master Darth Sidious dismisses her as "young and naïve," she continues to battle. When she addresses the Senate much later in another elaborate gown, she debates more senators (all male) and calls for appointing one elderly white male chancellor to replace another. Here she plays in the arena of visually male politics, strengthened and emboldened by her wardrobe as well as her game of substitution.

It's notable that, as queen of a planet, she literally has it all, and yet has little power to save her people. This too works as a metaphor for the contradictions of third-wave. Heywood and Drake explain in their essay on the economics of third-wave, "There has been a shift from a top-down, hierarchical culture of power to a power focused in multinational corporations and dependent upon global flows. In this context, power understood as possessed by individuals has become inaccessible to almost everyone" (2007, 120). Amidala discovers this as she finds her planet assaulted by a literal trade federation greedy for wealth. With this, girls' visions of a ruling queen's power are crushed.

Enemies in this trilogy are not just the Sith but also the droid foundries of Geonosis, the Techno Union, or the Banking Clan. "Throughout the prequel trilogy, the capitalistic villains are portrayed in terms of images and ideas that semiotically evoke and reference the "dark ages" of fixed capital and heavy industry: assembly lines, the desire to monopolize trade, the bosses (Neimoidians) who oversee the entire operation from a lofty position of hierarchical superiority, etc." (Silvio 2007, 70). There is also good capitalism, portrayed in the shining capitol of Coruscant and the decadent but well-meaning Naboo. Not all capitalism is bad, the film suggests, only meaningless identical droids, bred for war on endless assembly lines. Girls can still dream of princesshood and beautiful fashions, while dangerous sports arenas can offer boys like Anakin a chance to be heroes and even win themselves free of their systemic oppression.

Following this is a scene with the queen's councilors. The queen wears her imposing red outfit with the maidens in gold, each on her own throne, suggesting a near equality. Costume designer Trisha Biggar says, "For Episode I, George [Lucas] wanted the Queen's handmaidens to have a mysterious quality, their faces obscured when they are seen in public. This is accomplished with soft hoods, constructed to extend out and create deep shadows over their faces" (2005, 41). Even more than the queen's makeup, this look emphasizes the women's power of disguise. Beyond them sit human male characters Governor Sio Bibble and security head Captain Tanaka—emphasizing a world in which the queen rules over strong men.

Girl power often focuses on friendship, and indeed, the handmaidens are suggested to be a source of trusted companionship as well as protection. Their female-centric community arguably even celebrates a nonheteronormative community, emphasizing that she is complete with her four maidens in her chambers, with no sign of a male consort. The queen is certainly closer to her decoy, with whom she shares a secret double life, than to the nine-year-old potential "love interest" of *Phantom Menace*. However, with no personalities and barely a line for any maiden except the decoy-queen while she's playing that role, this film, like the original trilogy, focuses on the queen as exceptional—basically the only woman in the galaxy who evolves or has a personality. Her companions make up the background scenery.

Together, Amidala and her advisors try to find a solution to the Trade Federation's blockade. Following the third wave tradition, the prequels do political activism in their own way: As critic Melissa Hillman explains, "The prequels were clear that we were all complicit in a corrupt system whether we admitted it to ourselves or not, symbolized by noble Jedi finding themselves leading an army of slave clones that were purchased from part of a massive military industrial complex." The Jedi's moral compromise as they fight for goodness but find themselves bogged down by politics and political agendas revealed a new side to *Star Wars*—one where backroom deals with a "Trade Federation" could take precedence over a people's independence. The queen tries fighting for her people, as well as those oppressed throughout the galaxy, but she is shouted down by the older men in power—a disappointing image shared by many viewers of her generation. At first introduction, the Old Republic is bogged down with argument and compromise, choking peace as well as progress. As critic Melissa Hillman (2017) concludes, "This was a stunning accusation, and played to the 90s' growing concerns of big business' influence on government."

Even as she struggles to protect her people, Amidala's decisions seem naïve, as she is denying the facts and stubbornly insisting on decent behavior and diplomacy even as the planet is assaulted:

> **BIBBLE**: A communications disruption can only mean one thing. Invasion.
>
> **AMIDALA**: The Federation would not dare go that far.
>
> **CAPT. PANAKA**: The Senate would revoke their trade franchise, and they'd be finished.
>
> **AMIDALA**: We must continue to rely on negotiation.
>
> **BIBBLE**: Negotiation? We've lost all communications! . . . and where are the Chancellor's Ambassadors?
>
> **CAPT. PANAKA**: This is a dangerous situation, Your Highness. Our security volunteers will be no match against a battle-hardened Federation army.
>
> **AMIDALA**: I will not condone a course of action that will lead us to war.

Since she and her people are captured just after this, her decision is revealed as foolhardy—motivated by wishful thinking rather than an acceptance of reality. As she flees, her costume once again strengthens her. The immense black feather headdress with gemstone crispinettes over a black cowl makes her more imposing as she faces off with her enemies. It also suggests the concealment that is the heroine's talent. She wears a black spiderweb lacy robe, with its somber color suggesting her dismay in a subtle form of protest.

Rapidly, the Trade Federation capture the queen. She stoutly refuses to sign an agreement to submit to an occupation, emphasizing her morality. Of course, the Trade Federation doesn't clue in to her deception. Technically, as Padmé thinks in the junior novel, her decoy cannot legally sign the proposed treaty, giving her people an added layer of security, However, from her safe position, Padmé must watch her people suffer at the enemy's hands, even while unable to fight. "Can I watch my people starve, and maybe die, and not give in," she wonders (Wrede 1999, 36).

Still, in a display of traditional gender roles, it's the two Jedi (and one clumsy Gungan) who must rescue her party. Further, the moment is very traditionally gendered, a scene of knights and princesses in the otherwise more modern political plot. "This is indeed a scene filled with gallantry and heroism, the Jedi coming to the rescue in a 'knightly' chivalrous manner, with a hint of western 'gun slinging' as Qui-Gon holsters his saber with terrific speed," note Hanson and Kay in *Star Wars: The New Myth* (2001, 71).

Having saved the day, Qui-Gon and Captain Panaka take charge, directing her to the hanger and then arguing the queen into fleeing. When she replies that her place is with her people, Qui-Gon, Bibble, and Panaka all chime in to persuade her. After a coded exchange with Padmé, Amidala accepts her new mission, to plead their case to the Senate. Of course, the men's role in the decision as well as in rescuing her and arranging protection weakens her, as do subtler points: As Cavelos points out, "A strong leader would not allow her planet to be so defenseless. If her people don't want to have an army or weapons, then she ought to establish a treaty with another planet to defend them. If her only recourse is to 'plead' her case to the Senate and the fate of her people depends on that, then she should have arranged for her own escape from Naboo, which she did not" (2006, 316).

Off they fly, but soon land on Tatooine, with a damaged ship in need of repair. Here a new character comes to the forefront as Padmé the queen's handmaiden emerges from the ship to accompany Qui-Gon on his salvage mission. For this, she dons a homespun gray tunic with medium blue shirt and belt. Her hair is back in simple braids. Here she's not an elaborately decked queen or invisible handmaiden, just a girl. This is a classic fairytale tradition: "Stories abound of kings and princes escaping notice and palace life, dressed as ordinary subjects" (Reagin and Liedl 2013, 170).

For Joan Riviére, the pioneer of "performing femininity," ultra-femininity is "assumed and worn as a mask, both to hide the possession of masculinity and to avert the reprisals expected if she was found to possess it" ([1929] 1986, 38). For instance, Riviére describes housewives faking ignorance of repairs "in an innocent and artless manner, as if they were lucky guesses" to appear nonthreatening to the male ego ([1929] 1986, 39). Padmé's girlishness is a masquerade deliberately putting aside her fierceness, as she's a queen playing a handmaid playing an unassuming desert-dweller. These roles reassure both audience and authoritative males like Qui-Gon that she's no threat, just a curious, forgettable observer. On planet, she draws no attention from Jabba the Hutt, while remaining meekly, politely, at the background of their adventure. She gives no orders and allows Qui-Gon to ignore her quiet protests. When she voices her own opinion in the words of the queen, thus in her own words ("the queen would not approve"), she gives Qui-Gon an atypical freedom to reject them out of hand because only the handmaiden is saying them. Qui-Gon smirks to himself in the junior novel, "And so the little handmaiden discovers that her influence with the queen has limits," (Wrede 1999, 79) though he absently notices and dismisses the authority in her voice.

Third-wavers grew up in a time of equality, and indeed, Padmé doesn't feel the need to fight for respect from men as Leia does. However, her generation's battle already won, she responds to strong men in rather the opposite way. If Queen Amidala was imposing to viewers (though undercut by naïve actions and beliefs), little Padmé is far less impressive, and can win over the audience through gentle, if wimpy, likability. In fact, she breaks out from behind the robotic queen image to become a sympathetic viewpoint figure beside the wise, older Jedi and goofy Gungan. "Natalie Portman hasn't been given much of a character to play, just an ordinary girl in a transgalactic princess fantasy. But in *Phantom Menace*, her ordinary girlness really stands out. For all her froufrou gowns, she's the only figure in the movie who can make the audience say, 'There I am'" (Sheffield 1999).

Even while reassuring Jedi and audience, Padmé clearly enjoys subverting her queen role as the lowliest-looking inhabitant of an outer-rim planet (a backwater world in contrast with her privileged Naboo). Being simple Padmé gives her a new level of freedom, not only to wear slouchy clothes but to make friends and explore, not as burden-bearing queen but as a girl. The junior novel reflects on how freeing the handmaid costume is: "'Padmé' did not exist . . . except when Amidala was in disguise" (Wrede 1999, 35). For the first time, she is not excessively feminine or coldly androgynous in her gowns. The people around her respond in kind: No one holds her hostage or makes passes at her as "the girl" or subjects her to sexist remarks. Unlike in the palace, where the Jedi rescue her and the Trade Federation comment on her inexperience, she's free to simply be unnoticed.

Of course, Qui-Gon treats Padmé as a burden, accepting her with "This is not a good idea. Stay close to me." In fact, she's less disruptive than Jar-Jar (whom it's not clear why Qui-Gon is bringing). She's a positive figure, approaching the new environment carefully and acknowledging that she doesn't know everything. She's sweet, telling the child Anakin she's glad to have met him after a brief conversation. Anakin in turn promptly objectifies her, asking if she's an angel, which he's heard described as "the most beautiful creatures in the universe." His adoration will continue through the next films.

"One could read the cultural obsession with girlhood as a response to postfeminism, a kind of 'backlash' against the particular 1980s postfeminist woman who is unhappy with how career has displaced family or who has returned to a rather boring neotraditionalism" (Projansky 2007, 44). By focusing on girls instead of women, this new movement need not reject postfeminism utterly. "If the postfeminist woman is always in process, always using the freedom and equality handed to her by feminism in pursuit of having it all (including discovering her sexuality) but never quite managing to reach full adulthood, to fully have it all, one could say that the postfeminist woman is quintessentially adolescent" (Projansky 2007, 45).

As their adventures continue, her sweetness does not lend itself to being an equal team member. Despite extensive training in diplomacy and an entire planet's resources, she does nothing to help their mission besides befriending Anakin. "She offers no plan and takes no significant action. Like a milder version of Leia, her only input is criticism, and her criticisms are dismissed" (Cavelos 2006, 317). It's Anakin, a nine-year-old uneducated child, who comes up with the plan to get the money necessary to repair the ship. He offers them the racing pod he's built and heroically executes the plan by competing in the podrace for a substantial chunk of the film. Padmé, meanwhile, only cheers him on. As she is the identification figure, the audience does this as well, becoming the heroine whose heart is stolen by the young hero. With all this, girl power comes across as far weaker in fact than boy power.

Suddenly, the enigmatic Sith creature Darth Maul attacks, trying to murder the innocent queen and her handmaidens. Valiant Qui-Gon battles him, defending the lady. After Anakin has saved them all with his showy pod racing, it takes a male Jedi knight to defend the queen and then leap onboard the fleeing ship. Once more, Padmé has done nothing.

At last, she addresses the Senate, as has been the stated goal for much of the film. Thus, she appears in all her glory. Her gown once again is majestic and powerful to lend the young woman strength. It's thick red velvet with embossed rosettes and golden triple-braided soutache on the sleeves and collar. The imposing headdress binds her hair into a severe form with golden hairbands, and it's all topped by the Royal Sovereign of Naboo medal, emphasizing the source of her power (though once again establishing it as outside herself). A red robe of office lined in red silk adds to her majesty.

"The essence of third-wave philosophy, though hard to pin down, is that real social change is achieved indirectly through cultural action, or simply carried out through pop culture twists and transformations, instead of through an overtly political, electoral, and legislative agenda" (Rowe-Finkbeiner 2004, 88). In fact, the queen and her maidens to this point have escaped capture and toured Tatooine—to say nothing of changing costumes a dozen times—but spend only a few moments attempting politics before they lose in the political arena. The appeal to the Senate is short and easily deflected, as the Trade Federation call for further investigation, delaying any attempt to save Naboo. Even in her general queenship and mission, Amidala comes up short, as Cavelos (2006, 317) notes:

> A strong leader must know the resources she commands and the options she has. Amidala appears to have no idea that the Gungans have an army and significant weaponry. If she had, she could have used them to repel the original invasion. Instead, she stakes everything on an appeal to the Senate. But when she arrives at Coruscant, she asks Palpatine her options. Apparently she has no clear course of action in mind and has no sense of the alternatives.

Of course, Amidala's great well-meaning failure on Coruscant is calling for a vote of no confidence in Valorum, allowing Palpatine's election in his place. He tells her, "Our best choice would be to push for the election of a stronger Supreme Chancellor. One who will take control of the bureaucrats and give us justice." Visually, Palpatine is speaking into Amidala's ear, using her as her mouthpiece. Unwilling to accept her people's death or slavery, she agrees. Storywise, her kind heart and love for her people are seen beguiling her into destroying the Republic. "Our people are dying, Senator," she tells Palpatine. "We must do something quickly in order to stop the Federation."

This has third-wave implications as the complacent feminists often found themselves losing power in the workplace, confronted by religious and other backlashes. Men, ruling the White House and other social arenas, began to take back freedoms once thought of as permanently won. One proud third-waver, interviewed in *The F-word: Feminism in Jeopardy*, notes, "We thought the second wave was boring and dull for 'fighting the patriarchy' but maybe we should be keeping our eye more on the 'patriarchy,' particularly with all the changes coming from the White House" (Rowe-Finkbeiner 2004, 105). Indeed, a similar battle seems to have been lost in Padmé's galaxy: "The world of *Star Wars: Episode I The Phantom Menace* is dominated by males. Nearly all power is in the hands of the Jedi Council and the Galactic Senate, both of which are made up mostly of males" (Bodden 2012, 48).

Having done her best by appointing the old, white, upper-class male Palpatine to fight on her behalf, Amidala selflessly returns to the planet, apparently to let herself be captured and become a martyr. She decides this in a black gown—elaborate but somber to match her failure. Her role of sacrifice matches her victimization through much of the story.

Besides the elaborate gowns, Padmé continues to share the feminine kindness she revealed on Tatooine as she comforts Anakin onboard the ship. "Responding to Padmé's maternal concern for his well-being, the precocious Anakin, despite his tender years, soon becomes interested in her romantically, convinced that they will one day wed—no matter Jedi prohibitions of such relationships. Separated from Shmi, he has already found another woman upon whom to focus his apparent deep need for emotional attachment" (Wilson 2007, 137–38). Meanwhile, Anakin's gift of a necklace he's made Padmé suggests his giving his favor to the warrior on the eve of battle. "Here male and female are reversed, but the roles the characters play are still consistent, given that Amidala is the warrior and Anakin, who is a child, plays a more benign and vulnerable role" (Hanson and Kay 2001, 98).

Girl power heroines cross gender boundaries, "and so the very notion of gender has been unbalanced in a way that encourages experimentation and creative thought" (Rampton 2015). Like Leia, the queen and her maidens wear elaborate gowns and hairstyles, but also readily defend themselves with blasters. "Even as she takes on the role of a powerful, intelligent, and courageous leader, Queen Amidala retains her characteristically 'feminine' traits. She does not have to become masculine, mannish, or even 'sexless' in order to exercise her power and strength," Bodden notes (2012, 50). As Rampton (2015) notes, this flexibility and refusal to conform to traditional feminism is one of girl power's strengths:

> This is in keeping with the third wave's celebration of ambiguity and refusal to think in terms of "us-them." Most third-wavers refuse to identify as "feminists" and reject the word that they find limiting and exclusionary. Grrl-feminism tends to be global, multi-cultural, and it shuns simple answers or artificial categories of identity, gender, and sexuality. Its transversal politics means that differences such as those of ethnicity, class, sexual orientation, etc. are celebrated and recognized as dynamic, situational, and provisional. Reality is conceived not so much in terms of fixed structures and power relations, but in terms of performance within contingencies. Third wave feminism breaks boundaries.

Preparing for war, Amidala and her maidens wear red when they reach Naboo for the climax. Sabé the decoy's battle dress is intimidating black over red and short enough that she can move easily (though critics have pointed out that the heavy headdress and warm fabric make actual battle problematic). Her hairstyle is elaborate to intimidate the enemy, but the rest of her outfit is simpler and cut like a samurai's. Padmé's wine-colored velvet battle dress is cut similarly.

As they approach Naboo, the queen reveals she has a plan, though it requires the help of the laughable Jar-Jar. This raises up the marginalized character but also reveals the depth of their separation. Many aspects of third-wave feminism came from a place of white middle- and upper-class privilege. Fiction would cast minorities as the best friend far more often than the lead. In this tradition, the *Star Wars* galaxy is ruled by humans (especially in the novelizations, which emphasize Palpatine's racism). In fact, Naboo is an Imperialist paradise, with the decadent humans colonizers of the world. Obviously, the Gungans, now relegated to hidden villages in the swamps, are the natives. When the queen visits them, they are surprised and dismissive as they're fed up with her people's superiority. In fact, the oblivious Naboo have brought down a war and now ask them to fight in it.

Revealing her abilities as a leader and diplomat, the queen appeals directly to the Gungan Boss Nass. This is her testing moment, and Padmé seizes it by bursting from the decoy's side and revealing herself as the true ruler: "I am sorry for my deception, but it was necessary to protect myself. Although we do not always agree, Your Honor, our two great societies have always lived in peace. . . . I ask you to help us." With this, Padmé dramatically drops to her knees and the others slowly join her "no, I beg you to help us. We are your humble servants. Our fate is in your hands." Arguably this is another performance, filled with drama and supplication, but this is the queen's top skill and she executes it admirably. "Embodying the hard-won successes of previous generations, the third wave expands the fight against social hierarchies, moving it past American borders, with a focus on global feminism," Rowe-Finkbeiner (2004, 90) explains. As Boss Nass reveals, the important moment here is Amidala abandoning any trace of colonialism—the impression that she views herself as superior. This indeed wins him over. It's a moment of greatness, though enacted as the pacifying loving peacemaker.

Of course, problematic gender roles continue following the idealistic queen. She is still coming from a place of weakness, as she has no army and begs the Gungans (whose soldiers, leaders, and named characters are all male) to defend her. Still, it's delightfully empowering that she organizes her people's revolution and leads it herself. The queen is the one to derive the plan—the Gungans will act as decoys, distracting the viceroy's forces while she personally retakes the palace. This scene, like Leia's with the Ewoks, struck fans and critics as remarkably anti-technological, putting the power in the overlooked power of nature. The Gungans' war on Padmé's behalf can be seen as furthering third-wave's "environmentalism, anti-corporate activism, and struggles for [non]human rights" all at once (Heywood and Drake 2007, 122).

Fighting in this manner is logical, as ecofeminism was vital to second and third wave. Padmé allies with the Gungans and literally battles against brutal, planet-destroying technology using the powers of the undeveloped swamp and underwater world. "Gungan culture centers on the environment and the other living things that populate it" (Lewis and Keier 2013, 76). *The New Essential Guide to Alien Species* goes on to explain that they have particularly close relationships with their riding mounts and use biotechnology, growing rather than building their ships (Lewis and Keier 2013, 77).

"Grrl-feminism tends to be global, multi-cultural, and it shuns simple answers or artificial categories of identity, gender, and sexuality. Its transversal politics means that differences such as those of ethnicity, class, sexual orientation, etc. are celebrated and recognized as dynamic, situational, and provisional" (Rampton 2015). The queen leads her forces, shooting the enemy to directly reclaim her throne. However, in this scene, Padmé's exceptionalism shows up again—the suggestion that she's the only capable female in the galaxy. In her firefight, she leaves the maidens behind, including the bodyguard decoy—apparently only the men are useful guards. Further, when Padmé is pinned down, Anakin wrestles with the fighter controls and manages to shoot the droidekas. Once again, boy power saves the day as he actually flies his fighter over to the Trade Federation control ship and destroys it—ending the war though he's just a child who's never flown in space combat.

Only when her decoy arrives with her own army does she fulfill her true function, leading away half the army long enough for Padmé to snatch hidden blasters and overcome the last of the Trade Federation. She throws one to Captain Panaka and one to an officer. With a third, she shoots a battle droid and holds the Viceroy at her mercy. Steely, she tells him, "Now, Viceroy, we will discuss a new treaty." Despite all the pitfalls and costume changes, she has finally reclaimed her world as well as the course of the film.

She ends the film in a celebratory gown like Leia's in the first film, presiding over an award ceremony. "Many historic queens were defined by public ceremonies. Most common and significant were weddings, but queens were also celebrated with grand entry pageants and parades when they visited subject cities" (Reagin and Liedl 2013, 172). While Princess Leia's ceremony is simple, the parade on Naboo shows off the Old Republic at its height, with showers of petals, music, and cheering mobs. This is what it means to be queen, another conventional, glamorous role.

"After the victory over the Trade Federation, Amidala appears in a parade gown markedly different from her robes of office. The silken petals of the dress resemble huge, lovely flowers found near Amidala's home village. These flowers bloom only once every 88 years, heralding a time of special celebration" (Reynolds and Fry 2012, 41). The gown is lighthearted, frivolous, and pretty. It's weddinglike in color and the parasol collar gives her an angel halo—as she offers a glowing sphere to Boss Nass and smiles at Anakin, she is indeed framed as the reward for the men's heroism. With this, she ends the story as the elegant queen saluting the men who battled to protect her.

As Padmé slips between elegant princess and tough warrior, she embodies girl power's versatility, but also emphasizes its weakness. Girl power was meant to boost girls' self-esteem and personal empowerment while also allowing them to enjoy preoccupations with glamour, boys, and consumerism. Certainly, the queen spends as much time selecting Hollywood runway gowns and having her hair and makeup done as she spends negotiating or ruling. Further, she can have it all by going on adventures as a handmaiden, even to the rough parts of town. However, the other characters spend far too much time propping her up. Girl power heroines were often regarded as frivolous and weak, deliberately undercutting their power to appease the men. Likewise, Episode I introduces a warrior queen, but one who's fourteen, overly polite, and politically naïve. Arguably, a tougher, savvier leader would have served Naboo better, without appointing Palpatine to unheard-of power.

> It is hard to talk about the aims of the third wave because a characteristic of that wave is the rejection of communal, standardized objectives. The third wave does not acknowledge a collective "movement" and does not define itself as a group with common grievances. Third wave women and men are concerned about equal rights but tend to think the genders have achieved parity or that society is well on its way to delivering it to them. The third wave pushed back against their "mothers" (with grudging gratitude) the way children push away from their parents in order to achieve much needed independence. This wave supports equal rights but does not have a term like feminism to articulate that notion. For third wavers, struggles are more individual: "We don't need feminism anymore." (Rampton 2015)

Of course, while a girl can snatch Leia's blaster or Rey's lightsaber and play at action heroine, Padmé's political plot comes across as more complex and less desirable for children to emulate. Padmé offers another complication as feminist icon for girls—the costumes are complex enough to be difficult to replicate. Amidala and Padmé were unpopular for Halloween costumes and convention cosplay, in contrast with Leia's iconic gown and buns or the male Jedi. Episode II's white jumpsuit was more popular, specifically as the inverse of the gigantic ballgowns. Still, even in her action clothes, she remains more damsel than savior.

HAVING IT ALL: PADMÉ'S THIRD WAVE LOVE AFFAIR

Episode II begins with Amidala's decoy's sudden assassination. This abrupt death of a near-personalityless heroine impels the plot, giving rise to comments about fridging—female characters killed to affect the men. In the novelization, Typho is horrified on seeing Amidala dead as he finds himself "looking at Amidala's beautiful robes, at their placement about the very still form" (Salvatore 2002, 40). He objectifies her, sympathetic and desolated at the loss of the beautiful, fragile queen. Visually, shooting the senator's double suggests killing off the senator, both foreshadowing her end and driving this film's objective of bodyguarding the damsel. With this, as Cavelos comments, "Amidala becomes an object to be protected rather than a compelling character" (2006, 318).

Meanwhile, Padmé herself is disguised as a Naboo starfighter pilot as a safety precaution. Her featureless helmet gives her the most concealing mask of all, as she pushes her decoy routine to a new level. The uniform with grey leather tunic, gauntlets, and Naboo military boots nods to her active wear jumpsuit of the climax. It's a surprisingly androgynous moment for the heroine, emphasizing, as with her rough clothes on Naboo, her willingness to fade away when necessary.

Of course, she soon returns to the gowns, this time with even more plot and character symbolism than in the previous film. As senator addressing the Loyalist Committee, Padmé's "severe hairstyle conforms to diplomatic etiquette," as the Visual Dictionary explains (Reynolds 2002, 8). With it bound up tightly in gold fillets above a matching golden collar necklace, she looks trapped in the admittedly regal tokens of her office. In a frenzied combination that works for space queen or post-nineties global markets, the jewelry comes from the Mangbetu tribe from the Congo. However, the contrasting dress is Elizabethan in cut, emphasizing the world of classic politics and protocol. It's stern and authoritative, yet graceful. The gown's deep purple, though with an elegant leafy pattern, suggests the dark treacherous forest of government and threats on her life. The dark color contrasts with her pale skin, which looks disturbingly ghostly beside it. The sleeves are so long they conceal her hands—a symbol of deception. In the midst of all this darkness, the chestpiece, over her heart, sparkles, suggesting vulnerability that needs guarding.

"The more secure individual tends to favor colors that range from neutral to cool (green, blue, beige, and grey), of medium value tending toward dull, whereas the more insecure individual tends to select warm bright colors (red, yellow) that range from the extremes of light and dark" (Sharpe 1974, 69). In the first film, the adolescent queen dresses incredibly dramatically, while young Anakin is calm and self-assured in neutral tan. In the next two films, however, the tempestuous older Anakin sports more black and red—even against Jedi tradition—while the increasingly secure adult senator dresses in more placid jewel colors.

Of course, her costumes in and out of Senate chambers are dazzlingly intricate, emphasizing how she dresses gorgeously while serving politically, in a particularly nineties-style contradiction. "An aspect of third wave feminism that mystified the mothers of the earlier feminist movement was the readoption by young feminists of the very lipstick, high-heels, and cleavage proudly exposed by low cut necklines that the first two phases of the movement identified with male oppression. Pinkfloor expressed this new position when she said that it's possible to have a push-up bra and a brain at the same time," explains Martha Rampton (2015) in "Four Waves of Feminism." The fabulous gowns celebrate the glamour of third-wave, encouraging girls to dress for gorgeousness if they desire. The romance plot likewise supports finding love as well as career. Combining these concepts of beauty and brains, this film shows off Padmé's new role—no longer ceremonial royalty but a fighter for her people's rights.

Her new title of senator, one more in keeping with American politics and earned responsibility, shows her more as adult and less as innocent prodigy. It also makes her more a role model for girls, who can more easily aspire to Congress than a queendom. The Visual Dictionary (2002) reveals that her performance in office earned what might be considered a promotion—from working for one planet to playing intergalactic politics on behalf of a massive region: "As elected Queen of Naboo, Padmé Amidala won the lasting devotion of her people by showing extraordinary strength of character during the Trade Federation invasion. On the expiration of her second and final term of office, she yielded her authority in spite of the popular demand for a change in the law that would have allowed her to rule longer. She was soon elected Senator to represent the 36 Naboo regional star systems" (Reynolds 2002, 8).

It's notable that while Leia was a rebel, Padmé puts her trust in the system and, as the quintessential good girl, tries to work within it even as it fails around her. In *Phantom Menace*, she gives up and declares, "The Republic no longer functions" and then returns home to successfully lead an uprising and banish the Trade Federation from her world, It's unclear why, having given up on the Senate in the previous film, Padmé then joins it. Tony M. Vinci (2007, 18) comments in his essay on the franchise's political message, "Instead of using herself as a resource, Amidala continues to suppress herself and her people by working for and within a system that she has openly claimed to be corrupt." Films two and three have her insisting it still can do a great deal of good and debating a nihilistic Anakin who wants to tear it all down. Clearly, she hasn't learned from her experience.

The new senator lives atop a skyscraper, in itself a symbol of compliance with the patriarchy. Even living there makes her feel oppressed, as the Visual Dictionary protests, "While the quarters are comfortable, Padmé loathes Coruscant's gray, artificial environment" (Reynolds 2002, 9). Nonetheless, it's an image of luxury, showing how she's more royalty than defender of her people's rights. This compromised heroism is one of the problematic sides of girl power.

> Girl Power's popularity is credited to its very lack of threat to the status quo for the ways in which it reflects the ideologies of white, middle-

class individualism and personal responsibility over collective responses to social problems. The result is a redirecting of attention away from the "degradation and economic exploitation of women worldwide . . . and the commercial enterprises largely responsible for the continuing gendered and racialized exploitation of laborers globally," the very enterprises producing Girl Power products for Western consumption. (Gonick 2006, 10)

Even as Padmé is embroiled in a larger universe of politics and economics, the story places the heroine under the Jedi's paternal thumb: Padmé believes Count Dooku is behind the attempt on her life, but the Jedi Council insist that can't be the case because he's part of their boy's club. "You know, milady, Count Dooku was once a Jedi. He couldn't assassinate anyone: it's not in his character," Jedi Master Mace Windu tells her. The entire order continues insisting they know better than she does. Meanwhile, the emperor has no clothes—the Jedi are being blocked from seeing much of the future, but they refuse to admit their weakness and still carry on as if everything is fine. Symbolically, the old order is crumbling, though they maintain the façade of power.

Palpatine, the true force of power in their universe (and an elderly white male human with a background more aristocratic than hers) piles on more pressure as he insists Padmé have Jedi protect her. She acquiesces. Following this, comes her reunion with Anakin. "From nearly the first scenes of the film, viewers see Anakin's obsessive, nearly stalker-like fixation on Padmé, whom he has not seen in nearly ten years" (Wilson 2007, 138). Gaze is prominent for both as she tells him how good it is to see him, eyes wide, and he babbles about her loveliness. "While the prequel trilogy seems to take pains not to show Padmé in overtly sexual situations or as a highly sexualized figure (i.e., like Leia's bikini episode), much of Anakin's language regarding his love for Padmé is centered on her beauty and the image she portrays" (Dominguez 2017, 126). As he compliments her, she stands still like a picture, happy to be admired. Her gown and bound hair are formal, while his black Jedi robe is meant to be cool and dashing—both outfits meant to impress others while reinforcing gender norms.

After meeting with Obi-Wan and Anakin, Padmé claims her role as target just as she has many times before, and cleverly, selflessly sets herself as bait. However, this involves her sleeping in her satin bad, curled up in a girlish white nightgown, as an assassin breaks in and sends creepily phallic poisoned centipedes to crawl up her helpless body and kill her. The low bed and huge wide windows emphasize a lack of security. Likewise, the light through the slatted shutters resembles stairs—allowing easy access.

Outside, Anakin complains, "She covered the cameras. I don't think she liked me watching her." Even thrown out, he assures Obi-Wan, "I can sense everything in that room." Clearly being a Jedi comes with the privilege of spying on his crush object. The film switches between Padmé curled up asleep, a bare shoulder visible (all emphasizing her extreme helplessness and vulnerability) and the two Jedi outside, arguing. Though they can't see her, the viewers can.

The image is medieval or fairytale in its helpless sleeping maiden guarded by the brave knights. The classic gender roles become exaggerated here, even skewed—the two Jedi posture for dominance (specifically arguing about whose "senses" are best in a competition over Jedi skill as well as, on some level, their ability to voyeuristically monitor Padmé). Meanwhile, the camera winds around Padmé's room, finally zeroing in on the creepily greenlit probe at the window, spying on it all. It opens the window, changing its passive voyeurism into literal penetration as it inserts two poisoned insects into Padmé's chamber. Outside, the men continue arguing and ignore her until it's nearly too late. Just as a centipede prepares to strike, hero Anakin bursts in and slays it with his lightsaber, while Obi-Wan dramatically throws himself through a window after the assassin. Anakin gives chase too, only instructing Padmé "Stay here!" and leaving her handmaiden to comfort the presumably frightened damsel.

Afterward, Anakin takes the job bodyguarding Padmé at the Jedi Council's insistence, leaving her managed by men once again. "Until caught, this killer is, our judgment she must respect," Yoda announces, showing his own allegiance with the old boys' network. In fact, the Council members have Anakin ask Palpatine to talk her into it.

Padmé quickly gives in and abandons her campaign for which she's risked her life—stopping the Senate from approving a massive army that could plunge the galaxy into war. She merely leaves the rather pathetic Jar-Jar to fight in her place. Cavelos (2006, 315) protests, "We never see Amidala's devotion to this cause. She only tells Jar-Jar about it, at the same time that her actions show us she is abandoning the cause, leaving on the eve of a vote because Palpatine told her she should, for her safety. What we see is not commitment, but cowardice." Instead, she flees to safety with her massive wardrobe and hot Jedi protector.

Many are amused that Jar-Jar helps destroy the Republic with his call for discretionary powers for the Chancellor. However, it is Padmé's influence that makes it happen, as the novelization reveals: "There came a brief silence as everyone turned to look at everyone else. Gradually, a clapping began, and when the jeers erupted from opposing factions, the cheering grew even louder, soon drowning out the opposition. Though she wasn't even present, it was Amidala who had done this, Mace understood. All the years she had worked to win the trust of others had led to this crucial victory" (Salvatore 2002, 312). Her one great influence on the galaxy, the one moment her voice makes a difference, helps create the Empire. While her intentions are good, the moment is painfully ironic and demonstrates her naiveite.

After her decision to leave, Padmé and Anakin travel as simple refugees. As with her adventures on Tatooine, this means a shedding of responsibility and a chance to be herself. In fact, the novelization describes her warring repugnance at the primitive conditions and joy at her new-found independence and simplicity.

> Senator Padmé Amidala, formerly Queen Amidala of Naboo, certainly wasn't used to travelling in this manner. The freighter held one class, steerage, and in truth, it was nothing more than a cargo ship, with several great open holds more suitable to inanimate cargo than to living beings. The lighting was terrible, and the smell was worse, though whether the odor came from the ship itself or the hordes of emigrants, beings of many, many species, Padmé did not know. Nor did she care. In some ways, Padmé was truly enjoying this voyage. She knew that she should be back on Coruscant, fighting the efforts to create a Republic army, but somehow, she felt relaxed here, felt free. Free of responsibility. Free to just be Padmé for a while, instead of Senator Amidala. Moments such as these were rare for her and had been since she was a child. All of her life, it seemed, had been spent in public service; all of her focus had always been for the greater, the public, good, with hardly any time ever being given just to Padmé, to her needs and her desires. (Salvatore 2002, 140)

Once again, her costumes emphasize luxury but also reflect her feelings and goals. When she leaves Coruscant, she wears gray with a black bodice as "subdued colors express grave mood" (Reynolds, 2002, 9). In a clever mix of disguise and literal shielding, her heavy gray floor-length skirt hides an "uncomfortable blast-dampening underskirt," a subversion on the frivolous luxury of the costume for those who read the background materials (Reynolds 2002, 9). Grey symbolizes "death of the body and immortality of the soul," emphasizing how Padmé prepares for sacrifice (Cooper 1978, 40).

In contrast, the sequined sky blue, lavender, and gold chestpiece emphasizes again her vulnerable center, with a stained glasslike flower image. Its beads glow in the light, symbolizing her inner beauty and strength. The Visual Dictionary calls it a "corset of light armor that doubles as protection," suggesting a strong defense (Reynolds 2002, 9). However, she isn't completely free, as the elaborate gown suggests—her sleeves are bound with silver cuffs, like manacles. The cut is sixteenth century Europe, with touches of modernity, emphasizing the tradition and responsibilities that bind her, even as she seeks escape.

The semi-crescent double-bunned hairstyle is reminiscent of the cinnamon rolls her daughter will wear, with a turquoise emblem suggesting wings—echoing her flight and spiritual growth. The Hopi-inspired hairstyle and turquoise accents suggest non-European spirituality. With all this, she's a mass of third-wave-celebrated contradictions—protection and camouflage, renaissance Europe and new-age new world. Likewise, the crescents and surrounding silver chains offer feminine moon magic, as she leaves for her place of power—Naboo.

In the transitional time between Coruscant and Naboo, Padmé dresses feminine but shrouded to the point of fading away. Disguised as a fleeing refugee, Padmé dons a "Thousand Moons young matron's dress" (Reynolds 2002, 7)—luxurious gold but fully enveloping, complete with an elaborate hood. She's wrapped up completely, hidden and pushed into the background rather than sexualized. The gold has a trace of beauty and glamour, but also a cheetah's camouflage. Upon safely arriving at Naboo, Padmé is safer and removes the veil, revealing an elaborate Naboo crest on a crownlike headdress—her royalty shines through. The Flower of Life emblem decorates the crest in a continuous pattern. "Turning base metal into gold is the transmutation of the soul; regaining the primordial purity of human nature" (Cooper 1978, 40). This combination of hidden beauty casts her as a hidden jewel, a puzzle for Anakin to unlock (thus lacking the assertiveness girl power popularized). As such, Padmé is set as Anakin's prize, the goal he's desperate to attain.

When they arrive, they have a rather telling audience with the new queen. Queen Jamillia insists, "We must keep our faith in the Republic. The day we stop believing democracy can work is the day we lose it." Padmé agrees, "Let's pray that day never comes." The women's politics through "faith" "belief" and "prayer" is worded in flimsy terms, and of course is doomed to failure. The fighter on the senate floor and the role of Naboo's queen have significantly diminished. "Instead of doing something themselves to find out the fate of their most potent enemy, they decide to trust a system they know does not work to help them even though it has refused to do so in the past" (Vinci 2007, 18). Further, as their romantic tension escalates, Padmé and Anakin can't stop undercutting each other in a bid for dominance:

SIO BIBBLE: (to Anakin) What is your suggestion, Master Jedi?

PADMÉ: Anakin's not a Jedi yet, Counselor. He's still a Padawan learner. I was thinking . . .

ANAKIN: (nettled) Hey, hold on a minute.

PADMÉ: Excuse me! I was thinking I would stay in the Lake Country. There are some places up there that are very isolated.

ANAKIN: Excuse me! I am in charge of security here, M'Lady.

PADMÉ: Annie, my life is at risk, and this is my home. I know it very well . . . that is why we're here. I think it would be wise for you to take advantage of my knowledge in this instance.

ANAKIN: (takes a deep breath) Sorry, M'Lady.

This exchange builds up character threads—Anakin's arrogance and Padmé's eagerness to pacify and conciliate. Both seek control and have significant experience but are too passionate in their youth and responsibility.

Following this, Padmé has discarded the all-important Senate vote and politics altogether to picnic with Anakin and walk among the waterfalls. Cavelos protests, "Once she gets safely to Naboo, she makes no attempt to supervise Jar-Jar, lobby the other senators to vote her way or even monitor what happens with the vote. All she seems to care about is flirting with Anakin, making out and then saying no, as if the entirety of *Star Wars* were taking place in the backseat of a 1956 Chevy" (2006, 315). As a second critic worries, "Her story ceases to be one about political advocacy, diplomacy, and her struggles to keep her people's liberties and safety intact. Instead, Padmé becomes little more than a love interest and a pretty face. Ignoring the fact that the love story is painfully trite and stilted with zero chemistry and wooden acting, this romance becomes all that Padmé is about" (Rodriguez 2014).

In third-wave stories, the young women have wish-fulfillment romances (as Buffy, Xena, and many other heroines do) and wear fabulous gowns even while having a serious career and impressive skills. Third-wave was a sex-positive movement, advocating a woman's right to be active and have relationships. Reclaiming words like girl and more sexualized ones like slut was a significant hallmark of girl power. "This playful re-appropriation of stereotypes is often interpreted as marking a lack of seriousness, but such play is a serious part of third-wave feminism's critical negotiations with the culture industries" (Heywood and Drake 2007, 117). Still, there were reasons to be cautious. The new era had moved beyond the traditional rules, leaving girls surrounded by conflicting messages. Many were left fearful of predatory males even as they sought safe, nonthreatening romances.

Even as Padmé pushes her own boundaries and questions her identity, she's sexualized for the camera. Lucas says, "We have a much more romantic story, so Padmé's costumes are obviously more sultry in nature" (Lucas et al. 2002). They include a backless sundress, sexy black bedroom ensemble, and midriff-baring blue gauzy gown as she vacations and flirts far from the Senate. Trisha Biggar describes her "looking sexy and gorgeous and young in skimpy clothes" while Portman mentions "my sexed-out version of the queen" (Lucas et al. 2002). Of course, these flimsier, erotic outfits (even before her strategically ripped jumpsuit) draw the eye and emphasize Padmé's sexuality. Laura Mulvey writes of another franchise:

[. . .] the film opens with the woman as object of the combined gaze of spectator and all the male protagonists in the film. She is isolated, glamorous, on display, sexualized. But as the narrative progresses she falls in love with the main male protagonist and becomes his property, losing her outward glamorous characteristics, her generalized sexuality, her show-girl connotations; her eroticism is subjected to the male star alone. By means of identification with him, through participating in his power, the spectator can indirectly possess her too.

Considering Queen Amidala's first appearance as static, made up figure negotiating with the Trade Federation, and her discarding of the queen role as well as its elaborate gowns to play romantic heroine on Naboo, the criticism certainly fits well here.

Joan Riviére's ultra-feminism as performance is also strong, as Padmé spends her vacation in elaborate gowns, undermining the concept that she only dresses thus in her queen or senator role. Though she's given a chance to let Anakin see the real her, she's once more buried in lace and silk. Flowing and sensual as well as richly made, the gowns appear chosen to attract Anakin. Though he first fell for her in her rough tunic on Tatooine, she feels she must dazzle him to keep his attention. This is a further problematic gender message as she charms him by appearing as delicate damsel instead of impressing him with her strength in battle or wisdom in politics. Finn falls for Rey, who never changes out of sand-covered beige rags, and then for Rose in her coveralls. Leia flirts in an old jumpsuit and dirty hands. Padmé, however, spends her arc as the medieval heroine.

Pastels appear when the female role is strong (Sharpe 1974, 115). Indeed, for this film, Padmé's color palette embraces rose, yellow, and light blue. Her backless gown at the lake is dyed pink and yellow, with real abalone at the neck and arms, and a headdress suggesting the ridges of a conch shell (Biggar 2005, 175). Across the world, shells and pearls are used in the imagery of love and marriage. Likewise, pink is a sensual color suggesting the skin. Thus, even beyond the backless touchability, it's a very sensual ensemble for their first kiss. "I found that with Iain [McCaig, the concept artist] on Episode I, it came easy for him to make Padmé look like an innocent girl who was not aware how beautiful she was, whereas when I drew her in Episode II, she was much more aware of her beauty and sexuality," comments Dermot Power, co-concept artist on *Attack of the Clones* (Biggar 2005, 166).

As the actors flirt awkwardly (with caveman Anakin wanting to touch her arm because she's so soft), they go on to picnic and wrestle playfully in the meadow. Butler comments on "the binary restriction on sexuality" and how culture reinforces it (1990, 74). Indeed, Padmé's hyper-femininity uses her culture (in the form of elaborate gowns and lakeside excursions) to strengthen gender binaries—she picnics in a flowery meadow while Anakin shows off his daring by stuntriding. With their actions, each tries to draw the other's gaze. However, as Anakin attracts Padmé (and presumably much of the audience), it's not only by acting cool but by battling and trick flying through Coruscant to avenge his lady love. Padmé attracts Anakin in turn, but only through costuming and existing statically. Apparently, no more is required to be the female star of turn-of-the-century *Star Wars*.

Padmé's golden gown is decorated with clusters of feminine pink roses and pastel ribbons, suggesting a blooming spring season. The fabric is frivolously summery but still has the grandiosity of court fashion with delicate filigree over a stiff bodice, suggesting she's not ready to discard all propriety. Together with the gold netting in her hair (a thirteenth century crispinette binding it in two buns) and cascading waves down her back, it's reminiscent of a storybook princess. The draping gauze hints at the pre-Raphaelite art of John William Waterhouse, with its romanticized vision of the past—the artist tended depict his heroines as delicate, flowerlike figures, and Padmé falls in line.

In their 1987 article "Doing Gender," sociologists Candace West and Don H. Zimmermann introduce their notion of gender as an achievement, created by constant social practices and behaviors. They specify sex as biological criteria, while doing gender, as they put it, "involves a complex of socially guided perceptual, interactional, and micropolitical activities that cast particular pursuits as expressions of masculine and feminine 'natures'" (127). For instance, published manuals of deportment emphasize that appearing ladylike is unnatural, completely learned behavior. Thus, Padmé's alluring looks as she sits in the meadow, dazzling in the golden gown, are as deliberate a mating behavior as Anakin's show-offy trick riding.

The couple's forbidden love makes them star-crossed, forbidden to be together yet finally succumbing. In the most intimate scene, Padmé wears the black dress that bares her shoulders and a good bit of cleavage. The thirties-style mermaid shape emphasizes her womanly figure. It's all set off by a fireplace and dim lighting as she and Anakin sit on the couch together. It's a contradictory look as she's still insisting they shouldn't be together. "The senator protests her innocence and resolve while simultaneously and disingenuously dressing the part of a femme fatale. In this rather confusing and clumsy scene, Padmé Amidala the clean-cut, responsible heroine is suddenly crossed with a worldly seductress out of film noir" (Wilson 2007, 138).

> Older than Anakin by several years, fully aware of the prohibitions placed upon Jedi, and committed to the success of her own senatorial career, Padmé nevertheless begins sending mixed signals, both protesting and encouraging Anakin's advances, alternatively reminding him of their respective duties and admitting her own growing—and, to most viewers, rather inexplicable—romantic attraction. Indeed, the more violently possessive and somewhat deranged Anakin behaves,

the more Padmé is attracted to him, until the audience is left wondering half-seriously whether she has unknowingly fallen prey to some
sort of psychic suggestion or Force persuasion on Skywalker's part.
The alternative seems hardly less implausible in light of her relative
sophistication and Anakin's disturbing behavior. (Wilson 2007, 138)

Anakin appears a tragic hero, desperately in love with cruel Padmé
who toys with his emotions by kissing him in one scene and then rebuff-
ing his advances. "Throughout this scene Padmé is wearing possibly her
most seductive outfit yet, seemingly with the sole purpose of tormenting
Anakin further," Pianka explains (2013, 44). Since films teach impressionable young viewers how to approach a relationship, the outfit disturbingly hints at mixed messages and "leading him on," encouraging hero Anakin to respond to her clothing, not her wobbly refusal. Of course, he does.

In the scene, he declares his feelings and asks her to return them. As
he protests, "From the moment I met you, all those years ago, a day
hasn't gone by when I haven't thought of you. And now that I'm with
you again, I'm in agony. The closer I get to you, the worse it gets. The
thought of not being with you makes my stomach turn over—my mouth
go dry. I feel dizzy. I can't breathe. I'm haunted by the kiss you should
never have given me. My heart is beating, hoping that kiss will not become a scar. You are in my very soul, tormenting me." He places the guilt
of his suffering on her, suggesting she owes him love. Certainly, there's a
disturbing current to his plea for romance. It advocates a painful sense of
obligation that the girl must take pity on whoever is attracted to her.
Padmé refuses Anakin, and he keeps pleading and pushing.

On a classic level, they are the rule-following good girl and the rebellious bad boy—stereotypical but generally a crowd pleaser. Though
tempted, she tells him firmly, "You swore an oath, remember? You'd be
expelled from the Order. I will not let you give up your responsibilities,
your future, for me." As she adds, sticking up for herself as well as her
illicit suitor, "I am not going to give in to this. I'm not going to throw my
life away. I have more important things to do than fall in love." When she
challenges him directly, asking whether he could truly live a lie, he backs
down. Here, both agree that abandoning the duties they've earned
through long struggle, all to indulge their feelings, would be too selfish.

West and Zimmermann (1987, 136) point out that those performing
gender feel accountable to society—"To 'do' gender is not always to live
up to normative conceptions of femininity or masculinity; it is to engage
in behavior at the risk of gender assessment." Even as Padmé dresses in
her most feminine, all her thoughts are about society's judgment. She
feels she cannot be accepted as politician and lover of a Jedi, so she will
have to regress to covered-up senator or discard all propriety.

Her obsession with costumes and masks suggests the audience has
never seen the real Padmé and never will. Her portrayal in Episode II as

the object of Anakin's obsession suggests two possibilities. She is something of a placeholder character in an archetypal myth, Anakin's vision of Woman rather than a person—thus emphasizing how much this is his story, viewed through his eyes. Or, for a more subversive take, Padmé feels trapped in a such a narrative and thus refuses to reveal herself. Many novels, from *The Penelopead* to *The Mists of Avalon* address this concept, not only inventing the women's probable views of the epics in which they are bit players but emphasizing how much of their true selves are left out in a story dictated by men.

In contrast with the lifelong careers of the Boomer era, third wavers found themselves with more short-term and shifting occupations in a new type of workforce. With this, "workers' identities tend to be flexible and multifaceted, even contradictory" (Heywood and Drake 2007, 118). Reflecting this, Padmé's tenure as queen (traditionally a permanent position) has lasted two elected terms, but after this she has reframed herself as a senator without the heavy makeup and disguises of her previous identity. Now she considers another switch, to wife and mother. In a cut scene, Padmé says, "Actually, I was hoping to have a family by now . . . My sisters have the most amazing, wonderful kids . . . but when the Queen asked me to serve as Senator, I couldn't refuse her." Long ago, she made her choice, sadly abandoning her conventionally gendered desires for an intergalactic career. While third-wave encouraged the option of love and family, Padmé considers giving up a decade of work, to say nothing of the fate of the Republic, because Anakin is so dashing and needy. The message turns sour.

In another cut scene, Padmé introduces Anakin to her family. She has sweet, caring parents and Sola, her older sister with children. Beside them, with her exotic hairdo and bare midriff and back, Padmé looks far more sophisticated—the young woman who left the countryside to become a famous urbanite. As they all have dinner, and the sisters have the traditional "he's not my boyfriend" conversation, the women then retreat to the kitchen so Padmé's mother and sister reveal they can tell Padmé's in love. Of course, her duty still remains: In the novelization, Sola notes that she's thinking more like a disciplined, selfless Jedi than Anakin is (Salvatore 2002, 181). Furthering the romantic plot and traditional gendering, all her family encourages her to explore her personal desires instead of clinging to duty. This scene plays out more like one in a romantic comedy than one of politics and war. This too is part of third-wave feminism—valuing the stay-at home sister or the warrior princess model as equally valid.

Under Padmé's shrouding cloak (this one white with a dragonfly that symbolizes freedom and movement) is a simple diaphanous pale blue outfit. Its turtleneck look, combined with the flare skirt, are modern enough to evoke the year the film was made, with the bare midriff popular in the post–2000 era. Thus, it makes Padmé relatable to young female

viewers as she mirrors their struggle. It also suggests her relaxed infor-
mality while at home . . . and also her underdressed seductive look
around Anakin.

While getting to know the family in this extended cut scene, Anakin
also sees her childhood bedroom and childhood holo pictures. One
shows young Padmé, surrounded by a mob of little green creatures. She
holds one in her arms and they all beam. She describes accompanying the
Relief Group to Shadda-Bi-Boran. "Their sun was imploding, and the
planet was dying. I was helping to relocate the children. See that little one
I'm holding? His name was N'a-kee-tula, which means sweetheart. He
was so full of life. All those kids were. I did everything I could to save
him, but he died . . . they all did. They were never able to adapt . . . to live
off their native planet." This moment is suggested to have spurred her
into government. In the next picture, she's an unsmiling Apprentice Leg-
islator. The novelization, like the cut scenes included on the DVD release,
emphasizes her loneliness as she devotes herself so completely to duty
that she's never allowed herself to simply be Padmé in love. These echo
some of the contradictions of third wave feminism as they failed to have
it all.

As they flirt and stagnate through the romantic plot, Anakin dreams
of his mother and feels compelled to rescue her. Padmé generously vol-
unteers to go along, letting him continue as bodyguard while accom-
plishing his own quest. However, from here, she slips into background.
"The most frustrating aspect of Padmé's character is the inconsistency of
her actions and the gradual diminishing of her agency as the series progresses. What starts out as a hands-down feminist icon is reduced to a
plot device to further the male character's development" (Wood 70).

Further, Dr. Rebecca Harrison (2018) performed her women-onscreen
experiment on the prequels and placed them all around 20 percent of the
time, similar to Leia's time in the original trilogy. This means any wom-
en, including Padmé, are only found in about a fifth of each movie: 20
percent *Phantom Menace*, 18 percent *Attack of the Clones*, 17 percent *Revenge of the Sith*. As Harrison adds, Padmé or other women often make up
the background when they are onscreen: "Sadly, especially in Padme's
case, she's quite often just kind of 'there.' She really does get a rough
deal." Being present doesn't mean she's contributing to action or story,
let alone dialogue.

On Tatooine, Padmé dresses more casually, first in a rich but concealing hooded cloak. Fabric wraps tight around her face in Middle Eastern
fashion, covering all her hair. This nods to her concealing herself as well
as to her desert visit. Under it is a nearly white two-part bare midriff
ensemble, giving her the casual sexy look again. This suggests the
American girl bursting out of her abaya, contrasting old world values
with girl power assertiveness (Wonder Woman contributed a similar
scene in a post-September-11th comic). However, it must be noted that

Tatooine women wear casual pants and sweaters—they don't feel the need to conceal every trace of skin or to wear filmy gowns. In context, Padmé's look is more romanticized and out of place than liberating. Around the house, she wears a simple sky-blue dress with her long curly hair down. Once more she's informal and open in a domestic environment, away from societal pressure—even as she and Anakin bond. Warm colors suggest impulsiveness and cool, emotional control (Sharpe 1974, 63). Certainly, she is the pacifier and comforter, while the more dramatically-dressed Anakin flies into rages.

When Anakin goes into the desert to save his mother, he leaves Padmé with his family, saying only, "You are going to have to stay here." On his return, he's taken his first step onto the dark side, leaving her to either condemn or enable him. She takes the weaker path. Famously, he tells her he has killed all the Sandpeople and their children, and she hugs him and tells him he's only human. This not only pushes him toward villainy but toward his spousal abuse in the third film with her apologizing and supporting him through it.

After this, they rush off to rescue Obi-Wan, and Padmé's somewhat flimsy plot of Senate, assassination attempt, and romance vanishes into the start of the Clone Wars. Admittedly, she's the one who hauls Anakin off on the rescue: On hearing that Obi-Wan's been captured by the Geonosians, she responds, "[Mace Windu] gave you strict orders to protect me. And I'm going after Obi-Wan. If you plan to protect me, you'll just have to come along." While this is a delightfully strong moment, her framing her rescue of Obi-Wan as giving Anakin an opportunity to save and protect them both involves her verbally surrendering to the damsel role yet again, encouraging Anakin to be her powerful protector.

Padmé's iconic action outfit is a sleek white figure-hugging ensemble. The elastic bodysuit and simple looped hairstyle both are low-maintenance, allowing Padmé to run about, climb, and dodge. It's reminiscent of Leia's original gown, but even less restricting. However, it's more sexualized as it hugs Padmé's figure and soon gets artistically ripped through the middle. The look is particularly girl power as it hails from the nineties' short tops and uncovered midriffs. More shockingly for audiences, the shape of her nipples or at least some strategically positioned seams showed through during the original theatrical run. With this, "the postfeminist action hero underscores 'woman-as-spectacle,'" Cristina Lucia Stasia explains in her essay on postfeminist action heroines (2007, 243). Clearly, this was no longer just a film for the kids.

Casting the glamorous young woman as action hero but in such a tight outfit is another girl-power era trope—lovely teen girls fighting and winning while wearing gorgeous outfits, Buffy-style. "Images of girls 'kicking ass' proliferate in magazines and marketers have exploited the market potential of postfeminist girls who think it is cool that girls can kick ass—but are more interested in purchasing the designer stiletto the girl is kicking ass in" (Stasia 2007, 237). Called "action chicks" and "tough girls," these women are "softened, not hardened, by these labels" (Stasia 2007, 238). They are not warrior women, simply powerful "girls."

On arriving, there's an action sequence where the pair are being stomped by machinery in the droid factory. Padmé's flowing white cloak establishes her as the damsel, while Anakin's cool in black and red. He's actively fighting with the Force and lightsaber while she is limited to dodging and then fumblingly gets trapped in a giant crucible. At last, the Separatists capture them both. Count Dooku demands that Naboo join the Separatist faction, but Padmé displays personal valor and the courage of her convictions, saying, "I will not forsake all I have honored and worked for and betray the Republic." After this, she and Anakin are sentenced to death.

Facing execution, the star-crossed lovers finally reveal their emotions:

PADMÉ: I'm not afraid to die. I've been dying a little bit each day since you came back into my life.

ANAKIN: What are you talking about?

PADMÉ: I love you.

ANAKIN: You love me?! I thought we decided not to fall in love. That we would be forced to live a lie. That it would destroy our lives . . .

PADMÉ: I think our lives are about to be destroyed anyway. My love for you is a puzzle, Annie, for which I have no answers. I can't control it . . . and now I don't care. I truly, deeply love you, and before we die I want you to know.

They kiss. The love theme swells to epic levels. They have finally succumbed to rash, impetuous commitment. As the Visual Dictionary adds, "Her increasingly dangerous life and her exposure to the death of loved ones force Padmé to realize how precious every minute is. At the crucial moment, she becomes determined to live as fully as possible no matter what the consequences—and if she is to be destroyed, she will go down fighting" (Reynolds 2002, 32). It's a romantic, vulnerable human moment, but also one that suggests the heroine will inevitably throw aside judgment and career for the bad boy, especially if she's scared enough.

With this comes the arena battle. Asserting herself, Padmé snatches an active start—while Anakin has "a bad feeling," she's picking locks and climbing atop the pillar where she was bound. As Obi-Wan quips, "It looks like she's already on top of things." Of course, a monster climbs up it afterward and, emphasizing her damsel role, slashes her top open. Notably, this has no effect on plot, character, or relationships—unlike

Padmé's casual gowns around family or even Leia's gold bikini. The skin-baring thus appears gratuitous—objectifying the heroine because she's female.

She climbs away and fights with a chain, even helping to free Obi-Wan and Anakin. No one makes jokes about being "rescued by a girl." However, cool Anakin tames a monster. Obi-Wan spear fights another. Arguably, both are getting the flashier fight sequences. While Padmé shoots her blaster plenty, she doesn't hit much. She kills a monster herself but ends the sequence by riding off on the back of Anakin's mount and giving him a kiss on the cheek—visually, the rescued damsel in truth.

As they pursue Dooku, she falls out of the ship, excluding her from the climactic battle. Her falling from the ship is a crushing moment for Anakin, forcing him to pick between love and duty as she lies unconscious. After this, the stormtroopers come save her. With Obi-Wan, Anakin battles the film's villain Dooku, and loses an arm, forever transforming him. Padmé only arrives after the two Jedi have lost and all-powerful Yoda has saved them both. All she does is help Anakin limp away.

While the romance story appears to place Padmé (and her gowns!) front and center, she has surprisingly little growth. Her arc involves giving into a love she feels nearly from the beginning—with a whiny, self-involved character many audience members found unappealing. Since the assassination plot is about the men protecting her, and since she never checks in on the Senate vote, that's about all the growth she gets. There was room for much self-consideration of good and evil that's ultimately left out. Cavelos (2006, 315) concludes:

> At the end of Episode II, Amidala is saved by an army whose formation she has crusaded against. Is she troubled that an army was created before the authorization for it existed? Does she rush to the Senate to argue that the army be disbanded and its origins investigated? Or does she acknowledge she was wrong and an army is necessary? No, she goes home and secretly marries Anakin. Her commitment to fighting the evil forces that threaten the Republic has vanished.

Anakin, by contrast, has several character-defining moments—battling assassins, saving his mother, murdering the Sandpeople, saving Obi-Wan, leaving Padmé behind, dueling Dooku—and most times gives in to emotion and makes a fatal choice.

In the novel *Wild Space*, dealing with the aftereffects of the battle, Padmé gains a bit more initiative. She shouts down the Jedi Healing Temple, demanding to see Anakin. After, Obi-Wan comes to her, regretfully ordering her to break off their clearly evident relationship. She capitulates, but insists, "Let Anakin escort me home to Naboo. Saying good-bye is going to be difficult. I'd like our parting to be private" (K. Miller 2008, 33). Thus, they are married in her place of power and by her own deception. She spends the rest of the novel not simply waiting at home, but convincing Bail Organa and Obi-Wan to ally and finally rescuing them from near-death on a Sith planet—where Jedi cannot go, but she can. Of course, this sort of agency goes unaddressed in the film.

The film's final scene is the wedding. However, it comes after Yoda's ominous final line: "Not victory, a defeat, it was, Master Obi-Wan. Begun, the Clone War has!" Thanks to this, the wedding feels similarly ominous, set against the background of war and doomed by its forbidden nature as well as fans' knowledge of what Anakin will become.

> While Padmé and Anakin fulfill their secret pledge to one another, Bail Organa, who is symbolically positioned as the moral conscience for the Republic, looks to the ground in disgust as the Grand Army of the Republic parades in front of politicos on its way to the Clone Wars. In both of the dialogue-less sequences, (an editing choice which forces an emphasis on the visual), the audience's attention is drawn to a pair of seemingly dissimilar events that will have the cumulative effect of destroying the Republic. (Deis 98–99)

What does a queen and senator who dresses for a fashion show each day wear for her wedding? Even more of the same. Her Maltese lace veil is topped with Edwardian wax flowers and whirlpools of pearls (Biggar 2005, 187). Of course, pearls symbolize sorrow, and, more ironically, longevity. Transparent lace sleeves show only the heavy braid, which resembles chains or bindings on her arms. The edginess of the gown suggests the tension of their illegal act and the oncoming war. Though she chooses love, the ending is hardly the stuff of romantic comedies and girlish dreams.

SHMI THE TRAGIC MOTHER

Another figure of the prequels shares Padmé's weaker qualities. The most impressionable woman of the *Phantom Menace*, after the queen and her decoy, is Anakin's mother Shmi. Like Beru, she's the perfect loving mother, with little more to her, though she does get more scenes. "Only Shmi's selfless care for her son gives her the strength to let him go" the Visual Dictionary says, and that epitomizes her personality (Reynolds and Fry 2012, 74). Pernilla August (Shmi) describes the characters' mutual love, saying, "We have a good relationship, my boy and I . . . It's a beautiful part. I love it very much. It's so warm. And I feel very familiar about it because I have three kids myself" (Lucas et al. 1999b). Onscreen, she has no family, friends, backstory, or motivation beyond her son.

She's kind enough that she raises no objection when her little son brings home guests for dinner. Still, her every conversation is about Anakin, in an example of all the Bechdel test reviles. As Anakin proposes racing to win the travelers the part they need, Shmi protests, "I don't want you to race, Annie . . . It's awful. I die every time Watto makes you do it." However, Anakin wins her over by reminding her of her own words (which he puts in her mouth as the assertive male)—people should help one another. She instantly capitulates with "No, Annie's right, there is no other way . . . I may not like it, but he can help you . . . he was meant to help you." Her brief motherly protest and fast turnaround are her only contribution.

Following this is her conversation with Obi-Wan in which she naively has no idea how she became pregnant: "There was no father, that I know of . . . I carried him, I gave him birth . . . I can't explain what happened. Can you help him?" This lack of knowledge of her own body or will in creating the pregnancy both weaken her character. (Since the novels reveal that Palpatine and his master created her pregnancy, she is actually impregnated against her will by the galaxy's dominant evil males, and then cast aside by the story's good ones.) Further, this concept even takes away her procreative power, even while celebrating her motherhood. A victim of the mystical birth trope, in which aliens or all-powerful overlords inflict the pregnancy on a woman without her consent, Shmi has no agency in her motherhood. In such plot patterns, the mother is only a vessel for the child, subject to the patriarchy's abuse. This message has disturbing correspondences in real life and law, as some consider the fetus far more important than the living, breathing mother. "To top it all off, Anakin is the product of a virgin birth. Women are valued for their reproductive ability, but not for the actual reproductive act, which is either nonexistent or not mentioned or discussed in any way" (Wetmore 2005).

When Qui-Gon cannot save Shmi from slavery, he leaves her where she is. He asks if she'll be all right, but once more she has no plans or priorities except for her son, answering his question with "He was in my life for such a short time." Her only purpose is to have the child, and traumatize him with their parting now and later her death. She's a flat character from beginning to end. As Bill Spangler (2006, 336) comments in "Fighting Princesses and Other Distressing Damsels": "She's not a strong character in the sense that she's a leader or has active control of her own life. However, she's strong enough to survive life as a slave and to let her son go when he appears to be heading for a better life." Shmi bravely tells Annie, "Son, my place is here. My future is here. It is time for you to let go . . . to let go of me. I cannot go with you." Shmi thinks in the junior novelization, "This was what she had asked Qui-Gon after all—that he help Annie. Now her son had the chance she had always wanted for him. She would have to do her best to see that he took it" (Wrede 1999, 104). Pernilla August adds, "She's very brave in a way, to let him go," which she does to let him "take the responsibility of his own life" (Lucas et al. 1999b).

Of course, their loving, wholesome, if rather flat, relationship turns destructive, positioning Shmi, like Padmé, as the prop that turns Anakin evil. "Despite Shmi's self-sacrifice and Anakin's emotional security in her care, however, Lucas posits this loving mother-son relationship, strangely enough, as a primary cause or source of the events that will gradually transform Anakin Skywalker into the terrifying Sith Lord Darth Vader" (Wilson 2007, 137). She is his weakness through all the years between films. Tempted with quitting the Jedi Order for a life of freedom in one of the padawan-era children's novels, Anakin thinks, "He could see her again. He could free her, and make sure she was well and safe . . . But the Jedi would not take him back if he did such a thing" (Watson 2003, 27). Obi-Wan sympathetically comments, "You are the only Jedi with such a strong, deep tie, and it makes it harder for you" (45).

Attack of the Clones is haunted by Shmi, though she has very little screentime. "Shmi is not so much a character in her own right but rather exists to give purpose to Anakin. She exists to be a victim so that he might have a reason to go to the Dark Side" (Wetmore 2005). First, Anakin mentions her and has nightmares about her. Then he and Padmé go questing for her, and Watto reveals he's sold her. When Anakin finds her new husband, Cliegg Lars, his mother is still nowhere in sight. Cliegg tells him, "It was just before dawn. They came out of nowhere. A hunting party of Tusken Raiders. Your mother had gone out early, like she always did, to pick mushrooms that grow on the vaporators. From the tracks, she was about halfway when they took her. Those Tuskens walk like men, but they're vicious, mindless monsters. Thirty of us went out after her. Four of us came back." He is now stuck in a wheelchair, his leg lost in the fight. As he adds, "I don't want to give up on her, but she's been gone a month. There's little hope she's lasted this long." Everyone is treating her as the helpless damsel of the piece, and her thoughts and personality don't appear. When the Tusken raiders attack in the novelization, Cliegg yells at his womenfolk, "You stay here . . . or go get a weapon, at least!" (Salvatore 2002, 23). While there is mixed respect for their abilities, he and Owen ultimately go out on their own to check for raiders and leave the women safely at home. Clearly Tatooine is the land of traditional gender roles.

The film also introduces Beru, who, like Shmi, exists to further her son's story, both as underdeveloped, saintly mothers. Beru only says "I'm Beru" when she greets Anakin and Padmé. All conversations between women are carried out in a group with men present and also participating in them. In the novelization, Padmé and Beru have a short conversation (literally just enough for the Bechdel test) as Padmé tells her of Naboo and Beru says she prefers to stay planetbound (Salvatore 2002, 281–82). Beru wears a shapeless teal coat with orange collar in the first film, appearing dowdy and more than a bit seventies. In *Attack of the Clones*, she's more farmgirl, with a long tan skirt and baggy purple sweater. Her hair is cut short, to appear utilitarian and hard-working. Meg Cabot (2017, 91) gives Beru a monologue in *From a Certain Point of View*, and Beru observes, "I was born to make people feel good when every-thing around them seemed just awful." As her new family loses their matriarch Shmi, she's seen supporting and comforting, as she will for Luke in Episode IV. So much for Beru.

The novelization gives both women a bit more personality as it in-cludes scenes with their Tatooine family. The women joke together, and the family even indulge in a happy food fight. Still, Anakin dominates Shmi's thoughts. Even with the family she's made for herself, she thinks:

> Shmi had often wondered if Owen had been part of the reason she had so readily agreed to marry Cliegg. She looked back at her husband, rubbing her hand over his broad shoulder. Yes, she loved him, and deeply, and she certainly couldn't deny her joy at finally being relieved of her slave bonds. But despite all of that, what part had the presence of Owen played in her decisions? It had been a question that had stayed with her all these years. Had there been a need in her heart that Owen had filled? A mother's need to cover the hole left by Anakin's depar-ture? (Salvatore 2002, 16)

The Legends novel *Tatooine Ghost* by Troy Denning (2003) reveals Shmi's backstory. Confronted over and over by relics from Anakin's childhood while on a mission on Tatooine, Leia's forced to amend her hatred of Vader even while exploring the growing call of the Force from within. Luke's childhood friends also give her Shmi's lost journal. Pages of it, reproduced in the novel, give her a voice at last. When Watto starts Anakin podracing, a strong, vibrant Shmi recalls, "I was so angry I threatened to plastiment his wings together and drop him in a solvent vat. And I would have, too, had anything bad happened to you" (203).

She also has a relationship with her master Watto that's arguably both very human and notably disturbing. He starts having her buy wine for them to drink together as they reminisce about Anakin. She comes to care for him, the master who literally rules her with the power of life and death, thanks to the tracking chip that could destroy her in an instant. "Cliegg snorted when I called myself Watto's friend, but I *am*. I've grown fond of him over the years . . . and he misses you, Annie. That gives him a warm place in my heart," she writes (307). This appears a massive plot of Stockholm Syndrome. Later Watto reveals that he deactivated her track-ing chip some time ago, giving her only the illusion of confinement, not the reality (a weak defense as she had no idea and did not stay with him voluntarily). Further, with her lack of friends among her fellow slaves, Watto is the only person in her life. Her only other companions are *Ana-kin's* friends—the little children shown in *Phantom Menace* for whom she bakes pies, eager to reminisce about her lost child. Thus, she gains a little nuance but hardly breaks out of her flat role.

Her anger, power, and even journal writings all fixate on her son, to whom she writes. Still, even as she thinks about him obsessively, she adds details of a life beyond him, as the journal follows Cliegg's court-ship. When he arrives to buy a part from Watto, Shmi says, "There was something about this settler that made me want to help him, a sense of desperation, maybe . . . or maybe his proud blue eyes and the way he carried himself" (258). She helps in his negotiations, and later he returns to take her on walks and bring her produce from his farm.

In her escape from slavery, Shmi proves clever and tricky—in contrast with the film's vague account that places Cliegg as her savior. When Watto flatly refuses to sell her (as the story implies that by this point she is his only confidant and companion), she, Cliegg, and Owen prepare a classic con. Owen plays a rich ship buyer, only interested in Watto's most lucrative craft if it contains a Tobal lens. Shmi has one, which she gives Cliegg to trade for her freedom. The fact that the crystal was a gift from Qui-Gon suggests his desire to make amends and, as seen through the Force, give her her best chance for an escape from slavery. At the same time, the privileged male's aid only helps her after years of slavery at a time of his choice.

Tatooine Ghost also introduces Dama, Beru's younger sister who runs an upscale inn on Tatooine. She willingly hides Leia and her friends from Imperials "whom she hated for killing her sister and Owen Lars" (197). She gives Leia a little background on Beru and Shmi's family dynamic from Episode II, describing Beru and Owen's courtship and coloring them with a bit more nuance even as she helps bridge the eras. She emphasizes that young Beru had a family and life, with a legacy that has outlasted her.

Back in the film, Anakin the action hero goes out to save his mother in a traditionally gendered pattern. When he finds her, she's hanging from a wooden frame in the Tusken Raiders' hut. She's clearly been badly beat-en. If she fought back, she failed. She opens her blood-caked eyelids and murmurs, "I'm so glad . . . to see you, Annie . . . Now . . . I am com-plete . . . " With a final "You look so handsome. My son . . . my grown-up son. I'm so proud of you, Annie . . . so proud . . . I missed you so much . . . I love . . . " she dies. This is a classic moment of "fridging"—killing the hero's loved one to propel his plot forward. This treats her as a flimsy placeholder and supports violence against women as a plot device. With her death, Shmi has served her purpose.

"An anti-feminist version of white womanhood appears in the image of a dead Shmi in the arms of her avenging son. The primitive wood and leather torture and/or rape rack stands behind the kneeling Anakin who now drapes his mother in his arms in a reversed Pieta pose. The product of immaculate conception holds his crucified mother" (Estrada 2007). In the Jesus story and many others across the world, the son is sacrificed and the mother endures in what in world myth is commonly a metaphor for the all-powerful earth mother continuing as the vulnerable male hero dies and is reborn. This is subverted into Shmi's helpless sacrifice. Further, many critics saw a disturbing racial narrative in Anakin's quest to rescue his mother from the "desert savages," whom he then slaughters "like animals." His rage at the nonhumans capturing his white mother drives his violence and thus the plot. In this, she is a prop shoring up conventional gender roles. "White patriarchy ideally envisions white frontier women such as Shmi as tortured, dead, and bloody because it provides the need for white male protection from indigenous savagery" (Estrada 2007).

Adding to the count of women in the film, female Tusken Raiders exist long enough to get slaughtered—increasing the pathos as they and their children are noncombatants. In the novelization Anakin specifies that "the men are the only fighters among the Tuskens"—apparently, they are traditionally gendered as well (Salvatore 2002, 284).

The novelization, which shows Shmi's captivity from her point of view, would be expected to give her more personality that isn't all about the hero. However, as she lies suffering, she subsumes her character in her absent son's, committed to protecting him even as she dies:

> Shmi Skywalker had always kept a special place in her heart reserved for her Annie, her son, her hero. And so now, as it seemed the end of her life was imminent, Shmi's thoughts focused on those memories she had of Anakin, while at the same time, she reached out to him with her heart. He was always different with such feelings, always so attuned to that mysterious Force. The Jedi who had come to Tatooine had seen it in him clearly. Perhaps, then, Annie would feel her love for him now. She needed that, needed to complete the cycle, to let her son recognize that through it all, through the missing years and the great distances between them, she had loved him unconditionally and had thought of him constantly. (Salvatore 2002, 271)

As she pushes her love out through the Force (ironically, likely drawing Anakin to Tatooine and setting him on the destructive path that appears here), all her energy is spent on her son, not herself. "It is a pathetic end to a life showing no agency from this lowest-class woman, once a slave" (Estrada 2007).

AIDES, MAIDS, AND TOKENISM

TC-14, the chrome-colored C-3PO-style robot who welcomes Obi-Wan and Qui-Gon in episode one, has a disconcerting female voice. It's also disconcerting how badly she's treated as her Trade Federation master insists, "Are you brain dead? I'm not going in there with two Jedi! Send the droid." Treated as disposable, she can only sigh. Of course, her travails continue. With a meek "Oh! Excuse me!" she bumbles into the middle of a firefight and is nearly shot. While the Jedi and even the droid soldiers avoid attacking her in the middle of their battle, her masters clearly have no regard for her. Making her apparently female highlights her exploitation and powerlessness to avoid the cruelty.

Two of Anakin's little desert friends are girls, who are as skeptical about his chances as the boys. The elderly fruit seller Jira has a single line: "Oh, my bones are aching . . . storm's coming up, Annie. You'd better get home quick." In a deleted scene, Anakin bids farewell to the elderly woman and gives her his winnings to buy a cooling unit, so she calls him "the kindest boy in the galaxy." Of course, this grandmotherly stand-in supports Anakin's story and has no defining personality traits—any elderly person in distress would do. As Shmi's role emphasizes, the women of his planet are quite conventionally gendered. *Tatooine Ghost* reveals that the little girl Amee even planned to marry Anakin so, as Shmi says in the journal she's writing to her son, "she would be part of the family when you won our freedom" (Denning 2003, 204).

In *Phantom Menace*, a few other women exist in the background. Bounty hunter Aurra Sing watches the podrace in a red skintight suit. Bald with a ponytail and dead-white skin, she has a distinctive alien look, flaunting her femininity. (She was given this distinctive image to fill in the podrace audience and called "Babe Fett" in a concept sketch by Lucasfilm's Doug Chiang.) Though model Michonne Bourriague doesn't speak, the character was popular enough to make it into the video games and comics. The *Clone Wars* children's show, which takes place between Episodes II and III, fills in the main characters' growth but also allows the briefly-seen prequel characters expanded arcs. Sing appears, voiced by Jaime King, hired to assassinate Amidala and others. In "Hostage Crisis," she's utterly coldhearted—shooting an injured guard in the face as he begs. She thus subverts gender expectations, even while falling into stereotypes. Aurra Sing continues with classic female roles, as she stops her young protégé Boba Fett from drinking in a bar and has a romance with pirate Hondo Ohnaka who calls her "my dear." The rather unarticulated female bounty hunter thus offers little that's unique beyond her appearance.

Sebulba has twin Twi'lek slaves dressed in mesh jumpsuits open to the waist. They're clearly eye candy for the audience and the character— even the guide book says he's hired "expensive blue Rutian Twi'lek twins as masseuses . . . mostly to irritate his fellow racers and steep them in jealousy" (Reynolds and Fry 2012, 83). The racers, described one by one in the guide, are all male. Thus, traditional gender roles appear once more—the men are the heroes and women their masseuses in skimpy clothing.

Continuing the conventionally-gendered galaxy, a few senators, but especially their consorts and aides, are female—Chancellor Valorum's aide Sei Taria is an Asian woman in long purple robes. Representation is nice, but far too many of these females specifically work for the men.

Sly Moore, Palpatine's aide, is bald and tall in a gray furred cloak that resembles icicles, over a dark blue layer. The firm structure of the garment makes Sly appear robotic. The Visual Dictionary calls it an "Umbaran shadowcloak . . . patterned in ultraviolet colors" (Reynolds 2002, 11). She does not say a word, but her presence, along with Palpatine's male aide, emphasizes his own importance. Of course, in the backstory, she's given significant alien powers that she harnesses to aid her master: "Sly Moore is Palpatine's Staff Aide. She controls access to the Chancellor, which gives her tremendous power. Moore comes from the shadowy world of Umbara, deep within the dark reaches of the Ghost Nebula. Umbarans are known for their abilities to subtly influence and even control others" (Reynolds 2002, 11). Their society is coded as evil feminine, devoted to manipulation over direct combat. In fact, the Umbarans base their society on spying and political scheming to rise out of their castes. "Their specter-like visages haunted the galactic political scene for generations. They have long been objects of fear and suspicion because of their subtle ability to influence others" (Lewis and Keier 2013, 212). All this nasty elusiveness emphasizes the insidious nature of the Sith but codes it as feminine as well.

"One thing that seems like a disturbing pattern in the *Star Wars* universe is how the Skywalker women all die in tragic circumstances: Shmi Skywalker, Anakin's mother; Padmé Amidala Naberrie, Anakin's wife; Mara Jade Skywalker, Luke's wife. It can be even pointed out that even Beru Lars, Shmi's (step) daughter-in-law, also died tragically," comments Natacha Guyot (2015, 62) in *A Galaxy of Possibilities: Representation and Storytelling in Star Wars*. Damsels and women in general fare badly in *Attack of the Clones*. In the first scene, Padmé's decoy Cordé is killed. "My lady . . . So sorry . . . I've failed you, Senator" she says, selflessly perishing. The undeveloped bodyguard's only purpose is to die and thus motivate the heroine. Handmaiden Dormé rushes into Padmé's room after the next assassination attempt and blurts, "Are you all right, milady?" only to get the job of watching over her while the men get the more exciting task of tracking the assassin. Of course, the rhyming names and identical outfits stress the women's sameness.

> Amidala's handmaidens have names, but the only way one would know them is by reading the credits or going to the website or other Lucasfilm-affiliated sources. They are indistinguishable from each other. They serve no purpose than to surround the queen. One of them serves as decoy at the beginning of *Clones*, gladly giving her life. As Amidala's security chief says of her, "She did her duty, now you do yours." This statement might summarize the role of women in *Star Wars*—to serve as a brief presence, a motivating purpose for the male characters. (Wetmore 2005)

Zam Wesell, bounty hunter and "clawdite shape-shifter" uses the centipedelike Kouhuns to sting Padmé. Zam Wesell's bodysuit is quite tight. In the novelization, she thinks, "Often she had taken assignments where her assumed feminine wiles had helped her tremendously, where she had played upon the obvious weakness of a male to get close" (Salvatore 2002, 91). It's a feminine mauve, but fully concealing bodysuit and cloth headscarf, revealing only her eyes. Over it is a masculine leather jerkin, hybridizing her gender. It mixes the message, emphasizing her body but also her toughness. Jango Fett kills Zam before she can reveal who hired her, and she dies with barely a word, like so many women of the series, with little personality to define her. It's also unclear why the bounty hunter needed to hire another bounty hunter to deliver poisonous creatures from a distance unless she was always meant to die.

On Naboo, Padmé and Queen Jamillia talk directly to each other about Padmé's safety and the Separatist crisis. Of course, the scene lets Anakin try to assert dominance over his love interest. Queen Jamillia is a young teen overwhelmed by the elaborate gowns just as Padmé was—a successor much in Padmé's vein with no development.

Dexter's droid waitress is a sassy fifties-style gal. Likewise, the Outlander nightclub features scantily dressed women. As they all sport short skirts and tight dresses, they emphasize that Coruscant is happy to exploit its women.

The alien Taun We of Kamino assists the male prime minister. She's a pacifier, one who meets all of Obi-Wan's requests during his stay. The novelization gives her a hint of toughness as it describes Taun We as "thin, yes, but packed with a solid and powerful presence" (Salvatore 2002, 192). She wears a long skirt and skintight top that basically match her skin tone, making her appear both demure and semi-dressed. The fabric of their clothing has a light, ethereal quality, while the aliens' movement gives them specifically feminine grace. Animation director Rob Coleman describes the Kaminoans' movement as "a blend of the elegance and poise of a runway model with the gestures of tai-chi" (Biggar 2005, 158). Ko Sai, the Chief Scientist, has found a way to reproduce asexually and create thousands of children as the ultimate mother, or at least the technologically improved version. At the same time, this is only a business to her and she destroys clones found to be imperfect. This makes her the evil alien mother, who murders her own offspring. In the Clone Wars show, various factions track her—clones want the secret to a normal lifespan and Palpatine seeks the genetic key to make him live forever. Thus, she becomes a galactic pawn, another disturbing feminine role.

The prequel trilogy presents a variety of women on the Jedi Council. However, over three films they have no personalities, save in their dress and stance, and no lines at all. On the Council, only the male Mace Windu, Yoda, and Ki Adi-Mundi speak (as well as Obi-Wan and Anakin), subtly emphasizing a patriarchal slant. Ki-Adi-Mundi, is a Cerean with a binary brain (Lewis and Keier 2013, 28). Even for those who don't read the extended universe materials, his massively high head emphasizes his cerebral power. Thus, he's coded as masculine, devoted to the intellect. Mace Windu is the fierce leader, Yoda the elderly sage. All represent a spectrum of masculine archetypes, with the females silent in the background. "In *Sith*, for example, there are four female Jedi Masters—Luminara Unduli, Aayla Secura, Barriss Offee, and Stass Allie, none of whom are named in the film or given much to do other than sit in the council and then get killed by their clone troopers when Order 66 is executed. No lines, just quick deaths," Wetmore protests. Notably, none of these female Jedi Masters wear the traditional robes, so their dresses (and Aayla Secura's tube top) make them look unprofessional, like unofficial Jedi. Arguably, all are fridged, in contrast with Windu's dramatic battle.

Among the Jedi Council, Adi Gallia is played by Black actress Gin Clarke. Her presence adds diversity but arguably subverts it by casting the minority woman as an alien with a scaled cranium that sprouts fleshy white tendrils. "The people of color of the *Star Wars* universe are literally alienated—they are represented as aliens, as complete and utterly nonhuman. For the most part in the two trilogies, non-white means nonhuman. They are alienated from human psychology by literally being aliens" (Wetmore 2005). Of course, the female Jedi are already marginalized, and making them alien just exacerbates their othering: "The alien has often been used within science fiction to reproduce, rather than question, those divisions" (Wolmark 1994, 27).

Along with her fellows, she approves the missions of *Phantom Menace* and *Attack of the Clones*. After this, she's switched with another actress, who battles on Geonosis and then is killed by Order 66. In fact, the part was recast, since most of *Attack of the Clones* was shot in Australia instead of England, and local model Lily Nyamwasa replaced Gin Clarke. They shared a general look as well as the costume, but the filmmakers eventually realized the characters appeared significantly different, so they renamed her and decided they were meant to be separate women. In canon, similar-looking cousin Stass Allie takes Gallia's place on the Council after her death (by a Sith in season five of *Clone Wars*). This suggestion that the two actresses of color are interchangeable is cringeworthy, but the fictional wider universe has attempted to compensate.

As a treat for fans, another Council member is Master Yaddle, of the same species of Yoda but with long brown hair. She appears wordlessly in *Phantom Menace* and never again, but the Expanded Universe offers more. *Yaddle's Tale: The One Below* from the comic *Star Wars Tales* #5 has young Yaddle accompanying her master to liberate a planet. When her master is killed, she is sealed in a pit for over 100 years, becoming a local legend called "the one below." When she escapes, she defends the people and saves them from tyranny (Motter and Saiz 1999).

The young readers novel *Jedi Quest: The Shadow Trap* by Jude Watson (2003) sends her on a mission to Mawan with Anakin and Obi-Wan. Yoda calls her "Our most able diplomat" (8). A quintessential master, she's composed and wise in every situation. When she fights, she is "all grace and flowing movement, her lightsaber a blur" (29). When Obi-Wan suggests she leave and stay safe, she mildly rebukes him, and he accepts it. She smoothly rescues Anakin from imprisonment and leaves him with prophetic words: "If you lose your anger, find you it will. Embrace it and disappear it will" (34). Of course, the writers of novel and comic had only Yaddle's appearance and Yoda's personality to go on. Modeled after him, she speaks and even gestures in much the same manner he does.

When a villain releases a bioweapon, Yaddle absorbs the explosion through the Force and sacrifices her life. With this, the master is lost. Like Yoda, she was always particularly attentive and friendly toward the young. As Obi-Wan thinks of her in memorial:

> She had taken a special delight in the young Jedi students. She had turned a blind eye to their pranks. She had hidden sweets in their pockets. . . . There were hard lessons to learn. Yaddle had been there in a different way. There had been so many times when he had knocked respectfully on her door with a problem he didn't want to bother Yoda with. Obi-Wan realized how exceptional it was that a member of the Jedi Council had made herself to be so available to every student. (36)

All the Jedi mourn her, and Anakin bitterly thinks of her as "a member of the Jedi Council, a wise being so practiced in the Force that she was a legend. A being whose strength and wisdom the Jedi needed in these times" (35). One less master is left to stand against the darkness.

Other Jedi councilwomen also operate in the background. Jedi High Council Member Depa Billaba (in the first and second films) varies her Jedi brown robes with two distinctive gold decorations on her forehead and nose, which suggest a Hindu bindi. In fact, she's played by Dipika O'Neill Jot, a Turkish-Australian actress of Indian descent. She does not feature in the *Clone Wars* show but has a significant unseen role in the *Rebels* comics: she becomes the mentor of *Rebels* star Caleb Dume, and during Order 66, sacrifices herself to save her Padawan. Again, the wider fictional universe gives her a vital role, though one conforming to gender roles as her male student and *his* student save the galaxy.

More Jedi appear in the battle of *Attack of the Clones*: Aayla Secura is a warrior and Jedi master, though visually undercut by the amount of skin she always shows off. She's a Twi'lek, a race previously seen as Jabba's sacrificed dancing slave. Thus, even a capable member of her species appears half-dressed, perpetuating stereotypes. In fact, their society, drawn from these examples and expanded on in novels and television shows, is quite sexist. Their cities are each governed by a clan of five males. Slavery is a problem among the clans, especially for females: "In traditional Twi'lek society, women are expected to be subservient to men, and are often treated as afterthoughts or accessories. They are not considered particularly intelligent or capable, having value only to the degree they please others. Twi'lek women were commonly sold into slavery, even by their own clans, to become dancers or companions, as their beauty and grace is favored galaxywide by many different species" (Lewis and Keier 2013, 167). Thus, she feels that even as a powerful Jedi, she must entice others. She dies dramatically but helplessly onscreen during Episode III's Order 66.

A striking Jedi Master and Padawan are Luminara Unduli and Barriss Offee, both near-human Mirialans with greenish skin and elaborate tattoos. In sapphire and purple robes, they're a formidable pairing—emphasizing that their team doesn't require a man. They have extensive arcs in the Clone Wars show, with several novels devoted to their exploits. These two breakout characters do not die in Order 66, emphasizing their more extensive characterization in the show, especially in their dealings with Anakin's Padawan Ahsoka.

There's also Jedi Knight Bultar Swan, a young Asian woman with short-cropped hair. She slices off Vader's sword arm but hesitates to kill her disarmed opponent, a choice that destroys her. The Jedi battle of Episode II, starring women and men, aliens and humans, is an empowering moment of unity. Order 66, however, fridges them before they've had a chance for much character development.

Madame Jocasta Nu, the Jedi Archivist, is an elderly, frail-looking human—another welcome type to offer in the galaxy. When Obi-Wan searches fruitlessly for the planet Kamino, she tells him proudly (and incorrectly!) "The archives are comprehensive and totally secure, my young Jedi. One thing you may be absolutely sure of—if an item does not appear in our records, it does not exist!" The sole matriarch of the show is wrong in the area of her expertise—the only topic on which she's consulted.

"Madame Jocasta Nu is Archives Director and a former active Jedi Knight. Her astonishing memory seems to rival the archives itself, which she runs as a tool, rather than a service, expecting Jedi and support personnel to do their own research. Her pride sometimes blinds her to the Archives' limitations, however," the Visual Dictionary explains (Reynolds 2002, 28). Her beige robes are printed with a mazelike pattern of complexity, while her white hair emphasizes her longevity and wisdom. Though she is a librarian, the lightsaber at her belt suggests she wasn't always. Jocasta speaks more in an early script draft, used for the novelization, but it's all to provide exposition on Dooku, furthering a male character instead of herself. She goes on to appear in four episodes of the *Clone Wars* (2.01 "Holocron Heist," 2.11 "Lightsaber Lost," 3.07 "Assassin," and 6.10 "The Lost One"), advising Jedi including Ahsoka.

Shaak Ti is the films' first Togruta, a Jedi Master and warrior who paves the way for Ahsoka. She joins the battle of *Attack of the Clones*, though her presumed death in *Revenge of the Sith* is complicated: two versions were filmed—the first has her dying at the hands of General Grievous but was left a deleted scene on the DVD. She becomes a sacrifice with little personality or dialogue, meant to hurt and enrage the male Jedi. Of course, her sacrifice foreshadows those to come, including all the female Jedi, leaving a world of entirely male ones until Rey arrives. In the novelization, Anakin kills her during the attack on the Jedi temple. Since neither made it into the final cut of the film, it's possible that in canon she survives.

The third film presents few other women. Palpatine and Bail Organa have female aides. Padmé was intended to have a subplot when she joins a group of male and female senators in beginning the Rebellion. Cutting these scenes basically cuts Mon Mothma from the film and ruins the Bechdel test as well as Padmé's agency.

The twelve-year-old Queen Apailana, queen of Naboo, dresses as elaborately as her predecessors, wearing mourning white and purple to Amidala's funeral. After Order 66, she hides Jedi fugitives on Naboo in the Expanded Universe. The Queen continues investigating Amidala's death but also takes a more assertive stand against Palpatine. She and Boss Nass jointly attack and destroy Imperial Headquarters, to protect the secret of Padmé's child (Watson 2006). Later, the Empire assassinates her for her defiance and installs a puppet queen named Kylantha.

Of course, Queen Apailana does not speak in Episode III but silently attends the funeral. Likewise, Beru and Queen Breha each *silently* accept the babies the men have arranged for them, giving the women a second of screentime but no characterization. Baby Leia falls into a similar category. The medical droid that delivers Padmé's twins has a female voice, emphasizing traditional gender roles once more as the female droids cap off the prequels. This era offers a galaxy of quiet women, incompetent women, and especially fridged women, as all die in this conflict of Sith and outspoken male Jedi. The prequel films thus emphasize conventional, even painful gendering at almost every turn, though the novels and six seasons of *Clone Wars* add more balance and nuance.

AN ALTERNATE PADMÉ: HER *CLONE WARS* ADVENTURES

The Clone Wars takes the Padmé Amidala of Episodes I and II and injects her with refreshing doses of agency, wit and political idealism. As imagined by George Lucas himself and actualized by showrunner [Dave] Filoni, Padmé (voiced by Catherine Taber) is a beacon of morality in the corrupt Senate, a defender of democracy amid the chaos of radicalization and fear, a moralist blessed with pragmatism, and a selfless advocate for the common people. In fact, she is just the kind of politician we in America wish we had on the docket. #ImWithHer, indeed.

With this, Allyson Gronowitz (2016) celebrates a far stronger heroine in her essay on Clone Wars' feminist redemption of Padmé. The children's 3D CGI animated television series (Cartoon Network, 2008–2013) follows Anakin and Obi-Wan through the Clone Wars, together with Anakin's new Padawan Ahsoka Tano and many other recurring characters. While the films waited until Rey's debut to create a female Jedi protagonist, the show was more willing to break boundaries and empower female role models. Its reimagining of Padmé offers a character closer to the strong leader of Episode I than the romantic heroine who subsumes all desires in Anakin's agenda. "Of course, Padmé's power and influence earn her many enemies, making her a target of physical intimidation and assassination attempts. But unlike in *Attack of the Clones*, which begins and ends with Anakin and Obi-Wan protecting her from these dangers, the Senator Amidala of Clone Wars is stubbornly self-sufficient," Gronowitz explains. Padmé continues to fight for peace and deescalation.

She also devotes herself to those without representation, expanding her privilege to them. She hosts a conference alongside Bail Organa to discuss how to protect refugees. She even defends aliens outside of the Republic like the Zillo Beast. "Padmé constantly fights for the rights of others at the expense of her own reputation and likeability. Where Leia is generally respected by those around her, Padmé is seen as a troublemaker and a traitor to the Republic" (M. Wood 2016, 71–72). This puts her at personal risk and emphasizes how much she wants to improve the lives of nonhumans as well as people like herself.

She also forms a fast friendship with Anakin's new Padawan Ahsoka. When the young Jedi sees a vision of bounty hunter Aurra Sing coming for Padmé in "Assassin" (307), she goes to see the other women, who greets her with a delighted hug. However, the senator refuses to skip the conference she's holding on behalf of refugees. Instead, she welcomes Ahsoka along, adding, "I enjoy your company." Onboard, they play the holographic game and Padmé advises Ahsoka like a big sister, giving both a bit more nuance:

AHSOKA: I've been mostly unsure about my abilities on my own. Usually Master Skywalker is there to guide me.

PADMÉ: When I was queen, I felt the same insecurities as you do now. I had my advisors but, it was ultimately up to me to run the entire Naboo system. And I was very afraid at times.

AHSOKA: Really? You felt unsure?

PADMÉ: Oh, yes. I've learned to trust in myself, and you will too.

AHSOKA: Thank you. One more game?

PADMÉ: Absolutely.

Midway through the trip, Ahsoka dramatically leaps onto the sleeping Padmé's bed, lightsaber drawn, to defend her. However, the moment proves an embarrassing false alarm. Diplomatic Padmé offers a compromise, trusting Ahsoka's visions but insisting she won't back down. At the crucial moment, the bounty hunter shoots and injures Padmé. Still, she persists. As she gives a luminous speech about being "bruised but not beaten," Ahsoka arranges a droid to take the senator's place, and Padmé accepts these security measures, as she frequently refused to do for the male Jedi. Padmé gives a lovely speech, finishing, "To those that act as agents of chaos, I say this. I stand resolute and unyielding. And if you strike my voice down, know that a chorus of thousands shall rise up in its place, for you have no dominion over the righteous." She also shows up to Ahsoka's surprise to take the assassin down at the last moment. They capture the bounty hunter and return her to Coruscant. Yoda and Padmé end the adventure praising Ahsoka's insight in this delightful tale of teamwork, friendship, and trust.

In this and other moments, Padmé proves a supportive teacher for the younger girl as well as politician: She acts as Ahsoka's lawyer when the younger girl is accused of treachery in season five, emphasizing how she and Anakin are the only ones clearly on Ahsoka's side. She treats Ahsoka as family, offering endless support as well as teaching. In "Heroes on Both Sides" (310), Padmé takes Ahsoka for a mission. Anakin has been mansplaining the war in a painful fashion: "War is complicated, Ahsoka," he says. "But let me simplify it. The Separatists believe the Republic is corrupt, but they're wrong. And we have to restore order." However, Padmé the diplomat comprehends that the galaxy is not so easily divided into right and wrong. In this vein, she teams up with Ahsoka, teaching her about the finer complexities of conflict. The pair fly off on an illegal trip to see Padmé's old mentor Mina Bonteri, now a Separatist senator. She's sympathetic and friendly, emphasizing the real, likeable people caught in the conflict. She and Padmé work together to deescalate the war in their respective senates. Here the women show off their power to act in friendship behind the scenes, even while passing the lesson on to Ahsoka. However, the vicious Count Dooku murders Mina and bombs Coruscant to inflame tempers and continue the war. With this, the patriarchy destroys the women's alliance to make peace. Still, Padmé continues, teaming up later in season three with Duchess Satine, another woman of sense and courage in charge of a planetary system. All these moments don't just play into the Bechdel Test but emphasize women as political players.

In a touching scene in the following episode, Padmé chats with one of her assistants, asking how the war is affecting her at home. Having heard the woman's concerns, she rushes to address them. In a problematic gender scene, Padmé tells Bail the Senate will only listen to him. When he is injured, however, Padmé speaks in his place. She touchingly invokes her assistant, giving her a voice in the world of international politics: "Teckla is one of my aides. Like so many of the people that we tell ourselves we're here to serve, Teckla lives in a district that rarely has electricity and running water as a result of the war. Her children can now only bathe every two weeks, and they have no light in which to read or study at night." Once more, she expands her privilege to those in need. When she protests, "If not for people like Teckla and her children, who are we fighting for?" ("Pursuit of Peace," 311), she wins the senators to her side, leaving even Palpatine visibly impressed. Gronowitz (2016) notes:

> Padmé's politicking is her superpower, making her a stellar role model for little girls who get to see a strong-willed young woman making a galactic impact. Indeed, when Padmé is forced to step in and deliver a speech in place of the esteemed Senator Bail Organa (Princess Leia's eventual adoptive father), we catch a glimpse of a young Mon Mothma gazing at her in admiration. Mon Mothma, of course, will go on to play a pivotal role in the Rebellion—and prove to be a personal idol of *Rogue One*'s Jyn Erso. Indeed, Senator Amidala presents an inspirational figure for young women within the *Star Wars* universe and beyond.

Unlike in the films, Padmé is seen fighting for the needs of those living without basic necessities. This emphasizes her sympathy for the wider world beyond her own fashions and illicit romance. Third wave "can also promote an understanding of the links between Western women's pleasurable play with affordable fashions in clothing and make-up, and the sweatshops in which third world women and immigrants labor to produce those sources of middle class (and largely white) enjoyment" (Woodhull 2007, 159). Many young women expanded their horizons and took on causes to advance equality. With her eloquent sympathy for others, Padmé is a voice of wisdom and progressiveness in the increasingly warmongering Senate. Through all her stories, she displays an incredible loyalty to both political allies and friends. She's fearless and unrelenting in her quest to do what she thinks is right, even smuggling herself into Separatist space and putting her body on the line over and over.

Still, her trust in Palpatine and faith in the democratic process also emphasize her repeated naivete. Often as a result, she and the other senators spend the show being kidnapped and threatened with assassination, casting them as the weaker characters. In just the first season, Padmé is captured and rescued a total of four times (or roughly once every five episodes). Anakin must swoop in and save her. With a galaxy still filled with damsels and "fridged" women, the warrior Ahsoka stands out as the exception—a disturbing message in a show that's often archaically gendered.

In episode four, "Destroy Malevolence," Grievous takes Padmé hostage, and Anakin bursts into his ship impulsively and rescues her, even catching Padmé with the Force when she jumps to him. Anakin then takes on the cool flying, leaving Padmé to "clean up the droids," in a disturbingly old-fashioned take on their relationship. He even calls it "housecleaning." When she takes the guns in a space battle, she modestly calls her shooting "beginner's luck." Meanwhile, Ahsoka sits on Anakin's ship in a tube top and has a few monosyllabic comments. In "Bombad Jedi" (108), Padmé insists she wants no clone escort as it's a diplomatic mission. Of course, she's soon captured. Though she frees herself with lockpicks and grabs a gun, she insists to the droid soldiers a Jedi has come to rescue her—even while saving herself, she must pretend the great heroes are doing it. In "Hostage Crisis" (122), Anakin gives Padmé his lightsaber, and she proves his weakness as he's forced to fight without it. Once again, she's held hostage for Anakin to free as he improvises cleverly without his weapon.

"Blue Shadow Virus"/"Mystery of a Thousand Moons" (117–18) follows Padmé, Ahsoka, and some of the clone troopers as they investigate a deadly disease and are infected. Padmé and Ahsoka tend the weakening clone troopers with cool cloths. It's Anakin and Obi-Wan who have the heroic quest and deadly firefight, crossing through Separatist space to find the antidote as the women slowly succumb inside a bunker. After Anakin saves the two women, they thank him from their medical beds. "I never lost faith in you. None of us did," Padmé tells him sweetly and somewhat pathetically.

The couple are arguably more fun without the painful Episode II dialogue. In The Clone Wars, "their relationship is given a chance to breathe, and their interactions are actually . . . kind of adorable. They bicker, they worry, they snark, they find comfort in each other's embrace; in short, their domestic life is imbued with a healthy dose of normalcy," Gronowitz says. Anakin still displays macho behavior, but Padmé simpers less and is more willing to stand up for herself. Her personality is more central, and the costumes are simplified in this new medium, leaving the senator often in her action jumpsuit. She gets in some jokes and flirty moments, while other times their understated touches and public looks say it all. The pair, newly married, are finding a balance between the political and personal in third wave style, even as they hide their relationship from others.

At the same time, there are hallmarks of the violent jealousy and selfishness that will end their love. In "Senate Spy" (204), Padmé is sent to spy on an old love interest, Baron Rush Clovis, leaving Anakin fuming with jealousy. He actually tries to forbid her the mission, adding "I'm not going to let you do it." She responds incredulously, "You're not going to let me? It's not your decision to make—it's mine." They may be married, but she controls her own career. "An Old Friend" (605) has Padmé helping Clovis again, with his life in danger. Since he trusts her, she crosses the galaxy to aid him in exposing the banking clan's schemes. However, she's treated as a pawn and arrested for espionage, leaving Anakin to save her once more. Since he disapproves of her mission, Anakin turns unusually nasty, threatening to leave her in the Banking Clan's jail.

In the following episode, as Clovis suspects Padmé's romantic secret and disturbingly tries to force a kiss on her, Anakin shows up and Force-chokes him in a clear display of macho power that's on the cusp of the dark side. The pair fight hand to hand, offering more testosterone-poisoned posturing as Padmé begs them to stop. Anakin coldly tells her she has no say in the men's battle. Clovis even taunts him, "Why don't you try fighting like a man without your Jedi tricks?" After severely injuring his rival, Anakin finally backs down and apologizes, but afterward, Padmé tells him that their relationship is the problem: "This marriage is not a marriage, Anakin, if there isn't any trust. We said at the beginning that this could be a terrible mistake . . . We live in secret, Anakin. Like it or not, our relationship is built on lies and deception. No relationship can survive that." She tells him, predicting the future with chilling accuracy, that she doesn't feel safe and adds, "I think it's best if we don't see each other anymore, at least not for a while."

There are other signs of a fraying relationship, especially in the accompanying novels. In *No Prisoners*, Anakin drops in unexpectedly on Padmé only to discover she's wearing a goopy facemask. "Even a Senator is entitled to a girl's night in with a beauty mask and a holozine," she tells him (Traviss 2009, 32). Immediately, he helps her wash the mask off and she changes into "one of her elegant gowns, fierce electric blue sateen that cast a turquoise reflection on the glossy white cabinets" (Traviss 2009, 34). On her husband's arrival, she feels the need to dress up, to look polished and alluring. Even around him, she must wear her persona. Butler comments, "Gender cannot be understood as a role which either expresses or disguises an interior 'self,' whether that 'self' is conceived as sexed or not. As performance which is performative, gender is an 'act,' broadly construed, which constructs the social fiction of its own psychological interiority" (1990, 192). By wearing an elegant gown for Anakin, Padmé is not showing off her true self, but a disguise she assumes to please him. As a consequence, their relationship never reveals the real her but only the perfect queen.

In *Clone Wars Gambit: Stealth*, Anakin returns to Coruscant unexpectedly to find Padmé is off at a women's retreat. His thoughts turn selfish and misogynistic. "The reunion he'd dreamed of on the journey back from Kothlis—ruined. Stolen. Carelessly trampled for some stupid, pointless women's gabfest" (K. Miller 2010, 97). In his fury, he smashes a damaged gun turret, and then goes on fuming: "*Sacred retreat? What is she thinking? There's a war on. She's not supposed to be romping offworld with a bunch of vegetarian navel-gazers. She's a Galactic Senator, she's got a job to do. And I'm here.* And what was the good of him being here if she wasn't? Women" (K. Miller 2010, 98). His universe and his wife only exist to please him, as he thinks—a childish belief but also one that foreshadows his callousness in the next film. Since he buries much of his resentment, he's playing a part as artificial as hers.

After the pair are reunited, Anakin displays jealousy for all the men with whom she displays any closeness. Padmé dotingly dismisses his jealousy as "silly" instead of noting that he has real control issues. He also asks her to step down from her committees when she doesn't have time to spend with him during his spontaneous visit. Once again, she doesn't confront his bossy attitude, instead telling him the sweet "I can't, Anakin. I have to keep myself busy or I'll go mad worrying about you" (K. Miller 2010, 187). She insists that even her devotion to duty is all about him, feeding his ego. Clearly, the couple are communicating badly, both allowing Padmé to be the loving adult and Anakin the selfish child. Worse is soon to come.

THE GOTHIC DAMSEL AND POOR DROWNED OPHELIA

This is Padmé Amidala:

> She is an astonishingly accomplished young woman, who in her short life has been already the youngest-ever elected Queen of her planet, a daring partisan guerrilla, and a measured, articulate, and persuasive voice of reason in the Republic Senate.
>
> But she is, at this moment, none of these things.
>
> She can still play at them—she pretends to be a Senator, she still wields the moral authority of a former Queen, and she is not shy about using her reputation for fierce physical courage to her advantage in political debate—but her inmost reality, the most fundamental, un- breakable core of her being, is something entirely different.
>
> She is Anakin Skywalker's wife.
>
> Yet wife is a word too weak to carry the truth of her; wife is such a small word, such a common word, a word that can come from a down- turned mouth with so many petty, unpleasant echoes. For Padmé Ami- dala, saying I am Anakin Skywalker's wife is saying neither more nor less than I am alive. (Stover 2005, 160–61)

With this, the third film's novelization emphasizes how deeply she's fallen from her previous levels of power—first queen and guerilla gener- al, then respected senator and action heroine. This excerpt is disturbing—

now Padmé cares nothing for halting Palpatine's excesses as he seizes power—only her husband and pregnancy are the center of her world. Pianka sorrowfully observes, "Any hopes of a Leia for a new generation of young *Star Wars* fans, someone young girls could look up to, proved to be futile. Padmé is a plot device for Anakin; a character whose entire reason to live is literally tied to her relationship with a man" (44). The heroine queen who once shot villains in a velvet gown, as the epitome of having it all, now has nothing. Padmé's deterioration through the three films "can thus be read as an alarming reflection of the complex, confusing, and contradictory messages today's young women receive from society and the media" (Dominguez 2017, 111).

As such, she flips into another fundamental text of the nineties—Mary Pipher's 1994 book *Reviving Ophelia: Saving the Selves of Adolescent Girls.* The text focuses on the psychological motives for Ophelia's suicide, as she cannot meet the competing demands of Hamlet and her father. "On many levels the Girl Power and *Reviving Ophelia* discourses represent a social and cultural fascination with girls that also is an expression of the uncertainties, tensions, fears, and anxieties elicited by the rapid social, economic, and political changes taking place due to neoliberal policies" (Gonick 2006, 4–5). One emphasizes strength and choice, while the other, victimization.

As the film begins, Anakin has become an acclaimed hero who saves the Chancellor in a dramatic action sequence. On his return, all the dignitaries fuss. His once-mighty bride, however, has faded away. She shrinks behind a pillar when her colleagues walk by and twitches, visibly trying to draw Anakin's attention but no one else's. This impulse will define her for the rest of the film.

When Anakin comes to her, she's concealed by a long dark blue cloak. Generally speaking, a cloak is "ambivalent as both a symbol of dignity and position but also as a disguise, withdrawal and obscurity; darkness; the secretive; dissimulation. In magic, it is invisibility" (Cooper 1978, 38). In fact, all of Padmé's costumes tell the story of her slide into doom: Muted colors suggest the darker time, while crinolines and petticoats hide her figure. In times of emotionalism, subdued colors can be comforting (Sharpe 1974, 114). Blue and purple also suggest sorrow. Traditionally, warm colors take central stage while cool colors make up the background. "Warm tones are 'advancing colors' while cool colors are 'receding' (Sharpe 1974, 107). While Anakin grows in power, Padmé's fading into the colorless wallpaper. Designer Trisha Biggar says, "By *Revenge of the Sith*, Padmé's softer and more alluring costumes have given way, at least in public, to more structured shapes. The Clone Wars have been raging for a couple of year and her marriage to Anakin, who has been fighting battles on the Outer Rim for several months, is still a secret; what's more, she is, unbeknownst to him, expecting a child. For both their sakes, her quite advanced pregnancy has to be hidden in public life"

(2005, 97). As she hides, she splits into public and private sides. Even as her body threatens her career and Anakin's with its revealing pregnancy, Padmé rejects this part of herself on some level by concealing it.

In *Reviving Ophelia*, Pipher argues that due to pressure from U.S. culture, adolescent girls are coerced into putting aside their "authentic selves," splitting what was, in their younger days, a healthy and united individual, into true and false identities. This pressure to be a false self, Pipher claims, disorients and depresses most girls. They begin secret lives, often of drugs and alcohol or bulimia and shame. At puberty "girls become 'female impersonators' who fit their whole selves into small, crowded spaces. Girls stop thinking, 'Who am I? What do I want?' and start thinking, 'what must I do to please others?'" (2005, 27). Of course, Padmé, in danger of losing her Senate seat to her pregnancy, insists on defining herself as Anakin's perfect love, since the once duty-bound politician has no other identity. Anakin loves Padmé utterly, but without her, he is still a champion pilot and warrior, the chosen of Palpatine and the Force. When he loses Padmé, he loses his happiness and goodness, but keeps all these skills and privilege, gaining unheard-of power. As shown at film's end, Padmé feels she has nothing without him, and thus gives up on life. In fact, Padmé's addictive, dependent behavior is centered on Anakin. While in public, Padmé still fulfills her duties, behind closed doors she is a self outlawed by society, one they would turn on if they knew her dark secret.

Anakin tells her, "I'm tired of all this deception. I don't care if they know we're married," but Padmé demurs. As they continue embracing, dark shadows mar her face, suggesting a desire to hide even from the audience as well as from the public eye. She insists, "Annie, I want to have our baby back home on Naboo. We could go to the lake country where no one would know . . . where we would be safe. I could go early and fix up the baby's room. I know the perfect spot, right by the gardens." Once again, she values hiding and having their child above the fate of the galaxy and her decade of responsibilities. Her universe has shrunken to only Anakin.

She remains in her Coruscant apartment during the film, only for Anakin to drop in and reassure her with meaningless assurances. There, she's isolated, a solitary hero without the gaggle of supportive friends from the first and second films. This "is also sadly reflective of the rash of recent stories of women overwhelmed by the responsibilities of marriage and motherhood that have lost their support networks and suffer in silence until they snap in horrifyingly public ways" (Dominguez 2017, 129). Padmé pretends to be who she was—the glamorous, duty-bound senator. However, underneath she's increasingly unhappy. Pipher explains, "Adolescent girls are like saplings in a hurricane. They are young and vulnerable trees that the winds blow with gale strength" (2005, 22). Though Padmé is older, she too is pushed about by Anakin's wants and needs until they threaten to overwhelm her. "She's duped by Palpatine, and gradually her story shifts to one of torment over her forbidden love, facing pregnancy alone, and being emotionally and physically abused by her secret husband—all before she dies (of a broken heart) right after giving birth" (Schnelbach 2017).

> This equating of young women with their bodies, at the mercy of their hormones, signaling the loss of rationality seems very closely related to the disease of hysteria which, as we have already seen, was also thought to befall young women at this time in their lives. The representation of adolescence as chaos feeds into many of the demeaning cultural stereotypes about girls and young women. (Gonick 2006, 12–13)

Her most common line through the film is "Anakin, what are we/you going to do?" Even worse is "Anakin, I'm afraid." She thus puts her entire trust and willpower in the hands of a terribly flawed man. Pipher represents girls as unwitting victims. According to her, even their own bodies work against them. "Everything is changing—body shape, hormones, skin and hair. Calmness is replaced by anxiety. Their way of thinking is changing" (2005, 27). Of course, all these symptoms are also markers of pregnancy. It is the source of Padmé's weakness—a problematic message in comparison with the many fictional and real-life mama bears who fight savagely to defend their families.

Focusing on his role as dashing hero, Anakin spends the film treating Padmé as housebound and hysterical—a victim of dark forces he's driven to save from death. The prophetic dream she will die in childbirth—another gothic staple—drives him. Comforting him after his premonition, she wears a vulnerably bare-shouldered pale nightgown, hair loose and curly. The blue-grey silk is trimmed with pearls and a spiral brooch, nodding to luxury and the trim of her wedding gown, but mostly suggesting sorrow as her eyes fill with tears. In the eighteenth century, light blue was associated with the romantics and melancholy—the young lady wasting away from being spurned in love. ("The blues," referring to the music and the feeling, stem from this.) The nightgown also displays her vulnerable, guilty pregnancy for the first time.

"That gender reality is created through sustained social performances means that the very notions of an essential sex, a true or abiding masculinity or femininity, are also constituted as part of the strategy by which the performative aspect of gender is concealed," Butler explains (1990, 192). Leia fights for her ideals as a princess with a gun—it's implied that, especially in Episodes V and VI, she is wearing the clothing she prefers to fight for her people. She wears gowns when Lando and the Ewoks offer her them, but (setting aside the infamous gold bikini Jabba forces on her), she wears simple jumpsuits or military camouflage, not so different from the distinctive but simple clothing worn by Han and Luke. Padmé wears these jumpsuits at moments of action in Episodes II and III (and indeed the *Clone Wars* show dresses her in jumpsuits or far simpler gowns, emphasizing her actions rather than drowning her in fashion). However, most of Padmé's film appearances allow her costumes to dominate her personality, emphasizing how little willpower she has outside of her love for Anakin and desire to be the supportive wife and mother in his life. As she does in Episode II and the *Clone Wars* novels, she's dressing as his princess in satin, never allowing him to see her grubby, authentic self. Pipher describes how destructive burying the real self could be for her vulnerable patients: "The part that was unacceptable went underground and eventually withered from lack of attention" (2005, 36). Every time she dresses up for Anakin, Padmé loses a bit more of herself in her beautiful persona.

Clearly the clothing is selected to entice her husband, to attract his gaze and the audience's. She's still costuming to please him, even heavily pregnant and alone in their bedroom. This suggests love but also desperation as she feels the widening split between them. Still, she only endures. As Anakin vows to love and protect her, their relationship is already fraying; as she promises not to die in childbirth, she's already doomed.

> In Episode III, Amidala is back in passive mode. Except for the beginning and the end, she spends the entire movie in her penthouse apartment, changing clothes and gazing out the window. This Rapunzel, though, is more even-tempered than Leia. In fact, for much of the movie, she has that Prozac glow. As the war escalates and the Republic threatens to crumble, she brushes her hair, musing about how to decorate the baby's room. After Obi-Wan has told her his concerns about Anakin, Amidala relates them to Anakin without seeming concerned herself. Anakin confesses he's not the Jedi he should be and claims he's found a way to save her. When your husband claims he's found a way to save you from death in childbirth, wouldn't you ask him what he's talking about? Is he suggesting abortion? Has he learned about a hot new obstetrician on *Oprah*? Has he, by chance, turned to the dark side? Amidala asks none of these things. (Cavelos 2006, 319)

In fact, she does not ask how he plans to save her and the Republic— it's implied she doesn't want to know. "Indeed, Padmé's passivity seems largely to blame for Anakin's fall to the dark side. She only half-heartedly attempts and abysmally fails to dissuade him from seeking forbidden occult knowledge that may, no matter the personal or galactic cost, supposedly save her from an unlikely death in childbirth" (Wilson 2007, 140). Her denial of Anakin's capacity for darkness drives the story, catapulting it into far older tropes. Gothic narratives generally feature a passion-driven, willful villain-hero, like brooding Heathcliff shouting his love for Cathy over the moors. Meanwhile the traditional gothic heroine is the fainting damsel in the white nightgown, captured by the villain for the hero to rescue.

In this gothic tale, Palpatine is the true architect, the force behind Anakin's tragic fall. Through the film, the Jedi along with skeptical senators Padmé and Bail Organa lose trust in Palpatine as he seizes ever-more power. However, Anakin gives his trust to the chancellor, who hints he has the lore to save Padmé from death in childbirth. Thus, she becomes Anakin's vulnerable spot as well as his temptation. The story arc is framed as *his* attempt to halt the prophecy of her death, thus tragically bringing it about.

However, even as he quests to save his idealized, dying damsel in distress, the real Padmé doesn't confront him in the issue of politics—one in which she is far better trained than he is. Bound in tight dark red like a martyr, she asks Anakin whether he's considered he may be on the wrong side. However, he ignores her protests—their relationship deteriorates through the film as he dismisses her political opinions and refuses to confide in her. When he rejects her arguments, she doesn't keep persuading but simply asks to be held. Already she's softening, giving up on keeping Anakin on the side of light. As she describes how much she loved being held by the lake when they had no war to contend with, she's clinging to the past, not who Anakin is becoming. Neither one sees the other honestly—only through a romanticized lens.

Meanwhile, Anakin is still being beguiled by the shadowy Chancellor Palpatine, who doubles as Darth Sidious in his shadowy robe. As Anakin teeters on the border between good and evil, he separates himself from Padmé, rejecting her influence. The couple wait separately for the Jedi Council to arrest Palpatine, lit by a sunset. Each wears dark colors and Padmé's hair lies simple and unbound. She gazes at the city with wide eyes, on the edge of tears. However, as Anakin wrestles with his decision, she has no choice to make, no option but to wait. It's not even clear how much she's been told. As Cavelos comments acerbically, "She stands on the sidelines and cries as Palpatine destroys the Republic" (2006, 316).

After teetering between good and evil, and then pledging his allegiance to Darth Sidious, Anakin too begins hiding a secret self. He starts wearing his hood up, hiding his evil beneath its shade. As he mirrors Padmé visually, he is actually gaining power as she is fading. Masks and disguises continue as a motif, as both pretend at normalcy, yet are more separated than ever. Horrifically, Anakin finally murders children and reveals himself at last as the villain of the series.

She's next seen standing at the window, this time in a pale blue nightgown draping down like a waterfall, suggesting tears and sorrow as well as the costume of her funeral. It's accented by embroidered Naboo designs, beads and tiny shells, suggesting the feminine wisdom and peacefulness of the water as she recalls her lost lake on Naboo and endlessly weeps. Further, the lines of draping embroidery hint at trails of tears. Aquamarines, a shining water-stone, hold back her loose hair. In this costume, she sees a brightening fire on the horizon—the polar opposite and enemy to her water imagery. C-3PO reports that Anakin has gone to the Jedi temple, which she can see burning in front of her. However, she does not leap onto a speeder and rush to save him: As Anakin's apparently trapped in the burning temple, she simply cries rather than attempting a rescue. The more assertive Bail Organa is the one to rush to save the Jedi survivors. After this, Anakin returns to Padmé and reassures her, encouraging her once again to wait while he takes care of everything. "As Anakin, a mass murderer, tells her that he's going to end the war, she looks up at him trustingly, like a child, and nods. Then she cries" (Cavelos 2006, 318).

Her frozen fear and inability to act may also signal what the fire alludes to in American culture of the time:

> Communicating Lucas's worries regarding how post September 11th angst and fear has permeated American political life, the Jedi Temple is shown burning on the horizon in a visual that is eerily reminiscent of the World Trade Towers prior to their collapse. Powerless and evoking the position of the American public as spectator on September 11th, Padmé looks toward them and painfully realizes her husband's role in its destruction and that her world, as well as that of the Republic's, have been forever changed by one act of violence. (Deis 2007, 99)

Like Americans of just a few years previous, she is shocked and horrified that this pillar of her impregnable city has been destroyed. However, no possible action can remedy the world-shattering catastrophe. Thanks to this, she embodies the third-wave women's despair and distress, even as she succumbs to hopelessness in a world that can never be repaired.

"The unraveling and disintegration of her spirited character in Episode III was not only a disappointment but smacked of betrayal as well" (Dominguez 2017, 111). Many fans, recalling the warrior queen of Episode I were shocked at her feebleness. In the introduction for a DVD cut scene, Lucas explains that Padmé was supposed to have a subplot of forming the Rebel Alliance, but he cut it to focus on Vader's descent. In the scene (also present in the novelization), Padmé insists she still believes in the chancellor, her old friend, but the others, including Bail Organa and Mon Mothma, persuade her they are the best chance to save the Republic. As Padmé agrees to tell no one, even her loved ones, she crosses a line toward galactic preservation just as Anakin does into destruction.

When she presents the senators' "Petition of the 2000," to Palpatine, requesting he relinquish his wartime powers, her gleaming copper robe is more subdued than her clothing of the previous films, yet its light blue inserts suggest a little hope. The "peacock gown," which was featured heavily in the prefilm advertising for its elaborate beauty, changes colors in the light, echoing the shifting times. Her hair appears in thin ringlets—sorrowfully down, yet intricate. During the meeting, Anakin chillingly stands behind Palpatine, placing them symbolically on opposite sides. If the scene had been kept, it would have allowed Padmé to take a stand for democracy against the patriarchy, as she does in the first two films. Further, it would have played into the theme of masks, as her cloaks would have dovetailed with her sneaking about and conspiring to preserve the Republic and launch the next generation's Rebel Alliance, not just to conceal her selfish pregnancy for fear of public shaming. Without the subplot, she's no political player, but only a cringing damsel weeping in her tower.

This subplot of secrets also works as a gender metaphor. Anakin can be himself—not only proud war hero with no pregnancy to hide, but honest. While he and Padmé both fear that her speaking her doubts about the Republic's corruption will bring reprisals on her, privileged Anakin feels no threat, close as he is to the chancellor. Anakin rebels over and over against his Jedi masters and they have no choice but to put up with him. Padmé, less protected, uses disguise as a tool to bolster her position, emphasizing her political vulnerability. She uses her very femininity and beauty to play at harmlessness even as she sweetly offers up the Senate's petition to Anakin and then Palpatine. "The very fact that we can speak of a woman 'using' her sex or 'using' her body for particular gains is highly significant—it is not that a man cannot use his body in this way but that he doesn't have to" (Doane 1999).

With or without her attempted intervention, the Chancellor proclaims himself Emperor, and Padmé watches from her Senate seat, a hand pressed against her mouth in dismay. She does not publicly protest, but only manages a bitter aside to Bail Organa—"So this is how liberty dies. With thunderous applause." As Vinci notes, "This critique of anti-individualism is decidedly ineffectual; it carries little weight during the course of the film's narrative and functions more as a commentary on how Palpatine rises to power than on how the individuals of the Republic lose it" (2007, 19). She's turned from Senate warrior to observer. In this scene, she's again in subdued shades for the Republic's death—elegant but no longer glamorous. She wears layered purple velvet—rich but very somber. Her light is dimming.

After, Obi-Wan comes to her and tells her Anakin has embraced evil, stumbling over the difficult words. From the outside, her balcony is shown stretching wide with open curtains—as vulnerable to assault as she is. She wears a thick, more casual dressing gown in deep violet, with vintage embroidery and tassels. A pattern of flowers down her shoulders foreshadows her funeral look. Underneath the robe is an underdress of white satin with an empire waist, once again suggesting innocent, even girlish, vulnerability. The headdress is pewter with shining bands in Celtic knots—she's a prisoner of love, duty, and fate. Beneath it her hair is down. This is as close as she comes to total disarray. While Obi-Wan himself has reacted to Anakin's transformation with horror, shock and denial—and then soon accepts it—Padmé refuses to do so herself. Obi-Wan tells her Anakin has killed all the Jedi younglings, but she stubbornly replies, "Not Anakin. He couldn't" and "I don't believe you. I can't."

After Obi-Wan leaves, she finally takes initiative, rushing to Anakin to warn him—thus bringing Obi-Wan with her as stowaway and precipitating the climactic duel she was trying to stop. This choice creates the destruction she most fears (much like her votes of no confidence and emergency powers have already brought down the Republic). Nonetheless, her character wins the audience's empathy through this very human, emotional, even heroic act. Her action outfit, a taupe tunic, reveals her pregnancy as the other outfits do not, leaving her markedly vulnerable. It also suggests a return to her warrior status and an acceptance of her pregnancy—no longer hiding it under voluminous gowns but embracing it as part of herself. As she becomes a pregnant action heroine, this outfit is very third-wave, emphasizing how she really can have it all . . . though this quickly ends in tragedy.

Upon her arrival at the volcanic planet Mustafar, she falls to pieces, especially in the novel:

> Padmé stumbled down the landing ramp into Anakin's arms.
>
> Her eyes were raw and numb; once inside the ship, her emotional control had finally shattered and she had sobbed the whole way there, crying from the relentless mind-shredding dread, and so her lips were swollen and her whole body shook and she was just so *grateful,* so incredibly grateful, that again she flooded with fresh tears: grateful that he was alive, grateful that he'd come bounding across the landing deck to meet her, that he was still strong and beautiful, that his arms still were warm around her and his lips were soft against her hair.
>
> "Anakin, my *Anakin* . . ." She shivered against his chest. "I've been so *frightened* . . ." (Stover 2005, 389)

Gone is the powerful queen, leaving only a wilting victim. She bursts out with everything Obi-Wan has told her in confidence and begs Anakin to love her and trust Obi-Wan. These shared secrets, along with her helpless presence, give Anakin his final motivation to turn violent. Admittedly, her arrival at the volcanic planet is also a revelation to herself—a descent into darkness from which she never recovers. There, her Anakin finally unmasks what he's become. He tells her, "I am becoming more powerful than any Jedi has ever dreamed of. And I'm doing it for you. To protect you."

She begs him to come away with her, as she did at the movie's beginning. Padmé has not grown or changed, only revealed how much Anakin has transformed into someone no longer interested in her offer. He retorts, "Don't you see? We don't have to run away anymore. I have brought peace to the Republic. I am more powerful than the chancellor. I can overthrow him. And together, you and I can rule the galaxy . . . make things the way we want them to be." As with gothic stories like *Jane Eyre*, the hero demands the heroine compromise her ethics to pledge herself to him forever. However, the heroine balks as he wants her to choose evil and succumb to her passion for him. Despairing, she rejects him.

Padmé retreats, but her dialogue is still feeble, from "I don't believe what I'm hearing" to "I don't know you anymore. You're breaking my heart." As her husband's drippy enabler, she cannot assertively condemn him. Pipher describes girls' perceived dilemma: "They could be authentic and honest, or they could be loved. If they chose wholeness they were abandoned by their parents. If they chose love, they abandoned their true selves" (2005, 36). She can keep her ethics or her husband, but not both—a choice that apparently leads her to suicidal despair.

As with the Senate scenes, a more powerful plot twist here was planned for Padmé and discarded. Artist Iain McCaig describes an intended climax as Padmé arrives at Mustafar with a knife concealed in her hand (thus paying off her double life through the entire film as it finally rebounds on her husband): "She gets off that ship with the knife, she runs up and throws her arms around him, and he lets her. She's got the knife at his neck and she's going to kill him. He lets her, and she can't do it. She loves him too much to stop him, even when he becomes the monster." Then Obi-Wan arrives and Anakin turns on Padmé as in the finished film. As McCaig concludes, "Wouldn't that have been good?" (Reyes 2017). Certainly, it would have given Padmé a despairing but all-too-human struggle, even as the audience would have sympathized with her choice, especially knowing all the evil Vader would bring. Moreover, it would have placed the entire course of the future two decades in her shaking hands. Without this or the Senate plot, Padmé barely has agency in the film, and even her trip to Mustafar is only so Anakin can attack her as she pleads.

Back in the released version of the film, Obi-Wan arrives and the two men begin fighting over Padmé, treating her as the pawn in their more central male-male conflict. Anakin chokes her, nearly killing her. "Like many an abusive husband, in an all-too-ordinary outburst of domestic violence, Anakin turns on his pregnant wife, the one he had vowed to protect and save at all costs and strangles her. Only the more attractive prospect of destroying Kenobi distracts him from murdering Padmé in his irrational fury" (Wilson 2007, 141).

As he attacks Padmé, he reveals the deprivation of their relationship—bursting through her denial. This is the moment of her catharsis, understanding that he's so transformed that he would willingly harm her and her pregnancy. This moment also evokes the audiences' fears in an era of domestic abuse and violence. "In 1991, more than one million women reported being the victims of violent crimes at the hands of husbands or lovers; four thousand women were killed," *Reviving Ophelia* reports (2005, 218). Police estimated another five million that went unreported. This is Padmé's wake-up call, a chance to realize how Anakin has truly become a monster. However, Padmé falls unconscious before she can learn from the encounter. As she lies there, the men continue fighting over her:

OBI-WAN: Let her go, Anakin. Let her go.

ANAKIN: You turned her against me!

OBI-WAN: You have done that yourself.

ANAKIN: You will not take her from me!

OBI-WAN: Your anger and your lust for power have already done that.

Anakin's self-centered immaturity means that he cannot accept responsibility for his actions, a trend that continues beyond this turning point, as he continues to obey Palpatine for decades. Even in his mind, he's stuck in these patterns. In Luceno's novel *Dark Lord*, Anakin/Vader broods: "Padmé and Obi-Wan . . . had sentenced him to his black-suit prison. Sentenced by his wife and his alleged best friend, their love for him warped by what they had perceived as [Anakin's] betrayal. . . . He had only wanted to save them! Padmé, from death; Obi-Wan, from ignorance. And in the end, they had failed to recognize his power; to simply accede to him; to accept on faith that he knew what was best for them . . . for everyone!" (2005, 76–77). He sees them as the problem, unwilling to obey him and allow him to dictate their thoughts and actions, make them obey as he wants the Senate to do. Meanwhile, his conflict with Obi-Wan fuels the climax and also his attack on his wife as Anakin lashes out at both for the emotional burdens they've placed on him.

> Despite Padmé's growing ineffectiveness over the course of the three films, Anakin clearly remains threatened by what limited and dwindling power over him she still possesses and turns upon her the dark murderous fury he had previously reserved only for Tusken Raiders and, now, the Jedi Knights as well. Indeed, it seems as if much of Anakin's rage stems from his resentment over the "control" Padmé exerts over him without even intending to—the problematic and potentially "castrating" force of his excessive emotional dependence upon her. Thus, he tends to blame her, in the long run, for his own turn to darkness. (Wilson 2007, 141–42)

She lies at his feet and even as Obi-Wan wants to help her, Anakin does not, consumed as he is with rage against his old mentor. "Padmé's white female body lies limp as the light-bearded, blue-eyed Jedi stands alone against Vader. In fact, her body rests just below the right knee level of the Jedi, showing that she is literally out of the picture in terms of resistance" (Estrada 2007). The epic battle has a particularly gothic element beyond the fainting damsel as Obi-Wan and Anakin battle in primal fashion beside a river of fire, and Obi-Wan finally dismembers his best friend, leaving him the crippled, masked monster of the original trilogy. Miserably, Obi-Wan leaves Anakin for dead.

When Padmé wakes and asks, "Is Anakin all right"—showing her love but also her deep denial of the men's inevitable life or death struggle—Obi-Wan doesn't have the respect for her to make her face the truth. Instead, he sends her into unconsciousness as Anakin did—so the surviving men of the film can concentrate on the greater war of good and evil. Obi-Wan carries unconscious Padmé to the medical center, where during a gothic storm, she succumbs to despair. The medic reports to Obi-Wan, Yoda, and Bail as she lies motionless: "Medically, she's completely healthy. For reasons we can't explain, we are losing her . . . she has lost the will to live."

It also adds that she is having twins—with this, the men share knowledge of her body she lacks. Apparently, Padmé, a wealthy and powerful senator, has not bothered to visit an obstetrician, assuming her culture even has such a thing. Even her husband's panicking that she'll die in childbirth doesn't impel her to have the science fiction equivalent of an ultrasound. All this makes it clear that the entire realm of female-centric medicine doesn't exist. "In a galaxy of bacta tanks that can heal grievous wounds, and highly advanced cybernetic prosthetics to replace limbs, reproductive health is stuck in the middle ages," complains critic Sarah Jeong (2017) in "Did Inadequate Women's Healthcare Destroy *Star Wars*' Old Republic?"

Turned from heroine to damsel, Padmé dies for no clear reason. "Her death is an accident of health, imposed by the author. Once she fulfills the needs of the saga—falling in love with Anakin and having his children—the sooner she dies, the more convenient it is for a story that has no interest in her" (Cavelos 2006, 316). Her sudden death emphasizes that her main story purpose beyond motivating Anakin was to birth the hero-twins of the next films. Her accomplishments as queen, senator, and potential rebel leader vanish beside this.

Of course, her death makes no sense medically—she does not expire from a cardiac incident or from deathly levels of postpartum depression. She simply, inexplicably (according to the medical droid) dies. Smart, colorful fan theories have tried to account for the mystery, suggesting the Emperor saps Padmé's life to raise Vader, for instance, or that Padmé's throat injuries really are fatal but she forces herself to live long enough to save her twins. The droid's making an error (or an edit cutting the ridiculous line) would solve matters, but the film doesn't solve the mystery. Jeong (2017) decries how the film treats giving birth not as a medical situation but a disturbingly sexist murky mystery:

Reproductive health and childbirth is a crutch, and Lucas gets away with it because his audience accepts that these things are mysterious and cannot be intervened with the way that that the loss of limbs can be remedied with robot prosthetics, or the way Luke can be rescued from near-death on Hoth by being submerged in a bacta tank. Having babies is worse than being mauled by a wampa ice creature or being chopped up by lightsabers and falling into a river of lava. Lucas can write a world like that, and worse, the audience will accept it.

But uteruses aren't made of malignant magic. Women's bodies are real physical things that can be studied and understood and when necessary, cured. The public at large should be better educated about reproductive health in general. Like ankle sprains, tooth decay, or heart attacks, reproductive health should be a banal medical thing that a lot of people know something about. The fact that there's so much ignorance around it is a disgrace, a disgrace just as massive and overwhelming as the very existence of the *Star Wars* prequels.

Padmé gives birth (or rather the droid surgically removes her children) as she sobs—apparently more from despair than the pain of childbirth. She's wearing the simplest white gown she's ever worn in the series—the personality that shone through all her costume choices has faded away. Her birthing the twins foreshadows the downfall of the Empire even as it rises, but she has done nothing herself to halt it. As she performs this essentially biological act (though subverted by the droid midwife and sterile room), Vader undergoes the opposite transformation, as he is remade as cyborg. She succumbs to death, he finds a new vigor. Technology and evil triumph visually over motherhood, and the heroine surrenders.

Sweetly, sadly, Padmé names each baby, though her motivation is unclear, since the names' meanings are not explained, and they have no namesakes among her friends or family. This is her final act—one of love, but not protection or concern for the future. Her last line is that there's still good in the child-murdering Anakin. With this flimsy hope for Anakin's redemption, Padmé expires. She gives up on fighting to redeem the galaxy from darkness or leading the Rebellion she had begun. She does not even try staying alive to save Anakin's soul. She has given her will so completely to him that she cannot consider living to protect her two children from an Empire devoted to murdering them. This she leaves to the stronger men—Bail, Owen Lars, and the Jedi. Having fulfilled her biological destiny, she cannot add more to the story. Her death disturbingly suggests that without her man, she has no reason to go on. Between her lesson for the audience about how a man defines her so much she cannot imagine life without him and his lesson that manipulating one's uninterested love interest is the right path, they make a chilling pair of dysfunctional role models.

While the first and fourth films end with the royal woman rewarding the more active heroes, this film ends with a different lavish ceremony—Padmé's funeral. Like the award ceremonies, this is a spectacle in which the woman does not speak but is opulent and draws the crowd's and audience's eye. If the parade scenes emphasize the woman as subject for the man to gaze on, this one deprives the heroine of total agency. "Ceremony and grandeur may have been useful for political power plays, but ceremonies also helped people cope with loss. Royal women were often given elaborate funerals that were as much a comfort to their subjects as to their immediate family" (Reagin and Liedl 2013, 172). Lifeless, she is celebrated as symbol and beautiful art object. While her public costumes were dictated by her position (in contrast with those worn just for Anakin), she has not even dressed herself in this one.

The heroes have gone off preserving the galaxy, but weaker figures like Jar-Jar and the current queen of Naboo attend. Padmé's funeral gown is the dark blue of motherhood and sorrow with strings of sequins like sunlight on the waves. Producer Rick McCallum notes that as costume designer Trisha Biggar envisioned it, "the color—this beautiful azure blue—and the rippled fabric matched the ethereal and melancholy landscape of the Naboo lake retreat at Lake Como, where Padmé and Anakin fell in love. This is where Padmé had wanted to escape with Anakin, and the funeral gown symbolizes her spiritual return to that lake" (2005, 200).

"The devolution of Padmé's character throughout the prequel trilogy seems an eerie parallel to this adolescent loss of self, especially in terms of her death in Episode III, with its visual echoes to Victorian representations of Ophelia's and the Lady of Shalott's flower-strewn, tragically romantic deaths" (Dominguez 2017, 110–11). A cascade of tiny white flowers in her hair makes her appear to be floating. Portman notes, "Someone said to me that it was very 'Ophelia.' With the flowers and the hair, it does look like I'm drowning" (Biggar 2005, 200). This is an intriguing allusion considering how *Reviving Ophelia* presents girls as vulnerable, voiceless, and fragile. "Underlying this inquiry on changing discourses of girlhood is a conceptualization of girls and women that understands them not as a universal, biological grounded condition of female experience but rather as produced within shifting sociohistorical, material, and discursive contexts" (Gonick 2006, 3). Padmé, abandoned by all the ones she trusted, increasingly diminishes into a haunted abuse victim who perishes still trusting her abuser. Ophelia, so badly treated by Hamlet, proves an apt comparison.

The camera shoots in on her face, emphasizing the film's central victim. It then pans down slowly to her folded hands with Young Anakin's love-token—the handmade necklace from the first film—and her wide belly. It's not a sexual moment for the well-covered lady, but a sad one, emphasizing the romantic tragedy and tugging at audience heartstrings. In her death she is revealed as a plot device for Anakin rather than a person with a life or priorities outside of his (even her children!). "It is framed as a romantic death, a woman so torn by her love that she cannot continue to live. This romanticized death—complete with petals arranged around her funeral procession—heightens the tragedy of Anakin's failure to 'save' her (from himself as it turns out). Padmé Amidala's death has little purpose than a prop for Darth Vader's rise" (M. Wood 2016, 72). Further, all is a lie. In her clasped hands is Anakin's charm but his betrayal caused her death. She appears pregnant but is not. Her people salute her as a loyal senator of the Republic and of Naboo, but she betrayed them by loving Anakin, and with her growing disillusionment and subversive conspiracy.

"While some fans accept and romanticize Padmé's death as a natural, tragic outlet of the star-crossed lover motif, others find it very disturbing, and online discussions regarding the incident are often lengthy and heated" (Travis 2013, 51). Of course, Padmé's entire arc from beginning to end is one that emphasizes a lack of good choices. She begins as the prodigy good girl, appointed to be a figurehead overwhelmed by her position. The next film makes her romantic heroine, then tragic heroine to end it all. Her action scenes are nice, but notably inferior to those of the spectacular fighters around her. Her only options through her life—to be a figurehead for the Naboo, a senator campaigning fruitlessly against the dominant patriarchy and greedy Trade Federation, a lover in beautiful gowns, or a tragic gothic damsel—highlight the difficulties of a postfeminist world with fewer choices than women had once believed. Gonick (2006, 19) concludes, "Girl Power and Reviving Ophelia bespeak the two central and interrelated contradictions of the times. That is, that systemic contradictions require more than simply biographical solutions, even as these are increasingly the only solutions recognized as legitimate. And second, they suggest that the individual produced by means of such solutions is both a leverage for change as well as a closure on what it is possible to become." With this, the third wave dichotomy betrays Padmé and leaves her a weak role model for girls. As Cavelos (2006, 321) concludes:

> Amidala might have been the naïve peace-lover who learned the hard way that a world without defenses is a world open to slaughter, might have crusaded for an army of the Republic and triumphed only to find herself duped, might have investigated the suspicious army to uncover its preprogrammed secret orders, might have warned the Jedi only to find she was too late, might have shot herself so Anakin could not turn her children to darkness, might have died a tragic hero's death. Leia might have been the lost leader of an obliterated planet who found a new identity among the Rebels as their head of intelligence, might have been painfully conditioned as a child to repress her Force abilities, might have sensed something breaking free inside her during her torture on the Death Star, might have fought these new instincts and

sensations, which carried with them an awakened anger toward Bail, might have electrocuted herself on Cloud City to avoid a second round of torture by Vader, might have recruited Lando's aide into her intelligence network, might have discovered through him the new Death Star, might have faced her own crisis with anger when Luke told her the truth. The characters carry many exciting, unrealized possibilities, unfortunately, because the focus of George Lucas and the other writers was not on the female characters, who were undervalued, underdeveloped and undercut.

THREE

Introducing the Legends

Mara, Jaina, and the New Jedi Order

In 1991, with no new *Star Wars* available, Hugo-award winning author Timothy Zahn published the licensed *Heir to the Empire*, which debuted in the top ten on the *New York Times* bestseller list and remained cemented there for over twenty-nine straight weeks (Carter 2008). This did indeed revive the franchise, as no year between the 1991 release of *Heir* and 2013 offered fewer than ten *Star Wars* novels. Zahn modestly comments, "I didn't revive *Star Wars* so much as I simply tapped into the interest that was already simmering below the surface. The fact that the first 60,000 copy printing vanished within a week shows that it wasn't the quality of writing that people were first buying, but the name *Star Wars* on the cover. I'd like to think that the quality helped the sales later on, but the fact remains that the audience was hungry for anything that dealt with *Star Wars*" (Carter 2008). The first beloved trilogy led the way to a new *Star Wars* era of novels, role playing games, comics, video games, and much more. It established there was still interest, buoying the franchise forward. "*Heir to The Empire* is a true milestone in the dizzying evolution of the *Star Wars* phenomenon, an important first step that led to George Lucas announcing that he indeed would be continuing the *Star Wars* saga with a new trilogy of films that would tell the tale of Anakin Skywalker's fall to the dark side of the Force" (Carter 2008).

In the first of these novels, Mara Jade dazzles as a smuggler's second-in-command. She ties many scenes together and solves unanswered questions, as Zahn retroactively inserted her into Jabba's Palace as an Imperial assassin stalking Luke. In fact, she once was the Emperor's Hand, spying and acting as courier with the Force power he trained in her. When he died, she lost everything—save his final command that she kill Luke and avenge him. As Mara tells it:

> I was a personal agent of the Emperor himself. He brought me to Coruscant and the Imperial Palace and trained me to be an extension of his will across the galaxy. I could hear his voice from anywhere in the Empire and knew how to give his orders to anyone from a stormtrooper brigade all the way up to a Grand Moff. I had authority and power and a purpose in life. They knew me as the Emperor's Hand and they respected me the same way they did him. (Zahn 1993, 105)

When they meet, on a planet that's sapped his powers, Luke wakes to find her holding a blaster on him. She's taken his lightsaber too. She greets him smirkingly with "Welcome back to the world of mere mortals" and taunts him about losing "everything that once made you special" ([1991] 2011, 22–21). When he looks at her, he sees "bitter hatred blazing in her eyes" but also "a deep and lingering pain" (222). Pitted against Imperials on a hostile planet, Luke reasons with Mara, offering to help break Palpatine's hold on her, and heroically ignoring her blatant plans to murder him.

When asked about her popularity, Zahn replies, "One simplistic answer might be that women can identify with her, while men would like to have her at their side in trouble" (Carter 2008). He envisioned her more of a capable action woman than flimsy girlfriend. As he adds:

> Actually, I don't think Leia and Mara are very far apart in either personality or character. Though Mara served the Emperor and Leia the Rebellion, both were in fact serving causes they considered giving their lives for. Mara has a sharper and more sarcastic manner . . . Bear in mind too, that Leia was one of the first people in the New Republic who decided Mara could be trusted, which perhaps says something about their understanding of each other.

When Mara insists on killing Luke, Leia points out that she's already passed up several opportunities and doubts this is what Mara truly wants. She adds that she understands what it's like to lose all of one's friends and position as Mara has. Leia perceptively suggests that it's the Emperor's mental impression that is coercing Mara, a true insight that throws Mara into conflict with her desires (Zahn 1993, 105).

At the trilogy's climax, she breaks free by only symbolically following the Emperor's command and is left as Luke's ambivalent ally. Through the story, the two Force users spark. Brilliant, capable, and lethal as she is, she's an interesting match for Luke—his equal and opposite but adopted by the supervillain, not the kinder Obi-Wan and Yoda. "She was to become, after Thrawn, the Expanded Universe's most popular character . . . With her vibrant red hair, green eyes, and full-figured leather jumpsuit, Mara is fast becoming one of the more popular *Star Wars* costume choices for women on the comic convention circuit; she offers all of the feisty, fiery personality that Leia should have developed, but ultimately lacked," notes Christ Taylor in *How Star Wars Conquered the Universe* (291–92).

Following this in Zahn's *The Hand of Thrawn* Duology, they fall deeply in love. At last, he proposes marriage, and the wedding follows in Michael A. Stackpole's graphic novel *Union*, amid the expected chaos and assassins. They have one private ceremony in Jedi robes, with the officiate adding in a bridge to the prequels, "It was once thought that emotional attachments would make a Jedi vulnerable, but these two so complete each other that only strength will flow from this union" (Stackpole and Teranishi 2000). Luke glowingly describes the Force bringing them together, and Mara, Luke's acceptance of her. At their more lavish public ceremony, representing a bridging of Empire and New Republic, Luke quips, "Well, since Leia always wanted to kill Han, I knew where this could lead." It's a sweet, romantic story that brings people together, without the foreboding of Padmé and Anakin's.

The pair have a child, Ben, and adventure alongside Han and Leia, or the growing Jedi Order Luke is training. After Mara's death in 2012, she appears as a Force ghost, emphasizing her power and influence through the series. Zahn adds, "She's a strong female character (which were few and far between in the *Star Wars* movies), but she's also flawed and searching and—dare we say it?—human" (Carter 2008). While Mara does have it all—hero, villain, spy, respected teammate, Jedi Master, wife, and mother, she's not limited to being girly and parodic. Formidable would be a much better word, as she associates being Jedi with a womanly toughness, not just Luke's naïve student side.

As an established part of the universe, she appeared in other formats. Voiced by Heidi Shannon, she is a playable character in *Star Wars Jedi Knight: Mysteries of the Sith* and *Star Wars: The Force Unleashed*, also passing through *Star Wars: Galactic Battlegrounds*, *Empire at War*, *Masters of Teräs Käsi*, and *Galaxies*.

> So far, the only narratives she hasn't been featured in are television series and movies. It is now unlikely to happen given that this branch of the Expanded Universe was labeled "Legends" to make room for the official sequel stories that will be shaped by the upcoming movie trilogy. Yet the fact that she still exists, and all that was written remains a source of inspiration for *Star Wars* authors, Mara Jade might still reappear in future narratives. (Guyot 2015, 63–64)

While Mara is likely the most standout, many other new heroines joined her in the novels. "Characters such as Mara Jade, Jaina Solo, Tenel Ka, Aurra Sing, Asajj Ventress, Jocasta Nu and others give readers a variety of female characters with which to identify: female Jedi and female Sith abound. The added benefit of novelization is that many of these characters and their relationships can be explored in depth, an aspect that many female fans enjoy" (Travis 2013, 51–52). Cosplayers and fanfiction writers could find outlets, while these stories, covering the prequel era and Jedi's first establishment, as well as Luke and company's further adventures, emphasized that female Jedi and Sith had always existed.

In Zahn's first trilogy, Han and Leia have twins—Jacen and Jaina. The latter presented another beloved heroine of the extended universe. Both twins grow from babyhood through the massive series and join Luke's new Jedi Academy. They thus become teen heroes for a new generation. Kevin J. Anderson and Rebecca Moesta's children's series *Young Jedi Knights* (1995–1998), beginning with *Heirs of the Force* (1995), develops the children's personalities. Jacen collects animals and dispenses jokes, while Jaina loves inventing strange contraptions. Jaina's walls are covered in "neatly stacked containers of spare parts, cyberfuses, electronic circuit loops, and tiny gears taken from dismantled and obsolete droids" (Anderson and Moesta 1995, 6). "Her dark brown hair was straight and simple, tied back with a string to keep it away from her narrow face. Smudges of grease made hash marks on her left cheek" (Anderson and Moesta 1995, 7). She has no interest in her mother's complex hairstyles but adores her father's gifts of spare parts.

They come of age during the Yuuzhan Vong War, and Jaina accepts her role philosophically. She understands that she may die, telling Jacen, "I can count the number of the enemy, and I can count the number of friends who have been killed, and I can count the number of battles before we can hope to end the war and the number of shots that are going to be fired in my direction in those battles . . . but it's all right. It's what I've sworn to do" (Williams, 2002, 317). She is more than a warrior: When she becomes a knight, Luke announces:

> I name you the Sword of the Jedi. You are like tempered steel, purposeful and razor-keen. Always you shall be in the front rank, a burning brand to your enemies, a brilliant fire to your friends. Yours is a restless life, and never shall you know peace, though you shall be blessed for the peace that you bring to others. Take comfort in the fact that, though you stand tall and alone, others take shelter in the shadow that you cast. (Williams, 2002, 310)

Through the next books, she struggles to define this role. However, when Jacen turns to the dark side, a heroic Jaina is the only one who can stop him. To defeat her twin, she knows she needs skills he doesn't have, so she trains with the Fetts. Understanding from one of them that her former brother has lost everything but his hatred, she learns to pity him. When she battles him, she channels her "love of what her brother had been" and ends it (Denning 2008, 262). "When the disposal pit door opened, Jaina was sitting on the floor where shadow became light, holding Jacen's head in her lap and whispering that he wasn't really dead—

that he would always have a place in her heart, now that she could finally feel their twin bond again" (Denning 2008, 284).

Zahn's first trilogy also introduces Leia's aide, Winter. She was raised alongside Leia and spied for her during the Rebellion with her perfect memory. As Zahn commented in his twentieth anniversary annotated edition, creating new characters was one of the best parts of the new expanded universe. Winter was the first "good guy" he imagined. As he adds, "Aside from her general usefulness as a character, she also gave me the opportunity to express my opinion that Leia always seemed too tomboyish to fit comfortably into the role of a soft, pampered member of the aristocracy" ([1991] 2011, 23). As Leia thinks, her statelier friend was often mistaken for the actual princess when they were growing up. "Awakened in the middle of the night, dressed in an old robe with her hair in total disarray, Winter still looked more regal than Leia herself could manage on her best days" (23). She fights beside Leia, protects and raises her children, and functions as the perfect counterpart to the princess herself.

The Courtship of Princess Leia (1994) by Dave Wolverton (however it has aged as an early adventure) introduced two vital cultures in the Legends universe. When the Hapes Consortium proposes an alliance-marriage between their Prince Isolder and Leia, who would then rule their matriarchal society, she's tempted. Mysterious assassination attempts suggest the people or even its current queen may not accept her, but she's prepared to try. Han, however, kidnaps her to the planet he's just won—Dathomir. Its first introduction here offers a contrasting matriarchal culture of Amazons strong in the light or dark side of the Force. In their world, only women have this power, and one young Force-user, Teneniel Djo, is quite amazed by Luke's skill. "For many days I worked at casting the seer's spells, and then I saw you in my dreams. I think perhaps you are my destiny," she tells him (256). While he resists her efforts to enslave him and force him to be her mate, he aids her tribe in their battle against the local dark side Force users. (These evolved into the Nightsisters of the *Clone Wars* show. The villainess Charal from the television movie *Ewoks: The Battle for Endor* was later named another Nightsister, according to *The Illustrated Star Wars Universe*.)

Eventually, Prince Isolder (also captured as Teneniel's slave) decides to wed Teneniel, as he finds himself falling in love with her strength. Proving herself no pushover, she defeats the queen's four guards with a hand wave and tells the conniving queen mother, "I'm going to marry your son, and someday I'll rule your worlds in your place . . . Let me assure you that I am not a pacifist. In the past two days alone, I have killed several people, and if you ever try to harm me or mine, I will force you to confess publicly all your crimes, and then I will execute you" (322).

She indeed becomes Queen Mother of the Hapes Consortium, and her daughter Tenel Ka succeeds her, though she also trains alongside Leia's twins in *The Young Jedi Knights*. She has "long rusty-gold hair" and is very muscular and physical with "a brief athletic outfit made from scarlet and emerald skins of native reptiles" (Anderson and Moesta 1995, 19–20). "She had little interest in the bookish studies, the histories, and the meditations; but she was an excellent athlete who preferred action to thinking" (18). She prefers to use her body rather than the Force, which she considers a resort for the weak. She's "impatient, hard-driven, and practically humorless" (18). Further, she's kept her background as princess and heir a secret from her fellow trainees. Roughing it here and on Dathomir, she enjoys earning everything on her own merits. "She had always prided herself on being strong, loyal, reliable, unswayed by emotion" (138). She loses an arm in *Lightsabers* (1996), while sparring with Jacen. This gives her a striking disability arc for young readers.

> Not only does this limb loss happen to a female character who is an active protagonist (Moine, 2010), but the novel also depicts how Tenel Ka handles the events and forms decisions about how she wants to adjust to her new physical condition. Both are outside of the norm in the *Star Wars* universe, where males typically are disarmed, and are nearly immediately shown as accepting of the disability . . . Tenel Ka falls into the scope of amputation and symbolism visceral to the *Star Wars* universe but goes beyond the usual description—or lack of thereof—of the character's dealings with the aftermath of their limb loss. (Guyot 2015, 76)

When she and Jacen eventually have a daughter, Allana, she symbolically closes the circle after her mother's obsession with Luke at their first meeting. She entwines her fate with the Skywalker legacy . . . just as Jacen turns to the Dark Side. Like his grandfather, he finds love and fear are his greatest weaknesses, and the dark side takes hold through his desperation to protect his threatened family. While she, like Padmé is his catalyst, her warrior determination never leaves her.

"The Expanded Universe began to change the representation of female Force users during the early 90s" (Guyot 2015, 68). Indeed, there are many more striking women in the series: The Han Solo Trilogy by A.C. Crispin introduces Bria, the idealistic archeologist who steals and breaks Han's heart in his original backstory (rather a parallel to Qi'ra in the similar 2018 film). Barbara Hambly's Callista Trilogy introduces a love interest for Luke in the long-dead Jedi Knight Callista. Novels that cover the Clone Wars follow the female members of the Jedi Council seen in the prequels. As Luke and his friends live on through decades following their films, they encounter many more formidable women, from queens to hidden Jedi. Many are aliens with strikingly different perspectives. Unlike the film prequels, they emphasize a galaxy filled with competent queens, warriors, smugglers, and reliable partners as well as consorts and bureaucrats.

The computer games too added female representation to the galaxy. Jan Ors, a mercenary played by Korean-American model Angela Harry, has been in many computer games, including *Dark Forces*, *Jedi Knight: Dark Forces II* and *Jedi Outcast*. She pilots the Moldy Crow, a ship as distinct as the Falcon. In the first sequence of *Dark Forces II* (LucasArts, 1997), her partner Kyle Katarn (the player's character) finds himself as the "damsel in distress" and Jan is able to save the day for a striking beginning. In their trademark playful banter over the comlinks in *Dark Forces II*, Jan reminds Kyle that this is a common occurrence:

JAN: Oh, whenever I need to find you, you're always in some kind of trouble.

KATARN: Jan! What a pleasant surprise!

JAN: What would you do without me, Kyle?

KATARN: I'd be a content old man.

JAN: Somehow I don't see content or an old man.

She has goggles, like many pilots of the series. Also, like many, she has a prosthetic hand. Both give her competent complexity. At the same time, she has softer moments—arguably both giving her more facets and making her more girlish in what was still often considered a boy's world. When Kyle is injured, she watches over his sleeping form in the video cut scene "Kyle's vision." Further, she needs rescuing repeatedly in a huge damseling trope—the Empire captures her in the first *Dark Forces*, while in the second, the vicious Jerec captures her as a hostage and goads the hero to kill her. In *Jedi Outcast*, her death is faked to draw Kyle out and she's kept as a hostage too. Thus, the competent, sassy pilot is relegated to the role of "girl" in the larger plot.

Sariss (voiced by Valerie Wildman) is the lieutenant of the villain, a traditional female role. Taciturn and tough, the cool blonde prefers to stand back and let others posture. She's also a formidable warrior, quick to draw her surprisingly blue blade. A vision of the late Jedi Qu Rahn relates: "Out of all the Dark Jedi I have met, Sariss is the one I can say . . . I fear. Powerful, strong in both the physical and mental arenas of the Force, she is a master, a perfectionist, quiet and reserved. This makes her a very dangerous foe." She's an abuse victim as, according to her backstory, Sariss's father allowed his Prophets of the Dark Side to do vile things to her and likely abused her himself, leading to her hardened personality and devotion to evil.

Dressed as a traditional Sith in black and red, she wears makeup but otherwise is not particularly sexualized. "Her depiction is about power, despite her good looks; the blonde doesn't wear a revealing outfit, for example. Even the moment she removes her cloak in 'Kyle Crashes the Moldy Crow' is more ritualistic and practical than anything else. The way she hands it to her apprentice Yun is another way to show she is in charge" (Guyot 2015, 53). A strong, nonsexualized female Sith still hasn't appeared in the films—as Ventress is notably underdressed.

> Just as Jan Ors is featured in multiple cut scenes, Sariss is also present in a number of them, though fewer than Jan. The female Dark Jedi appears in the opening cut scene of the video game, along with the rest of the antagonists. Until Katarn has to choose between light and dark, she appears in five cut scenes, and will show up in two more no matter whether the protagonist falls to the dark side or remains true to the light. That means that overall Sariss is featured in nine of the existing cut scenes for the video game, two less than Jan Ors. (Guyot 2015, 52)

Through the story, the player's choices turn him toward light or dark, offering two contrasting story paths. Finally, one woman or the other dies depending whether the protagonist follows the light or dark. In fact, the hero kills Jan at Jerec's direction. While this gives the story some options, here both women are somewhat damseled, both pushed into the role of sidekick and sacrifice. While losing the woman may be more emotional for the player, it weakens the characters when this is their destined role.

Star Wars: Knights of the Old Republic (2003) and *Knights of the Old Republic II: The Sith Lords* (2004) likewise offer a few striking female characters. In both, the player can choose a face and be male or female. Heroes and villains are searching for the Jedi Knight Bastila Shan (voiced by Jennifer Hale) for her unique skill at Battle Meditation. As the story goes on, she is seduced to the Dark Side—a twist but an enfeebling one. The light-side protagonist defeats Bastila in a lightsaber duel and, in cliched fashion, she finally redeems herself by helping the Republic fleet. If the protagonist is a dark-side character, he may kill her or recruit her as his apprentice. Bastila is also a romance option for a light-sided male character. There are many choices here, but all along rather conventional lines.

Mission Vao, voiced by Cat Taber, is a rough street Twi'lek who joins the player's party. Unlike most of her species onscreen—even in *Clone Wars*—she's fully dressed in nondescript brown with vest and goggles like a smuggler. She has more than a little Han Solo vibe as she's sarcastic and closed-off. Her character class is "scoundrel," and she even travels with a Wookie. Having a cool "female Han" join up definitely gets high marks, as does showing a Twi'lek who's not a sex slave.

In the second game, the hero Jedi Exile seeks the last remaining Jedi to battle the Sith. There's some variety to the story, as a light side player will be joined by the sharp-edged bounty hunter Mira, while dark side gets her Wookie rival, and a female character is partnered with Mical the Disciple but a male character gets Brianna the Last Handmaiden of a Jedi academy.

The protagonist is joined by Kreia, the Exile's new mentor (voiced by Sara Kestelman), with white braids protruding from her deep brown hood. She and the Exile are linked by a Force bond, to the point at which they feel each other's pain. "Compared to Jocasta Nu, she teaches more directly and at length, since she takes the Jedi exile — the game's protagonist — under her tutelage. She works in a rather direct way even when they first meet under dire circumstances" (Guyot 2015, 71). As an older, blind advisor, she appears something of a cliché . . . until she surprises players by revealing herself as the final boss, a Sith Lord. It's nice representation, emphasizing that older women shouldn't be discounted. She was quite popular, as fans appreciated all her nuance. Fan Emperor Devon (2007) remarks: "Kreia is without a doubt the most well-developed character in TSL, with her unique goal of destroying the Force, her cryptic persona, interesting backstory and deep personality and motivations making her one of the most well-done characters to yet grace a video game."

> It would be easy to simply label her a dangerous witch and draw from entrapping considerations when she — and the notion of witch — is more complex (Haase, 2004, 14–17). Kreia isn't only an educated woman who has traveled across the galaxy for years; some of her advice and guidance are also primordial for the protagonist. Without Kreia's support, the Jedi Exile that the player controls wouldn't reconnect to the Force. At the same time, Kreia can't help but consider survival of the fittest as the one true choice, and she often negatively criticizes the rest of the protagonist's crew. (Guyot 71)

Chris Avellone, the creator, comments: "Her one redeeming feature is that for a (former) Sith Lord, she loves the player and what he/she represents. She sees in the player a chance to turn away from predestination and destroy that which binds all things, giving the galaxy back its freedom" (Emperor Devon 2007). She, like the other women of the videogames, emphasizes a much more colorful galaxy.

The Expanded Universe has of course been echoed in a growing female fandom universe. Emily of the Tosche Station blog (2012) explains: "I wanted to be Tenel Ka and Mara Jade when I grew up [. . .]. I hope that I've become that person. And more than that, I hope that I've learned to embody that strong female role — and that my own daughter will want not only to be Tenel Ka and Mara Jade, but to be her mother as well" (qtd. in Travis 55). Erika Travis (2013) explains in "From Blasters to Bikinis: The Role of Gender in the *Star Wars* Community":

> The majority of online *Star Wars* fan communities are operated by men, but more and more frequently with women on staff or serving as mod-

erators. Others, such as "Club Jade," "The Moons of Lego," and "*Star Wars* Chicks," are operated (mainly) for women by women. There are also numerous "geek girl" websites run by female science-fiction, fantasy and/or pop culture fans that include significant discussion of *Star Wars* related themes: popular examples include "FANgirl the Blog," "Pink Raygun," "Geek with Curves" and "Girls Gone Geek." These websites post *Star Wars* news, editorials, reviews, and their "female viewpoint." Vlogger Jennifer Landa is one female fan who expresses her "geek girl" viewpoint by posting what "The Official *Star Wars* Blog" calls her "witty, adorkable" videos of her cosplay, *Star Wars* fashion and crafting. (52)

There's the female-led *Saga Journal* (2004–2010), focusing on the academic side of fandom, and plenty of podcasts and YouTube channels. Fans cosplay the Legends characters, comment on them, and revel in a less-known Expanded Universe that offers much more diversity. Moms who grew up on the films can join in costuming the next generation or bake treats together from *The Star Wars Cookbook: Wookie Cookies and Other Galactic Recipes*, or work together from *The Star Wars Craft Book*, to say nothing of the infinite bedtime stories. It's a new era of inclusivity, and everyone's joining in.

FOUR

The Butt-Kicking Teen

Ahsoka

The 2008 animated movie, *Star Wars: The Clone Wars*, introduced Ahsoka Tano as the fourteen-year-old apprentice of Anakin Skywalker. She soon became the central figure of the resulting animated series. "George Lucas had two daughters, and he harbored a strong belief that science fiction and fantasy could—and should—appeal to preteenage girls" (Taylor 2014, 377). Showrunner Dave Filoni comments, "The outpouring around the character really was surprising to all of us. She has grown exponentially as a fan-loved character, to the point where her cosplay is becoming so commonplace as is merchandise and memorabilia. For the era of *Clone Wars* kids, they get her as an identifier for them" (*Empire* 2016).

> She is compassionate and feminine, without being overtly sexualized. She breaks the mould Leia and Padmé cast in several important ways: she is a Jedi rather than a politician, she is adolescent rather than a young adult, and she is a Togruta rather than a human. These differences allow her to break clearly away from fairy tale typology and explore other aspects of the female identity, such as coming of age and diverse ideas regarding femininity, important to new generations of *Star Wars* fans. (Travis 2013, 52)

As such, she became the first starring female Jedi (or female nonhuman) of *Star Wars*. One review notes, "Ahsoka's place in *The Clone Wars*, both as a series and film, and as an event in history, brought girl power to a different audience—kids. *The Clone Wars'* immense popularity allowed Ahsoka to become a loved and respected character and example of how important girls can be, whether it's in a battle for galactic freedom or being the smartest kid in class" (*Game of Nerds* 2015). This was an important step forward for the franchise, which previously had offered only Leia and Padmé among a spectrum of boy heroes. Her voice actress, Ashley Eckstein, adds:

> I think what people don't realize, because we've come so far, but when you go back to when Ahsoka was first announced and *Clone Wars* first came into theaters, Ahsoka was such a revolutionary character. The fact that Anakin Skywalker had a Padawan that nobody knew about, first of all, was mind-blowing. Second of all, the fact that it was a 14-year-old girl just rocked people's worlds and that was so revolutionary at the time, because strong female characters in this genre, aside from Princess Leia, were relatively new. I mean, now we have Rey and Black Widow and Katniss, but there weren't strong female characters in entertainment like that. Especially a 14-year-old girl. So Ahsoka was the first female Jedi that was a lead in the *Star Wars* universe. That's *huge*. (D. Brooks 2016a)

However, times were changing. "The incredible proliferation of images of girls in film, in media stories, and in education policy debates is at least partially related to the ways in which girls have come to represent, for the first time, one of the stakes upon which the future depends" (Gonick 2006, 5). The film shows an adolescent new to her rank and eager to prove herself. Ahsoka is a bit of a know-it-all, especially in the beginning. She's spunky and squirrely, forever climbing over and into things. "Easily the most popular *Star Wars* character who has not appeared in any films, Ahsoka [is] a huge hit with young, female (as well as male) viewers due to her feisty, adventurous attitude," Pianka comments (2013, 47). She combines a youthful arrogance with uncertainty and hopefulness. Eckstein adds, "Ahsoka bursts onto the scene as this snippy Padawan in the *Clone Wars* movie . . . she had an opinion about everything and she was very green as they would say. And she was definitely the sidekick" (2013b).

Girl power heroines are strong and capable but also dress provocatively to please themselves. Ahsoka's midriff-baring tube top is startling for a Jedi trainee in a war zone. It objectifies her, displaying a great deal of skin, though she is an underage character in a children's animated adventure. Skintight pants in the film are teenagerish but also objectifying. Even her weapon is youthful, as the creators explain, "The white lightsaber is indicative of the fact that she's not really a chosen side" (Eckstein, Filoni, and Hidalgo). Still, she does change up the outfit as time passes.

> Luckily, halfway through the third season, all three main characters (Anakin, Obi-Wan, and Ahsoka) undergo costume changes, in order to make the former two's outfits more similar to the ones they wear in

Revenge of the Sith and thus show the passage of time. Ahsoka, now fifteen or sixteen years of age, actually begins wearing more conservative clothes which, while still considerably more suggestive than the outfits worn by male characters, improves on her original outfit, making it less revealing and therefore, less uncomfortable for the viewer . . . The costume change was praised by many fans, with Scott Thill of *Wired.com* stating, "In a limitless *Star Wars* universe dominated by males maneuvering for political and military primacy, it's good to see that the few females in *The Clone Wars* are serving a higher function than eye candy for salivating fanboys." (Pianka 2013, 48)

Red skin and markings that resemble intricate face tattoos mark Ahsoka as a particularly exotic other—not just a minority but one who resembles an island native with her bare skin and loinclothlike skirt panels. Her lekku—head tails—and her montrals—horn-like protrusions—resemble an exotic headdress, stately and Pharoahlike in contrast with her childishly large eyes. She has an actual headdress in the Akul-tooth decoration, which apparently can only be worn by a Togruta who has slain an akul (Lewis and Keier 2013, 159). This has cultural value to Ahsoka and adds a thread of toughness and cultural background to her character, though also a trace of the savage. A strand of beads dangling from it replaces a Padawan braid, showing Jedi accommodations for species without hair.

Ahsoka is a rare *Star Wars* main character who's a minority (at least metaphorically, as she's an alien). However, much of the visual choices and expanded universe backstory emphasize her culture's primitive roots, making her seem more like Tonto, Friday, or Chewie himself than an enlightened Jedi trainee. *The New Essential Guide to Alien Species*, based on the creators' notes, reveals that Togrutas are from Shili, a planet of red and white grass, where the Togrutas' striping helped them blend. "When hunting, their head tails aid them by providing echolocation abilities and a finely tuned special sense, which they use to encircle herbivorous prey" (Lewis and Keier 2013, 158). Like Wookiees, they live in communal villages hidden by the forests where they hunt as entire tribes. "Togrutas are a peaceful, quiet people who are fierce in combat. Loyal to a cause and happy in large groups, they work well with others . . . and will tend to follow other members of their group around simply for companionship" (Lewis and Keier 2013, 158). This description suggests a primitive tribal nature—both condescending from her creators and problematic for her role model status. In the galaxy, Togruta are unusual, so much that Ahsoka is always set apart. This too emphasizes her othering. Sadly, she thinks in the novel *Star Wars: Ahsoka*, "She was alone, something she was never meant to be. Her people were tribal, blood and bond, and her ability to use the Force gave her a galaxy of brethren from all species" (Johnston 2016, 7).

Among her people, those who can no longer keep up are often left to die (Lewis and Keier 2013, 159). They prefer to go without shoes and connect spiritually and directly with the land. They also have "prominent incisors that give the impression of a snake's venom-projecting teeth" though suggestions that they have actual venom appear to be ignorant rumors (Lewis and Keier 2013, 158). All these comparisons to herd animals, tigers, and serpents mark them as capable and fierce but largely instinctual, incapable of higher reasoning.

The guide also describes their primitivism as giving them a strong Force connection—Jedi are basically the only ones to go out into the galaxy. This suggests a few of them are "rescued" and educated by the enlightened patriarchy, civilizing them in a painful example of Imperialism. Ahsoka is happy as a Jedi, revering the masters who discovered her, and never seen visiting her home planet or seeking her parents as Anakin does in *Attack of the Clones*. She doesn't celebrate her culture's rituals or holidays or know anything about what makes her people distinct, except for a few biological traits.

Further, just as Chewie is a follower, Ahsoka apparently has similar traits ingrained in her species. "In their culture, individuality is considered somewhat deviant, and yet those who take leadership positions among their people are sometimes forced to achieve their goals through calculated individualism. Sociologists claim this is a sign of the further social evolution of the Togruta people" (Lewis and Keier 2013, 159). The Togruta, when their wider culture appears, are completely victimized by the humans in power, much like the Twi'leks or Wookiees. (Their surrender of individual desires may leave them especially open to exploitation.) Thus, like Chewie, Ahsoka has lower status than her "master," who does not always show the cultural sensitivity and knowledge he could.

> Third wave feminists were invested in identifying with a movement that emphasized diversity of participants, ideas, and tactics. They also stressed intersectionality and the complex nature of identity. Many third wave feminists destabilized the notion that there is a unified "woman," rejected the gender binary and rigid gender roles, embraced sexuality, and sought to include men in the movement. (Crossley 2017, 109)

Anakin is not a perfect third-waver, but he tries. Padmé, who becomes Ahsoka's friend and advocate, does as well. Still, the galaxy is becoming a darker place. In fact, the Empire will subjugate the alien races, instituting slavery and prohibiting them from becoming Imperial soldiers. "By *A New Hope*, the alien Other has been removed from the center of galactic civilization and literally, as well as symbolically, 'ghettoized' to the hinterlands of the Galactic Empire" (Deis 2007, 84).

Third wave struggled with essentialism—defining all women by their commonalities instead of their differences across a vast spectrum of backgrounds. Certainly, this had its problematic side as far too many perspectives went unacknowledged—a Black working mother with five children has different political needs than a single white corporate lawyer. Ahsoka's alieness suggests an innate difference from other women and other Jedi, even as her personality is that of a traditional eager teen. Still, she is trained just like all the other Jedi for a uniform experience. Ahsoka was separated from her people at age three and is never seen learning from Shaak Ti, the only other Togruta shown. In fact, on joining Anakin, Ahsoka is skeptical of his own outsider status—she was raised by the Jedi from toddlerhood. He, meanwhile, resents getting a trainee at all, and so they clash. Eckstein notes:

> It's been well documented how snippy she was in the beginning and, quite frankly, how people thought she was very annoying and didn't like her. We knew that there was a fine line. I mean, we didn't want her to be bratty, we didn't want her to be annoying. We did have these certain nicknames and she would ask questions and talk back, and that very much was and became an endearing part of her personality over time. But in the beginning it was just like, "Oh, my gosh, who is this 14-year-old girl talking to Anakin Skywalker this way?" (D. Brooks 2016a)

One assumes the Council would match the two based on her personality. Instead the pairing is more for his benefit than hers, in another blow for inequality in their relationship: "Ahsoka is assigned to Anakin as his Padawan in hopes that responsibility for her will temper Anakin's impulsive and rash ways. Instead, while fighting for the Jedi Order against the Separatists, Ahsoka is even more reckless than her master" (Reagin and Liedl 2013, 65). In *Star Wars* context, of course, this makes her heroic, and Anakin is not a bad mentor for her—just a young, inexperienced one just out of training himself. This exactly repeats Obi-Wan and Anakin's partnership . . . and this hints forebodingly at their violent future.

However, he begins to accept her. In the novelization, he thinks sympathetically, "Maybe she's like me. Maybe nobody else wanted to train her, either" (46). As she's assigned to him in the midst of a combat situation, he's instantly dismissive. He insists she's not a civilian, but in the battle must pull her weight. Soon the pair of them slip behind the battle droids' defenses to fight them within the buildings. With her sharp predator teeth, she's fierce. She can also use the Force: Even as a droid forces her off a cliff, she swings herself up by her fingertips, calls her lightsaber to her, and slices its leg off. She's not human, so she has inborn physiological abilities, like better night vision and intuitive spacial relations. She uses the latter to collapse a wall onto Anakin, even while knowing he'll be standing in the space of the carved-out window. She thus shows off her innate superpower, even as this moment of pure trust begins to change their dynamic. She sassily calls him "Skyguy" and resists being called youngling. However, he starts calling her Snips "for being snip-py."

The pair are assigned to rescue Jabba's baby son Rotta from Dooku's forces. While Anakin is disgusted by the horrible-smelling slug baby, recalling his childhood as slave to a Hutt, Ahsoka plays nursemaid. "Ahsoka did her best to keep Rotta calm, rocking him. Nobody could ever accuse her of giving less than a hundred percent; cuddling a Hutt was beyond the call of duty, because she'd be in the 'freshers for a week scrubbing the smell off herself" (Traviss 2008, 106). She coos to him, insisting he's cute as she carries him in a backpack. She is also the one to remember to give him water and to notice he's sick. This gives them another quest—not only protecting the child but getting him to medical care. Her role caring for the baby gives her likeable qualities but also traditionally gendered ones. At the same time, the young warrior who fights and dodges while caring for a baby (in fact, a slug baby) is an excellent example of the era's trends. Melissa Klein (1997, 222–23) writes in *Third Wave Agenda*, "We are interested in creating not models of androgyny so much as models of contradiction. We want not to get rid of the trappings of traditional femininity or sexuality so much as to pair them with demonstrations of strength or power." Ahsoka and Anakin save each other through the story, as they learn to bond. When Anakin duels Dooku at the end and hears Ahsoka is walking into a trap, he charges off to rescue her. As he negotiates with a vengeful Jabba, Ahsoka stumbles in, Rotta still safely on her back. She bids him a sweet farewell as she returns the baby to his father.

The book *Wild Space*, taking place just after the film, fills in more of their evolving relationship. As Ahsoka thinks, "All right, she'd skated pretty close to the edge a few times. Asked for the reprimands he'd given her. That had been nerves. The desire to impress him. Show him he'd landed the right apprentice" (K. Miller 2008, 44). As Anakin goes off to war or sneaks around with Padmé, he considers Ahsoka an annoyance, and sends her to study in her room. Anakin decides, "He didn't want her as his Padawan, though he liked her well enough. He didn't want *any* Padawan. But thanks to the Council they were stuck with each other. All they could do was make the most of the fact" (81). However, she comforts him when Obi-Wan is wounded, emphasizing how much they share the same mission and the same emotions. After this, he offers reluctant permission for her to call him Skyguy and they begin a respect-filled partnership.

Ashley Eckstein found herself an icon, as she began receiving fan letters from girls worldwide. She explains, "They were so excited to finally have a girl Jedi they could look up to and pretend to be. I very quickly realized that just by being the voice of Ahsoka, I had become a role model to these girls, and it was an honor that I took very seriously" (Eckstein 2018, 92). She notes that many children watch *Clone Wars* or *Rebels* before the films, giving them a particularly girl-centric introduction to the franchise and to their own potential: "I think there's this extra bond because Ahsoka was always meant to be kind of the eyes of the audience. You could put yourself in Ahsoka's shoes as an audience member and you almost felt like that was you experiencing the Clone Wars" (D. Brooks 2016a). As she adds:

> She started this revolution. She honestly did, and what I think was so beautifully done was, not only did she make a statement for girls, which was groundbreaking. She put a lightsaber in little girls' hands. So when they play *Clone Wars* on the playground, there was now a girl that could hold a lightsaber that she could be. So that literally started a movement. It's almost become so commonplace now, but at the time, it was mind-blowing. And then what Dave [Filoni] and his crew so beautifully did is, they made you forget about the fact that she was a girl and they never pointed it out. They just created a strong character and, all of a sudden, boys related to her, as well. They no longer looked at her as the girl character. They looked at her as Anakin Skywalker's Padawan and she then became, like I said, the eyes of the audience, where kids who grew up with her could learn these lessons through her. (D. Brooks 2016a)

AHSOKA'S ARC: *THE CLONE WARS* SHOW

The Clone Wars show continues from the film, following Anakin and Ahsoka as they fly on missions alone or with Jedi like Obi-Wan or sometimes the others. The 501st back them up, giving the young Jedi troops to command. In this mix, Ahsoka is the only child. "Without her character, the show would be about adults and a war. Ahsoka allows young viewers to see the war through her perspective, as a child thrust into a wartime scenario. Thankfully, despite a few missteps early on, Ahsoka has become the strongest female role model the *Star Wars* universe has ever had" (Pianka 2013, 47).

She idolizes and emulates her mentor, Anakin. However, as she leaves her culture behind for the patriarchal Jedi Order she also is arguably devaluing her feminine side. She learns occasionally from female Jedi but most often defies their teachings of selflessness and obedience to behave as Anakin would. Thus, she's a girl who acts like a boy, training to be a knight but rarely doing anything girlish including making female friends.

Their give and take reflects much about their power dynamics. In the second episode, "Rising Malevolence," Anakin meets with the Jedi Council as well as Chancellor Palpatine, since Master Plo Koon, who actually recruited Ahsoka at age three, is missing. In this august patriarchal crowd, he tells his female teenage Padawan to speak only when spoken to and she responds with a bit of sarcasm, "Don't I always." However, she cannot contain herself but bursts out in the middle of their deliberations. As Obi-Wan humorously notes, this exemplifies how she's following in Anakin's footsteps:

AHSOKA: Wait! Just because there haven't been any survivors before, doesn't mean there won't be any this time.

PALPATINE: Boldly spoken for one so young.

OBI-WAN: She is learning from Anakin.

ANAKIN: Excuse my Padawan. We will deploy, as you've instructed, Master. (after they've left) Ahsoka!

AHSOKA: If anyone could survive, Master Plo could. I don't understand why.

ANAKIN: What you don't understand, is Jedi protocol, or your place, my young Padawan.

After this condescension, Anakin follows Ahsoka's plan, revealing that he'd always meant to rescue the survivors but that Ahsoka has no idea how to appear to obey the Council—a necessary step in rebelling. While this is amusing given Anakin's constant rule-breaking, he's also trying to teach her *how* to break the ruling class's rules and successfully get away with it, rather than dismissing her goals and ideals. Thus, while he makes excuses for her, he's also trying to empower her. As a male mentor, he can teach her how to operate in the men's world, though he isn't yet prepared to use his privilege to elevate her in his superiors' eyes. Meanwhile, Ahsoka displays the compassion and heroism that will soon outstrip her master's: Even as the clone soldiers insist they're expendable, Ahsoka spins the ship in a massive U-turn, sensing her old Jedi master and saving him and the clone troopers as well.

Eckstein describes how much the character develops, and how she needs the initial brattiness to grow beyond it and achieve wisdom:

You appreciate the arc and where she's come from, and that was the biggest thing I asked for in the beginning from the fans, because we were always, in [the production of] *Clone Wars*, a season ahead from what the fans saw. We were always pretty much an entire year, an entire season ahead. So I knew how far she had come by the time *Clone Wars* launched and I just begged fans. I said, "Look, I hear your concerns. I hear your frustrations with her snippiness [*Laughs*], but just trust me, she comes so far." With *The Clone Wars*, so many of those characters, we already knew their outcomes because of the movies, so they had to stay pretty true to what we already knew. But Ahsoka was just a complete blank canvas and we didn't know anything about her.

And so I told fans, "Look, we're going to go on a journey with this character, so if she started in this perfect place where everyone wants her to be, that would be a pretty boring story. You know, she has to grow and she has to overcome and she has to go on a journey and an arc." Over time, fans saw that and I'm truly grateful we had so much time to tell her story. (D. Brooks 2016a)

Ahsoka notably does not treat Anakin as an equal. Calling him "Skyguy" is humorously mocking but she's doesn't use the familiarity of first names, though he does. Ahsoka is a normal student, brought up in the Temple among a large group just like her. While she is a Jedi, she's assigned to train with the top hero of the Clone Wars. He is the Chosen One of prophecy, the most gifted pilot with the largest midichlorian count. "When Master Yoda told her she'd been apprenticed to Anakin Skywalker, Ahsoka didn't know whether to laugh or cry. No Jedi in the Temple cast a longer shadow than Anakin" (K. Miller 2008, 44). All this gives her an added responsibility to protect him, as she thinks, and treat his life as more valuable. In the novel *Clone Wars Gambit: Stealth*, she thinks, "I will not be the Padawan who gets the Chosen One killed" (K. Miller 2010, 5). At the same time, it's a relationship born of friendship and trust, in which he doesn't objectify her or demean her for being female or alien, only young and impulsive.

Still, she has more adjusting to do. The novel *No Prisoners* has Anakin dumping Ahsoka on Captain Rex so he can have time with Padmé. He frames this as needing a break from the irritating Padawan, which is an insult, if also a cover. When she boards Captain Pellaeon's ship, he insists (though she's technically his superior) that she wear a uniform and boots. In a "paternal" voice, he tells her, "We do *not* expose flesh in this ship, not only because it's unbecoming, undisciplined, and *distracting*, but because a ship is a dangerous place. Sharp edges, noxious chemicals, hot exhausts, weapons flash. Safety first, Padawan. Cover up" (Traviss 2009, 21). She's irritated but complies. This moment emphasizes the ridiculousness of wearing her outfit to battle (much as she has chosen it herself in girl power fashion).

While her story features a girl growing out of adolescence, it's also a wartime story of hard decisions and pain. Ahsoka commands her first squadron in "Storm over Ryloth" (119). She takes a risk and loses an entire ship and its crew. After, she's devastated, and Anakin is supportive but chiding.

ANAKIN: Ahsoka, I am very disappointed in you. You not only disobeyed the Admiral, you disobeyed me.

AHSOKA: I thought I could knock out those ships so Master Obi-Wan could get through.

ANAKIN: I know you meant well, Snips, but there's a bigger picture you're not aware of. First rule of war, listen and obey your superiors.

AHSOKA: But sometimes you get carried away.

ANAKIN: All that means is I understand what you're going through.

AHSOKA: But I failed.

ANAKIN: It was a trap, Snips. It wasn't your fault.

AHSOKA: I lost so many of my pilots.

ANAKIN: Take heart, little one. That's the reality of command.

After this, he insists that she take command once again, while he risks his life in a lone hero gambit. She protests, "Master, I-I can't. If something goes wrong, I can't be responsible."

He retorts firmly, "You are responsible. These men are depending on you and this time so am I." Cornered, she decides on a bold plan, summoning confidence she doesn't feel to reassure her troops. The gambit pays off and Ahsoka's confidence returns. While she hesitates to join Skywalker as a military commander, he tries to raise her up, helping her cope with the responsibility but also accept its price. Thus, he's often shown as a responsible teacher, using his privilege to raise her to his level.

Anakin and Ahsoka's dynamic continues to challenge their roles, including and beyond gender. In "Cargo of Doom," the bounty hunter Cad Bane holds Ahsoka hostage. Anakin caves, emphasizing how much Ahsoka is his weakness. In the second season's "Weapons Factory" (206), Anakin keeps interrupting Ahsoka during her briefing to her annoyance. She complains that he doesn't seem to trust her enough to let her do her job. Clearly, he's sometimes too close in his mentor role. Another time, she saves Anakin and Obi-Wan who are trapped in a cave filling with poisonous gasses. The men appear embarrassed that the young Padawan was the one to save them. "This also serves as an interesting contrast between male and female gratitude after a rescue. When Ahsoka rescues Obi-Wan and Anakin, they are embarrassed and deny the fact that they required her help. Conversely, as we saw in the clip of Anakin rescuing Padmé, females who get rescued by men are quick to jump into their arms (and presumably later, their beds) in gratitude" (Pianka 2013, 49–50).

In "Slaves of the Republic," Anakin makes Ahsoka play his slave. Ahsoka, covered in a concealing burka-style robe, complains, "Remind me why I'm the one playing the part of the slave?"

Anakin smirks, "I tried it once, I wasn't any good at it. Besides, the role of master comes easily to me."

Still, she gets in a zinger with "Really? Well, this time try to be convincing at it" (412).

He rips off the burka in front of the queen, revealing Ahsoka's pretty blue two-part dress. In this moment, she is objectified by her master as well as the audience. Subverting the docile image, Ahsoka snarks at the queen and slaps away her hand, prompting the queen to suggest "processing." When a rescue mission diverts their mission, Ahsoka pulls a lightsaber, but the queen electrocutes her. In the next episode, Anakin frees her from the cage in which she's been dangling, then orders her to wait while he frees Obi-Wan. Of course, she doesn't. As with Leia in the bikini, the heroine tries to subvert and sass her way through the scene, but the objectification is purely painful.

As characters of color (or rather a variety of colors) guest star with the main heroes and they adventure through the galaxy, there's a closer link than in the films to global feminism—raising up the minorities of the world and aiding them to become part of the greater community. Instead of insisting planets conform to either the dominant culture or the ideals of the Republic, Ahsoka finds herself learning about the locals, from underprivileged families to Separatist rebels. Over and over she learns to sympathize as she learns they are all just people, though frequently in need of her Jedi privilege. Third wave is "defined by the historical moment of its emergence, a moment of unprecedented interrelation between the local and the global, between the West and 'the rest'" (Woodhull 2007, 165).

Season five starts dramatically with "General Ahsoka," apparently Anakin's equal, going to help train insurgents to free Onderon. In "Front Runners" (503), Obi-Wan and Anakin leave her in charge of the 501st and local rebels to liberate a planet, emphasizing her new level of authority. She wears a brown Jedi robe as they do, and after this, she takes a group of younglings to forge their own lightsabers—she is the experienced mentor now. In the next episode, she hurls pirates out the airlock and into space in a dramatic zero-g battle. She has a new, more mature outfit, though the tank-top look is backless, with a peekaboo hole on the front. Ashley Eckstein (2013a) comments, "Ahsoka in the past couple seasons has been given more responsibility. Y'know, the Jedi are stretched pretty thin, so they will leave Ahsoka by herself and trust her that she's learned enough that she can handle the mission on her own." Now she's the teacher and mentor passing on the lessons the older Jedi once told her.

"Ahsoka, as a Commander in the Army of the Republic, has command of an entire battalion of Clone Troopers, to whom she can dispatch orders, and with whom she goes into battle. Women giving men instructions is something we have seen before in Princess Leia, but unlike Leia, Ahsoka accompanies her troops into battle, often putting herself in unnecessary risk for her men" (Pianka 2013, 50). Ahsoka, a teen trapped in command, must accept that she could get her soldier friends hurt or killed through her orders. Through the show, Ahsoka earns the respect of the 501st legion, especially their commander, Rex. In the original *Clone Wars* film and its novelization, Anakin counsels her to treat the clones as individuals, learning about them and listening to them. While he's willing to sacrifice them, he only does so as a last resort. Studying with him, Ahsoka comes to understand all this for herself. In *Star Wars: Ahsoka*, she thinks, "They respected her. They listened to her. They taught her everything they knew. And when she made mistakes, when she got some of them killed, they forgave her and they stood beside her again when it was time to return to battle" (Johnston 2016, 64).

As she grows up, she also gets a taste of romance. In "Heroes on Both Sides" (310), Padmé introduces Ahsoka to a separatist teen, Lux Bonteri. Ahsoka, hesitant and tough, greets him by insisting on carrying her own luggage. However, the other teen grows on her, while Padmé uses the lesson to teach Ahsoka the two sides aren't as different as she had believed. "A Friend in Need" (414) reintroduces Lux. As Dooku prepares to execute him, Ahsoka bursts in and dramatically rescues him. After, she calls Anakin and demands the Jedi give him asylum. When Lux stuns and kidnaps her, she's furious. As he works with the violent extremists of Death Watch to get proof Dooku murdered his mother, Ahsoka protests. However, in the midst of their squabble, Lux kisses her. While he takes the initiative, Ahsoka doesn't appear to mind. This is cover on a sexist planet where the locals comment, "Tell your woman to leave us," so they can negotiate with Lux. As they drag her out, Ahsoka looks worried, emphasizing Lux's helplessness in dealing with the far tougher adults.

Ahsoka also befriends a village girl, one of several forced to serve Death Watch. Ahsoka joins them in serving the men food, though as she brings Lux his plate, she warns him, "Careful not to choke on your stupidity." When Death Watch thugs murder her after her grandfather requests her return, Ahsoka fights and is captured. With a little help from Artoo, she makes a dramatic escape. Surrounded by four Death Watch members, Ahsoka leaps up and decapitates all four, before engaging in a one-on-one lightsaber battle with a man who once fought Obi-Wan to a draw. Symbolically, she is smashing the patriarchy and the men who prey on and abuse women. Lux insists on going his own way after this, but vows they'll meet again. Filoni insists, "With Ahoka, I was very careful to try to represent, especially to young girls, they don't have to make these decisions be black and white, they don't have to have to be with someone because." He describes her learning she has agency and value rather than learning her self-acceptance from a boyfriend (Eckstein, Filoni, and Hidalgo).

As season five begins, she discovers Lux, who's in a bit of a love triangle with Saw Gerrera's sister Steela. Saw offers to provide a fourth side and make the other pair jealous. Even as they struggle with romance, the four young people, all excellent in war, controlled and capable, provide all the plans and leave Obi-Wan and Anakin sidelined in favor of the more interesting teens. Lux, meanwhile, is admiring, as he says of Ahsoka, "Ahsoka is the reason I'm here and not with Death Watch . . . She saved me from a huge mistake." His presence gives Ahsoka her own supporting characters and personal plot, appointing her sidekicks of her own.

Of course, everything falls apart as season five ends. Her actress comments, "We have this major turn and who knows what's next for her. Her life is changing, and the Jedi order is changing a little bit. I think she's seeing that things will never be the same" (2013b). "It's a fun way to tell a tale," executive producer Dave Filoni says. "Start in a light way we can all identify with and slowly take them into a darker place with more meaning and depth" (Day). Ahsoka is framed for a terrorist attack on the Jedi Temple, and to her horror, everyone but Anakin immediately blames her. "Ahsoka's accusers are all male, consisting of Mace Windu, Yoda, Plo Koon, Ki-Adi-Mundi, and Obi-Wan himself. This seems to highlight Ahsoka's depiction as a feminist character, fighting for justice against a patriarchal society" (Pianka 52). Though she's served devotedly for years, fighting with no thought for herself, her proud Jedi superiors betray her by banishing her. She must investigate and clear her name with no resources. Desperate and alone, she actually teams up with the villainess Ventress, now turned bounty hunter. When the Jedi, led by Anakin, capture her and bring her to trial (with Padmé as her lawyer), it goes badly. However, Anakin manages to clear her name by discovering the true culprit—Ahsoka's trusted friend Barriss Offee. Through it all, Ahsoka is horrified by her lack of support from the Jedi who raised her and made her believe in their cause.

The male Council members issue a weak apology and invite her back. Her old mentor Plo Koon looks remorseful for his actions, but Mace Windu calls Ahsoka's ordeal "a great trial," and excuses the Jedi by saying it was the will of the Force that she be accused. Her arms crossed, Ahsoka obviously finds this a pathetic excuse. To Anakin's and the audience's shock, Ahsoka abruptly refuses to rejoin the Order. She bids Anakin a sorrowful goodbye and turns away.

Eckstein writes in her memoir, "We watch and root for Ahsoka as she *transforms* from a student to a leader. And we are inspired at the heart-wrenching moment when Ahsoka *trusts* in herself and her conscience and chooses to walk away from the Jedi Order" (2018, 201). Ahsoka no longer buys into the Jedi path, rejecting it in a similar way to Luke's in *Last Jedi*. Clearly, she's lost her idealism as well as her trust for the Jedi— from her mentors to her best friend. Ahsoka thinks much later in her continuing novelization: "Barriss had been angry with the Jedi Order and had sought to win Ahsoka's sympathies, if not her outright alliance, but she'd done so in the cruelest way imaginable: by tampering with Ahsoka's own choices. To have a person she considered a friend use her to unleash such deep anger and channel it at the Order had changed every part of Ahsoka's outlook" (Johnston 2016, 55).

After this startling twist, the series suddenly ended, prompted by Disney's purchase of Lucasfilm. *Star Wars: Rebels* was set to follow it, and the already-made episodes from the next season were released on Netflix and finally DVD as "The Lost Missions." Though the show had officially ended, it offered well-received stories that completed many pre-Episode III arcs. Some of Rex's clone troopers discover there are chips being placed inside clones when they are still embryos and uncover the truth about Order 66. Yoda quests to prove his worthiness to train in the Force with Qui-Gon's ghost. Yoda even confronts Ahsoka's death in the Jedi Temple in a guilt-filled vision—it doesn't come to pass but suggests her fate if she had stayed and if, ironically, he had believed in her more.

Of course, the sudden end to *Clone Wars* cut off Ahsoka from completing her arc. However, Filoni and others on the creative team gave interviews and panels about what they intended for her. In a planned plot, she gets wrapped up with the Coruscant underworld as she discovers life beyond the Order. "She has a very clear moral center. Even though she not technically a Jedi anymore, that doesn't mean that she's not gonna behave like one," Filoni says. "It is kind of a teenage story about her, and what she does on her own" (Eckstein, Filoni, and Hidalgo).

The heroine was to explore the infamous level 1313 (part of the cancelled *Star Wars 1313* video game). There, she would team up with a young, carefree smuggler. "Ahsoka had a boyfriend for a hot minute," exclaimed Eckstein, "and his name was Nyx Okami!" An Asian male lead, he's cool with a wolf jacket. Eckstein adds, "It was really how stories should be told for teenage girls should have crushes . . . It was a real learning and growing experience for her" (Eckstein, Filoni, and Hidalgo). Eventually, the Jedi would have called her back as a consultant on a special mission—working with Anakin and Obi-Wan to reach the foreboding surface of Coruscant and rescue Yoda from the seething Sith temple there. She would have confronted Darth Sidious himself, paving the way for the *Revenge of the Sith*.

AHSOKA'S UNFILMED FINALE

The popular teen heroine may be named for the ancient Indian King, Ashoka. After his rise to power, he launched a conquest against the Maurya Empire. However, his trauma at the resultant bloodshed goaded him to convert to Buddhism. With this, he became a more pacifist leader, uniting his people through his new beliefs. If Ahsoka is his namesake, this is the arc that clarifies her role. Witnessing the horrible violence of the Clone Wars and the betrayals that followed launch her to fight for the galaxy far differently than she began.

Filoni reveals the backstory of what Ahsoka was doing during *Revenge of the Sith:* Ahsoka meets with Anakin and Obi-Wan and plans to capture Darth Maul. Yoda calls the Jedi back because Chancellor Palpatine has been kidnapped and before they leave, as Filoni explains, "There's this nice long walk down the hallway where Anakin expresses how proud he is of Ahsoka, all she's achieved, even though she left, he understands it to some degree, he's not completely happy about it. He says, 'I'm not going to leave you on this mission unprotected.'" The 501st unit, which once belonged to Rex, appear all in orange helmets patterned with Ahsoka's markings, acknowledging themselves as Ahsoka's unit. "What was a little girl is standing there and now she's grown, and now she's has command of this whole thing" (Eckstein, Filoni, and Hidalgo). He and his team showed concept art of Ahsoka, happy and eager, leading the charge and hurling Maul across the room.

Further, Filoni envisioned the clones turning on her during Order 66, surrounding the former Jedi in a forest clearing, while she was meditating. However, a giant wolf pack would have sprung from the forest to save her, tearing the clones to pieces. These delightful moments would have put Ahsoka and her agency center stage in shining moments of power. The protective wolves, of course, appeared in *Star Wars: Rebels,* watching over the young hero Ezra's home planet.

Filoni insists that he wants her to exist as more than an animated character. Though the novel *Star Wars: Ahsoka* is the first project he didn't supervise, he was "very involved" (Eckstein, Filoni, and Hidalgo). The novel continues past this point, envisioning her on the run and slowly finding a new role for herself. It also emphasizes how much she can carry a story all alone. The novel treats the battle with Darth Maul as fact, launching from this point. As they duel, he calls her "not even a real Jedi" and she responds by calling him "half a Sith" (2016, 3). She has the opportunity to kill Maul, but instead chooses to save Rex (Johnston 2016, 65). Rex, in a last act of loyalty, has faked killing her and then dying himself, and the pair agree to flee separately and hide in the Outer Rim, even as he ages unnaturally and grows disillusioned with his masters (Johnston 2016, 67). Her lightsabers, given to her by Anakin for the final battle, lie abandoned on her grave.

Though it doesn't answer all the questions about Ahsoka's past, the novel does help fill in the end of the war. It also strands her without her Jedi community, leaving her nearly the sole survivor—an especially painful burden for her community-based species. It also lets her come to terms with her choice on the show. As she thinks, "Why had it been her? She'd had that thought a hundred times since Order 66. Why had *she* survive? She wasn't the most powerful; she wasn't even a Jedi Knight, and yet she was still alive when so many others had died. She asked the question so often because she knew the answer. She just hated facing it, as painful as it was. She'd survived because she had left. She had walked away" (Johnston 2016, 63). She wanders the outer rim, working as a mechanic and staying out of the Imperials' path, and then works her way to the farming moon of Raada. When Imperials arrive and demand the locals plant a food crop that will destroy the soil, Ahsoka aids their rebellion. Though she struggles to keep hidden, safeguarding the locals instead of mounting attacks, they soon discover she's a Jedi. She flees to keep them safe.

She comes to care for Hedala Fardi, a Force-sensitive child just a bit older than the Jedi would have recruited. In the course of the book, an Inquisitor—a gray creature with a double red lightsaber—begins seeking her. These Jedi hunters are the villains of the *Star Wars: Rebels* series onscreen at the time of writing, helping Ahsoka bridge into the next franchise. Ahsoka warns her family the girl is in danger and once more leaves for their protection. She then tracks the Inquisitor back to her friends on Raada, where he's holding one of them hostage. Clearly, she's following the path of the reluctant hero, running from all her obstacles. At last, Ahsoka comes to realize that trying to keep her friends out of the fight isn't working—only putting them in more danger.

Through the book, Ahsoka collects scrap metal pieces without understanding their purpose. However, Yoda sends her a dream of gathering her lightsaber crystal from an ice cave, and instantly, she understands. She returns to Raada and battles the Inquisitor. As they fight, "She felt something awaken in her, every combat lesson Anakin had ever taught . . . She wasn't weaponless. No Jedi ever was" (Johnston 2016, 323). She breaks his lightsaber, which explodes, killing him. After, she takes a few parts, including his two crystals, and combines them with the parts she carries. Meditating, she builds the lightsabers. "They would need more work, but they were *hers.* When she turned them on, they shone the brightest white" (Johnston 2016, 326). She rescues everyone on the moon, carrying them off to join the rebellion, as Organa's forces attack the Imperials. After, she shows her lightsabers off to Bail Organa, explaining the repurposed crystals. "When the creature had them, they were red. But I heard them before I ever saw him on Raada and knew that they were meant for me." As she adds, "I restored them. I freed them. The red crystals were corrupted by the dark side when those who wielded them bent them to their will" (Johnston 2016, 348).

As Ahsoka's ship is caught in a tractor beam, she slips on board and disables the two pilots, only to discover R2-D2 is on board. He tells her they're the beginnings of a rebellion led by Senator Bail Organa. Though R2-D2 assures her secrecy, he also releases a shot of her on the camera to Organa, revealing that she survived. Ahsoka meets with him and they note with amusement how independent Artoo is, based on his "bad role models" (Johnston 2016, 285). She also meets Captain Antilles. As she tells him of her recent battles, he replies, "You can't fight the Empire alone, Ahsoka . . . But you don't have to either. You can fight it with me" (Johnston 2016, 287). This part of the plot carries her from the lone rebel to part of the network in the show that followed hers.

She refuses to command troops and order them to their deaths, and he resolves to find her another position. At last, she tells him potential Jedi children are in danger from a mysterious force—if he will help her track it down, she will join him. Instantly, he agrees. As she muses, "She had to be willing to work in a system again, to accept the order of common purpose and the camaraderie that went with it" (Johnston 2016, 315). She hesitates. Still, as she meditates, she realizes she will get involved whenever she sees innocents in danger. She seeks a middle path, one that will keep her from the deaths of her friends yet let her play a part. She clutches the communication device on her wrist and knows her answer. After, she tells Bail that too many people want to rebel but need better ways of communicating, need someone to run the intelligence networks, assigning some people missions and finding out what others need. Organa eagerly agrees, and she names herself Fulcrum. Thus named, she arrives in *Star Wars: Rebels*, to confront Darth Vader and complete her classic arc.

HER UNIVERSE

Meanwhile, Eckstein found a related path to empower her young fans. In fact, in 2010 she started Her Universe, now a multi-million-dollar company that sells "geek chic" feminine clothing and accessories, beginning with licensed *Star Wars* merchandise and expanding through science fiction. "We were really, to my knowledge, probably the first company in the sci-fi genre to say we don't want the men and the boys, we only want women," Eckstein said. "And they had to do a special contract for us at first, just to siphon out women only" (Yossman). She began selling t-shirts online and at events, progressing to Disneyland and then Hot Topic when her products were greeted with overwhelming approval.

Eckstein stated that her reasons for starting the line were simple: She was tired of wearing men's shirts. "Almost 50 percent of *Star Wars* fans are women, and it made no sense that 80 percent of the consumer market and 50 percent of SW fans are female . . . Why was there nothing for them to buy? Then I began reading all of the girls' comments online, and I realized that girls have been begging for female SW merchandise for years" (Travis 2013, 54). She asked fangirls for their input and listened. As she'd expected, fans of all ages loved her products. Indeed, while many female fans were willing to purchase male-marketed t-shirts and action figures, they were far more excited to purchase merchandise created for them. Eckstein began by steering away from pink, as she wanted to offer female geeks different options. Today, the online store offers products from girl power-style lightsaber lipstick to clothing for plus-sized women and maternity. T-shirts proclaim "Ahsoka Lives" or "Self-Rescuing Princess."

From there it grew and grew. With licensed *Star Trek*, *Doctor Who*, *Transformers*, *The Walking Dead*, Disney, Marvel, DC, BBC, Studio Ghibli and Syfy Channel, products include a comfy Tardis cardigan along with Baby Groot purse and earrings. There's Wonder Woman replica boots and a tiara but also a Themyscira romper, red and blue jacket, and several styles of dresses and sneakers—real clothes in Wonder Woman colors and logo patterns. For *Solo*, there's a ruffled t-shirt proclaiming, "Just Be Charming" and a tank top with Millennium Falcons and flowers. There's also a suede dress, blue wrap skirt with Han's military stripe, Chewbacca bandolier purse, and a retro peasant blouse with the Mandalorian symbol and gambling cards. All these encourage girls to take part in the fandom a bit more subtly and look stylish in the process. "I wanted items that girls could wear every day, not a costume," Eckstein said. "This was something that you want to show off, your fandom in your daily life, whether it is at school or work or going and running errands on the weekends" (Whitten 2017). One might argue that warrior-heroes like Ahsoka and Wonder Woman were not made to promote lipstick and purses. However, this too is a token of girl power—blending empowerment with fashion and fun.

> Eckstein said that the brand had bottled lightning in 2015 when Lucasfilm President Kathleen Kennedy wore one of Her Universe's designs during a *Star Wars: The Force Awakens* panel with director J.J. Abrams in Anaheim, California. The design, a series of lightsabers curled and situated to spell out "Star Wars" quickly sold out online and continues to be a top-seller for the site. (Whitten 2017)

Eckstein explains that she'd spotted a particular glamour movement at conventions: "I'd been noticing a trend for quite some time that girls who show up in their own costume fashions that weren't cosplay," she says. "They were these outfits that were cosplay-inspired but that you could wear going out, and the women were using Comic-Con as their runway" (Dockterman 2014). Celebrating this, Eckstein now hosts an annual Comic-Con fashion show in which designers compete with their original "geek couture" designs to win the opportunity to design a Her Universe fashion collection for Hot Topic. Models arrive in ballgowns reminiscent of Moana or Furiosa, or wear short, sporty high-schooler takes on the characters. The winners of the 2015 fashion show, Leetal Platt and Kelly Cercone, helped design *The Force Awakens* fashion line, with evocative clothing like a silver jacket with red Phasma piping, instead of a literal costume. There was a Rey-style hooded cardigan and a jacket for Finn. "You want to be inspired by your favorite character, you even want to look like your favorite character, but you don't want to wear a costume," Eckstein explained (Whitten 2017).

Some creators at the fashion show add LED's or heat-sensitive fabric to show off the new technologies and usher geekdom into a more science-fictional space. The audience winner of 2016, "I Solemnly Swear I Am Up to Couture" by Camille Falciola, featured vanishing ink heat technology to make the Marauder's Map appear "magically" in her gown. 2017's winners sported a Don't Panic shirt with ruffled grey galaxy skirt made entirely of towels, a "Sorceress Supreme" short dress with Eye of Aga-motto purse, and a fur wrap from *Princess Mononoke*. Once again, design-ers (male and female) are celebrated for girly looks, bridging femininity and fandom. "Such an event would have been unimaginable at Comic-Con in the 00s," Dockterman (2014) comments.

Some products are notably childish—harkening back to younger fans' interest in Pokémon or The Little Mermaid with cuddly sleepwear. Here the emphasis on being "girls" not women appears. "Pop culture really equals nostalgia, and it takes us back to our childhood," Eckstein ex-plains. "In a world right now where so many crazy things and terrible things and scary things are going on, everyone needs an escape, and everyone needs something that just gives you hope, and makes you hap-py" (Yossman). It's not surprising that she takes this angle, as youthful photos of her in Alice in Wonderland dresses and hybrid princess cos-tumes in her memoir emphasize her love of dressing up. She attended the 2016 Comic-Con fashion show in a custom Ahsoka gown made out of more than 10,000 Lego bricks, celebrating this return to the pleasures of youth.

Eckstein adds to this girly fan expression in her book, *It's Your Uni-verse: You Have the Power to Make It Happen*. Published by Disney and filled with princess art as well as photos of Eckstein in cosplay and fan gear, it offers blank lines where teen readers may record their goals. As the book explains, "Before you read this book, I need you to do one thing: throw out all your doubts and negative preconceptions about your dreams . . . Has anyone ever told you no or said that you couldn't achieve something? Has anyone ever squashed your dreams? If so, you are not alone" (2018, 7). As it goes on, Eckstein tells her story of growing up at Disney World and turning from actress to fashion designer. Princess style, she compares her struggles to Belle, Rapunzel, and other favorites as she urges young readers to pursue what they love. Finishing her life story, she leaves girl fans with a final thought: "I made myself take one day a week to do whatever I wanted. I took a day off to go to Disney World or perfect a new recipe. Sometimes I spent the whole day on the couch in my pajamas, binge-watching my favorite shows. So be prepared to put in the hard work, but don't forget to have fun in the process" (191). Here, she shows the frivolous, joyous side of pursuing dreams, empha-sizing finding beauty on one's path.

Granted, glamorous feminine fandom and the modest looks of Jyn and Rose haven't erased the gold bikini cosplay or the minidresses of Her Universe. "Yes, you'll see girls dressed in sexy costumes," says Eckstein. "But part of that is that these classic characters in comic books are dressed in sexy costumes, and it's really important to the fans to be accurate" (Dockterman 2014). Her clothes offer a range—some skimpy and some loose, some alluring and some casually fannish. They're definitely girl power, and certainly popular among some sets of fans who want to look cute and still dress for the franchise.

LADY JEDI ARRIVE AT LAST

Attack of the Clones and *Revenge of the Sith* give viewers a quick glimpse of female Jedi Masters. A few are tragically murdered in Order 66, offering pathos but no characterization. Delightfully, these weak roles are expanded in the show, letting Ahsoka work with and be mentored by strong alien women, with personalities and distinct plot arcs.

Jedi General Aayla Secura is a Twi'lek, leader of the 327th Star Corps of clone troopers during the war. She has a midriff-baring top with notable cleavage, but is presented as tough and powerful, third-wave style. In several *Clone Wars* episodes, the blue-skinned Jedi is considered a cunning warrior, and helpful mentor with her characteristic French accent. In "Jedi Crash" (113), when Anakin is critically injured, she becomes a new kind of mentor for Ahsoka—a big sister figure who also warns the Padawan that she cannot sacrifice many lives just for Anakin. She counsels Ahsoka to accept that attachments are a distraction, but loving, emotional Ahsoka defies her. "In many ways, Ahsoka is supposed to parallel Anakin; a young, reckless Jedi who often disobeys orders but nevertheless remains heroic throughout" (Pianka 2013, 50). The other female Jedi teach detachment and obedience, but Ahsoka is defiantly heroic. She tends his wounds and defends him from danger until he can recover.

Jedi Master Adi Gallia, a Tholothian, teams up with Anakin and Obi-Wan in "Grievous Intrigue" (209). She fights capably in Jedi robes that resemble a mini-dress, but with sturdy pants and boots beneath—feminine and different but not sexualized. After battling Grievous, she saves Obi-Wan and several troopers from death. She's certainly capable, but her dialogue is mostly devoid of personality. She also helps out in "Nomad Droids" (406). As season five launches with "Revival," the deadly team of Savage Opress and Darth Maul attack the pirate Hondo Ohnaka and win over his men. Obi-Wan and Adi Gallia arrive to help Hondo, with Adi once again offering little personality in her dialogue. Adi duels Opress without a word, and without a word, she slides off his blade, dead. While this emphasizes the brothers' growing power and strikes a blow at the Jedi leadership, it also sacrifices the character without ever giving her much characterization.

Shaak Ti doesn't mentor Ahsoka, the other Togruta, but she also helps out in a few episodes. She oversees the production of new clone troopers on Kamino, and leads during the Battle of Kamino, when the Separatists attack. She also easily takes out a bunch of Aqua droids as a stalwart Jedi warrior. Since she's a member of the Council, her few episodes generally show her in charge of large operations, in a position of power.

The white-haired archivist Jocasta Nu, the elderly keeper of the Jedi records, appears a few times in an expanded role of her own. In "Holocron Heist" (201), Ahsoka searches the Jedi Temple for a shapeshifting bounty hunter. However, she's taken Jocasta's form. The sudden attack by the elderly woman in long skirts, who leaps and summersaults with a lightsaber is quite startling. However, Ahsoka takes her down and notes, "You may have Madame Jocasta's face but not her skills." Jocasta also gives her advice about tracking down a thief in "Lightsaber Lost" (211). Her appearance is brief but helpful. "The question of representation is another reason for the importance of Jocasta Nu's return in a handful of *Clone Wars* episodes. Not only does a minor character experience new adventures in the saga, but an older woman who occupies a valuable role in the Jedi Oder, obtaining more screen time participates to greater inclusiveness" (Guyot 2015, 76). She adds diversity in a rare elderly woman but serves to move along the main characters' plot as a rather flat character.

Luminara Unduli, an exotic-looking Jedi Master from Mirial, has olive skin with interlocking black diamond warrior tattoos on her chin and a lower lip permanently stained black. Her concealing, nunlike headdress actually contains sensory devices, while her black robe in the Jedi style is particularly shrouding. This pushes her into the background, making her appear more teacher than warrior. When the Council speak in the films, she can be seen nearly pressed into the wall, ceding the discussion to the central males. Her apprentice stands a step behind her. In the prequels, she's played by actress/model Mary Oyaya from Kenya who interpreted Luminara's appearance as a "mystical look which can be taken for deep knowledge, determination, decisiveness, insight, and all qualities that can be expected of a Jedi Master." She's more of a gentle thinker than authoritative leader.

Still, she and her fellows were the first female Jedi to wield lightsabers for viewers. The actress notes, "It's quite exciting to be one of the first female Jedi to wield a light saber! I think it is something special for women; there is no discrimination amongst the Jedi ranks" (Oyaya 2002). There was also an action figure, of which the actress was quite proud.

In *Clone Wars*, Luminara commands the 41st Elite Corps. When Padmé captures Gunray in "Cloak of Darkness" (109), Ahsoka and General Luminara escort her. While Ahsoka plays bad cop and threatens him with her lightsaber, Luminara remains the unruffled Jedi master. She's strong and tranquil with the Force but uses it to be aloof and unapproachable. This, however, sets her up for failure against a more aggressive force wielder. "Luminara's strict discipline makes it hard for her to believe that a wild, untrained user of the Force like Asajj Ventress could ever be her equal in lightsaber combat. Aboard the Tranquility, she discovers her error: Ventress's rage gives her surprising power" (Fry 2010, 106). Squaring off with the villainess lets Luminara and Ahsoka explore all their contrasts, modeling different female paths to power. Dooku calls Ventress "child" and tell her she must "prove worthy of being my apprentice." A defiant, feisty Ahsoka calls her "hairless harpy" and "bog witch" and duels her. Meanwhile stately Luminara comes to her rescue and saves the impetuous Padawan several times. While Ventress taunts her with Anakin's absence, Ahsoka spits back, "Good thing I don't need saving!"

Nonetheless, Ventress defeats her, and Luminara must free her from a prison cell. Luminara insists she will duel Ventress alone as Ahsoka protests. However, Luminara is quite conventional in her combat style. Ventress detonates a small bomb to escape and then blasts a steam vent in Luminara's face, cackling with witchy glee and emphasizing that she fights dirty. After blinding her with steam, she knocks away her lightsaber and pins her under a heavy pipe. Luminara calls Ventress's fighting "amateurish" and "sloppy" but Ventress continues the trickery and defeats her. Dramatically, Ahsoka shows up and saves the Master. Afterward, Luminara admits she should have listened to Ahsoka's warnings about such a different kind of adversary. Each has learned from their adventure, in a contrasting partnership in which each teaches the other wisdom.

In "Legacy of Terror" (207), Luminara is captured while looking for a Separatist leader, so Anakin, Obi-Wan, and Commander Cody must plunge into a colony of Geonosian zombies to find her. She hangs there, suspended in an energy field, while the Geonosian queen Karina the Great makes demands of the Jedi and proposes to take over Luminara's mind as the captive Jedi protests. Here she's weakened as the lady needs the men to rescue her—the Jedi even teasingly use her as bait.

A trace of her returns in *Rebels'* "Rise of the Old Masters," where she's rumored to have survived the Jedi massacre of Order 66 (in the film executions, her and Barriss's appearances were planned but cut). As it turns out, she was taken prisoner and executed offscreen, but her remains are so powerful with the Force that they are used to lure the protagonists into a trap. Once again, she's a pawn in others' schemes, emphasizing her lack of power beside the male Jedi.

As likely the best developed of the female Jedi, Luminara and her Padawan Barriss Offee appear in several *Clone Wars* novels, with arcs for the characters. *Battle Surgeons* by Steve Perry and Michael Reaves has

Barriss actually tempted to turn to the dark side, using drugs to solve the mystery around her and claim power through the Force. She pulls away and discovers that she's already a Jedi Master, clear in judgment and self-possession. *The Approaching Storm* by Alan Dean Foster has the pair team up with the more volatile Anakin and Obi-Wan, even as Luminara worries how to best train her student. Of course, this gives her depth and personality. Luminara even displays her skill at dance amid coils of Force-lifted sand, emphasizing some secular abilities. Oyaya (2002) adds that the book *The Approaching Storm* "clearly brings out her character as a political Jedi who is disciplined, alert, and determined" and calls her "an inspiration to women." Both provide delightful arcs and novels with extensive scenes from the heroines' points of view.

The second season's "Weapons Factory" (206) teams Ahsoka up with Barriss. In *Attack of the Clones* and *Revenge of the Sith*, Barriss stands behind her mentor silently. She shares the Mirialian olive skin and diamond tattoos, though Barriss's cover her cheekbones. Barriss's Jedi robes consist of a black top, a long black skirt worn with a leather-tooled belt, and a blue patterned cloak with a deep hood that gives her quite a bit of mystery. Her distinctive dress and tattoo pattern in contrast with her mentor's emphasizes the diversity of their culture.

Barriss, a little older than Ahsoka, is more traditionally trained and sticks closely to the rulebook. Further, Barriss dresses modestly, covered in purple-brown from head to toe with as grey headscarf, in a more understated path to competence and power. This contrasts with Ahsoka's unorthodoxy, but they soon prove a steady team. Barriss and Ahsoka strike up a friendship on Geonosis despite their differences. The story has the Padawans disarming a new superweapon while their masters fight an army—a mission that requires trust on both sides. When the masters are pinned down, both trainees selflessly agree to sacrifice themselves destroying the weapon. They succeed, and afterward, Ahsoka calls Anakin through one of their cobbled-together channels so he can come rescue them.

The two Padawans work together again in "Brain Invaders" (208). As the clone troopers are taken over by mind-controlling parasites, Ahsoka relies on friendship and loyalty, calling on her friends for aid, while Barriss sticks with the rules. However, she is taken over by a parasite and battles Ahsoka, who pleads for her friend to recognize her. Despairing as she briefly returns to herself, Barriss begs, "Kill me, please!" but loving, brave Ahsoka cannot. Eventually Anakin's plan succeeds and the cold Ahsoka has released drives out the parasite. The Jedi come to the rescue to find Ahsoka nearly unconscious, cradling her friend. While both stories see Anakin saving the day, the focus on the contrasting women's friendship gives both some depth.

"The Wrong Jedi" (520) reveals in a shocking twist that Barriss is the traitorous saboteur who has bombed the Temple and framed Ahsoka, all as a protest again the Jedi's new warlike roles. At Ahsoka's trial, Anakin goads Barriss to confess and she does: "I did it. Because I've come to realize what many people in the Republic have come to realize, that the Jedi are the ones responsible for this war. That we've so lost our way that we have become villains in this conflict, that we are the ones that should be put on trial, all of us!" Given that Chancellor Palpatine has orchestrated the war—and will soon slaughter all the Jedi—Barriss is more right than wrong in philosophy. However, she is still a murderer of innocents and betrayer of her friend as well as the Order. Ahsoka thinks much later in her continuing novelization:

> Barriss Offee was wrong about a lot of things. She let her anger cloud her judgment and she tried to justify her actions without considering their wider effects. She was afraid of the war and she didn't trust people she should have listened to. But she had a point about the Republic and the Jedi. There was something wrong with them, and we were too locked into our traditions to see what it was. Barriss should have done something else. She shouldn't have killed anyone, and she definitely shouldn't have framed me for it, but if we'd listened to her—really listened—we might have been able to stop Palpatine before he took power. (Johnston 2016, 349)

Of course, the show's new characters are also beloved, while giving the main characters enhanced backstory. Duchess Satine Kryze of Mandalore (voiced by Anna Graves), is introduced as a good-hearted, elaborately gowned queen like Padmé . . . and also Obi-Wan's lost love. She deepens the other characters and provides a strong feminine presence as well. Like Padmé, she has an extensive retinue but willingly drops the formality and elaborate outfits for a jumpsuit in which she can move. The novelization, *Darth Maul, Shadow Conspiracy*, tells of the young couple's first meeting, when Qui-Gon brought his apprentice to Mandalore on a mission:

> To Qui-Gon's amusement, Satine and Obi-Wan had quarreled about nearly everything. They had also fallen deeply in love, despite their vows to avoid doing so—or maybe because of them. When Satine was safe again, Obi-Wan had simultaneously hoped she would ask him to stay with her and dreaded that she might do so. Emotional attachments were forbidden for Jedi, to say nothing of marrying Mandalorian noblewomen.
>
> He would have been expelled from the Jedi Order—and that was a fate he had been willing to accept. But Satine had not asked him. Obi-Wan had continued his Jedi training, and shoved the thought of Satine down so deep in his memory that the regrets came rarely. For the most part, he was grateful for the life of service he had pursued. (Fry 2012, 152)

As introduced in "The Mandalore Plot" (212), Satine comes from a warrior culture but is committed to pacifism. She is also the leader of the

Council of Neutral Systems—a conglomeration of 1,500 planetary systems firmly neutral in the war. The unpopularity of her opinion emphasizes how firmly she stands by her convictions even though she is targeted for assassination, framed for murder, and betrayed by those closest to her. As *Darth Maul, Shadow Conspiracy* explains, "Satine had accepted long ago that she might have to die for her beliefs. But she had never accepted that her people might have to do the same. She wouldn't let them die for the Republic or the Separatists, trapped amid the madness of their current war, and she certainly wouldn't sacrifice them because a few fanatics wanted to return to the madness of the Great Clone Wars" (148).

Though a strong player in her own right, she has an amusing effect on the otherwise composed Jedi. Obi-Wan is fumbling and clumsy around her. She, by contrast, remains in control, flirting softly with her flustered ex. In the next episode, he responds to Anakin's curiosity with defensiveness. At the same time, the pair are very touching as they each choose duty over love, in contrast to Anakin and Padmé. Still, they clearly care. Defending her, Obi-Wan engages in a lightsaber battle with her treacherous general and finishes by flinging himself atop her.

Duchess Satine and Padmé have a lively team-up in "Corruption" (305). This involves lots of cozy talks about a queen's struggle, and lighthearted joking as the pair sneak through the tunnels under the palace. They discover greedy opportunists have exposed schoolchildren to poison and the two rulers work together to save the children and end the exploitation. Padmé leaves, vowing to bring Satine's concerns to the Senate and do anything possible to help her planet. Both prove excellent role models for young viewers in the process. "They lament the greediness and selfishness of certain Galactic Senators while also expressing admiration for the goodness embodied and enacted by others. Padmé and Satine are not exactly political allies, but their devotion to public service allows them to find common ground—as the best leaders do" (Gronowitz 2016).

"The Academy" (306) has Anakin drop off Ahsoka to help Duchess Satine on Mandalore. Anakin tells her, "According to Senator Amidala, Mandalore is a deeply corrupt world. If the cycle is to be broken, the future leaders at the Royal Academy of government must learn the evils of corruption. Yoda feels that only a young Padawan like you can get through to them." Ahsoka finds herself lecturing the older children at a school, instructing them in morality. Soon after, Ahsoka confronts the older male prime minister, laying a trap with the students' help. When she discovers he's imprisoned the duchess, Ahsoka tries to rescue her. Even as the prime minister threatens the duchess with death and tortures her with a shock collar, she refuses to sign the confession he provides. After the heroes triumph, the duchess reveals that she called on Ahsoka as someone she could trust—an outsider and Jedi who could save her people. Once again, Ahsoka learns from an older woman even while helping her succeed with her unique perspective. They share a sweet hug.

In "Shades of Reason" (515), Darth Maul, newly in command of a gang of smugglers, fulfills his bargain with the Mandalorians by targeting the duchess. He decides, "I will use my army of crime lords to attack different targets across Sundari and sow chaos to undermine the Duchess' rule. Our gangsters will make her look too weak to maintain control. Then you and your Death Watch will capture and arrest us, bringing order where Satine's weak government could not." This echoes the Trade Federation's condescension against Amidala—that she, a naïve young woman, needs an outsider male to step in and take over. *Darth Maul, Shadow Conspiracy*, reveals the Duchess's thoughts and thus a bit more of her character:

> The Duchess found herself wondering exactly how many times the terrorists of the Death Watch had tried to kill her. She'd lost count, but at some point she'd accepted that the attempts would never stop. The misguided fanatics had tried to end her life here in Sundari, and on Concordia, and had hunted her all the way to Coruscant, and now here they were again. She had never given up hope that she might reach them, might get them to listen. But the idea of a Mandalore who believed in peace and progress was too infuriating for them to accept. (Fry 2012, 147–48)

She maintains her ideals, insisting calmly as the Death Watch gang burst into her throne room, "The people are on their side now" but adding, "There will be no bloodshed . . . I will not be provoked to violence by these terrorists." The new Prime Minister, Pre Vizsla, leader of Death Watch, takes her prisoner and publicizes that she's fled. Within the same episode, however, Maul defeats him in single combat and establishes himself as shadow ruler. In the next episode, Satine escapes (or rather is freed by her nephew and a Death Watch rebel) and sends her old friend a holographic message: "Obi-Wan, I need your help!" In this scene, she's Leia, the feminine inspiration for the hero's actions.

Obi-Wan rescues her, but Darth Maul captures them both. He taunts Obi-Wan, saying, "Your noble flaw is a weakness shared by you and your duchess. You should have chosen the dark side, Master Jedi. Your emotions betray you. Your fear, and yes, your anger. Let your anger deepen your hatred." He murders Satine in front of him with the fabled darksaber and tells him, "And now the perfect tool for my vengeance is in front of us. I never planned on killing you. But I will make you share my pain." Filoni acknowledges that Satine, the forbidden love interest, was always doomed (Filoni and Witwer 2013). This is a perfect example of fridging, killing the love interest to hurt the male hero and suggesting her life is worth no more than that. Filoni points out that Obi-Wan blames himself for Maul's resurrection too. "We wanted to put him in that incredibly vulnerable and incredibly frustrating spot to show the audience how he has to learn to let go of everything that he holds dear" (Filoni and Witwer 2013). This is a necessary step in his path to becoming a selfless Jedi but trivializes the strong heroine.

Bo-Katan, a fierce member of Death Watch, defies Darth Maul in his power-grab and calls all who support him traitors. She has short, straight orange hair and her armor is a bit figure-hugging, but she behaves as a tough, competent soldier. Having fought to free Satine and save Kenobi too, all she does is fight uncompromisingly for her people. Clearly, Mandalore means far more to her than personal power or even family. At episode end, she tells Kenobi, "Go back to your Republic and tell them what has happened." She accepts a Republic invasion if it will stop Maul and save her beloved people. In this, moment, Obi-Wan realizes she's Satine's sister, another strong woman for the series.

There are other heroines less central to the main characters' struggles. Aurra Sing, pirate and bounty hunter, may have trained as a Padawan but is now an enemy to the Jedi (Fry 2010, 16). She teams up with Boba Fett in "Death Trap" (220) to help him get revenge by killing Mace Windu. She acts as the brains of the operation with a startling ruthlessness, ordering him to kill cadets so they can't report. Even as she sweet-talks him and calls him "honey," she looks out for him and won't let him drink. With all this, she is framed as the evil mentor of the episode, and young Boba hesitantly does her will and is corrupted. She's also the clichéd woman who feels she must act through a man. She repeats this trope in her next adventure: "Lethal Trackdown" (222) reveals that Sing used to date the pirate Hondo Ohnaka. She rejoins him while seeking advice (shooting someone for calling her an "old hag"). She abandons Fett and flees from Ahsoka in Slave I, but Ahsoka disables her ship, which crashes.

"Innocents of Ryloth" (120) has two clone troopers befriend Numa, a cute but fierce Twi'lek girl. She shows Obi-Wan the tunnels they can all use to reach the Separatist cannons and save the day. QT-KT, a pink astromech droid, appears in four episodes of *Clone Wars*, assisting Jedi Knight Aayla Secura. The droid is an homage to R2-KT, a similar pink astromech droid built by *Star Wars* fans to watch over Katie, a little terminally ill girl. In "Sphere of Influence" (304), a chairman's two daughters are kidnapped as leverage, sending the Jedi on a double rescue mission. Another civilian, farmer's wife turned warrior Suu Lawquane, wears only a few strips of cloth above the waist—barely covering her bosom. There are a few little girls and one loving, sacrificing mom, but scantily dressed bounty hunters and docile assistants are the most common.

Another sexist trope appears in the "Betty droids" in pink leotards that emphasize their supermodel anatomy "They serve wealthy owners as secretaries, butlers, and attendants on worlds such as Coruscant" (Fry 2010, 22). They, like Jabba's dancing girls, fill the fictional world with a touch of painful objectification and sexism. As the *Character Encyclopedia* smirks, "Most Betty droids are programmed to act like pretty, slightly dim girls in situations that fall outside of their main functions. This annoys republic citizens who note that the galaxy is full of smart, strong females such as Padmé Amidala and Luminara Unduli" (2010, 22).

In "Slaves of the Republic" (412), Anakin flirts audaciously with the slaver queen, whose neck is bound in a high collar. The queen eagerly buys Ahsoka and gloats about slavery until one of her slaves attempts assassination and then suicide out of despair. She enslaves Obi-Wan and Ahsoka, encouraging Anakin to swear loyalty to her alone. She also insists Dooku isn't her master. Of course, he arrives and gives orders, even choking her to the point of death and calling her a slave to make her comply. Clearly, her hypocrisy and self-delusion are heavy. Anakin arrives to rescue the damsel, of course. Dying, she confesses, "You were right, Skywalker. I am a slave, just as you are." Thus, she emphasizes her weakness in the hierarchy, though she's ruler of a planet. The fact that she's female and serves Dooku stresses her low place below the patriarchy. Her torturing slaves, male and female, is the illusion of power but not its truth.

Saw Gerrera's dark-skinned, poofy-haired sister Steela enters the show from a position of strength, looking down from her alien steed to eye the Jedi with suspicion. Soon after, she introduces her brother (later to become the galaxy's most extreme terrorist) with a disrespectful punch to the arm as "He fashions himself as our leader, though no one elected him" ("A War on Two Fronts," 502).

"Front Runners" (503) ends with the people appointing Steela their leader, giving another salute to putting young women in charge of their forces. In the third episode, she appears as a massive hologram to urge the people to rise up in a heroic speech: "People of Onderon, the time has come to take back our freedom. We have all been deceived. King Rash is a traitor who has sold Onderon to the Separatists for the crown. But Onderon is ours. We need your strength to reclaim our planet and restore our sovereignty under our true king, King Dendup" ("The Soft War," 304).

While her brother acts foolhardy, rushes in, and gets captured, Steela leads her people in rescuing the king from execution. The teens successfully lead a rebellion, with Ahsoka standing by to help but finally unneeded. In the fourth part, Steela finds herself dangling from a cliff. The young women's shared love interest Lux struggles to rescue her but tumbles down himself. Ahsoka dramatically saves Lux, lifting him up with the Force and thus gender flipping the traditional damsel in distress image. Next, she tries to save Steela, but is shot at the crucial moment. Steela tragically dies as her brother and love interest both succumb to guilt. The episode ends with her funeral. To some extent, Steela is fridged—her death serving to motivate her brother through the events of *Rogue One*.

On the other hand, she's a dynamic enough character to supersede this role.

ASAJJ VENTRESS: THE *STAR WARS* VILLAINESS

> Noticeably absent from the galaxy are any female villains. While this doesn't seem like a problem at first glance, the fact is that *Star Wars* villains are some of the best and most iconic in the history of film. These are characters the audience loves to hate and occasionally just plain loves. Characters such as Darth Vader, Darth Maul, and Boba Fett can captivate an audience, sometimes even without needing to speak, as is the case of the latter two characters. In addition, these villains have the all-important job of running the galaxy. The galaxy is run by Emperor Palpatine and Darth Vader. The Empire itself, is devoid of any and all women, in addition to the noticeable lack of aliens. Perhaps Lucas believed no one would accept a woman as a legitimate villain, or perhaps he doesn't believe they can actually be a threat to a man. (Pianka 2013, 36)

The *Clone Wars* film brings a striking villainess in Dooku's apprentice Asajj Ventress. She's named for Asajj from the samurai film *Throne of Blood*, one of Lucas's favorites (Bray et al. 2015, 69). One of the Nightsisters, she hails from a mysterious sect of warrior witches who wield dark Force magic. She is a formidable opponent and fights Anakin and Obi-Wan (often at the same time) to a draw with her double-bladed lightsaber. She's skilled at stealth and martial arts as well as the Force-choke, though she is not fully trained in the ways of the Sith. When she and Ahsoka duel, the child is full of energy, darting around, while she is more measured.

As flashbacks on the show reveal, she was sold as a slave to protect the clan. Christie Golden's novel *Dark Disciple* (2015, 102) tells her suffering from her point of view: "When I was an infant, my clan was forced to surrender me to a criminal. I became his slave, but he was a surprisingly kind master. He was killed when I was still quite young." When her bounty hunter master died, the Jedi who killed him discovered young Ventress's talent with the Force and trained her. It's unclear how much love he showed her (in the distant, critical Jedi way) but he certainly imposed his own culture, at the sacrifice of her own. Like Ahsoka, she becomes a victim of imperialism. This can leave the heroine confused, willingly turning her back on her own inferior upbringing, as she thinks, in order to succeed. If she can only do so by dulling her feminine instincts (here portrayed as the magic of Dathomir), she will believe herself lesser—never able to measure up to her male masters and enemies.

Ventress adds, "For ten years, we helped the people of Rattatak. We became heroes—to most. But to some, we were the enemy" (Golden 2015, 103). This shows an ambivalence about her role, in an era in which the

Jedi's morals are slipping. When her master was killed, she longed for revenge, and Dooku recruited her. He said, "I can sense the darkness within you. I will teach you the ways of the dark side. But you must prove yourself first" (2015, 314). Steven Barnes' novel *The Cestus Deception* (2004, 148–49) elaborates on this, revealing her fury:

> Ventress closed her eyes, laying plans. Jedi. She'd killed many Jedi, and yet did not hate them. Rather, she hated the fact that they had lost their way, that they had forgotten their true purpose in the world, becoming pawns of a corrupt and decadent Republic. While most Jedi were discovered in early infancy and raised in the Jedi Temple, Asajj Ventress had been discovered by Master Ky Narec on the desolate planet of Rattatak. An orphaned child starving in the wreckage of a war-torn city, Ventress had clung to anyone offering her hope, and over the next years came to worship the formidable Narec as a father figure. He had groomed the Force-strong child, uncovered and developed her potential. At that time she imagined that one day she might travel to Coruscant and stand before the Council, become part of the ancient Order.
>
> Then her Master was murdered. The Jedi Council, who had abandoned Ky Narec to his fate, now became the object of her blind rage. Consumed with vengeance, she became a destructive force beyond anything her Jedi Master could have dreamed.
>
> It was Count Dooku who discovered her on the Outer Rim. She had attacked him, been defeated and disarmed, but rather than slaying her he took her as an accomplice, completed her training, and set her feet on the proper path. It was Dooku to whom she owed total allegiance, as she owed nothing save death to the ruthless, corrupt Jedi.

She notes in the present, "I died a long time ago. So did everything I cared about. It's only the likes of me, with nothing to lose, who'll really be prepared to tear the galaxy down and start over" (96). While everyone uses Jabba's son as a pawn in the *Clone Wars* film, her first appearance, she actually is eager to kill him. "Ventress felt no pity; nobody raised in the brutal ganglands that were Rattak could afford that level of emotion. They learned to shut down just to cope" (Traviss 2008, 172).

The Cestus Deception follows Obi-Wan through the Clone Wars and offers several scenes from Asajj's point of view. She thinks as she grows in Force sensitivity, "For months Count Dooku had taught her the Quy'Tek meditations. It was good to see the result. Her grin was as feral as a kraken's fixed and meaningless smile" (2004, 148). She has a savage delight in conflict. While she fears Obi-Wan's power, she thinks, "Nevertheless, his strength made the taste of her inevitable victory all the sweeter" (2004, 168). Danger and risk form a source of overwhelming pleasure for the dark Force user. The scenes emphasize how a *Star Wars* villain thinks, not just ambitious and cruel but glorying in giving herself to pure evil.

At the same time, she does her best to hide from Obi-Wan's sight, to shield herself as a nonexistent presence—a hole in the Force. This suggests her own emptiness as her skill is vanishing. This self-effacing behavior emphasizes her abused status and subservient place. She thinks, hands shaking, "Action. That was what she needed. That was what she hungered for. She would accept Count Dooku's scathing approbation, then volunteer for the most dangerous assignment General Grievous could devise, and on whatever planet that was, in whatever maelstrom of wrack and ruin she could immerse herself, she could find cleansing, and peace" (2004, 395). Only by winning male approval, as she thinks, can she triumph.

The aristocratic Dooku treats her as a tool and servant—as well as a lesser being because of her primitive origins and training in the swamps of Dathomir. Dooku tells her, "You were never cut out for anything more than grunt work." She is not born to darkness but "just flirt with it" (Golden 2015, 289). As a result, she internalizes his message about her worth. "Young women often make this choice at a crucial moment of their development, hooking elbows with the Devil and walking off on a power trip—assenting to and joining in the cultural chauvinism that rejects or mutilates feminine values and the unique power of the feminine" (Nelson 1991, 48). She believes the Jedi (as well as former Jedi Dooku) are superior to her birth people, and abandons the latter to serve power, as she thinks. "An argument against Ventress as a strong character can be made here, as it seems as though she is subservient to Dooku and therefore is placed into a traditional female gender role. And indeed she spends the better part of three seasons carrying out Dooku's wishes and remaining a fairly non-important character" (Pianka 2013, 56) The audience is given no reason to sympathize with her, as they are with Vader or the compelling villains . . . at least in the early seasons. Her voice is a charming purr, and she appears in the first episode of *Clone Wars* carrying Dooku's holo image, serving him as mouthpiece and messenger. Ventress longs for Dooku to see her as a true Sith and burns to defeat Obi-Wan and Anakin and take their lightsabers as trophies. However, Dooku won't name her his apprentice.

Still, she passes her people's test of initiation, wielding her dark side powers against six Nightbrother clan leaders in the Test of Fury to become a full assassin. After this, she tattoos her face. The icon on her shield is a snake, suggesting her underhanded deception. This is a negative feminine symbol, of fertility and regeneration but also the trickery and betrayal of Eden with "the aggressive powers of the gods of the underworld and darkness" (Cooper 1978, 147). This emphasizes women's trickery and sinfulness, in contrast with straightforward war. "It also takes on the feminine characteristics of the secret, enigmatic, and intuitional" (Cooper 1978, 147). Her ship is the Banshee, with similar symbolism of the raging, screaming killer woman.

She is rather sexualized, since between her high purple collar and long skirt, Ventress's shirt has a cutout in it over her midriff and much of her back. Her pale, bald head is creepy, while the purple tattoos on her face suggest the lines of the dark force. The droids call her supreme leader, and it's nice having a woman in a position of power, but she's unnecessarily underdressed in a way the male villains in the franchise are not. A predatory female, she actually kisses her foes before dispatching them with her lightsaber. Obi-Wan, who banters with her as they fight, notes in *Dark Disciple*, "With Ventress, it's a power play, a way for her to exert control" (2015, 28). After defeat in several episodes (as the ongoing villain), she runs off in cowardly fashion, adding spinelessness to her other character traits.

The three-episode arc beginning with "Nightsisters" (313) introduces Ventress's people. It begins with a furiously savage Ventress fighting in space, directing cruelly, "Trident group one, attack the starboard engines. Trident group two, knock out their port shield generators. I'll go directly for their bridge." Battling Anakin and Obi-Wan she screeches in rage. This shows her anger overwhelming her to an animalistic degree.

Abruptly, the Emperor requires Dooku to kill her over his objections, smirking, "I can sense her powers growing stronger. I would hate to think you are training your own Sith apprentice to destroy me" (313). To prove his loyalty, Dooku sacrifices Ventress. Her competence and the Sith traditional competition have proved her undoing. She thinks in *Dark Disciple*, "Dooku had *not* loved her. She had thought he had—not as a woman, of course, or even as a daughter, but as an apprentice. Someone who showed promise, whom he enjoyed training and shaping. How eager she had been to learn, to serve him, to obey, and how quickly he had discarded her. She had meant something to him only when he could use her" (Golden 2015, 54).

Ventress represents evil, but also a slippery slope of abuse and cruelty. In *Dark Disciple*, Dooku murders children, gloatingly calling it a message to all who side with the Republic. The Jedi, meanwhile, plot his assassination, though this means that they too are leaving their ideals. Yoda warns that such actions lead to the dark side, even with a tiny step to begin. Sometimes an adolescent girl with no parental support will "become coldly intellectual, ruthless, power-driven, or functioning without heart" (Nelson 1991, 47). This sort of young woman clings rigidly to justice without mercy. "Rules and laws push past her femininity and lead her with a kind of driven, possessed attitude. Intellectual pursuits may be taken up—and with a mania that destroys relationships and is destructive of everything around her. She is ruled by her masculine side, not guided by it" (Nelson 1991, 48). Ventress follows this pattern, especially as she seeks revenge. Her treating men as objects to corrupt or discard reflects how she herself was treated.

The Nightsisters' predatory sexuality actually comes from the 1994 extended universe novel that invented them, long before conception of the show. Witches of Dathomir first burst onto the scene in *The Courtship of Princess Leia*, riding rancors.

> One of the riders bent low, her dark hair shimmering in the light of the burning walkers. She wore a high-collared tunic of glittering red scales, and over it a supple robe made of leather or heavy material. On her head she wore a helm with fanlike wings, and each wing was decorated with ornaments that bobbled as she moved . . . If the costume and mount were not impressive enough, the woman's very presence struck Leia like a blaster bolt to the ribs. The woman seemed to radiate power, as if her physical body were a mere shell, and beneath it hid a being of terrible light. Leia knew she was in the presence of someone strong in the Force. (Wolverton 129)

The witches of Dathomir have an equally fearsome foe—when those among them turn to evil, they become Nightsisters. Both sides in their battle of good and evil are "space Amazons"—powerful women who enslave the men and force them to be their mates. One tries this with Luke, who must persuade her through his reasoning to take a more egalitarian path. This trope has women winning the gender war, flipping conventions in a way that synchronizes with girl power—sexy but not submissive. At the same time, it suggests one gender or the other must dominate. Further, the space Amazons may be powerful, but often appear scantily dressed and objectified, even as they leer at men and demand sexual services.

Ventress escapes Dooku's attempt on her life and reaches her misty, secretive home planet. On *Clone Wars*, Dathomir is entirely red, with branches providing creepy shadows. The women's magic comes in creepy green light. The Nightsisters' village lies inside a mountain carved with women's figures. It's filled with round stone columns and monstrous plants, feminine symbolism. "Plant and flower symbolism is closely connected with the Great Mother, goddess of the earth, of fertility and vegetation" (Cooper 1978, 133). Roundness and plants suggest the lifecycle, though there's more than a touch of savagery.

The Book of the Sith, a fannish replica journal, has a section written by the Nightsisters' leader Mother Talzin in which she explains it is the right of the clan mother and no one else to broker the services of the Nightsisters as assassins. She adds of their philosophy, "What the Jedi call the dark side, the Nightsisters know to be the essence of life . . . The Winged Goddess and the Fanged God bestow the passive and aggressive energies that animate every creature and allow each to draw breath" (Wallace 2015, 101). As she continues, "Our shamanism saturates the galaxy, influencing other traditions even if their practitioners are unaware of it. It flows from a single wellspring—the life web of Dathomir" (98). Dathomir is especially significant in the larger franchise as a Jedi alternative—a different path from the dualistic, patriarchal Jedi versus Sith. Their teachings rely on sisterhood, ancestry, primitivism, and spirituality—concepts scorned by the haughty Jedi.

Mother Talzin, with her long red robes and Russian accent, has graceful, deliberate gestures, emphasizing her discipline but also providing foreign distancing. Streamers of her cloak float around her like tentacles. She often gazes into an orange crystal ball—more antiJedi mysticism and feminine roundness. Talzin uses the words of witchcraft with a "potion" of invisibility and another to distort Dooku's vision. The women thus appear to have powers beyond the Jedi knowledge, but also unknowable feminine magic framed as mysticism not science and training. It's implied that their traditions are just as ancient and mighty or more, though discounted for their feminine coding. *The Book of the Sith* describes totems from something like a Voodoo doll to Talismans of Transformation that give the sisters the guises of animals (Wallace 2015, 115). These are primitive primal magic, evoking ancient legend.

The sisters are masked and hooded, and dwell in harmony with the monstrous animals of their planet, including rancors. "Every time we eat the meat of a whuffa worm or wear its skin, we are reminded that life is connected," Talzin writes in *The Book of the Sith* (115). She adds that savage rancors fiercely protect their own. "The Nightsisters connect with them, speak to them, and ride them. Be like the rancor and you will hold authority in any confrontation you face among outsiders" (113). This is another hallmark of their strength.

Ventress and two other Nightsisters, all invisible, blind Dooku and battle him (emphasizing how much stronger he is in comparison if these odds are necessary). However, the women lose, requiring a new plan of attack. Next, Mother Talzin negotiates directly with Dooku and offers him an apprentice in order to lure him into a trap. Her speeches to him weigh gender heavily as she smirks, "Perhaps a male from our planet will be more to your liking, since you could not tame the female." Her word choice emphasizes that he would be more comfortable with a male—who will better understand the strictness of hierarchy—rather than the fiercer, less obedient female.

Enticed by the offer, Dooku visits her planet—her own place of power. "Men are easy to acquire, hard to control," Talzin smirks, framing herself as the queen manipulator of men—not just the new apprentice but Dooku as well. In contrast with the women, the men exist in rough fighting camps where they train and kill as well as growing the women's food. Ventress arrives to choose one and treats them as slaves, striking them to the ground with words like "a fine-looking specimen" and "too small." Their matriarchal society thus stands out as in the original novel.

While the women have magic that they bestow on the men as they please, the men know only the external world of combat. The women have other powers as well. As the *Book of the Sith* explains, detailing the Nightsisters' philosophy, "Mesmerism is another gift provided by spirit ichor. This power allows a shaman to override the thoughts of those weaker than oneself—particularly men and offworlders" (107). When the Nightsisters use this, they emphasize their power in the war of the sexes and their use of the Force for selfishness:

> The Nightsisters are portrayed as something of an abomination; they do not use the Force for good, as do the Jedi, nor do they use it to further their own ambitions, as do the Sith. Rather, they use the Dark Side for witchcraft; they are capable of manipulating the things around them, including people, for whatever use they see fit. Therefore, the first (and possibly only) planet in the galaxy that is dominated by women is portrayed as a cult; it is an affront to what the audience has come to expect, and it is therefore evil. (Pianka 2013, 57)

After Ventress chooses a champion, Savage Opress, the sisters remake him with new powers in a second birth and also an example of their control over him (and by extension, all men). As the guide *Star Wars Absolutely Everything You Need to Know* explains, "Nightbrothers like Savage Opress are raised as servants of the witches who rule Dathomir—the Nightsisters. The strongest Nightbrother warriors are tested and selected from their clans, to receive the power of the Nightsisters' dark side magic and to become their mates" (Bray et al. 2015, 57). His horns grow in a physical manifestation of virility and he gains height and muscle mass, becoming a powerhouse but only as they will it. Talzin orders him to kill his own brother and he does. His camaraderie of the training camps has been purged, replaced by the women's agenda. They have taken his humanity and left him a savage. Ventress recalls "forcing the dark side upon him with Mother Talzin's rituals and torturing him when he disappointed her in training" (Golden 2015, 146). Horrified, Dooku and Obi-Wan alike call him a "beast" and "monster." After this, his masters and enemies alike reject him for the tainted self they've created. "Writer Katie Lucas used Frankenstein's monster as inspiration when writing the vengeful character of Savage Opress" (Bray et al. 2015, 57). The scene alienates him as well as casting the Nightsisters as corrupting monsters, turning their charges into heartless supersoldiers.

Ventress and Savage turn on Dooku, and then Savage attacks Ventress, suggesting her hypnosis has failed or that he's too monstrous for even this control. Responding to her treachery, Dooku tries to eliminate Ventress but she escapes. The Jedi arrive and attempt to take out Savage, and then Dooku's droids attack him too, emphasizing how he's a threat to all. Wounded, he returns to Mother Talzin. She sympathetically offers him a new mentor—the resurrected Darth Maul.

In the appropriately-named "Massacre" (419), Ventress swears herself utterly to the witches and Mother Talzin conducts an arcane ritual of swirling green light. Grievous leads an invasion of droids to kill Ventress and all her sisters, but her mother tells her, "There is no time for regret." The Mother goes to the "oldest and wisest" and asks her to resurrect their undead to fight for them as an army. This presence of the old, wise ancestor, to say nothing of sisterhood with the dead, emphasizes a multi-generational community of support and interrelationality.

Meanwhile, Ventress challenges Grievous to single combat to save her sisters, while Mother Talzin tortures Dooku with a voodoo doll, empha-sizing her power over him. The witches use all their arcane magics de-fending their planet. However, Grievous murders the old grandmother Daka, felling the army of the dead. He then kills Talzin, who appears to Ventress in a final vision:

TALZIN: It is over, sister.

VENTRESS: No one remains? This is all my fault. Where do I go? What do I do?

TALZIN: This chapter is over. Your destiny will always be linked with ours. But you have your own path to follow now.

VENTRESS: No! Wait! You can't leave me here!

Ventress ends the episode crumpled on the ground in despair. This gives her an arc and personal suffering, though also suggests she and her people have limited power. The death of the entire sisterhood empha-sizes their helplessness before Grievous and his droids—despite the women's incredible magics, unseen even in the Jedi Temple. Still they're no match for the patriarchy, who slaughter them.

Returning home in *Dark Disciple*, "Ventress sat for a moment in the cockpit, opening to the pain, letting it slice her soul like a knife across an open palm, her grief, hatred, and guilt dripping out like blood. It had been less than a year since the slaughter, and the wound was still fresh and raw" (Golden 2015, 104). She shows her companion sacks hanging from the trees like teardrops.

> "These contain the bodies of my sisters," Ventress said. She reached to caress the smooth casing. "When one dies, so I was told, we perform a ritual to honor her. We bathe her in a sacred pool, then enclose her in this pod. In this way, a sister never truly leaves us. She is dead, but she is nestled inside something vibrant and alive. She is suspended be-tween sky and soil, because she is truly of neither. She is always near, always part of the clan. I was taught that our dead sisters can share our celebrations of joy, and our ceremonies of grief. And that one night— they shared our fight."

Ventress gestured to the skeletons around them. For a moment, her voice caught. "But . . . I do not know the secret of preserving the fallen, and no one else was left to tend to them." (Golden 2015, 104)

Paralleling the Jedi, the Nightsisters' sacred lore is lost, leaving their last survivor hopeless, unable to complete the rituals and training.

In season three of *Rebels*, Darth Maul brings the young hero Ezra to Dathomir to cast a spell. He harnesses the Nightsisters' "old magic," while adding that he is the planet's last survivor. He casts a spell but flinches from the swirling green ghosts that appear afterward. He tells Ezra, "The spirits of the Nightsisters must be compensated for the use of their magic . . . The price is our flesh and blood!" The last remnants of the Nightsisters are monsters—vampires who drain the living. They capture two of Ezra's friends, and Ezra must vanquish the Nightsisters by using his lightsaber to sever their magic ("Visions and Voices," 310). Here, they exist only as corrupted corpses, ironically exploited to serve the male. This scene emphasizes the ghosts' evil, but also suggests they have been irretrievably cut off by the genocide, with no Nightsisters left to properly harness their power.

In Ventress's next episode, "Bounty" (420), she tries working for young Boba Fett. However, when she discovers the teenage Pluma Sodi will be delivered as a captive bride, and the girl protests at the horrors of being separated from her family, Ventress ties Fett up to deliver as a bride instead and returns the girl to her family (though for an additional fee). This delightful gender flip emphasizes that she's capable of pity and mercy as well as sisterhood even with alien women. However, she's still largely out for herself.

Contributing this amoral mix once she's been freed from Dooku's servitude, Ventress actually comes to rescue Obi-Wan. As Darth Maul and Savage Opress torture him, Ventress suddenly arrives to gloat, "I was looking for a challenge, not some wretched castoffs from the Night-brothers clan. What a disappointment" ("Revenge," 422). In perfect control, she's cool and collected. She rescues Obi-Wan, even while insisting she's not a "good guy." Still, they fight their common enemies side by side.

Ahsoka, on the run from the Jedi, teams up with Ventress as well. While the Sith apprentice-turned-bounty-hunter considers turning her in, she agrees to help in return for Jedi consideration. Working with Ahsoka, Ventress shows she is amoral—not evil. "See? Didn't kill one. It's the new me," Ventress smirks. While she's selfish, she helps solve a bombing that killed civilians, emphasizing how far from the path of evil she's come. Thanks to a judgmental, unfeeling galaxy, she's blamed for the bombing herself in the end. "Ventress has changed so much, from a one-dimensional attacking force to this really personal dimensional character who has feelings and her own agenda," Filoni notes. "She goes out on a limb for Ahsoka and she kind of pays the price. I kind of feel bad for her" (Filoni 2013).

The novel *Dark Disciple* finishes the story of Ventress, with an arc planned for the final television season. The kindly Jedi Quinlan Vos is chosen to pair up with Ventress and together assassinate Dooku and end the war. Kenobi comments, "I wouldn't go as far as to call her trust-worthy, but it's true that our interests do align, on this one point. And no one knows him as well as she does" (Golden 2015, 24). Obi-Wan advises Vos to show off his intelligence and competence, but also to appear to be attracted to Ventress and banter with her as she will expect. Accordingly, Vos plays a bounty hunter and cajoles her into partnering with him. He finally tells her his true identity to convince her to assassinate her former master, and she agrees. The pair gradually fall in love and she cautions him that to defeat Dooku, he will need the dark side as ally. She decides to train him as she once was, by the Nightsisters. "Nightsisters know the dark side better than anyone. We grow up steeped in it, but we can use it as a tool and stay ourselves—unlike the Sith. That balance is what you must learn" (2015, 109). She sends him on an initiation ritual to battle an ancient creature under a dark lake on her homeworld, preparing Vos to use his anger and also commit murder.

They battle Count Dooku—however, the pair cannot stand against him and General Grievous both. Ventress flees and Vos is captured. Dooku tortures him for months and when Obi-Wan finally rescues him, Ventress angrily reveals that Vos has turned to the dark side. The Jedi put their trust in Vos, but when evidence of treachery appears, Anakin and Obi-Wan accompany him and Ventress to assassinate Dooku and settle the question. At the crucial moment, Ventress harnesses her own experience and gives Vos an impassioned speech about setting aside being a slave to rage and hatred. All at once, in a warm, soft light, the Force rewards her with a vision of all the paths open to them both. With this, she chooses. Dooku strikes Vos with force lightning, and Ventress catches it with her body. Vos prepares to kill Dooku in his rage, but stops himself, insisting, "I do not feed off vengeance . . . I am a Jedi" (294). He has chosen at last. Dying, she insists he stay with the light side of the Force and promises endless love, and then perishes. Like Vader, she has saved herself at last.

After, Vos works with the Jedi to regain his commitment to the light. Dooku escapes of course. Obi-Wan tells the Council that by sacrificing herself, Ventress not only saved Vos's life but his soul, and perhaps theirs as well—their attempt to play assassin and send in a spy has been a betrayal of all they are, one with the potential to destroy them. Only Ventress was wise enough to understand this. Vos and Obi-Wan take Ventress's body to Dathomir and carry her to the fortress. It's a place filled with the dark side, but it welcomes them, sensing they are carrying the last Nightsister home. Vos places her in the lake and it turns "green, like the Dathomiri magicks Ventress had spoken of; green, like the Water of Life" (301). This is a symbol of "hope, renewal of life, and resurrection" (Cooper 1978, 40). With this, the Force embraces her in death. Thus Ventress journeys from darkness to light and redeems the Jedi, but through her wisdom and understanding of the dark side. She has no self-deception, but finds the courage to save her lover, as well as to strike out against her former master and nemesis. It's a fascinating end to such a strong, nuanced character.

III

The Fourth Wave Hits the Sequel Era

FIVE

Rey, Maz, Rose, Leia, Holdo, and Phasma

THE LIGHTSABER HEROINE

"*The Force Awakens* became the third-highest-grossing film of all time (worldwide) when it premiered in 2015, in part because it boasted one of the most diverse casts ever to star in a blockbuster film. It represented a galactic shift for the franchise" (Dockterman 2017a, 38). *The Force Awakens* indeed broke the billion-dollar sales mark in a record twelve days. It was memorable for the fact that its new trio had no white males—Poe is Hispanic and Finn, Black. "It was very important to me that this movie look more the way the world looks than not," J.J. Abrams said (Grossman 2017, 60). Even before release, the film emphasized that its characters had moved beyond the old moviemaking standards to fully embrace diversity. With a $200-million production budget and marketing to every demographic by Disney, *The Force Awakens* became the largest movie ever to reflect such an inclusive approach (Keegan 2015). At the same time, it was so extensively reshot that they had to scrap the "Making Of" companion book (Bundel 2018).

As was long advertised beforehand, the third era of *Star Wars* launched with a woman in Luke's place as chosen one and force wielder. *The Force Awakens* scored 37 percent in Harrison's study (2018) of how often women appear onscreen—not equal but a high score as Rey is the central hero. Further, she wasn't wearing a white dress, tight jumpsuit, ballgown, or bikini. It seemed *Star Wars* had finally reached the modern day. "She wears no high-heeled shoes, no copper-plated bikini, no princess robes. Rey is costumed as a woman might dress herself, for herself," comments Rebecca Keegan in her *LA Times* article.

Lawrence Kasdan, who wrote the *Empire* and *Jedi* scripts, comments that the lead was always going to be a strong woman: "There was never a question. It was not just J.J. and I, but Kathy and everyone involved as well. We aimed very strongly toward one of the protagonists being a woman right from the get-go. It cries out for that. Leia was a wonderful character, but she was among the only women in the movie. This saga demands more in female leadership. We want to see more characters like that" (Ashworth 2015, 74).

The film skips the glamour makeover that defined Katniss's existence, and thus made Rey more an everyday person. "I really want to see her; I don't want to see her with amazing makeup or anything," says Amanda Knight, head of the makeup department. "She's gotta look like she lived there and be dirty and be sweaty. She had a spray tan every day to make her look like she was living in that environment (*People* 2015a). In fact, she begins her film swathed in beige protective robes and goggles to keep out the sand, a mysterious figure scavenging through the desert. When she takes her helmet off, she still isn't objectified. Katherine Wright explains in *The New Heroines* that the image of a female lead is changing: "The New Heroine offers an ideal body type very different from that of the New Woman" (Wright 2016, 125). She is "thin and without curves, a body type typically associated with adolescence" (Wright 2016, 125). This makes her more childlike—filled with potential—and also more able to compete in the masculine world. In her simple up-and-down clothing, Rey fits the model.

"For Rey's hair we jokingly called the style the Three Knobs," says Lisa Tomblin, chief hair designer. "I was trying to do something that would be iconic, simple, realistic, but not something where you're always just looking at her hair. Princess Leia had one of the most iconic hairstyles in the history of cinema. So it's quite a big thing to come up with the next one" (*People* 2015a). In the real world, girls were pleased that they could make the hairstyle on their own. Many Rey costumes appeared—not glittering ballgowns, but simple tan garb often fashioned from tank tops, cargo pants, and cut-down adult shirts. Critic Nicole Sperling (2016) writes:

> Leaving the theater, my girls felt as empowered as their brother usually does after seeing one of the many blockbusters built for him. They never commented on how pretty Rey is. They never had to flinch because Rey was a sexual object to some man in power. They just felt strong. Equal. Imagine how the film will feel to girls in parts of the world where women are not allowed control over their own bodies or hearts or minds. Imagine a generation, of both sexes, growing up believing that girls are powerful. Imagine the force of a billion girls realizing that, one day, they can rule the galaxy.

This is most important for the issue of representation—in an increasingly diverse America that finally acknowledges its diversity, minority children can finally see onscreen heroes that resemble themselves: "Part of the power of *Star Wars* movies has been how they have invited generations of audiences to imagine themselves as heroic characters in the fantastical, detailed world George Lucas conceived nearly forty years ago. In 2015—spoiler alert—it is not only white males who get to harness the power of the Force," Keegan (2015) adds. Kids of both genders now could identify with their action heroine instead of the more passive women of the last set of films.

As she scrounges old parts and curls up in her home—a former AT-AT, Rey seems completely self-sufficient, earning everything for herself. Her prequel book adds, "She had found a spacecraft that had lain in the sand for years—decades even—and nursed it back to health. She had, with her hands and her smarts, taken it into the air once more. That was something to be proud of" (Rucka 2015, 105). She also establishes her character early by saving the childish droid BB-8 from scavengers and then refusing to sell him for a mountain of food. After this, the First Order comes for the droid and she defends him yet again. Micciche's "Feminist Pedagogies" (2014, 12–29) describes each feminist wave as having its own focus while calling to attention and linking aspects such as "race, class, age, disability, queer, linguistic, immigrant, global, and other categories of identification that include and exceed women's issues." Rey's care for the tiny droid and escaped Stormtrooper as she pledges herself to the Resistance addresses many of these, emphasizing that she will promote the causes of others, not just her own.

> Many of the concerns of the second wave women's movement are echoed in contemporary or fourth wave feminist voices, but there are also different issues and less clear or rigid "feminist" parameters. This is partly to do with the evolution of new cultures around sexuality, work, reproductive technologies, communication technologies and what can be seen as the continually changing market-driven commodification of all that is feminine and targeted at women. It is at this intersection of popular culture and feminism that many apparent contradictions arise for those of us who have grown up with the principles of second wave feminism, where every imposition on women had to be confronted or scrutinized. (Phillips and Cree 2014)

When First Order soldiers give chase, Rey trounces them all, showing off a lifetime of practice defending herself with her staff, instead of mysteriously-bestowed Force training. In fact, Ridley went through three months of physical training. As Rey, she spends twenty minutes defeating three enemy soldiers (Grossman 2017, 56). Finn tries to save Rey only to watch, stunned as she saves herself and him. He then keeps trying to take her hand in rescuer fashion but she keeps snatching it back. Clearly, the gender roles have been redefined. "She disarms Finn with her spear, hides them both from Stormtroopers, rescues him—no more hand-holding!—and flies the Millennium Falcon. Just like that, Finn is forced to abandon those quaint traditional gender-role ideas that were programmed into him since birth by the dictatorial First Order (if only Earth could adapt as quickly)," Sperling (2016) smirks. Rey and Finn respect each other as partners and potential love interests with neither of them weakened or objectified because of it.

They all escape in the wrecked Millennium Falcon and meet up with Han and Chewie. As two gangs of pirates attack, Rey successfully fixes the ship and uses the precision of slamming pressure doors to save Finn from a slavering space monster. The middle-grade novelization *Rey's Story* by Elizabeth Schaefer (2016) humanizes the character even more by putting all the film's events in her point of view. She's heroic even when scared: "Rey gave herself exactly ten seconds to panic. Finn was gone, and the ship was crawling with thugs who wanted to capture her and rathtars who wanted to eat her. But she had to keep her cool. Finn needed her" (2016, 81). Back on Jakku, this novelization gives her hobbies and more emotions for a better-rounded character: she enjoys sandsledding since "it was practical—and a whole lot of fun" (2016, 9). Other scavengers give her friends and conversation. She also has action-packed simulator flights and scavenges data chips of heroic stories of other planets. Using all these, she teaches herself to fly and do repairs, as well as learning about the larger galaxy.

Impressed by her myriad of skills, Han soon offers her a job. While many watching suspected Han knows who she is—his niece or daughter perhaps—and thus wants to help her, *Last Jedi* rewrites the story to have him simply impressed by her competence and cleverness. This once again stresses that she's earning her place through hard work not privilege of birth. As they disembark on Maz Kanata's planet of Takodana, Han offers her a blaster. "I can handle myself," Rey objects.

He responds, "I know. That's why I'm giving it to you," as he chooses to encourage her. This film shows him as her buddy and mentor, a father figure with no sexual tension. He also avoids the competitiveness he had with Luke ("Don't get cocky!") to respect Rey and help her forward.

Maz Kanata, the wise older woman and a voice for diversity as a female equivalent to Yoda, also mentors her. She encourages Rey to become a Jedi on a level with Luke and Anakin and adds, "The Force, it's calling to you. Just let it in."

Exploring, Rey follows her senses to Maz's basement. There, she has visions of Luke and Obi-Wan welcoming her as Obi-Wan says, "You've taken your first steps." All encourage her to be part of the new franchise and own her power. Clearly, the white male old guard are passing on the torch. In the classic refusal of the call, she thinks in the middle-grade novelization, "She was just a scavenger from Jakku, not a conduit for some mystical life force. She wasn't ready to be more. Not yet" (Schaefer 2016, 102).

The book shares her admiration at Maz's planet with more trees than she's ever seen. There's also her joy as she resolves to remember its beauty forever. Everything, from the aliens to the food at Maz's palace delights her and fills her with wonder. She isn't just doing her job, she's reveling in the opportunity, as another metaphor for a young woman offered the chance to become a film's action star and central hero. Rey, the icon for a new generation, echoes the most idealistic of the Millennials. Though she doesn't understand the Force, she's determined to become part of it, along with the fight of legendary heroes Luke and Han. She believes the Resistance, using the same techniques as the previous generation's Rebellion, can succeed. She's only slowly discovering how to find her own way to fight.

With Maz's help, Rey has a distinct character arc as she accepts her destiny and moves forward (in the most Bechdel-friendly scene of the film):

REY: I have to get back to Jakku.

MAZ: Han told me. (takes her hands) Dear child, I see your eyes—you already know the truth. Whomever you are waiting for on Jakku, they're never coming back.

Rey cries.

MAZ: But there's someone who still could.

REY: Luke.

MAZ: The belonging you seek is not behind you, it is ahead. I am no Jedi, but I know the Force. It moves through and surrounds every living thing. Close your eyes, feel it. The light. It's always been there. It will guide you. The saber—take it.

Rey accepts the lightsaber and with it, the *Star Wars* legacy. Doing so of course means doing it for all the little girls watching: "Ridley's Rey became the first major female character to wield a lightsaber in the series, a coup for any little girl who wanted to pretend to be a Jedi along with her brothers" (Dockterman 2017b, 37).

The First Order attack, and General Leia arrives, leading the Resistance fighters in saving them all. In the chaos, Han's evil son Kylo Ren takes Rey captive. He carries her off and locks her up to interrogate her while Finn insists that he and Han must find a way to rescue her (albeit one that will stop the First Order as well). At this point, it appears the plot will be conventionally gendered, like the original film. "You know I can do whatever I want," Kylo Ren taunts a strapped-down Rey, with an innuendo many interpreted as disturbingly sexual.

However, using the self-sufficiency that's defined her entire life, Rey saves herself. First, she pushes Ren out of her mind, reading his in turn despite her lack of training. "You're afraid. That you will never be as strong as Darth Vader," she decides, seeing him as a posturing man-child, not a supervillain. Echoing Jabba with Leia, he's looming over her in a massive base he controls, but as with Jabba, Rey discovers her enemy only plays at being powerful. Like the blustering patriarchy, he's all façade.

In his youth and anger, he symbolizes alt-right nihilism personified. Like one of the Gamergate set, he tries to block the young woman from sharing in the power that he assumed was his by birth. Masked and safely anonymous, Kylo Ren strikes out against innocents who have never harmed him. He's angry at the Boomer parents who put their causes above him (the novel *Bloodline* shows Leia in politics and Han devoted to racing, leaving him to study with Luke). Guided by the genocidal monster of Snoke, who seems attractive because of his opposition to Ren's stodgy family's goals, Kylo Ren embraces his teachings as Millennial rage incarnate.

> Now, in early 21st century America, the villain is an unstable young white man who had every privilege in life yet feels like the world has wronged him. Unbeknownst to his family, he finds and communicates with a faraway mentor who radicalizes him with a horrific, authoritarian ideology. By the time his family finds out, it's too late, and now this unstable young white man has this horrific ideology, access to far too many weapons, and the desperate desire to demolish anything that he perceives as a threat—or is told to perceive as a threat. (Hillman 2017)

He even digs up the remains of Vader, somewhat like a few of today's youth with the Nazi flag, vowing to revive the war the Baby Boomers thought they had won. In Vader's name, he becomes a mass murderer and bombs the galaxy's capitol. "Kylo (né Ben) is so full of rage and abandonment issues that he's completely unable to control himself and chooses to kill indiscriminately rather than face his parents" (Fletcher). Damien Walter of *The Independent* (2018) explains, "Were Kylo Ren real and alive today, you strongly suspect he would be one of those enraged, hysterical followers of Jordan Peterson's morose YouTube ramblings about reclaiming masculinity in the alt-right." Ironically, Ren longs for Rey but repulses her with his beliefs. She, by contrast, fights for love and tolerance. The allegory of modern youth is clear.

They represent two different approaches to the disparities and hopelessness of the post–2000s, with its swelling financial inequality and uncertainty. Many of the young American audience, knowing Social Security housing and jobs were vanishing, that they would inherit a dying environment and ballooning national debt, could see themselves in Rey's determination to fix the galaxy the previous generation had left so damaged or Ren's desire to blame everyone and burn it down. They have different visions of the previous generation's flaws. The junior novel of *Last Jedi* presents their contrast: "He too had tried to erase his past, reinventing himself in the mold of his grandfather. The difference was that he had lost hope in his parents, while she had kept in hers, however false, alive" (Kogge 2018, 161).

Left alone with a guard, Rey escapes—hilariously using the "force trick" to make him free her. She sneaks through the base and "begins climbing to comparative safety, because she's spent her entire life climbing in and out of abandoned starships to scavenge and feed herself. She wasn't raised in a loving foster family like Luke, or by the Jedi order, like Anakin" (Schnelbach 2017). She goes from self-raised heroine to self-rescuing one. When Finn and Han arrive, Han must undercut their own heroism by pointing out Rey is already scaling the walls, perfectly prepared to save herself. Of course, their charging in isn't a waste, since it emphasizes their love and acceptance and offers her emotional resolution. The middle-grade novelization explains, "Rey felt ears pricking at the corners of her eyes. After all those years, someone had finally returned for her" (Schaefer 2016, 119).

As they all escape, however, Han confronts his son, who murders him. Rey watches in horror as, her kindly mentor, the tough, blustering cocky hero of the past franchise, falls. It is Rey who will need to step up as central hero now.

In the forest, Finn and Kylo Ren duel with lightsabers. However, Finn does not have the Force and quickly crumples. On fiery Mustafar, Anakin and Obi-Wan battled over Padmé's unconscious body in a painful dynamic. Reversing the cringeworthy scene, now Finn is the limp damsel and Rey the active hero. Once again, the macho age has ended. In fact, as Ren blusters how the legacy (and thus presumably the franchise) should be his, Rey summons the saber to her hand, emphasizing that she, not Anakin's grandson, is the true Skywalker heir. She and Kylo duel, but he's clearly intrigued by her. In villain fashion, he offers, "You need a teacher. I can show you the ways of the Force."

> It's Kylo Ren who discovers how powerful she is, that she is his superior both mentally and physically, and it scares him. (She's also much less prone to fits of rage, which has its benefits.) In Ren's last-ditch effort to lure her to the dark side, we feel his desperation at being outmatched. Their final battle, in the snow, is all about good and evil. It's never about physical strength, and it's never about gender. Did anyone in the audience doubt for a second that she could defeat him? That she wasn't capable? Now that's radical. (Sperling 2016)

She saves Finn and herself, defeating Ren long enough to escape with Chewie in the Falcon. While Finn lies helplessly recovering (playing the Sleeping Beauty role and leaving romantic and plot agency to Rey), she bids him a touching goodbye as she leaves to find Luke Skywalker, completing one of the main plots of the film.

In a delightful bridge between old trilogy and new, Leia hugs Rey, metaphorically welcoming her to the franchise. "It's Leia who welcomes her into the Resistance with an embrace. . . . In this moment, as the two fall into each other and hold each other up, Rey becomes part of the circle of women who have kept the Rebellion, and then the Resistance, going," Schnelbach (2017) explains. Thus encouraged, Rey flies off with Chewie—this original era hero defers to her, copiloting to her destination on her chosen mission. R2-D2, Luke's tool and sidekick as much as his lightsaber, appears to be Rey's now as well. Off they fly to Ahch-To, where, in an epic moment, Rey goes to Luke and offers him his old lightsaber. It will be a long two-year cliffhanger.

ONLINE ACTIVISM AND BACKLASH

Twenty-first century feminism focuses less on generational conflict and more on the political and social inequalities that remain even after a century of activism. The internet has made it ever more global. Women of this era insist they can fight for rights on their own without men to represent them. In this model, Rey rejects Han's protection and defends an unconscious Finn. Unlike Leia, she never needs saving. A young woman from Jakku rising to power echoes women from distant countries like Malala Yousafzai becoming advocates for women's education. Critic Nicole Sperling writes, "Played by 23-year-old newcomer Daisy Ridley, Rey is many things: a survivor, a scavenger, an isolated figure searching for community, a pilot, a mechanic, a warrior . . . and a girl. Her femininity isn't a weakness, and it isn't a strength. In fact, it isn't a thing at all. Not only is that remarkable for a female movie character, it's revolutionary."

In the era of Katniss, Tris, and other female superheroes—with the long-anticipated Wonder Woman on the horizon—filmgoers were treated to a new kind of *Star Wars* as Rey took center stage. From the first trailers, it was clear this film would break boundaries. Modestly-dressed but completely competent, Rey heralded a new, fourth-wave kind of heroine, seen in the many appearing beside her in *Black Panther*, *Mad Max: Fury Road*, *Ghostbusters*, *Old Man Logan*, *Doctor Who*, *Star Trek: Discovery*, *Frozen*, *Moana*, *Supergirl*, *Marvel's Jessica Jones*, *The Handmaid's Tale*, and more.

With each strong, diverse woman comes a new era of expectations and standards by which empowerment can be judged. "Audience expectations had changed: parents now demand diverse heroes for their kids and global box-office success can make or break a movie" (Dockterman 2017a, 38). Women fill the internet, automatically applying lenses of representation, gaze, and empowerment to the new female characters and holding their creators responsible as never before. Alison Dahl Crossley (2017) explains in *Finding Feminism: Millennial Activists and the Unfinished Gender Revolution*:

> Gender inequality and public discourse about feminism and inequality have come to the forefront of mainstream news outlets. On any given day a reader may come across a number of articles in the mainstream press about gender issues or sexism. The *New York Times*, not known to be a feminist news outlet, has had a swell of coverage about gender inequality; In its "Economics" section, a headline reads, "A Possible Path to Closing the Pay Gap," and in its weekly "Your Money" section, "Moving Past Gender Barriers to Negotiate a Raise." On the west coast, the *Los Angeles Times* has featured articles about gender in Hollywood, such as "Battlestar Galactica: Moore, McDonnell Talk Sci-Fi Gender Equality." Books instructing women on how to rise above gender bias and embrace feminism have proliferated—including *Lean In, Lean In for Graduates, What Works for Women at Work,* and *Wonder Woman.* (1?)

"What's most striking about this new wave, however, is how predominantly cultural the concerns are: how issues of representation of women or the lack of representation of women or the grossly distorted representation of women have taken top billing, with violence against women coming a close, and connected, second" (Benn 2013, 223–24). Admittedly, as filmmakers respond to public outcry, sometimes they make heartening, beautiful stories, and sometimes they include just enough seconds of female-female conversation to pass the Bechdel test, though not to empower anyone. A few of the films have fallen flat, though many are well-written and well-received.

Still, it's clear filmmakers have reached a new era. Feminism online "reconfigures elements of traditional feminist modes such as self-help and consciousness-raising groups" (Crossley 2017, 127). Communities form as participants discuss and repost articles that intrigue them. Today this can be accomplished without face-to-face encounters, for people living far from likeminded activists. People discuss common issues in their own lives and thus discover all they have in common and ways to support each other through difficulties. So much consciousness-raising spills over into intersectionality—the way minority groups share the same concerns and should support each other in the struggle. Plenty of moments in *Force Awakens* speak to this audience: "When Finn grasps a lightsaber, it's a cue to anyone in the audience who feels like an outsider in the culture—the power of adventure lives within you too" (Keegan 2015).

While *Empire* cast the well-known Billy Dee Williams, the character was problematically selfish and also rather stereotyped as a riverboat gambler. Cast alongside him were token Black characters—mostly name-less starfighter pilots who died in the final battle. The prequels, while more diverse, offered the problematically stereotyped Jar-Jar Binks and pseudo-Asian caricatures of the Galactic Trade Federation. By contrast, Finn and Poe stand out as admirable, relatable heroes who happen to be nonwhite. In *The Last Jedi*, they're joined by Rose, the franchise's first big-screen Asian-American female. Jyn's team in *Rogue One* also offers a di-verse, likeable spectrum. Representation for women merges with repre-sentation for people of color (and perhaps other representations as fans wondered about the gender-orientation of all the stars after various am-biguous hints). This is one of the hallmarks of fourth wave—the realiza-tion that everyone must be included—whatever their gender, race, relig-ion, orientation, or trans status. "Because online feminism remains, for the most part, unanalyzed, there is a perception that feminist organizing may not be happening on the web. The widespread belief that young women are disinterested in feminism is driven by the lack of understand-ing of the changes in feminist tactics. This phenomenon was featured in an online article: 'Young Feminists to Older Feminists: If You Can't Find Us, It's Because We're Online'" (Crossley 2017, 122). The movement is larger than ever. Still, feminism is regarded by many as a problematic term—to young women, it conjures the militant angry imagery of the seventies. To trans women and women of color, it can suggest a callous interest in only white wealthy cis hetero women's goals.

> Some people who wish to ride this new fourth wave have trouble with the word "feminism," not just because of its older connotations of radi-calism, but because the word feels like it is underpinned by assump-tions of a gender binary and an exclusionary subtext: "for women only." Many fourth wavers who are completely on-board with the movement's tenants find the term "feminism" sticking in their craws and worry that it is hard to get their message out with a label that raises hackles for a broader audience. Yet the word is winning the day. The generation now coming of age sees that we face serious problems be-cause of the way society genders and is gendered, and we need a strong "in-your-face" word to combat those problems. Feminism no longer just refers to the struggles of women; it is a clarion call for gender equity. (Rampton 2015)

Of course, eras of extreme progressiveness are met with inevitable "backlash"—"an attempt to retract the handful of small and hard-won victories that the feminist movement did manage to win for women" (Faludi 1991, 12). Critic Susan Faludi suggests that once feminism has reached a certain strength, achieving social and political progress, there is inevitably a pushback of angry people wanting to remove those rights, as with post-feminism in the eighties. Certainly, Rey's era also unveiled a clear gang of Gamergate misogynists determined to keep women creators out of online gaming and film, who threaten rape and murder, or plunge the reviewer scores on films like *Ghostbusters* before they even arrive. However, the new internet era is allowing a different pattern to emerge beside it: "Alternative to a model suggested by Faludi in which a wave of feminism is quickly followed by restrictive legislative change and counter-activism, the Internet allows for simultaneity of activism and backlash," notes Prudence Chamberlain in her essay on the fourth wave (2016, 462).

As *The Force Awakens* was announced, several internet campaigns emphasized the power of social media to influence films. In this year of incredible diversity in film and television (with Obama the first Black U.S. president) the hashtag #BoycottStarWarsVII shot to the top of Twitter's trending topics after the first teaser trailer for the blockbuster sequel featured Boyega as the Black Stormtrooper and first actor to appear on-screen. This was perpetuated by "a handful—as in, fewer than a dozen—of people creating their own echo chamber of racial discontent" (Koski 2015). As *Vox Magazine* adds, the cry for #BoycottStarWarsVII was led by people offended "that *The Force Awakens'* cast features not one, but *multiple* people of color, a situation a small but vocal minority sees as evidence of a 'white genocide' in the *Star Wars* universe, perpetuated by Abrams, a white-hating Hollywood Jew. Yes, it's ridiculous and disgusting on many, *many* levels" (Koski 2015).

Anti-strong heroine posts and racist posts dovetailed, as both protested so-called "PC culture." As Kayleigh Donaldson of *Syfy* (2018) explains: "Suddenly, the fandom is bigger than ever and full of people who care about things like representation, but they weren't there when those 'true' fans were, which means they don't belong. They have to be 'shown their place' in the pecking order, be they naïve young fans or the actresses getting the attention on screen." She continues:

> That seems to scare this toxic subset of fandom the most: the idea that the thing they ardently believe makes them special is actually something everyone possesses, including young women, people of color, LGBTQ+ fans, and so on. In reality, *Star Wars* was always for everyone, but now online fandom and wider media coverage means those poisonous fans can't ignore that, even before the films stopped exclusively positioning white men as heroes. Rather than share it, these fans seem dead set on destroying the thing they claim to love so much. That's not the mindset of a fan. That's just garden-variety bullying.

The racist campaign was met with some support but plenty of incredulous responses. Abrams said, "I think the people who are complaining about that probably have bigger problems than there's a Black Stormtrooper." Boyega's response was a dignified but forthright Instagram message: "Get used to it" (Dowd 2015). "It was unnecessary," he says of the negativity. "I'm in the movie, what are you going to do about it? You either enjoy it or you don't. I'm not saying get used to the future, but what is already happening. People of color and women are increasingly being shown on-screen. For things to be whitewashed just doesn't make sense" (Dowd 2015).

Many responders pointed out that the complainers were mirroring the Fascist Empire, rather than the multiracial Resistance battling for freedom from oppression. In a bizarre twist, a new trend started with some protestors insisting they would watch the film but identify with and root for the Empire and New Order. Perhaps by coincidence in the Gamergate era, perhaps not, J.J. Abrams' new villain was an angry privileged white twenty-year-old who saw his power lessened by others' diversity and freedom.

The feminist sites pushed back. "Women of color, young women, and others who are marginalized from the mainstream have found blogs and social media to be an effective platform for feminist communication, community, and mobilization" (Crossley 2017, 12). In the fourth-wave era, inclusivity has become a core part of the feminist agenda with feminists now giving serious attention to the discourse of privilege. "The phrase 'check your privilege' was born on the internet, and young activists who grew up communicating via internet chat rooms appear to have considerably less trouble with the phrase than older feminists" (Munro 2013, 25). "*Star Wars* feels different and shouldn't change" was no longer an acceptable complaint.

Still, besides anger and backlash, the internet also revealed its potential to increase diversity: Early photos were released, announcing stars John Boyega, Daisy Ridley, Adam Driver, Oscar Isaac, Andy Serkis, Domhnall Gleeson, and Max von Sydow joining the original stars of the saga, Harrison Ford, Carrie Fisher, Mark Hamill, Anthony Daniels, Peter Mayhew, and Kenny Baker. With Rey the only female in the new cast, fans began protesting the "one woman in the galaxy" approach seen in the previous two eras. The angry article "Hey *Star Wars*—Where the Hell Are the Women?" blasted it: "There is only one new female character being added to what is arguably the world's most beloved mythic series. It's as if 51 percent of the population cried out in pain and was suddenly silenced." Critic Annalee Newitz (2014) writes of her seven-year-old niece who enjoys princesses but likes other role models too:

> Surely in the second decade of the twenty-first century, she'd be given more awesome female characters to choose from in this contemporary incarnation of *Star Wars*. Leia would still be there, as the fighting princess—but maybe there would be a female fighter pilot whose swagger could rival Han Solo's or a female Sith strutting through some scenery-chewing lines. Nope. There's one female name other than Carrie Fisher's on that cast list: the relative unknown Daisy Ridley, whom fans are speculating might play the daughter of Han Solo and Princess Leia. Of course, more cast members will be announced, but this is probably our core cast—the main characters.

As she worries, "When *Star Wars* cannot offer us anything remotely like a diverse cast of characters, at a time in history when we know better, it's not just a bad casting decision in a Hollywood office. It's a move that will absolutely shape how children think about themselves." She points out how girls are taught to give way and support men, and adults believe the world cannot change. As the article was massively reposted, many raised a fuss. J.J. Abrams hurriedly responded that the casting wasn't over and that he would add one more "substantial" female role. Maz Kanata and Captain Phasma were cast, with the latter specifically gender-flipped and the former possibly as well. Likewise, a striking number of women appeared in bit parts, including Carrie Fisher's daughter. By the time the film hit theaters, audiences were well satisfied with a new era of female representation.

Likewise, while the Han/Lando ship was speculated on by fans since *Empire Strikes Back,* it gained far more attention as fans saw the trailers of *Solo.* "People have been shipping Han/Lando and Han/Luke since the 1980s, and the subtext has always been there," geek culture reporter Gavia Baker-Whitelaw told *Vox.* "The main difference is that now, queer representation is part of the public conversation," adds critic Aja Romano (2018). Spurred by the massive speculation online, both Lando's actor Danny Glover and the scriptwriters emphasized they were open to the possibility. Of course, the new internet fandom, coinciding with the prequel era, had already brought in plenty of shipping. Romano explains:

> The internet wasn't just crucial to popularizing queer shipping and bringing fanfiction beyond Lucasfilm's control; it also allowed a different part of *Star Wars* fandom to flourish, which was arguably crucial for the modern-day reappraisal of Lando as a character. Though Lando is certainly getting attention now with Solo, this level of discourse around his sexuality, as well as other characters like the popular Poe/Finn ship, is new.

While early *Star Wars* and Disney spokespeople condemned fanfiction, especially the type that added new relationships or non-family-friendly content, they're recently softening on its attitude toward fan works. "And the critical and progressive impulses of transformative fandom frequently drive the public conversation today in ways that would have been unheard of 15 years ago." The internet allowed transformative fandom culture to spread and even become mainstream. "The general spread of broadband internet helped increase the number of voices in the fandom and the number of people paying attention to queering the canon—which ultimately led to a fandom-wide reevaluation of Lando." (Romano 2018). The internet's validation of alternate lifestyles is one effect; another is including more people in the conversation.

Beyond the issues themselves, the fans' willingness to speak up highlights the new era. "The escalation of individual incidents online demonstrates how women are becoming less forgiving and more public about the treatment they receive. Now that women can call sexism into account, document it through photographs and mount defenses that gain wide support, initiatives by individual women are being effected through the Internet" (Chamberlain 462). Women repost insults, allowing hundreds or thousands of colleagues to respond and shame racist and misogynist comments. The internet allows a new degree of discourse, admittedly for rudeness and threats, but also for self-empowerment. "What is certain is that the internet has created a 'call-out' culture, in which sexism or misogyny can be 'called out' and challenged. This culture is indicative of the continuing influence of the third wave, with its focus on micropolitics and challenging sexism and misogyny" (Munro 2013, 23). Certainly, there are insults and even death threats hurled. Whether people are changing their minds is arguable. Still, many realize their favorite franchises or their word choices contain bias they hadn't noticed. Understanding and expanding one's viewpoint all starts with conversations.

There are also new possibilities for feminist community online: "Technology, such as Twitter and Facebook, has changed the ways in which feminists can communicate with one another. Both social media websites allow for activism to be organized rapidly and efficiently without feminists being required to occupy the same physical space as one another" (Chamberlain 2016, 462). "Vivid examples of strong online feminist communities abound, running the gamut from feminist blogs to multinational feminist organizations circulating feminist news. They suggest that Internet activity significantly upheld women's feminist communities" (Crossley 2017, 122). Feminist blogs help individuals, whatever their background or economic status, educate others about feminist movements and events, creating diverse communities of like-minded thinkers as well as the curious. Links are posted and reposted, spreading trending ideas. Blogs foster far larger online feminist communities than those offline, since they can reach across vast distances in moments.

> Students reported that they managed their feminist organizations' Facebook pages and disseminated news articles, feminist blog posts, and relevant current events to their membership and friends of the organization. On a site in which individuals have hundreds, even thousands of friends, it is an effective means of communication. In this respect, it is a particularly useful tool for feminist campaigns whose goals are to educate and spread awareness. (Crossley 2017, 124)

Even for young fans, the internet allows new levels of getting heard: When the toys were released, eight-year-old Annie Rose wrote to Hasbro, inquiring why there was no Rey figure in her Force Awakens Monopoly set (which instead contained Luke Skywalker, Darth Vader, Finn, and Kylo Ren). Her mother Carrie Goldman posted the poignant handwritten letter on Twitter in January 2016. As it said, "Without her THERE IS NO

FORCE AWAKENS! It awakens in her! And without her, the bad guys would have won! Besides, boys and girls need to see that women can be as strong as men! Girls matter!" (Smith 2017). An online outcry erupted with the hashtag #WheresRey. "Labeling *Star Wars* a male-based franchise is an error, given the important female audience it has had since its early days. Even if one is set on considering *Star Wars* mainly for boys, erasing girl products from its lines is a peculiar and damaging idea, for interesting female characters are also pivotal in all media consumed by boys" (Guyot 2015, 16). Online campaigns demanded Rey action figures that actually showed her face and inclusion in other toys and marketing. This expanded to other characters as fans complained of little merchandise from Marvel superheroines Gamora and Black Widow, while Harley Quinn was painfully underdressed in hers.

This is exactly the sort of movement the internet era is facilitating, and manufacturers are struggling to catch up with the speed and volume at which masses of people repost these protests. "The Internet pushes feminism in new directions. It speeds up the processes of organizing and network building, creates and nourishes communities across geographic divides, and introduces new tactics and strategies. However, because online feminism is less visible than offline feminism, this type of mobilization has been undervalued" (Crossley 2017, 127).

"We love the passion fans have for Rey and are happy to announce that we will be making a running change to include her in the Monopoly: *Star Wars* game available later this year," a representative told the *Associated Press*. In fact, Hasbro made the piece but didn't release the new version in the United States "due to insufficient interest." Apparently, people who bought the all-male game could request a Rey from customer service (Smith 2017). However, marketing for *Last Jedi* included prominent mockups of Rey at Target, including new action figures with her clear face and new costume. Maz and General Leia have joined her in the toy aisle. Clearly, even if the Monopoly set wasn't fully repaired, the advertising division learned from their mistakes.

After a year of Rey's iconic costume and hair knots (both pleasantly easy for girls in tank tops and capris to emulate), it became clear how popular the character was among female cosplayers. "I think that's my favorite part," says Ridley of meeting young girls dressed as Rey. "It's amazing to be able to embody someone people look up to. I feel now more of a sense of responsibility. It still surprises me, but oh my God, it's so cute" (*People* 2017). Clearly, representation had found a home.

While critics almost universally enjoyed *Last Jedi*, leaving it with a 93 percent on *Rotten Tomatoes* and an 86 on *Metacritic*, some viewers began a campaign to destroy it (Jasper). An alt-right group named Down With Disney's Treatment of Franchises and its Fanboys flooded *Rotten Tomatoes*, bringing its score down to a 54 percent user score from over 132,000 reviews. One updated Rose's page on the Wookieepedia with racist slurs.

A moderator for the alt-right group said, "Did you not see everything that came out of *Ghostbusters*? That is why. I'm sick and tired of men being portrayed as idiots. There was a time we ruled society and I want to see that again. That is why I voted for Donald Trump" (Sharf 2017b). The moderator explained that the group was upset with *Star Wars* for "introducing more female characters into the franchise's universe" and that Poe Dameron (Oscar Isaac) had become a "victim of the anti-man-splaining movement" and that characters like Poe and Luke Skywalker were in danger of being "turned gay" (Sharf 2017b).

> In a fit of anger over the movie, more than 10,000 people have signed a *Change.org* petition urging Disney to remove *The Last Jedi* from official *Star Wars* canon. "Episode VIII was a travesty," reads the petition. "It completely destroyed the legacy of Luke Skywalker and the Jedi. It destroyed the very reasons most of us, as fans, liked *Star Wars*. This can be fixed. Just as you wiped out 30 years of stories, we ask you to wipe out one more, the *Last Jedi*. Remove it from canon, push back Episode IX and re-make Episode VIII properly to redeem Luke Skywalker's legacy, integrity, and character." (Jasper 2017)

Reasons for signing included "I am 42 yrs old this is not the *Star Wars* I have grown up watching!" and "All I got in this was a lesson in politics. No plot and no emotion, except anger, lots and lots of anger." Some signed the petition without seeing the film. As *The Mary Sue* concludes, "This is precisely the sort of nonsense that epitomizes toxic fandom. There are, obviously, plenty of legitimate criticisms and questions to lob at *The Last Jedi,* but this sort of overreaction and hyperbole, with its emphasis on the past and rage against change, isn't the way to go" (Jasper 2017). As *Vox* concludes, "The saying "don't feed the trolls" was coined roughly five minutes after the internet was invented, but there's a reason it continues to come up, time and again . . . #BoycottStarWarsVII has truly accomplished is giving them a nice, hearty meal. Rather than heaping more scorn on their plates, consider reporting them to Twitter, blocking them, or forgetting they ever existed" (Koski 2015).

In 2018, Kelly Marie Tran, who played Rose, suddenly deleted all her Instagram posts after months of sexist and racist harassment online. Daisy Ridley deleted her own account in 2016 after facing criticism for her appearance and her stance on gun control. In an interview with *Glamour,* Ridley said: "I posted a thing about gun regulations, because I was at an event in tribute to the Orlando shooting at Pulse. People weren't nice about how I looked. And I was like, 'I'm out.' Simple as that. That is not what I signed up for" (Clark). Beyond criticizing her politics, they stretched to her appearance, while Tran is harassed not for playing a part that she obviously didn't write but simply for being Asian. When the official *Star Wars* Twitter tweeted a "Happy Birthday" wish to Lucasfilm president Kathleen Kennedy, some fans piled on attacks in replies. The sequel era was becoming a dark time for actresses. As Donaldson (2018) comments:

> The more this attitude is fostered, the more it is allowed to grow and become irrevocably empowered, particularly in online communities where harassment and abuse is euphemized as "trolling." We're now at the stage where fans sending vile abuse via social media is not only expected but quietly excused as "just what happens." The more this behavior is normalized, the harder it becomes to tackle. *The Last Jedi* haters position what they do as "critique," but there's a world of difference between reviewing a film and running an actress off Instagram because you didn't like her character. Anyone who can't or won't tell the difference is part of the problem.

Donaldson concludes that this behavior keeps reappearing online, over the Hugos, *Ghostbusters,* Gamergate, and any other attempts at diversity that anger online fans. She adds, "We have seen what happens when these supposed minorities of the fan communities, ones dominated by angry white men, decide to launch concerted harassment campaigns against those with apparent 'political agendas' that they accuse of 'ruining their childhood.' We saw what happened when the extended public humiliation of a woman by her ex-boyfriend became a platform to attack women and minorities in the video game industry." As she insists, corporations and fans must stop normalizing it, but instead calling it out as bullying, not overeager fandom. It's not love of their childhood heroes but "the obsessive screed of toxic white masculinity under the guise of a hobby."

REY AS MARY SUE

The catch in making a character so powerful arrives in the flip side — making her so mighty that she's unbelievable and worse, unrelatable. As critics well versed in the female terminology and tropes examined *The Force Awakens*, one thread gained traction. Critics noticed how easily Rey grew in the Force, suffering less than Luke and gaining powers in one film that took him three (or more) to master. These critics began using the term "Mary Sue," an internet term meaning a wish-fulfillment character, who, as the writer's stand-in, can accomplish anything and is basically perfect. Rey even seems a fan brought to life, especially as she gushes over Han Solo and recalls his exploits. She keeps a Rebel fighter pilot doll in her AT-AT home, signaling to viewers that she's one of them, lucky enough to be added to the franchise.

The problem is how perfect she is at everything: scavenging, rappelling and climbing, shooting, flying, operating and repairing ancient ships. She lives alone on Jakku from age *five* to nineteen with no companions, helpers, or even decent food and protection and she manages quite capably. She speaks all the alien and droid languages she encounters. If anyone attacks her, she successfully fights him off with her staff. On the Falcon, after repairing it perfectly, she releases monsters to kill bad guys. With this, she saves Finn, Han, and Chewie from death, repairs the Millennium Falcon, again, and whisks them all away. Though she isn't seen learning the sword or lightsaber forms, she beats the formally trained Kylo Ren at lightsaber and Force combat.

She needn't deal with consequences or failure, as she never makes a bad decision and never has serious negative repercussions from her decisions: she saves BB-8, steals the Millennium Falcon, and follows a strange calling into Maz's cellar. Each time she wins the encounter and gains new friends to boot. When she's captured by the more powerful Kylo Ren, she escapes unscathed and then battles him a second time. She's never injured. Certainly, Rey's training is raw, from her wonky flying to lack of understanding of the Force. Still, the complaint was how easy she had it. Critic Tasha Robinson notes that Rey is "a fantasy wish-fulfillment character with outsized skills, an inhuman reaction time, and a clever answer to every question—but so are the other major *Star Wars* heroes" (Howard 2015). Certainly, though Luke takes time to master the Force, he similarly uses it to escape tricky situations. Using it, he outpilots everyone else. However, he does not excel at reading people or speaking alien languages. He's a bumbling, emotional teen who loses everything in *Empire* through his own reckless choices.

Another token of the Mary Sue is how beloved she is by the established characters—once again, every fan's dream. Leia and Han treat her as an adopted daughter, and Chewie ends the film as her new co-pilot and subordinate, visually transferring decades of loyalty from his old friend to this chance-met girl. R2-D2 does the same. Finn immediately falls in love with her. Luke appears to have awaited her all these years so he can train her, and even a vision of Obi-Wan speaks to her. Unkar Plutt cajoles and bribes her, while Kylo Ren is fascinated by her.

Of course, this level of skill appears among other characters in fantasy. Critic Tasha Robinson (2015) compares Rey with James Bond, Legolas, Batman and other mighty male characters, pointing out that fans give them a pass because they're so fun to watch. She adds, "Instead of being concerned about whether her Mary Sue flawlessness is a problem, why not, just this once, enjoy it for what it is?" As she continues: "When we question a female character's coolness and competency, we're giving into that embarrassing tendency to second-guess and undermine ourselves. The impulse to judge Rey comes from the same place as the societally trained impulse to say: 'Am I being unfeminine by being too loud? Too confident? Too present? Too assertive? Should I tone it down? Do I deserve to be heard?'" She continues:

It takes more than one kind of character to make a world, and joyously proficient lady badasses are just as important to a diverse, rich, fulfilling cultural landscape as troubled, complicated lady heroes. And there's something deeply suspicious about the early stirrings, on Reddit and 4Chan and especially all over Twitter, about how Rey is just too damn effective and nifty to be acceptable. She's a fantasy wish-fulfillment character with outsized skills, an inhuman reaction time, and a clever answer to every question—but so are the other major *Star Wars* heroes. Are they all getting the same level of suspicion and dismissal?

Daisy Ridley too resisted this classification, saying, "I don't buy the Mary Sue thing anyway. I find the term sexist in itself, because it's Mary Sue. I don't think there's a thing called Ryan . . . Craig . . ." Indeed, the term "Mary Sue" (invented before its counterpart Larry Stu) is sexist because it's a shorthand that skips a nuanced discussion and assumes a female character shouldn't be ridiculously overpowered like Superman. Ridley goes on to say, "When I was doing it . . . playing her, I never felt sure of what was going on. It wasn't like *This is happening, and I'm so powerful, and look at me go*. And essentially, all I found Rey was trying to do in the first one, was she was trying to do the right thing . . . It's not a sort of self-centered power that she's exhibiting. She didn't ask for anything in the first one. She wasn't asking to go on this adventure" (Jusino 2017). Critics are divided on whether she's too perfect, or just perfect enough. The delightful part is having a strong enough character to bring up the question.

"THIS IS NOT GOING TO GO THE WAY YOU THINK": REY MEETS LUKE

Having joined the Resistance and become their hero, Rey withdraws from civilization, retreating, as Luke did in *Empire,* to a distant planet to train with a hermit mentor. On the remote island where she meets Luke Skywalker, she can "ask some questions and sort of get in touch with how she's feeling," says Ridley. "Everything's been other people asking her to do stuff, and it's been up to her to get to grips with what she wants" (*People* 2017).

The Last Jedi picks up where the previous episode ended with Rey meeting the legendary Jedi on a deserted island—but the introduction doesn't quite go as planned. "She's greeted not so warmly by Luke. There's obviously a little bit of work to be done for an unexpected visitor to be [encroaching] on someone's private space," says Ridley (*People* 2017). Luke rebuffs her, starting by tossing his long-lost lightsaber away, and then by hiding in his hut and ignoring her as he does chores around the island. Rian Johnson, the writer-director, explains, "Luke's slamming a door in her face seemed like the most obvious thing in the world . . .

there are folks in your life that you expect to fulfill a certain thing, and as we grow up, we realize that that doesn't always happen" (Johnson 2018c). Still, she persists (a tagline for a woman challenging the patriarchy that gained extra meaning in 2017).

At last, he agrees . . . but only to teach her why the Jedi "must end." As the middle film commences, Rey is more flawed and less in control. Fans can take amusement in her lack of knowledge about the Force as she trains with Luke—she defines it as "a power that Jedi have that lets them control people and . . . make things float" only to be the target of Luke's sarcastic "Impressive. Every word in that sentence was wrong." It's a funny scene, as he encourages her to reach out, and when she holds out her hand in literal fashion, he tickles it with a blade of grass and laughs at her. At the same time, Rey is over-serious, and insists over and over she needs the great Jedi Master to train her. She's seen practicing skillfully on a cliff, with her staff then the lightsaber, but much of her Mary Sue vibe from the first film has lessened. Still, one dramatic scene, repeated for a year in the trailer, had her splitting the ground and sending pebbles bouncing. Luke says in response, "I've seen this raw strength only once before. It didn't scare me enough then. It does now." Of course, this is untrained power, nothing she's earned but something that suddenly appears in her. Being the Chosen One emphasizes powers as a result of luck or fate, not the hard study that impressionable audiences can emulate. Luke pushes her to look deeper and understand the spirituality of their world, not just the special effects:

LUKE: What do you see?

REY: The island. Life. Death and decay, that feeds new life. Warmth. Cold. Peace. Violence.

LUKE: And between it all?

REY: Balance and energy. A force.

LUKE: And inside you?

REY: Inside me, that same force.

While he insists he wants the Jedi to end, Luke also teaches her that the Force and Force wielders will continue without Jedi training. It's an important lesson echoed in the film's final scene with a young stablehand calling a broom to himself. Through the course of the story, Rey seems to accept that she can wield the Force without thousands of years of patriarchal teachings. This works as a metaphor for old attitudes toward women, minorities, LGBT, traditional governments, corporate power, and more—it's time to evolve. In fact, Yoda supports this belief, burning down the Jedi library with, as Luke assumes, the last collection of ancient teachings within it. In fact, Rey has cleverly absconded with them, choosing to keep the Jedi lore but learn from it in her own way. The books appear at film's end, glimpsed in the Falcon's locker. In the novelization, the collection calls to Rey: "It felt like a promise, one made long ago and now ready to be fulfilled" (Fry 2018, 91). While Luke, keeper of the wisdom, hasn't even read them, Rey is eager to adapt them for her era.

All this works as a metaphor for reviving *Star Wars* for a new generation, keeping many of the powers and tropes but reenvisioning them for a new more multicultural audience, referencing the canon of *Star Wars* but not slavishly following every aspect. More interestingly, it's a metaphor for shaking off the patriarchy, as Rey learns to be a hero *not* by following the traditions of the old masters, training in their fighting styles and passing their tests, but by trusting her own instincts and finding the power within herself. At this, Yoda is knowingly amused, Luke is shaken but finally supportive, and Kylo Ren and Snoke want to tame her and coax her into serving them.

They are the ugly force of the patriarchy—Snoke belittles Kylo Ren after their fight on Starkiller Base, taunting him for being bested by "a girl who had never held a lightsaber." As they conquer the galaxy, crushing the ragtag Resistance with its female leaders, the film begins with Poe mocking Hux, deliberately mispronouncing his name in a broad frequency address to both fleets and hinting at his illegitimacy. The force of elderly male leadership crumbles during the film: Ackbar is killed. Snoke is bisected at his moment of triumph.

Revealing the backbiting that accompanies their classic hierarchy, Snoke verbally cuts down Kylo, smirking, "You are no Vader. You are just a child in a mask." It turns out he orchestrates Rey's next challenge, forging a link between her and Kylo Ren so the pair can communicate across space. Johnson explains, "I wanted to delve more into that relationship. I couldn't see how to get them together." As he adds, "I thought, what if a new kind of connection opens between them." He describes framing it as "painfully intimate just like you're sitting across from someone and talking" rather than drowned out by special effects (Johnson 2018b). When it begins, Rey pulls a blaster and shoots Kylo— fully prepared to hate him. However, the helmetless young man proves surprisingly vulnerable. As he spins the true story of Luke trying to murder him in his sleep, Rey begins to sympathize with the flawed character so reflective of herself. He is the victim of the patriarchal system as much as she is.

In this private space, Rey also finds herself drawn to Kylo personally. He is the one objectified in the film, shown shirtless, while Rey is always fully dressed. Thus, she is presented with more leverage. "Women have usually been featured as desired rather than desiring" (Andermahr et al. 1997, 45). Anakin's pursuit of a reluctant, sexily-dressed Padmé, and

Luke and Han's competition over Leia emphasize this point. Whatever Ren may feel for her, Rey is presented as the one with the power to choose. The same is true for Finn, whom Rey abandons in a comatose state in *The Force Awakens*, and then chooses to rejoin at the end of *The Last Jedi*.

"It's only when they touch that see what kind of could be," Daisy Ridley says. "And through that they build this kind of incredible intimacy. Luke should be the one nurturing Rey and it's actually Kylo that is" (Johnson 2018c). Johnson explains the necessity to write "the transition of Kylo from someone who killed Han Solo . . . how to transition him slowly from there to here in a way that was plausible through Rey's eyes, the notion that Rey sees this opportunity in him." (Johnson 2018b). Further, Luke and Ren both need Rey to guide them, a role she chooses to accept. Both are caught in a web of responsibility and failure. Mark Hamil says, "My character always represented hope and optimism, and now here I am, very pessimistic and disillusioned, and sort of demoralized" (Johnson 2018c). In this film, male characters from Poe to Kylo to Hux to even Luke are ruled by emotion: "Luke is a guilty, angry recluse who initially won't help Rey or the Resistance and who almost decided to kill his own nephew based on his sense that he might turn evil, thereby setting into motion a chain of events which result in Han's death and the creation of the franchise's most complex and dangerous baddie ever" (Fletcher).

> For Luke, this means running away to a remote island and abandoning his family, religion, and cause because he cannot face his failure. For Kylo Ren, this means trying to take over an entire galaxy (as you do) because he cannot deal with Luke's betrayal or the murder of his father. He cannot face the things he has done. While Luke is having trouble forgiving himself for his perceived part in Ben Solo's turning, a form of ego itself, Kylo Ren is unable to take even the smallest amount of accountability for murdering his classmates, his father, and much of the galaxy. (Burt 2017b)

As Kayti Burt continues in "Toxic Masculinity Is the True Villain of *Star Wars: The Last Jedi*" (2017b), Kylo Ren may be laughable with his tantrums and parental hang-ups, but after the last film's violence, he can't be dismissed. "He is scary because he reminds us of the real-world men whose anger and frustration and sadness have curdled into something ugly inside of them, causing them to lash out at those they perceive to have robbed them of what they deserve." Even as Leia and Holdo teach Poe how to listen, Rey tries to connect with the child Luke has abandoned, as she forces Luke to take back his responsibilities.

Kylo tells Rey, "Let the past die. Kill it, if you have to. That's the only way to become what you are meant to be." He has a valid point. Feminism has a history of opposition to patriarchal religions. The Jedi system—which includes women at all levels but only male standout leaders in the films—thus becomes synonymous with the old, corrupt ways—everything Rey as the new Chosen One will move beyond.

While Luke never appeared tempted by the Dark Side, Rey's story is more complex: as Kylo Ren tearfully pleas for understanding and love, she stops to consider. Johnson explains his desire to "reveal Kylo's vulnerability through Rey's eyes so we had to follow her on that journey" (Johnson 2018b). Of course, her willingness to see the best in others may be her undoing. Rey's internal struggle over where her path will lead is a rare storyline for a female character, but she accepts the darkness at the heart of the island, acknowledging its right to exist as much as the light. Since the dark forest or cave in folklore symbolizes the unconscious but also the buried feminine aspect, this is a worthy part of her heritage. Luke refuses to teach her but Kylo Ren offers, so Rey momentarily considers getting trained. Now it's time for new storytellers. While Luke in Episode V enters the cave with lightsaber drawn and battles the darkness he finds there, Rey simply asks for answers and receives them.

She chooses from among her options and follows the dark Force she feels deep within the planet. It guides her through a pool to a cave of mirrors. There, she reflects over and over, emphasizing the many possibilities she could become, as well as her persona, or surface appearance. "Mirror imagery, in particular, is employed to signify the cultural construction of femininity" (Andermahr et al. 1997, 57). Is she to become Luke's ideal, Kylo's ideal, the Force's, or her own? When she asks to see her parents, the reflection that appears is herself—she need not conform with the expectations or legacy of some supposed ancestor. Instead, she is encouraged to choose. "Rey discovers her parents literally sold her out—but doesn't let her issues affect her behaviour. She refuses to give up on Luke (until she has to), refuses to give up on Ben (until she has to) and maintains her own sense of honour and morality in the face of serious adversity. She makes Kylo look like the big, petulant child he is" (Fletcher). Johnson explains:

> It's all about finding herself . . . for me, this represents adolescence . . .
> the hero's journey is not about becoming a hero . . . if you're really look
> at it, I think it's about the journey from childhood to adulthood. It's
> about adolescence. It's about finding your place in the world, about
> finding who you are. You have these powers in you, and who's gonna
> find you the right way to use them, and that's really Rey's journey in all
> this." (Johnson 2018b)

For the first time, the films abandon the Skywalker bloodline—Rey is the central hero but not the royal child brought up in secret like Luke and Leia or the Force-created child of prophecy like Anakin. For the first time in the films, the Force could belong to anyone.

Of course, this rite of passage prepares the heroine for a darker one—journeying as Luke once did, into the Belly of the Beast—the dark lord's stronghold. To Luke's disappointment, the newly mature Rey chooses to save Kylo. Johnson explains, "There is some kind of primal connection between Kylo and Rey. It has to do with the fact that even though they're on opposite poles . . . the fact that they're both the only ones that have this power in the movie—and they're on opposite islands, they have this connection between them." (Johnson 2018b).

In a desperate act, Rey climbs into a coffinlike escape pod, desperately clutching her lightsaber. Her last thoughts are of Finn, as she sends him a special message through Chewie. The pod opens to Kylo Ren arresting her, handcuffing her, and taking her before Snoke. On the way, she reasons with Kylo as Luke did with Vader, with the good Jedi certain of the evil one's hidden goodness. However, he insists she must serve beside him, and he brings her to his master, Snoke on his imposing throne. "He might as well be asking her to join the patriarchy each time he tries to lure her to the dark side" (Watercutter 2017).

Snoke's gigantic size in the previous film and while berating Hux on his own bridge are all illusion—the real figure wears what appears to be a bathrobe and slippers and is heavily scarred. "Snoke's physical skills may have faded, but his Force-aided abilities to persuade, manipulate, and perceive are tremendous," explains the *Visual Dictionary* (Hidalgo 2017, 35). The novelization emphasizes his weakness even further, adding, "Snoke himself was almost slouching—indolent in his golden robes, secure in the safety of his sanctum" (Fry 2018, 204). "I love the fact that he's not just in dark evil robes but he's got a bit of flare to him," Johnson says (Johnson 2018b). Still, he is like the voice of weakness and self-doubt from within. He has no power aside from what Rey is fooled into giving him.

As Luke did, Rey takes a swing at the Dark Lord, representing all the evil in the universe, as well as the patriarchy in its power. Fascinatingly, she attacks with Kylo Ren's lightsaber, emphasizing how she's delving into the dark side, trying it on like a costume to see if it fits her. Snoke has confiscated her own, which sits impotently beside him. Before her horrified eyes, he begins destroying the fleeing Resistance fighters in their evacuation ships, much as Leia once watched Alderaan be destroyed, or Luke watched the destruction of the Rebel fleet. Snoke continues taunting Rey, swatting her with her own lightsaber, pinning her to the floor, and mocking her hope that Kylo Ren will take her side.

"Pathetic child. I cannot be betrayed, I cannot be beaten. I see his mind, I see his every intent. Yes. I see him turning the lightsaber to strike true. And now, foolish child. He ignites it and kills his true enemy!" At this moment, Ren activates Rey's lightsaber, and slips, for a moment, into the hero role. He destroys the dark lord, bisecting him with a simple, elegant thrust of the blue lightsaber in an example of toxic masculinity's hyper-competitiveness. When Snoke's Praetorian Guard turn on them both, Rey and Kylo Ren battle back to back, showing off their honed abilities. All the while, the First Order begins to fall apart. Their battle won, Ren reveals that he never intended to turn good, only take over his master's empire.

Ren then proposes Rey join him, that they rule the galaxy together (not as siblings or cousins as many had expected, or even explicitly love interests but simply as partners). It's unsurprising he would make such an offer—she has raw power, and as he noted in the previous film, she only needs training. In the Sith model, having murdered his master, he's prepared to take an apprentice in his universe-destroying hierarchy.

In his role as potential mentor and tempter, Kylo also finally reveals the truth of Rey's parentage. He reads her mind and shares the answer she was seeking. "Do you know the truth about your parents? Or have you always known? You've just hidden it away. . . . Say it." Of course, his phrasing here emphasizes that the answer exists within her—he provides nothing besides the question.

"They were nobody," Rey says, fighting back tears. She is not Luke's daughter, or Leia and Han's, or a rebel hero's or a Jedi's. Johnson remarks, "While Vader's revelation that he is Luke's father is the worst possible revelation for Luke, being told she's no one is likewise the most horrible, as a famous parent "would have shown her her place in the universe" (Johnson 2018a).

In the junior novel, Rey recalls her memory of someone promising he'd return for her, but it is not the voice of a parent. "The voice was her own. She had imagined that voice and repeated those words over and over as a child until they became part of her reality" (Kogge 2018, 159). Clearly, she is the original self-rescuer, one who has created solace and protective parents out of her own mind. The novel concludes, "Her whole life had been one giant lie of her own making, a castle of dreams and echoes that had no foundation" (Kogge 2018, 160).

"They were filthy junk traders," Kylo says. "Sold you off for drinking money. They're dead in a pauper's grave in the Jakku desert. You come from nothing. You're nothing. . . . But not to me." It's possible that he is lying, or mistaken, or fooled by someone like Maz or Yoda shielding Rey with a protective layer, as fans crowded the internet to suggest. The next film has the potential to undo this revelation with a greater one, even as *Return of the Jedi* gave Luke a sister to balance his evil father. "But for me, in that moment, Kylo believes it's the truth," director Rian Johnson added. "I don't think he's purely playing chess. I think that's what he saw when they touched fingers and that's what he believes. And when he tells her that in that moment, she believes it" (Breznican, 2017d). Johnson explains in the Blu-Ray specials, "You're wondering who you are? You have to find out who you are for yourself" (Johnson 2018c).

Of course, Rey is the child of no one important, yet her dazzling power, and likely her instinctive skill at using it, suggest the Force is using her to eradicate Kylo Ren and balance the Force back to neutrality.

Further, with no parental legacy to carry on, she can choose the path her future will take. There in the throne room, even with her great destiny taken from her, she chooses, rejecting Ren and battling him for control of her lightsaber. It, one more Skywalker inheritance, shatters, and she hurries off to rejoin the Resistance. Like Luke, she can construct her own in a great act of self-definition, now that she's forcibly lost the legacy of the other.

On the planet, she saves her friends in an epic moment by lifting the boulders trapping them. Reunited with Finn (who may be entering a complex love triangle with Rose!) she flies off to help the Resistance regroup. She has faced temptation from power and the dark side and decided who she is—the one who can save her people using the Force, but not the path of the hidebound Jedi.

ROSE, THE GLOBAL FEMINIST

Kelly Marie Tran posed as Rose on the front of *Vanity Fair* in May, becoming the first Asian-American woman to appear on the magazine's cover. In this moment, she struck a major blow for representation. "It's something that I think about a lot," Tran said. "I just remember growing up and not seeing anyone that looked like me in movies" (Flaherty 2017). She's also the first female main character of color anywhere in the franchise who appears as the human she is, not an alien. Upon her arrival, fans were delighted with her power and her personality. Caitlin Busch (2017) adds:

> Rose Tico is here to kick your ass with righteous determination burning in her eyes. Rose's entire story in *The Last Jedi* is defined entirely by her love for her sister and her desire to do the right thing. Not only does the film introduce Rose as a complicated character with an even more complicated backstory, it also endears audiences to her immediately. She's a spitfire, a stand-out hero with the kind of sacrificial storyline usually reserved for male characters.

As a heroine designed for a tougher era, Rose has bangs and cute curled midlength hair but minimal makeup. She wears stolen First Order officer boots, a masculine touch (Hidalgo 2017, 39). Between all this and the bulky olive jumpsuit she wears for the entire film, she's not sexualized, joining Rey and Jyn as modern heroines. Costume designer Michael Kaplan says, "When we were figuring out Rose's outfit, we didn't even know who the actress was. But we knew it was going to be a basic coverall. Rian wanted it to be pretty shapeless, something that a man or woman could wear. But it's in her character. She's not someone that has to look good for work. Rose is a no-nonsense character. She just plugs along and she's spunky. So it does work" (Szostak 2017, 112). By contrast, Finn is objectified in a pointed flip on traditional gender norms. He returns to the story goofily wandering about in a liquid bacta suit over his boxers as BB-8 spies him and comments on how "naked" he is. Poe stares, and the hero becomes even more objectified. While Kylo Ren also is seen coming out of the shower, *Last Jedi*'s heroines do nothing of the sort.

Objectifying the men instead of the women validates the female gaze, inviting the audience to picture themselves as the female action heroines sizing up the underdressed men. It's no longer true, *The Last Jedi* suggests, that men are central characters and women, objects of romance. Finn doesn't spend the entire film staring at Rose's rear end or have the audience do so through his eyes. Instead, they act as equals on a buddy adventure. This emphasizes that storytelling is universal and that the male perspective is not the only or default perspective. The female gaze is about presence, women telling their own stories about their feelings and thoughts, not about how sexy they look to others.

This isn't the only way this story revolutionizes gender tropes. Katherine Wright explains in *The New Heroines* that the twenty-first century sees a new kind of narrative: "The monomyth, the emphasis on 'mono' as the 'only, one, or single' myth, transforms into a collaborative process by a number of significant others linked together in their stories through the transmission of affect. New heroism, is, at its core, polymythic" (2016, 72). Rey arguably raises Finn and Older Luke to heroism, but not a community of young women (onscreen anyway). The one seen doing this is Rose Tico.

First, her sister Paige is introduced with an expression of shock as she's told "It's all up to you. Drop the payload, now!" With the sky exploding all around her, a harrowing sequence follows as she climbs through the bomber, falls, and cannot reach the detonator. In the junior novel, Paige thinks in a moment of love, "Rose would die if Paige didn't drop the bombs," (Kogge 2018, 17) while the adult one humanizes her with her desperate struggle. Flashes to Leia and the space battle emphasize how desperate her mission is. At last, she manages on her fourth try—clutching her crescent talisman all the while—to kick the release detonator to a place where she can catch it and release the bombs.

Epically, the ship explodes, and she can only grip her pendent and close her eyes. Before her death, this solitary hero has delivered the payload that destroys a dreadnaught and allows Leia to escape. The *Mary Sue*'s Laura Jernigan (2017) observes, "Paige Tico (Veronica Ngo), Rose's sister, is an unknown in her last moments as she deploys the bombs to destroy a Siege Dreadnought, and yet we watch her struggle, and we connect with her fight. In the first twenty minutes of a major franchise movie, an Asian woman is our hero, and though she dies, it's not so focus can shift to only white characters." Further, though she wears a little glamorous makeup, her olive flight suit and pilot's hood cover all. It's a very WWII outfit, casting her as a respected soldier.

Though dead onscreen, Paige has more to her story. She appears in a *Forces of Destiny* flashback comic and the teen novel *Cobalt Squadron* as well as a mock diary. Further, Rose keeps mentioning her during the film and thinking of her even more during the novelization. It explains, "After rarely spending more than a couple of days away from Paige, Rose was looking at the endless, yawning expanse of a lifetime without her. She had no idea how she was going to survive that—or if she even wanted to" (Fry 2018b, 95). Further, the bomber squadron commander gives Rose the Resistance ring in Paige's memory, and she uses it later to gain the stablehands' trust (Fry 2018b, 19). Paige's legacy thus saves the Resistance and recruits new members.

Finn and the audience meet Rose as she's crying over her sister's death—a human, sympathetic start but not the strongest for the character. It's a voyeuristic camera angle, very close on her face as she thinks she's alone and sobs in private. Finn spies on her too, as he hears her crying and cranes his head to see who's there. Though he's trying to sneak past her and steal an escape pod, not admire her, he still watches her as audience stand-in.

Despite her grief, Rose spies him and quickly takes charge of the scene. She recognizes Finn and gushes fangirlishly over the Republic's big famous hero. Johnson explains, "I rewrote it more to affect Kelly's spirit and her personality" (Johnson 2018b). In fact, her intrusive babble marks her as a particularly awkward devotee. While an expert on technology, "she is the first to admit that her people skills need work," as the *Visual Dictionary* notes (Hidalgo 2017, 38). He wishes her "May the Force be with you," and she gasps, "Wow" through her smiles and tears. He preens a little. In fact, Rose emotes so hard that he must remind her to breathe. Tran notes, "For Rose, when she meets Finn, he's a symbol for everything she's ever worked for. I imagine that Rose has had tough days and thought, 'Think of Finn and Rey who have done amazing things, and that's what we're fighting for'" (Bennett 2017, 37).

Her gushing also makes her a fannish stand-in like Rey, with whom audiences instantly begin to identify. Johnson calls her "Genuinely a nerd. Like someone I would've hung out with in high school. She felt like someone who didn't belong in the *Star Wars* universe, and that genuinely appealed to me" (Johnson 2018c). More, her wide eyes suggest she's objectifying *him*, even as Finn tries desperately to get away. This has her putting the heroic male on a pedestal, but realistically, she's a worker from behind the scenes whom the extended universe depicts as very shy. "When Rose first meets Finn, he is 'a big deal,'" Tran adds. Clearly his boast to Han Solo from the previous adventure has come true, as he always dreamed. By contrast, Rose has always been overlooked in comparison to her hotshot sister who fights on the front lines. Rose has never had to assert herself . . . until now.

With all this, Rose comes across as a combination of competent and goofy. To get her job, Rose had to "crawl from one end of a bomber to the other, identifying every part, from the active trackers to the ion thrusters, and telling . . . what might go wrong with each one and how to fix it," according to Rose's replica journal. (Fry 2018a). Her tech competency is unequaled onscreen. Still, her ramble about how excited she is to meet a real hero, in contrast with the three spineless deserters she's had to stop (as she wields a frightening stun weapon and waves it excitedly in Finn's face) is first intimidating and then humorous as it becomes clear she's worshipful enough not to have noticed that Finn is deserting too. However, she then spies Finn's packed bag. She protests in horror, "My sister just died protecting the fleet, and you were running away!" With a single authoritative zap of her stunner, Rose takes Finn down. She stands powerfully over him as he lies there protesting. With this, she discovers her hero is a flawed, ordinary person . . . much as the audience do over and over with this film. Once again, she stands in for their feelings.

At the same time, being reminded of his responsibilities forces Finn to reclaim his heroism. "When he meets her, Finn is trying to escape the whole war," Boyega says. "He's trying to leave, and she comes in and basically gives him a depiction of himself that wasn't necessarily true" (Breznican 2017d). Some fans even believe she's tricking him, pretending to admire him to guilt him into making the right choice. Either way, she doesn't let her esteem interfere with her job.

Showing off her strength and determination, Rose dumps him on a cart and proceeds to haul him to the brig. When he mentions (from the cart) that the First Order can now track them through lightspeed, she immediately starts calculating. Clearly, she's a technological genius the fleet is underusing by not giving her the latest intel. As related in the prequel novel *Cobalt Squadron*, Rose has already invented a power baffler that will stop them from showing up on a scan (Wein 2017, 4). After they use it on a mission, Vice Admiral Holdo orders that this substitute cloak be adopted throughout the fleet and invites Rose to join her crew, thus saving her life.

Bouncing ideas off each other, Rose and Finn simultaneously realize how they can disable the First Order's ability to track their ships through hyperspace. During the scene, she continues standing over him, subtly claiming the authority. This emphasizes that Rose has equal initiative and smarts as the established hero and sets them up to be partners with their complementary skills. Soon they're exchanging tech talk that goes over the flashier Poe's head. Rose also kindly covers for Finn, saying it was "just luck" they met. She's fully in control of the situation—in fact, when Finn stands in front of her, mansplaining, she calmly reclaims the conversation. Further, both agree that Poe's impulse to go shoot the First Order ship would be completely pointless, unraveling his classic gendered actions. In turn, Poe covers for Rose and Finn, helping them escape to recruit a codebreaker. Here, Rose's experience proves vital once again:

> Rose's shuttle is the modified control pod of a Resistance transport, which began life as a B-wing Mark II cockpit. Its small size and Rose's skill at keeping engine flux below sensor thresholds mean that Rose and Finn can depart the fleet without being detected. Though Rose doesn't consider herself a great pilot, she has much more experience behind the controls than Finn. (Hidalgo 2017, 39)

They spend the rest of the film as a team, with a romance beginning to spark. Beneath the surface, they share more: "There's a similarity between the two in terms of losing everything and not having a set home, but apart from that, they are literally opposites," Boyega says. "But they are stuck to each other" (Breznican 2017c). The story emphasizes how Finn used to clean the First Order's toilets while Rose still labors as a maintenance tech. They are the galaxy's "nobodies," but they maintain exceptional courage even when facing certain death. "Even though [Rose] is good at what she does, she's not known," Tran says. "She's this nobody, this background player, which is what makes her interesting. She's someone who is just like everyone else" (Breznican 2017d). Rose's job is one that generally goes unnoticed in the *Star Wars* universe—the flashy pilots like Luke, Anakin, and now Poe have always taken center stage. As with Finn in *Force Awakens*, this film promotes a member of support staff, one with no Force powers or special training but who has the marginalized perspective of growing up exploited by the First Order. Tran adds:

> For me, it's the idea of someone who comes from a humble background. In a lot of movies today, we see people who are royalty or have magical powers. But she's a background player. I love the idea of someone who isn't in the forefront of the action from the beginning. She's like a cog in the machine that keeps the Resistance going. But at some point, to have to face your fears and be pulled into a situation where you face any challenge, means so much to me. It's cool to be able to be someone who is special because she's like everyone else. (Bennett 2017, 37)

Finn, too, is no one special, one of the thousands of brainwashed young soldiers, yet one who breaks free and seeks to save the galaxy from the oppressors he once supported. Together, they offer a nonwhite team-up as the *Star Wars* newcomers—no one's heirs, no one's Chosen Ones or Force sensitives. They save the Republic on a deeper level by inspiring the next generation—an all-inclusive metaphor for the franchise itself.

In 2014, feminist compositionist Laura Micciche noted feminism's percolating fourth wave and its contrast with previous waves, stating that, along with the third wave it "increasingly addressed a much wider spectrum and entangled set of interests [that] emerge from the material, political, corporeal, and emotional effects of living in a globalized economy characterized by a spectacular disparity between wealthy and impoverished people, corporate interests and workers" (129). Melissa Benn's 2013 essay on the new era adds:

> Not all of the new feminism is concerned solely with issues of representation or sexualization. The campaigning group UK Feminista has taken up the cause of the living wage; young feminist journalists such as Laurie Penny have been vocal in support of Occupystyle critiques of capitalism; fourth-wave activist and writer Rhiannon Lucy Cosslett has written powerfully on class and care issues. Add to this the voice of young policy analysts, like Tess Lanning—formerly of IPPR, now working for Ed Miliband—who have written of the new settlement that is needed if we are to extend feminism to working-class women: a system of affordable childcare, more flexible working, greater domestic democracy and higher pay for so-called "women's work." (225)

Beyond their representation of a more multicultural America, Rose follows this fourth wave tradition and alerts Finn and the audience to the social injustice around them. Together the pair leave their distressed fleet and head to Canto Bight, "a *Star Wars* Monte Carlo-type environment, a little James Bond-ish, a little *To Catch a Thief*," as the director says (Kamp 2017). There, they reveal their different upbringings. The planet Cantonica is "located within the distant Corporate Sector of space—a fiefdom where corporate entities are given free rein to govern their own territory" (Hidalgo 2017, 9). On an artificial beach lies an opulent resort, "the playground for the galaxy's super rich, who have enough power and influence to remain untouched by the rapidly expanding war" (Hidalgo 2017, 9).

Rose tells a wide-eyed, naïve-looking Finn that the worst people in the galaxy congregate there. Flipping the similar line from the original film, however, they are not smugglers or criminals, but the elite of the galaxy, all dressed in high fashion. To Finn, they appear the successful pillars of society he's dreamed about from his utilitarian life. He exclaims that the casino looks wonderful. On a deeper level, he's admiring the world of the ultra-wealthy, one he never hopes to reach. He's given up on improving the unjust galaxy—his only recourse to defy the First Order, as seen in the previous film, is to flee. He still hasn't committed to the Resistance, though over and over, his love for his friends drives him to heroism. However, Rose reveals that under the sparkling surface, the wealthy are the monsters who destroyed her home planet with exploitative mining—weapons dealers who sell to both sides. She's the most self-aware of the young heroes, given perspective by her recent personal tragedy.

In Paige's replica journal, she details how their parents were killed by First Order, who invaded their planet of Hays Minor, and, digging for ore with no safety protocols, severely damaged it. This appears a nod to environmentalism as well as a blow to exploitation of third-world countries. After this, Paige continues, the arms dealers showed up to buy, continuing the degradation of the system and its people. One entire village was bombed into dust for refusing. At last, the sisters escaped and joined the Resistance together (Fry and Nouvel 2017). Delilah S. Dawson, writer of the first Rose and Paige *Forces of Destiny* comic, adds: "Rose and Paige are all about their bond with each other and their shared tragic history that propels them to heroism" (Baver 2018b).

In an America with an ever-growing gap between rich and poor, with an international audience who know all about American corporate greed, Rose's upbringing makes far too much sense. "The one-percenters on Canto Bight achieved their wealth by selling weapons to the First Order. They're war profiteers; their money is blood money. To Rose, and to those watching through her eyes, their way of life isn't beautiful, it's evil—and deserving of destruction," notes Ngela Watercutter (2017) in *"Star Wars: The Last Jedi* Will Bother Some People. Good." Rose protests in her replica journal, "I hated those arms dealers the moment I saw them. I still do. If General Organa would lend me an X-wing, I'd blast every one in the outer rim and the galaxy would be a better place" (Fry 2018a).

Further, the two heroes are not just minorities outside the system in the First Order's authoritarian galaxy—they're millennial-age, fighting the older, established 1 percent, whose opulent lifestyle and jingoism have destroyed the galaxy they're grown up in, creating a world of striking disparity. This reflects fearful millennials who can watch the wealthy but never join their ranks as the rich only get progressively richer. In a year in which the American rich were receiving enormous tax cuts at the expense of the poor, this criticism seems decidedly pointed. Watercutter (2017) adds, "Writer-director Rian Johnson's movie seems to be turning those covert ideas into overt messages—first by portraying a universe with a more inclusive cast of characters, and then by making them actually talk about what it means to 'resist' (aka be in the Resistance) and how to achieve those goals."

Over the decades, feminist critics have led colonial discourse. "Many feminist anthropologists . . . have highlighted the negative effects of imperialism, arguing that communal non-class societies in which women exercised considerable power and had access to resources in their own right were destroyed by colonial conquest" (Andermahr et al. 1997, 107). Rose is the voice of the conquered planets, exploited by the Empire and then the First Order for their resources and workers. "The political potential of the fourth wave centers around giving voice to those women still marginalized by the mainstream" (Munro 2013, 25). With this, she dictates morality for Finn, and in many ways for the show.

The actress also derives a great deal of meaning from Rose's background. Tran notes that because of her upbringing, Rose "has an interesting relationship with war"—a relationship Tran's family knows all too well. "I dug into that with my parents, and their relationship with war because of the Vietnam War," she said (Flaherty 2017). Tran is not only the child of immigrants but channeled their experience of growing up in poverty-struck, war-torn Vietnam. Her father grew up on the streets, something shining through the actress's performance as Rose reaches out to the abused stablechildren, marginalized on their own planet by the rich and powerful. "I could have had this life," Tran says, "and now I have *this* one, and it's purely because my parents dropped everything and moved to a country where they didn't know the language [and] didn't have any opportunities. I very much have felt this whole time that I've been living for multiple generations of life" (Flaherty 2017).

Rose's awakening Finn to social inequalities and inspiring him to fight is a traditional woman's role, but also a heroic one. On this mission, Rose is a respected partner for Finn—more worldly, creative, and capable than he is. As they search the casino (with BB-8 playing comic relief), their skills are more complementary than alike, shaking up the dynamic. Finn is impulsive; Rose is methodical. "That is Rose in a nutshell. She is such a problem solver," Tran says. "She thinks of things like an engineer or a mechanic, like, 'Everything is okay with the math'" (Breznican 2017c). Fourth wave films like *Wonder Woman* and *The Hunger Games* feature men who treat the heroine as an equal. They're respectful and, even when in love, don't leer or objectify. By assuming she's capable and giving her half (or more) of the task, by being willing to listen and learn, the man furthers her empowerment as well as their shared goal. These stories also provide a model for young viewers, showing them how to respect the opposite sex. All of this, Finn does.

Rose continues her adventures without once being sexualized. Costume designer Michael Kaplan says, "There was supposed to be a scene where Rose and Finn broke into a shop window when they got to Canto Bight. She put on a gown and he put on a futuristic tuxedo. So that was going to be a reveal for Rose, going from this frumpy-dumpy coverall to a beautiful gown, which never happened" (Szostak 2017, 129). Omitting this scene (in which Rose would have been dressed in something figure-hugging and gorgeous whereas Finn would get the comedy plot of donning his tuxedo backward) skips the traditionally gendered scene of most films. Even when tastefully and modestly presented, the gown reveal emphasizes the heroine's required role as an object of beauty and glamour. *Hunger Games* forces this on Katniss, and Wonder Woman gowns up for a disguise, but both subtly suggest even an action heroine must be admired for her looks. Rose, however, is a professional soldier, always in uniform like the men. In Finn's sloppy brown jacket and Rose's olive coverall, they stand out in the casino, emphasizing their opposition to the elite in their black and white instead of even tacitly pretending to join them.

However, among the rich, "there are unspoken rules and lines that should not be crossed" (Hidalgo, 2017, 56). In fact, both have broken one of the elite's unwritten laws—not the dress code but illegal parking. Promptly, Rose and Finn are locked in a jail cell under the casino. This moment again evokes millennials, lost in the shifting culture enough to be hurled into jail for something they assumed was no big deal. In the larger scheme of the Resistance survivors all being killed, parking seemed unimportant, but it's everything to the spoiled casino guests, as it mars their attractive beach.

In prison, they meet the amoral DJ (Benicio Del Toro), who frees them and assures them he's a codebreaker. DJ adds to idealistic Finn that moral absolutism is a joke. "It's all a machine, partner," he warns. "Live free, don't join." *The Atlantic*'s David Sims (2017) notes, "At the start of *The Last Jedi*, Finn might have believed that: He's still a runaway from the First Order trying to get as far away from the action as possible. By the end, he's committed to taking them down." It's Rose who defies this perspective and shows the audience what they're fighting for.

They head back to their ship, but Rose sees, once again, what Finn has missed. She is the one to go to the stablehand children tending the cruelly exploited racing fathiers and show them her ring. "We're with the Resistance," she says. As they gaze at her, the children's eyes light, and even the fathier perks up its head. All have been oppressed by the surly, warty alien groom. Despite this, the children tell stories and play with Jedi and Walker models they've made. They are the next generation, inspired as Rey and Rose were on the old stories.

> The gleeful alien gamblers and slavedrivers of the casino city aren't in stormtrooper outfits pointing guns at people, but the system under-writing them is, and by the end of the film, Finn understands why it's worth toppling. *Star Wars* has sometimes lacked this kind of world-building; in the original movies, viewers learned the Empire was ca-pable of evil acts like blowing up entire planets, but we didn't really see the wider impact of their tyranny. This kind of vagueness even led to some people defending the Empire as the true heroes of the saga. (Sims 2017)

Rose gains the children's help through empathy—she was once in their position and found the rebels a source of hope. This ties in with a major theme of the film—the Resistance as an inspiration that must rouse the ordinary people of the galaxy to its side. Rose best exemplifies this message by spreading it. As Sims concludes, this film truly makes the point the others haven't quite spelled out: "The First Order is evil, yes, but the Resistance isn't just good because they're against them; the rebels are also trying to create a better world, and to protect a cause the rest of the galaxy can rally to."

As they ride off on a fathier's back, Rose giggles, swept away on the pure joy of escape and the animals' newfound freedom, even as Finn protests, "Stop enjoying this!" The camera focuses on her happy face as she rides before Finn, taking charge yet again. As it alternates between her face and point of view, the film shares her fun. The novelization goes further as Rose invokes her sister: "Rose was laughing out loud now. How many times had she and Paige imagined themselves the heroes of adventures in which they rescued fathers from sleazy owners, guiding them to victory and watching their abusers laid low?" (Fry 2018b, 167). In fact, her ability to take joy in a moment of escape, even in such a dystopian universe, is another message of hope, for the audience as well as the characters. Rose can see the world's hidden evils, but also its unperceived delights.

Intersectionality is central to fourth wave. In this film, Rose's struggle with colonialism and her experiences from it dovetail with the Resistance goals. Before this, Luke, Anakin, and Rey—poor white kids from the backwater who nonetheless had supernatural gifts and mythic destinies—were central, supported by privileged senators like Padmé, Leia, and Mon Mothma who dictated the rebel agenda. Many of these characters end up being related to royalty if they aren't born to it. Such heroes, for instance, sympathize with Chewbacca's plight, but don't make his planet or even his opinions a high priority. The heroes work beside Bothans and Mon Calamari but sacrifice them without giving their characters a chance to develop. In a moment of necessity, Padmé teams up with the Gungans, but is not seen fighting for their specific interests afterward. Neither is Jar-Jar, whom she includes in her senatorial mission but abandons to promote the agenda she dictates for them all. The white woman gives him a voice by raising him to the level of Junior Representative, but no higher.

This time, Finn and Rose are left to their own quest, and they take full advantage. For Rose, freeing the fathiers for a few moments and spreading hope by revealing her identity outweighs even the search for a code-breaker to serve the larger plot. In the novelization, Rose rides "the herd's matriarch" and decides, "She loves wrecking this awful place as much as I do" in a moment of shared feminine rebellion (Fry 2018b, 167). As she smiles, letting her mount run off to join its fellows, she adds, "Now it's worth it." None of the other *Star Wars* heroes display such pure unrewarded compassion. The end of the film reveals that she's correct: only rousing the marginalized people of the galaxy can save their dying Resistance, which has lost so many of its elite.

Though she's a dreamer, her rough life has left her grounded in reality. DJ demands Rose's necklace, her only reminder of her lost parents and now deceased sister, as payment. Though Finn gallantly tries to intercede, practical Rose offers it up. There's a twist as DJ uses it for its conductive material and then hands it back, but a second twist as he betrays them both for a much more sizable reward than the Resistance could give him. With a parting shot that Finn may be right in who will win in the end but that it doesn't matter, he callously leaves them both to be executed and leaves the fleet vulnerable to destruction, ship by ship. This moment emphasizes the importance of morality—without a true desire to help the oppressed, ordinary citizens, even likeable underdogs, cannot be trusted. D.J. is no inherently ethical Han Solo or Lando Calrissian—he's more realistic. The Resistance must stop recruiting flashy, high-achieving heroes, but truly motivated street sweepers and stable-boys.

As is traditional, the hero samples life as one of the villains, symbolically absorbing their powers and toying with their perspective. Rose's stolen officer's uniform is more form-fitting than the jumpsuit but still quite modest. All of her is covered, from high neck to gloves. It's dark blue, a feminine color of wisdom. A large black blaster hangs at her side, while BB-8 humorously hides under an upended garbage bin. Rose feels ill-at-ease in the uniform but summons her courage. "Disguised as a major, Rose is not used to the pressed and tidy officer's uniform, preferring instead the far more comfortable baggy work coveralls of a Resistance technician. However, she plays the role well enough that a junior officer seeks her approval, little suspecting that Rose is not what she seems" (Hidalgo, 2017, 67).

In her brief appearance, Captain Phasma arranges a brutal public execution for the young heroes. However, Admiral Holdo's sacrifice blows up the deck moments before it's carried out. Finn wakes to strong, pragmatic Rose dragging him and insisting they get to a ship. Visually, he's being rescued by the feisty young woman, flipping him into the damsel role, as in *The Force Awakens*. After this, however, Finn gets his epic swordfight with Phasma, while Rose contributes little, returning her to conventionally gendering. Thus, Rose lacks a truly epic moment . . . at least, until they reach the planet.

After they arrive, dramatically crashing into the Resistance base under the lowering door, all available pilots fly at the First Order's approaching army, in a David-and-Goliath-style battle reminiscent of the Battle of Hoth in *Empire*. In the novelization, Poe specifically appoints Rose a pilot, pointing out that she "landed that shuttle with six TIES on your tail and a big damn door closing on top of you" (Fry 2018b, 275). Clearly, she's very skilled and just lacks confidence.

As the massive siege cannon prepares to destroy the last of the Resistance, Finn heroically aims his ship at it, sacrificing himself to bring it down. The audience prepares for the death of the hero in the classic pattern. However, Rose slams her own ship into his, diverting him and near-fatally injuring herself. As she lies close to death, Finn demands an explanation. "Why would you stop me?"

"I saved you, dummy. That's how we're gonna win. Not fighting what we hate—saving what we love." In her critically wounded state, Rose thus confesses her feelings for Finn and kisses him. She's the one to initiate their romance, after a film that has avoided tracing her body through Finn's eyes. In romance, as in the central message of discretion outweighing valor, Rose makes the choices for Finn. Certainly, her iconic line is an inspiring message, one that fits her role in the story—she stirs the wider universe and emphasizes the ordinary people the Resistance must save. Once again, the imagery reflects an America torn by prejudice and partisanship, in which many gloat about the other party's pain or support increased hardship for everyone if it takes down those on the opposite side. Rose thus comments directly on American politics as she encourages everyone to stop focusing on anger at the other and instead fight to preserve the best parts of their civilization. Rose describes herself in the replica journal as "Not happy in the traditional sense, because I was terrified every single second. But I finally knew what I was fighting for, and I believed in it with my whole heart" She puts aside revenge and explains, "Instead I was thinking about the lives we'd save by stopping [the First Order]" (Fry 2018a).

Rose's stopping Finn appears to have cost them the war. Finn's plan, though requiring his sacrifice, would have saved his friends in their base. In fact, with no one destroying the cannon, the First Order blasts the Resistance stronghold open and would kill them all if not for the deux-ex-machina appearance of Luke Skywalker. Logically speaking, Rose chooses badly. Despite this, it's a delightful human moment as Rose acts out of love and chooses to sacrifice for the personal, not the political. Having already lost her sister, Rose refuses to lose anyone else. She also, according to many viewers, strikes out against the trope that insists people of color must be sacrificed in films. Instead of obeying the Force, destiny, or orders, she transcends reason and chooses her own fate, more than most series characters manage.

At this point, having sacrificed herself, given the hero emotional turmoil and played her part, Rose succumbs to her wounds and leaves the story until the next episode, just as Finn the romantic interest did in *The Force Awakens*. It's a little too convenient, but her part isn't over. As Finn places her on the Falcon and tucks a blanket around her while a newly-returned Rey watches, a love triangle appears to be shaping. Inverting *Empire,* this one isn't two men (three with Lando's flirtations) squabbling over the only woman in the galaxy, but two self-actualized women deciding who will get the naïve, sheltered Finn, who may soon find himself in the role of prize.

The final scene of the movie, touted as central to *The Last Jedi*'s message, has one of the young stablehands (played by Temirlan Blaev and named Temiri Blagg in the novelization) wielding his broom like a lightsaber, and calling it to his hand with the Force. He then caresses a ring with the Resistance logo and looks to the sky longingly. Arguably he may be seeing Holdo's explosion there, a strike of light against the darkness. The galaxy is filled with heroes who will soon step up and join the cause, the film explains. This was the moment missing from *Wonder Woman*, showing the hero empowering the next generation, raising the under-privileged to fight beside her.

Before this, young heroes in the *Star Wars* universe had to be found and selected by the Jedi Order (who gave them aptitude tests and some-times rejected unconventional or hard-to-teach ones as shown with Ana-kin). Those who were deemed unworthy generally received no training and their potential went unrealized. In this post-Jedi world, however, children can conceivably rise without the establishment's approval.

Modern giftedness aids in maintaining inequality—if only one hero-ine is the Chosen One with divine abilities, the others are left unexcep-tional, as she cannot share her innate privilege. Her friends have no ex-pectation of being equal to Superman or Wonder Woman and must be content as Lois or Jimmy. This trope appears in fiction to mask social and racial inequalities, excusing why the upper class white person is most often chosen. Similarly, in real life, "Notions of giftedness are tied into exclusionary ideologies that use genetic intelligence to mask social and racial inequalities" (Wright 2016, 44). While Leia (with Force abilities in *Last Jedi* never before seen) exemplifies this exceptionalism, as does Rey, Rose emphasizes (as do Finn and the heroes of *Rogue One*) that those who aren't "chosen" can still save the galaxy. "Instead of self-making, the core of new heroism is community building through collaboration and net-working" (Wright 2016, 72). As Donaldson (2018) adds, this is the mes-sage young fans need:

> *Star Wars* is not what it used to be, and that's a good thing. In the 21st century, under new management and appealing to wider and more diverse audiences, the franchise has to evolve. Its casting and creative ensembles must reflect our world, not just because it's the right thing to do but because it's good for art and business alike. A whole new gener-ation of fans will get to experience these stories for the first time, to find heroes they never thought they could have before.

Thus, Rose's arc offers a new kind of universe welcoming a new kind of hero. Even her name is symbolically suggestive: "Prequel trilogy char-acter Padmé is derived from a Buddhist word for lotus, a flower that represents divine beauty and purity. The rose is a symbol of balance, a word that keeps coming up as a talking point about character journeys in *The Last Jedi*" (Barr 2017). Even as the most common flower, Rose can join with others and save them all.

It's particularly 2017-appropriate that the Asian woman, an outsider to the Skywalker legacy (as Finn and Rey are revealed to be) is not only accepted as part of the team but inducts new members—the underprivileged children from a foreign world who don't even speak English. The *Mary Sue*'s Laura Jernigan (2017) explains, "The story of the rebellion is being heralded by a young Black child—and if that didn't strike a chord with you, you haven't been paying attention to the world recently . . . There is hope for the future, and that hope comes in the form of people who are too often forgotten." That one of these children is shown wielding the Force and creating the next generation of heroes emphasizes a welcome to immigrants and those who look different. As Melissa Hillman (2017) concludes in her expressive "'This is not going to go the way you think': *The Last Jedi* Is as Subversive as AF and I Am Here for It":

> *The Last Jedi* has a clear message: The nearly all-white, overwhelmingly male, privilege-based way of thinking that celebrates war culture and toxic masculinity and that created the First Order has to go, both in the larger world and as it's internalized in our hearts and minds, and in its place will be something entirely new, created by diverse young people who are walking away from war culture, walking away from toxic masculinity, walking away from systems of privilege.
> So everyone can hope.

PHASMA'S CHROME CONCEALMENT

The chrometrooper Captain Phasma trains the teenage recruits of the New Order. As her prequel novel reveals, "She turns them into monsters like her . . . killers without conscience" (Dawson 2017, 316). She is remarkable as she gives the hero Finn a female mentor. She's also rare among the Stormtroopers—not just for her 6'3" height and distinctive chrome armor but because she's a woman at all.

One striking aspect of her character is that her gender doesn't matter. As fans went on Twitter to complain that she should have female-shaped armor (presumably aping the gold bikini or sword and sorcery ensembles like in *Red Sonja*) the creators quickly shut them down. The official *Star Wars* account responded back: "It's armor. On a woman. It doesn't have to look feminine." Likewise, critics refuted this on social media, pointing out that there was no practical reason beyond objectifying women for such a thing. "It felt to me that here was a character where we would respond to her due to her actions and what she represented rather than a more conventional delineated flesh outline," her actress Gwendoline Christie says. "That felt really really oppressive to me. I'm very proud to play this part. We're a long way from the old bikini" (Grossman 2017, 61).

Christie adds, "I like playing characters that challenge the way we have conventionally looked at women" (*People* 2015b). Since screenwriter Lawrence Kasdan confirmed that Phasma was originally intended to be a man, this character certainly qualifies (as does her warrior woman character Brienne on *Game of Thrones*). Christie's casting of course emphasized her nonconventional gender and powerful knighthood from *Thrones,* in which she's almost the only female character never sexualized.

Further, the fully armored "chrometrooper" also never removes her helmet, much like Boba Fett in the original trilogy. This emphasizes coolness and mystery. Her actress even comments, "She is a Boba Fett-style character, striking and in command . . . Other than that, all I can say is that she is badass" (*People*. 2015b). She plays the character with this aloof mystery, careful to remain distant from her charges. Of course, this leaves the audience distanced too. "What feels so modern about Captain Phasma is that we are used to forming our immediate relationships with female characters, conventionally, due to the way they are made flesh," Christie adds. She finds the audience's relationship with her character far more "modern" since they must "respond to her through her character and her actions" (Lussier 2015).

She has a small presence outside the films. In a Poe Dameron comic, Phasma condemns one of her most valuable agents for a small error and decides, "The First Order took a risk with you. The gamble did not pay off, and so now you will serve us in another way, in chains." However, she does offer mercy of a sort, beyond not killing him, when she adds, "You may request one more audience with me, Terex. Make it count" (Soule and Unzueta 2017). She shows that she does not wish to throw away an asset in a fit of anger, though failure is met with punishment.

The sequel era, and particularly *The Force Awakens,* filled the galaxy with many female characters across the film. Thus it emphasized characters' options in an egalitarian world—to be the heroes or to be villains (previous to this, no female villains had appeared in the live films. Moreover, Asajj Ventress, a wicked Force user in the *Clone Wars* film and show, was depicted in skimpy clothing.) In the *Phasma* prequel novel, a childhood companion of the heroine recalls "being pleased that among the First Order, women were considered equals and warriors. Her mother had told her stories, you see, of a different world in which women were considered somehow weaker or lesser" (Dawson 2017, 113). Certainly, the novel and trilogy strike a blow for gender equality.

The novel follows the dark heroine through her younger years—as a warrior of a primitive tribe on a dying planet. When a few First Order soldiers, led by Hux's father, crash-land, she reveals she is willing to betray her brother, friends, team, and everyone she knows so that Hux will take her off planet and make her a soldier. From the first, she makes it clear she wants to conquer the neighboring tribes rather than forge a peace with them. Surviving is central to her makeup. (This suggests why in *The Force Awakens* she lowers the shield when threatened by her blustering student, an old man, and a Wookie.) As she abandons weaker alliances for stronger ones, General Hux sees how useful she could be to the First Order. "Within the First Order, she is used as a symbol of what the regime can offer—she was a native of a primitive world that was 'tamed' and 'civilized' with modern methods and technology. But behind that artificial polish, her treachery and craven selfishness are the true reflection of the First Order principles" (Hidalgo 2017, 68).

Some aspects of her planet foreshadow her future, like her skill with traditional melee weapons. Generations back, her people were factory workers, betrayed and abandoned by the corporation that brought them. Now the desert has grown destructive enough that her people wear masks almost constantly. Meanwhile, the prequel characters' only possibility of survival comes from harvesting vital minerals from the dead and anointing themselves with this "oracle salve" for protection from the sun and for vital nutrients. This chemical practice well reflects Phasma's ruthlessness. She insists, "Death is inevitable, but it means the rest of the tribe will be stronger" (Dawson 2017, 99).

The novel finally reveals that as a young teen, she betrayed her parents, letting them die so she could find herself stronger allies from the first. She also murders Brendol Hux, once she's learned all she can from him. She is embarrassed about her savage past and longs to put it behind herself. As the novel's narrator adds, "Brendol was the last person who knew about her humble beginnings. The last one who knew her history. Brendol watched her betray her leader, fight her people, murder her own brother in cold blood. Brendol was the only witness to her crimes, the only witness in the entire galaxy who knew that she wasn't the perfect soldier poster child" (Dawson 2017, 296).

When the Order no longer serves her needs, she will betray them too. "Phasma's ultimate loyalty is to her own survival, an ethos that has kept her alive and secured her elevated position as captain of the guard, overall commander of the First Order's Stormtrooper forces" (Hidalgo 2017, 68). Though the film reveals little of her motivations, in the novel she is wholly selfish, in contrast with the boys' club of junior Hux, Snoke, and Kylo Ren, who all dream of ruling the galaxy. This removes her from the hierarchical structure, poising her as a potential knife in their backs, not an adoring follower or obedient soldier.

At the novel's end, Phasma returns to her home planet, and from the remains of Palpatine's favorite chrome-colored shuttle, once owned by General Hux, she constructs the chrome armor. She will continue their murderous legacy.

> Just as she had constructed this shining suit, the first of its kind in the First Order . . . she had also constructed a completely new Phasma. She spoke the updated Basic of the First Order fluently, her accent just as clipped and polished as Brendol Hux's. She fought better than any other stormtrooper . . . And she took her orders directly from the general and no other, a position she'd reached in less than a year. In part by getting rid of anyone who stood in her way, of course. But that was something she'd learned on this very planet. Kill or be killed. So she killed. And still she rose. (Dawson 2017, 377–78)

Writer Delilah S. Dawson comments, "Phasma is all about sacrificing anyone and anything to stay alive and get ahead" (Baver 2018b). This becomes her most fundamental motivation. Still, the longer backstory is quite foreign to the characters and events of them film: only Phasma's murder of Hux's father has the potential to affect the onscreen characters—and it doesn't.

Her other extended universe arc comes in *Captain Phasma* (2017), a four-issue miniseries comic written by Kelly Thompson and drawn by Marco Checetto, as part of *Journey to Star Wars: The Last Jedi*. This one bridges the events of the two films as it shows Phasma escaping the trash compactor and then finally rejoining the fleet. "Phasma used an anti-armor acidic compound to dissolve the door at the Starkiller trash compactor into which she was dumped," as the visual guide relates (Hidalgo 2017, 69). The comic begins with Phasma fleeing the exploding Starkiller base, pursuing a suspect whom she insists destroyed it. In fact, Lt. Sol Rivas actually has stolen evidence that Phasma was the one to lower the shield. Consequently, Captain Phasma sets out to frame and silence him before he can inform the First Order command of her treachery. The entire comic is dictated by her, giving a window into her dark mind-set.

On her adventure, she takes the time to corrupt the society where Rivas lands, encouraging them to take up their long-forgotten technology and become warriors again (even as she makes numerous references to her own warlike upbringing and has a brief flashback of those she betrayed). She teaches a little girl about the lost technology and mentors her. However, as she tells the admiring female pilot who accompanied her, "I need an army to get through there. They're nothing more than cannon fodder." Clearly, her guidance is completely heartless—an issue that hints at Finn's upbringing. Phasma ends the comic by executing Rivas, abandoning the locals to their losing battle, destroying the Imperial BB droid who may have witnessed her actions, and shooting her pilot protégé for good measure. As Phasma notes, "I'm a survivor. No matter what the cost. Today the cost is loose ends." Her savagery toward those who trust her emphasizes her role as treacherous mother and betrayer of the innocent—a common role for evil women in fantasy.

Kaila Hale-Stern of *The Mary Sue* (2017) writes that a full comic arc and backstory novel are unusual for a such a minor character, presenting a jarring clash: "This is a vaunted treatment that almost none of the new trilogy's characters have received—not Rey, not Finn, not Poe, not Kylo Ren, not Hux. It seems as though the creatives at Disney/Lucasfilm were interested in cashing in on Phasma's fan favorite status and her ability to move product and merchandise but did not view these offerings as any reason to actually include her in the film in a significant fashion." The history between Phasma and Finn—the most logical backstory to present—remains unexplored as does any onscreen sense of personality.

In *The Last Jedi,* Phasma appears when Finn and Rose are captured onboard the enemy ship but has a very small antagonist arc. "So good to have you back," she coos. Still, she manages to get plenty of venom in the short line. Christie explains, "She has been humiliated by someone who was her subordinate and has gone rogue, and someone who is at liberty and is a free spirit and has chosen another path. So, yeah, she's annoyed" (Truitt 2017). She savagely orders Finn and Rose's public executions. "That Finn, the most famous First Order turncoat in its brief history, sees through her façade angers Phasma no end" (Hidalgo 2017, 68). However, once again, there is no trace of the personal in their dialogue—no weakness either knows of the other, though Phasma presumably raised Finn. She is basically just a First Order representative.

When the Admiral destroys the fleet, Finn seizes his chance to duel his evil foster mother who trained him to kill the innocent. She burns with "a malevolence coming from deep within her that seems to have no real logic attached to it," as Christie puts it (Truitt 2017). As they fight, she wields a quicksilver baton for close combat. It expands from a small baton, in some ways echoing a lightsaber though cool, blank silver, without the color or nuance.

Armed with a Z6 Riot Control Baton, he strikes her with an epic, mask-shattering blow, revealing part of her face for first time and emphasizing her vulnerability (unlike Boba Fett). However, there's little dialogue, catharsis, or pathos for either of them—just sparking weapons and special effects as Finn destroys the officer blocking him from escape. In the novelization, Phasma is dehumanized further, with the scene from Finn's unsympathetic point of view. At last, Finn triumphs and she falls to her presumed death into a fiery explosion on the Supremacy. "You were always scum," she tells him.

"Rebel scum," he confirms proudly. He has chosen a side and banished his nemesis, presumably into ignominious death. This plot almost exactly mirrors their brief confrontation in *The Force Awakens,* followed by the trash compactor. Kaila Hale-Stern (2017) concludes:

> Instead of getting to carve out any kind of interesting character arc, Phasma is simply used as the B-plot villain for Finn to fight before the A-plot showdown between Kylo Ren and Luke Skywalker . . . What makes Phasma's small Jedi role all the more confusing is that this was a frequent, fierce criticism lobbed at her presence in *The Force Awakens*: despite prominent placement in advertisements and merchandise, Phasma didn't get much to do. *The Last Jedi* was the chance to stage a deeper look into an uncompromising woman with a fascinating background. But then *The Last Jedi* managed to give Phasma even less to do than *The Force Awakens,* which is almost an impressive feat.

MAZ, THE FEMALE YODA

Many were thrilled to see Yoda's role replaced by an alien woman—nearly the first elderly woman seen in the franchise and certainly a delightful mentor. Lupita Nyong'o, playing the computer-generated Maz Kanata, says, "She is a larger-than-life strong character with a colorful past" (Grossman 2017, 56). The *Visual Dictionary* confirms that she is Force sensitive and had many Jedi acquaintances but "never went down that path" (Hidalgo 2015, 72). Instead, she has quietly used her Force abilities to preserve herself during centuries of adventures as a pirate.

Further, Maz is played by a woman of color, increasing the diversity. The actress reports, "There's a universality to the world that George Lucas created that makes it possible for this multicultural cast to exist without necessarily turning the universe on its head. By very nature and with all sorts of creatures, it is, I think, a universe that is made for a multicultural experience" (*Time* 2015). As she adds, there have always been nods to all the world cultures in the art, costumes and languages in the franchise: "I think you can tell from the cast that it is a lot more multicultural. One of the things I remember as a child connecting with *Star Wars* is one of the characters [Nien Nunb] spoke Kikuyu, which is a Kenyan language. And I remember feeling like that made *Star Wars* mine, it made *Star Wars* Kenyan for all I was concerned" (*Time* 2015). In fact, the lines were delivered by Kipsang Rotich, a Kenyan student who was living in the United States, and are actually correct translations—increasing representation but only through the medium of an alien.

It's delightful to see progress . . . though still in slightly problematic fashion. The film is falling back on a mainstay of American science fiction—having ethnic actors disguised by prosthetics or played by puppets and computer-generated characters. As critic Chauncey DeVega (2015) sorrowfully writes in *Salon Magazine*, "This is a carryover from classic 'golden age' American science fiction where racial erasure was accomplished by turning non-whites into robots and aliens for the purposes of either well-intentioned allegory about the social evils of racism and prejudice or just plain old fashioned, ugly white supremacy." As with Vader, Nien Nunb, and Jar-Jar, Maz's voice appears but her skin is concealed, letting her only partway into the franchise.

Despite this hiccup, she's delightful. In *The Force Awakens*, she's humorous, teasing, wise, and perfectly in control of every situation—much like Yoda himself. She's over a thousand years old, and very discerning. In her giant goggles, Maz is a master of perception, as she notes, "I have lived long enough to see the same eyes in different people." She does not live as humbly as Yoda did, but has created a stone stronghold on a shining green planet. Green means a balance with life and death, as well as growth, hope, and immortality, Maz's strengths (Cooper 1978, 40). There, like the queen of nature incarnate, she lives in a castle decorated by a statue of herself, welcoming all comers. The home is also a feminine symbol as "a world center, the sheltering aspect of the Great Mother; an enclosing symbol, protection" (Cooper 1978, 86). Modern sensor arrays and communication gear emphasize that she's quite technologically savvy. The *Visual Dictionary* adds, "Maz enjoys this contrast. To her, it is yet another manifestation of a cosmic balance" (Hidalgo 2015, 73).

Of course, Maz encourages Rey to listen to the inner voice of her spiritual heritage. She tells Rey, "The Force, it's calling to you. Just let it in." This moment offers the heroine a singular turning point. "Meeting Maz Kanata has a profound effect on Rey. She comes to understand that she is an essential part of a much larger galactic tapestry that is unfurling before her eyes and that the power of the Force is real" (Hidalgo 2015, 33). The crone's castle is also where the traditional heroine goes for initiation, finding the passage to the underworld. In this tradition, Rey descends to Maz's basement and there finds her destiny. Maz has shown her the path.

In Episode VIII, her role is strikingly smaller—just a few lines over a screen. When Rose and Finn contact her for help, Maz replies that she is definitely a skilled enough codebreaker to save the fleet, with a simple "Of course I can do it." However, she is busy, and thus won't be appearing further in the film. They find her under heavy fire, clutching a heavy blaster that emphasizes her doughty toughness. When they ask what is going on there she simply replies, "Union dispute. You do not want to hear about it" (Since she specifically leaves the political wrangling out of the film, this could be considered a jab at *The Phantom Menace*). With this, she leaves Rey to train with Luke and the Resistance to seek help on Canto Bight. She actually flies off on a jet pack in a quick moment of coolness. Maz mentions in a novel that her own name means "Owner of the Warrior's Crown" . . . at least, according to some (Older 2018, 62).

Maz originally was on the cruiser, but Johnson explains in the Blu-Ray commentary, "So much of the stuff I had to her doing . . . it would be more economical if I gave those scenes to the main actors." It's amusing to see that Maz has a complete life separate from the Jedi heroes (whereas Yoda and Obi-Wan spend two decades sitting in rough huts meditating and waiting for Luke to seek training from them). She also describes the cracker's mysterious other skills with a lascivious smirk. At the same time, a few quick lines and the assertion that she could help them save the entire Resistance from destruction but won't is problematic for the character. Certainly, it's not a significant cameo.

Continuing brief cameos, Maz introduces the *Forces of Destiny* book collections. She frames each of the online cartoon episodes, announcing, "The choices we make, the actions we take, moments both big and small, shape us into forces of destiny." One episode has her setting Leia up with the bounty hunter armor seen in *Jedi*, setting up a long-standing relationship between them. Likewise, the tie-in novel *Last Shot* has Han and Sana in Maz's bar, bringing her into the story for a couple brief scenes. Still, the new Extended Universe keeps her mainly as a clever background character.

GENERAL LEIA

The Force Awakens shows a Leia who continued with the Rebellion and never became a Jedi. In the first of the Legends novels, Luke makes her a lightsaber and continues training her in the Force, insisting the knowledge will be useful. She's too busy helping with the new government, and delays becoming a Jedi. Still, over the decades, she finally seizes her chance: In Denning's *The Joiner King* (thirty-five years after *A New Hope*), she apprentices herself to reptilian female Jedi Master Saba Sebatyne, adding that she wants someone with a new perspective who can challenge her. "After all I've seen and done," Leia says, ". . . it always comes down to this. To one Jedi, to one blade, standing against the darkness . . . I'm beginning to understand the Jedi's place in the galaxy—and to see my place in the Jedi" (2005, 441). She insists that after all this time, she's finally earning her rank among them and following her heart.

Author Troy Denning offers an alternative hangup for Leia in *Tatooine Ghost*. As she explores her brother and father's planet, she realizes that "many of the diplomatic gifts she attributed to intuition were really the glimmering of untrained Force potential" (2003, 28). On the other hand, she worries, "developing her potential would have meant facing the dark side of her heritage and . . . that thought frightened her as much as having children" (28).

In the new canon, her struggle with and finally agreement to become a Jedi are sidelined. The *Last Jedi Visual Dictionary* notes: "Skywalker's first student was to be his sister, Leia. However, she ultimately decided that the best path for her to serve the galaxy left no room for the extended isolation of Jedi training" (Hidalgo 2017, 46). Instead, Luke journeys through the galaxy and gathers "disciples who would go on to become his first true students."

In the relaunched book universe, Leia serves as the senator of the Alderaan Sector in the New Republic for twenty-three years as a leading member of the Populists. The novel *Bloodline* has Leia's people encouraging her to run for the leader of the New Republic. However, her identity as Darth Vader's daughter is revealed at the worst time. She loses all public support and must withdraw in disgrace, just as the First Order is subtly gaining power.

Writers of the sequel era deconstruct the Baby-Boomer era hero-rebels who brought down the Death Star by emphasizing how little the universe improved for those on the bottom, despite the promises of liberation and utopia. In the *Star Wars* universe, many of the heroes have lost their idealism of a hopeful future to empower a new militarism as the political establishment has grown increasingly out of touch. Meanwhile, some of the angriest young generation have rebelled against conflicts they barely recall by embracing the villains. In *Bloodline*, a horrified Leia finds cults of reenactors not only collecting Imperial artifacts but militarizing and drilling with them in preparation for a Nazi-style uprising. On realizing the increasing corruption of the Senate, Luke has already retreated from politics in despair. Han Solo reverts to his previous independence, abandoning his temporary convictions as a dream.

Leia maintains her Rebel ideals, though the road is hard. With the revelation about Vader, she loses all political power, even as the depth of the New Republic's corruption is revealed. She decides on a new course. She meets her original-trilogy-era allies in a hanger—Nien Nunb, Caluan Ematt, Admiral Ackbar, as well as the young pilots Han has been training. "The sun is setting on the New Republic," she tells them. "It's time for the Resistance to rise" (Gray 2016, 332). With this, she leaves the capital for their new hideout, though only with those she trusts: "The High Command of the Resistance fleet comprises a mixture of Alliance veterans, ex-leaders of independent defense forces, and New Republic converts—all of whom share a personal connection to General Organa" (Hidalgo 2017, 12).

Of course, she's still tough. When being threatened by crime lord Rinnrivin Di in *Bloodline*, Leia reminds him of how dangerous she is. "All those times you watched me kill Jabba the Hutt, and you never learned from his example. It doesn't pay to jerk me around" (2016, 283). Still, she has not told her son Ben about his ancestry and worries that the jarring revelation will push him over the edge. Of course, it does.

After these compelling interim scenes, the crawl of *Force Awakens* establishes Leia as the impetus of the new era, though now as general giving orders, not princess begging for help: "With the support of the Republic, General Leia Organa leads a brave Resistance. She is desperate to find her brother Luke and gain his help in restoring peace and justice to the galaxy. Leia has sent her most daring pilot on a secret mission to Jakku." This time Luke is the damsel being rescued (or at least the prize being sought) while Leia takes the rescuer role, "leading," "sending," and acting on the galaxy.

Midway through the film, General Leia dramatically arrives with a fleet of Resistance ships to save Rey, Finn, and a flustered Han. She and Han share a messy, complicated reunion filled with news of their vanished son. She's left behind the princess look for pants and a purple vest that resemble Han's space-smuggler getup. Purple hints at maturity and royalty, but the greys as well as fabric and practical bun suggest rough work clothes. Fisher reportedly quipped during filming that Leia dressed like "a fancy gas-station attendant" (Breznican 2017c). She's supposed to be about fifty-three (since she was about twenty-three in *Return of the Jedi*), a mother, general, and leader.

As Fisher jokes, "What I didn't realize, back when I was this twenty-five-year-old pinup for geeks in that me myself and iconic metal bikini, was that I had signed an invisible contract to stay looking the exact same way for the next thirty to forty years." She notes that having a child, to say nothing of eating, over the decades, had ruined the fans' plans for her (Fisher 2011, 27). As she adds, "There are two choices post forty-five: letting ourselves go or making ourselves sit like good, well-groomed, obliging pets, coats smooth and wrinkle-free, stomachs flat, muscles taut, teeth clean, hair dyed, nails manicured—everything *just so*" (Fisher 2011, 30). However, "not only is this completely unnatural, requiring warehouses full of self-control and perseverance, but it demands a level of discomfort you have to be willing to live with 'til death by lap band or liposuction" (Fisher 2011, 30). Despite her concerns, she appeared in the high definition film, to fans' great glee and a minimum of sexist comments.

After this, Finn comes to Leia with his desperation to rescue Rey. She's supportive but tells him she also needs intelligence about Starkiller Base, as they're planning a terrible strike. As she struggles to solve both their problems—protecting the galaxy but also the individuals who make it up—she shows her mingled responsibility and compassion. Fisher explains, "A princess is someone who takes responsibility for their life and makes choices and has a life. She doesn't fall into things. Nothing has changed except the hair" (Ashworth 2015, 45–46). She sends Finn to save Rey as he wishes and Han to save their son. With her motherly insight and love, she insists, "You're his father. There's still light in him. I know it."

While in the original film, Leia waits silently and helplessly on base as the Death Star prepares to destroy her, now she directs the battle, ordering fighters in at the moment the shield falls. Meanwhile, Han tries to get their son back in arguably the more nurturing role. Offering to take him home to his mother appears to sway him for a moment, but then, resolute, Ben Solo stabs his father and kills him. Across space, Leia feels it, of course, and is devastated.

Leia ends the film by sending one more messenger to Luke—Rey, who needs training and finally has directions to where he's hidden. Leia also gets the last line of the film—"May the Force be with you" as she embraces the younger woman. "But this is not the act of a widow seeking solace; it is the work of a tireless empath, giving comfort to relieve another's pain" (Barr 2018, 73). She thus passes on the torch, sending the young heroine off to be trained. With a dark blue gown and fancier updo in this scene, she's reigning queen mother, mourning the loss of husband and son, yet enduring.

SPACE POPPINS

"The First Order reigns. Having decimated the peaceful Republic, Supreme Leader Snoke now deploys his merciless legions to seize military control of the galaxy. Only General Leia Organa's band of Resistance fighters stand against the rising tyranny, certain that Jedi Master Luke Skywalker will return and restore a spark of hope to the fight." Here, the opening credits specify that Leia's forces are fighting Snoke's—Leia is the supreme general of the Resistance, no longer searching as in the last film, but battling. Many systems have surrendered to the First Order just after its destruction of Hosnian Prime. The *Visual Dictionary* reports, "Despite its idealistic intentions, the New Republic never took root on a scale comparable to the Old Republic. Now the Senate and fleet are gone, along with the Republic's top military commanders, and it seems unlikely that the remaining systems will be able to hold together, let alone hold off the First Order" (Hidalgo 2017, 8). Currently they are winning as systems capitulate to its might, reeling from the sneak attack.

The original goofiness as Poe contacts Hux with a stalling message is interesting as the message comes from Leia. In fact, Poe's mocking· "I have a message from General Organa, It's about his mother" is a reference to Hux being illegitimate. Leia, politically connected enough to know the patriarchy's dirty secrets and to wield them as weapons, seems to have initiated this plan, though she sends irreverent Poe as her intermediary. At this, Hux is filled with fury and suddenly screams "Open fire!" emphasizing the power maternal love will have in this film.

"The New Republic is in shambles, independent systems are capitulating, and Han Solo has been murdered by her son—this would be enough to crush any lesser being in an avalanche of despair. But like a diamond, Leia shines under such pressure" (Hidalgo 2017, 16). In this film she's dressed as a mature queen and matriarch who rules in the world of the military and men—her pewter coat and dress are textured and rich, with gold bracelets and earrings. With a checked pattern over a grey silk gown, it suggests business attire, an ability to interact with men in their sphere. Her hair is up, with an Alderaanian mourning braid across the top (Hidalgo 2017, 16). As she prepares the next generation to take on the fight, she wears a homing beacon bracelet that will let Rey find her. Kaplan notes:

> Rian wanted Leia to be a little more queenly or authoritative looking. And I wanted something that would frame her, some kind of regal robe without it being too busy—just big graphic shapes like capes. As a takeoff point, I'd seen pictures of Queen Elizabeth wearing these capes on the Scottish moors. I wouldn't say the outfit on the bridge is an evening fabric, but it does have a shine to it and the shape is quite beautiful—a nice silhouette. (Szostak 2017, 200)

General Leia's Mon Calamari cruiser is named *Raddus*, named for Admiral Raddus from *Rogue One* in a quiet continuity salute. "The Raddus's key strength is its advanced deflector shield system that can push the envelope of protective energy far from its hull (Hidalgo 2017, 8). This echoes Leia's power in the film—protecting her people not engaging in a firefight.

After the battle, she sits onboard looking pained at the death tally. "There were heroes out there," Poe says. Leia replies, "Dead heroes. And no leaders." Through Leia's arc in the story, she emphasizes responsibility to the larger team and the necessity of working together. There are no lone heroes—everything is a team effort. Her big picture thinking being more correct is quite a departure for the franchise:

> She's pragmatic, more interested in saving the Resistance than winning big; he's the opposite. (Well, he wants to save the Resistance, but he also wants to win big.) He wants to make bold moves against the First Order; she wants him to "get your head out of your cockpit." They're both portrayed as right (and wrong) to varying degrees, but in a franchise where the heroes have historically succeeded by being cocky and often reckless, placing cooler heads at the helm feels like a pointed demotion for the stuck-up, half-witted, scruffy-looking nerf herders. (Watercutter 2017)

Poe disobeys orders in flashy fashion to continue his attack on the First Order. However, lives are lost, including Rose's sister Paige and her bomber fleet, and the surviving Resistance must deal with the loss. On his return, Poe and Leia have tension because, as she puts it, "Not every problem can be solved by jumping in an X-Wing and blowing stuff up." Poe thinks in the novelization, "An angry General Organa was a force to be reckoned with—and one for which Poe had a healthy respect. But he felt certain he could talk her down. He always had before" (Fry 2018b, 76). Instead, he's shocked when she slaps him. She also demotes him, emphasizing that he has responsibility to his fellow rebels and to the chain of command with the steely-eyed General Leia running it.

Viewers accept this, understanding that he's crossed a line. Moments later, they're attacked, and Poe snarkily requests permission to "jump in an X-Wing and blow stuff up." She agrees, and he's arguably proved his point that heroics have their place in the universe. Still, he's slow to learn—rushing off to blow something up in the novelization he thinks, "Leia had been genuinely angry with him and he promised himself he'd find time to think about what she'd said and why she'd said it. But she'd also remembered something more important. She really did need him to be reckless sometimes" (Fry 2018b, 78). Nonetheless, he still must work with the team.

"The reluctance to recognize women's legitimate power in certain area of social life is perhaps because its domain is female and familial"

(Andermahr et al. 2017, 15). Men often dismiss women's power because their commands feel like a mother's to wipe one's feet and eat all the vegetables. This is complicated by Poe's filial relationship with General Leia. In this film, she's training Poe to lead and someday take her role, much as Luke struggles with training Rey. Rian Johnson describes trying to find a weakness for Poe in "This whole thing between Poe and Leia." He adds, "The notion of turning from a hero into a leader seemed like a really interesting thing to me" (Johnson 2018b).

It's a complex dynamic of conflicting authorities, made more complex by Kylo Ren's piloting as he considers firing on his mother. The two have a brief battle of not only wills but also recognition. She confronts her son through the Force as he aims his weapons at her ship but can't bear to fire. Metaphorically, while he was willing to destroy his father and take his place, he isn't ready for the authority of his mother. In the junior novel, Leia is saintly in her motherly love, which triggers Ben's rage: "She held no anger against him, despite what he had done, despite that he had killed his father and her husband. For some reason, she still cared for him, as if he hadn't changed, as if he were still Ben Solo, her son. How dare she" (Kogge 2018, 44). His anger flares "into an emotional missile" and he nearly fires. He holds back at the last moment, emphasizing a more primal connection with his mother than his father. One of his teammates substitutes and fires on his behalf, doing the deed symbolically but not literally.

Leia, who has never trained onscreen in the Force (though she does in the novels and could have spent the intervening decades practicing with Luke, with books, with Force ghosts, or on her own), manifests an impressive array of powers never seen in her or any character. When she's blown into space, she flies majestically through the blackness, protected by a bubble of air, and returns safely to the ship, opening the airlock in a final dramatic moment. As Johnson explains, "Leia is a Skywalker as well—she's got that same heritage . . . The notion that in a moment like this when it seems like all is lost—she just realizes, she's not done yet. Almost through instinct . . ." He compares the moment to parents lifting cars off their children and also Leia tapping into her unexplored potential (Johnson 2018b). She is still the self-rescuing princess of the early films. She's also fighting for her friends' safety. In the novelization, Leia thinks, "She had to go on—for Rey and everyone else on the Raddus. And all those the First Order would consign to misery and despair" (Fry 2018b, 84).

Admittedly, she then collapses, and must be laid out in the medical bay in a white gown, comatose. Viewing fans fear that, having made her awesome mark on the galaxy in a single transcendent scene, the cost is her life. While that is true for Luke in his great Force moment, Leia returns in another all-powerfully awesome scene. Hotshot hero Poe has defied her subordinate Admiral Holdo and taken her ship in a brief mutiny. Leia, leaning on her cane and dressed in the white of the medical bay but also of her time as the young princess with a blaster, bursts through the reinforced door. In a single blast, she knocks out Poe with a stunner, reversing the scene when soldiers did this to *her* in *A New Hope*. Poe's accomplice, Lieutenant Kaydel Connix (hilariously played by Billie Lourd, Carrie Fisher's real-life daughter) and Threepio slowly raise their hands in surrender.

One could make a case in these two amazing scenes that Leia has been overpowered and cast as a Mary Sue. At the same time, these moments are wonderful in a series that has offered virtually no older women—and those who have appeared, Jocasta and Maz—have only offered advice, while Shmi and Beru were silently sacrificed. The great ruling matriarch is here and the First Order, led by her sniveling son—is no match.

Still Leia and Holdo don't dismiss Poe but take the time to explain the larger plan and the need to all work together to achieve it. Instead of glorifying the lone male cowboy, the film emphasizes women's roles as teachers and insists men should consider their effects on the larger society and work as part of it. This subverts the concept of the hero male and emphasizes the silent, enduring power of the women who must suffer as he leaves them behind to clean up.

> Leia doesn't need to use the Force; she already has a superpower. From Leia's quashing of Poe's ill-advised mutiny to Rose's quashing of Finn's suicidal run for glory, *The Last Jedi* is filled with women trying to explain to men that their actions have consequences outside of their own hero's journey, that glory and pride and victory are never the most important thing—at least not for the larger cause. That the decision that is best for the group is the one made by the group and its chosen leaders, not by the alpha male hero who thinks he knows best. (Burt 2017b)

In the comic *Poe Dameron: Legend Lost,* after Poe loses one of his pilots, General Leia grounds him, insisting he needs time to think. She tells him that to win the war, they need something rarer and more precious than a good pilot and that he must think about what that is. When they meet again, he acknowledges the war doesn't just belong to him. Leia agrees and adds, "I think you're one of those rare beings who help *other* people fight. Who will inspire and give hope when all seems lost and convince out people to keep going when they don't think they can" (Soule and Unzueta 2017). This lesson carries over to the film.

Leia displays a nuance and suffering capable Rey often lacks, and Leia has another quality nearly unique in the galaxy—a female-female friendship. While younger Leia hung out with the boys and Padmé's handmaidens didn't utter a non-work-related word, Leia and Amilyn trust each other enough to each offer her life to save the fleet. When Amilyn chooses to stay, the already-devastated widow suffers another blow. "I can't take any more losses," Leia says, speaking in a sense for the audience. "Sure you can," Holdo tells her. "You taught me how." In *Legend Lost*, Leia hints to Poe that the war may take decades. She adds, "And, I'm sorry to say, probably sooner than we'd like . . . I'll be luminous," a reference to the accounts of how Jedi die and suggestion that she too could become a Force ghost (Soule and Unzueta 2017).

"The Force Awakens and *Rogue One* transform the entire arc of the series, shifting from stories of young men acting more or less individually, to focus on women building resistances against unfair power structures, working together with people across class and species lines, welcoming new members, honoring each other's work" (Schnelbach 2017). *The Last Jedi* expands on this, guiding its characters into a true Resistance core and emphasizing the message they must spread.

Leia leads her people in an evacuation to the planet of Crait. Here, as in the original film, she is forced to wait and be brave for her people as the enemy's ship attempts to blow all of them up. In this high-tension scene, she lacks agency, save that it is her plan. It's her surrogate Holdo who saves them all. Still, Leia joins the firefight, emphasizing that she's still a warrior. In the novelization, she even snarks that she was last on Crait in her youth "before the hyperdrive was invented" (Fry 2018b, 266). However, once again, the story shifts focus as a new savior arrives in the form of Luke. As the twins emotionally reunite, Leia takes charge of the moment with a joke. "I know what you're going to tell me . . . I've changed my hair." Luke makes an exasperated face before grudgingly telling her that it looks good. Fisher herself added the line. "[Carrie] loved one-liners and jokes," Johnson tells *The Daily Beast*. "She could just pop out so many jokes. So the whole thing where she sits down with Luke and [says], 'I changed my hair,' obviously, that was her" (Sharf 2017a).

Luke gives her the dice from the Millennium Falcon and promises he's finally come to rejoin the fight. The pair sadly acknowledge that Kylo Ren is beyond saving. With this, Luke kisses Leia's forehead, winks at Threepio, and heads out. On the one hand, the male hero has come to save them all. On the other, it is Leia who has summoned him and her image that has reminded him of his duty. Further, his rescue and flashy battle are subverted by his projected presence. Instead of engaging Kylo Ren in the macho, gun blasting, saber-clashing battle the toxically male villain craves, Luke remains passively, peacefully on his island, taunting Ren with his lack of response. He already understands the lessons Leia has tried teaching Poe and seeks to distract Ren long enough to save the survivors.

Inside the stronghold, Finn suggests they fight, but Poe understands a better way. Parroting Holdo, from whom he's learned too late, Poe tells the remaining members of the Resistance, "We are the spark that will light the fire that will burn the First Order down." He even discovers the proper path—his perception has grown. When Poe tells the rebels, "follow me," everyone looks back at Leia, their leader. "What're you looking at me for, follow him," she says, acknowledging her own authority but delegating to the hero who has noticed the local crystalline foxes can lead them to safety. This moment suggests the give-and-take of authority that existed at the film's start. She even smiles proudly as he leads them off. Notably, Leia passes on leadership to Poe, not the son of royalty but of ordinary rebels.

As they depart, Leia leaves behind Han's dice, either breaking with the past or, more likely, aware that they aren't real and that Luke's presence is an illusion (in the novelization, she knows when he hands them to her). It's angry Kylo who lacks this deeper perception.

> Luke sacrifices himself in one last spectacular moment of force-wielding brilliance in order to save Leia and the Rebellion. This kind of sacrifice is something we're used to seeing from extraordinary female characters (see every extraordinary woman from Charlotte in *Charlotte's Web* to Eleven in *Stranger Things*). In *TLJ*, the central white male hero of the original films dies to save an exceptionally diverse, gender-balanced group of people who are, as Poe says, the "spark that will light the fire that will destroy the First Order." Not "save the galaxy"; not "save the Republic." This is not about saving something from corruption. It's about ending the old order and creating something completely new. (Hillman 2017)

As Luke sacrifices himself as Amilyn did, Leia has the harder job, safeguarding the last survivors of the Resistance and somehow beginning again. She insists, "We have all we need"—the last line before the final scene. Though few survive, there's still a trace of hope among the characters as their message spreads through the galaxy. A child is seen wielding the Force without training, emphasizing that while the Jedi and Resistance may be ending, people of all sorts will defend the galaxy from tyranny. Hope is thus reignited. This of course is balanced with the audience's sadness at the knowledge that the actress died just after filming. The general is prepared to retake the galaxy, but it can never happen. During the credits, "In loving memory of our Princess, Carrie Fisher" appears on the screen.

While it's been reported that Fisher's passing has changed the proposed storyline for the upcoming Episode IX (which was due to feature Leia prominently), all of Leia's scenes were presented unaltered in Episode VIII, leaving Episode IX writer/director J.J. Abrams to complete her story. Director Johnson confirms that Fisher's scenes were all filmed: "We had wrapped up shooting for a few months. We were farther along in the editing process and we had a complete and really beautiful performance from her, so we weren't lacking anything. And we didn't end up changing a thing in the cut. Her performance is beautiful, and we didn't touch it" (Bennett 2017, 36). With this, Leia's story ends.

FAREWELL, PRINCESS

"What you'll have of me after I journey to that great Death Star in the sky is an extremely accomplished daughter, a few books, and a picture of a stern-looking girl wearing some kind of metal bikini lounging on a giant drooling squid, behind a newscaster informing you of the passing of Princess Leia after a long battle with her head" (Fisher 2011, 75). This line in her autobiography echoes poignantly as Carrie Fisher passed away before *The Last Jedi* could arrive.

Fisher said of her iconic status in the franchise, "For me, it's about family. That's what makes *Star Wars* so powerful. When I go to Comic-Con, I meet lots of people and it's very powerful for them too. They show the films to their children and their grandchildren and share something that moved them as a child" (Hugo 2018, 37).

She died on December 27, 2016, several days after suffering a heart attack at the end of a trans-Atlantic flight. She had been traveling to promote her recent book, *The Princess Diarist*, a memoir of her time working on the *Star Wars* films. "The 60-year-old actress, author, and raconteur left a pop culture void in the form of her perpetually arched eyebrow" (Breznican 2017a).

Of course, her loss devastated the cast. "Carrie lived her life the way she wanted to, never apologizing for anything, which is something I'm still learning," Daisy Ridley said. "'Embarrassed' is the wrong word, but there were times through it all when I felt like I was . . . shrinking. And she told me never to shrink away from it—that it should be enjoyed" (Kamp 2017). Johnson notes: "Carrie was very conscious of what Leia meant to people and, specifically, what Leia meant to girls, especially when she was the only girl hero in *Star Wars* for many years. Carrie really knew that and carried that. So many of our conversations were in the context that we do have to do right by this character because she knew firsthand what she meant to people" (Bennett 2017, 37).

Leia was the heart and soul of the Rebellion, recruiting Luke, Han, and Obi-Wan in the first film, and keeping the heroes close. She was the feminine face of *Star Wars* for many adoring fans. Further, she proved that girls could have space adventures beside the boys and be just as smart, brave, and downright funny. Indeed, her snark on and off camera defined her as a person and made the character all that she was.

> Fisher was also unabashed about her family and love life. As the child of the late crooner Eddie Fisher and singer-actress Debbie Reynolds, who died at age 84 one day after her daughter, Fisher was born into turmoil, with a father who abandoned them when she was a toddler for

a romance with Elizabeth Taylor. The insecurities and upheaval of those early years provided fodder for endless anecdotes but also haunted her throughout a life that was anything but steady—except for the bond with her daughter, actress Billie Lourd, and maybe her French bulldog, Gary, a stoic constant companion in her later years. (Breznican 2017a)

The actress debuted on Broadway at age fifteen and soon made it to the big screen in the 1975 comedy *Shampoo*, opposite Warren Beatty and Goldie Hawn. Two years later, she became known for *Star Wars*. Of course, Fisher was also an inspiration in her courage as she battled drug addiction and mental illness, chronicling her struggle with inspiring frankness. These appeared in her first book, *Postcards from the Edge* (1987), later adapted into a film (for which Fisher wrote the screenplay) starring Meryl Streep. Four more novels and a pair of screenplays followed. She also performed "Wishful Drinking" as a one-woman show from 2008 to 2010 and had a career as the esteemed script doctor of *Hook*, *The Wedding Singer*, *Sister Act*, and the *Star Wars* prequels, among others.

"Out of everyone, Carrie was the one I really became friends with and expected to have in my life for years and years," Johnson concludes. "I last saw her in November, at the birthday party that she threw at her house. In a way, it was the perfect final, encapsulating image of Carrie—receiving all her friends in the bedroom, with Debbie holding court in the living room" (Kamp 2017). Indeed, her mother Debbie Reynolds passed away the day after her daughter's shocking death, doubling the tragedy for the family and for so many who adored them both.

AMILYN HOLDO'S NEW LEADERSHIP STYLE

Laura Dern's Vice Admiral Amilyn Holdo is one of the striking new female characters. When Leia falls into a coma, Amilyn leads the briefing in her place. With a voice that's soft and sympathetic, even a little self-deprecating, her opening speech is anticlimactic. She proclaims, "We are the spark that will light the fire that will restart the resistance," and insists on spreading their message throughout the galaxy—recruitment, not combat.

Poe says incredulously to another pilot: "*That*'s Admiral Holdo? Battle of Chyron Belt Admiral Holdo? Not what I was expecting." In this scene, he's the audience's viewpoint character and their guide to viewing the admiral. Dern notes, "It was important for Rian that she had room to be feminine, ethereal, and otherworldly, even spiritual" (Hugo 38).

Here is Vice-Admiral Amilyn Holdo, a tall thin woman in late middle age, wearing a draped floor-length dress that leaves every curve and angle of her body visible; a woman with dyed-purple hair in a style that requires at the very least a great many pins and more likely a curling iron in addition; a woman wearing star-chart bracelets and lipstick and eye makeup. She looks like a slightly-down-on-her-luck noblewoman from the Old Republic. She's not just female, she's *femme*. And she's not just femme, she's *soft*. All her age is visible; there's no architectural framing of that body to disguise how gravity has had its way with it. Holdo, in the middle of the remnants of the Resistance, is a kind of exposed that Leia Organa—who does wear those architectural frames around her body, giving her a grandeur and a solidity—never is. (Martine 2017)

Kaplan says Rian Johnson suggested a feminine gown, to contrast with Leia and the military personnel. "He wanted to see her body language. He wanted her to look a little flirtatious in some of the scenes with Poe, yet he wanted her to look dignified. She has a comb in her hair. It's like a halo," Kaplan says (Szostak 2017, 203). Silver bracelets, pink rings and drop earrings add to the feminine look. Dern notes, "She is flirtatious and sensual, which is an interesting choice" (Hugo 38). Her elegant gown, as well as this "flirting" makes it easy for the men, and even the male audience, to discount. Additional cultural significance explains her coloration: As the *Visual Dictionary* explains, "Her dyed hair and eye-catching clothing show her fierce devotion to her homeworld of Gatalenta and its independent spirit. Gatalenta is known across the galaxy for its poetry and the tranquility and compassion of its inhabitants" (Hidalgo 2017, 40). Of course, these qualities aren't typical ones sought in a military leader.

"Women who look like Holdo—femme fatales, even in their middle age, women who look like women who do *politics* rather than fight, who like frivolous things, jewels and bright hair and makeup even in the darkest moments—we are primed to read women like that as women who will betray. This is an old trope" (Martine 2017). With all this, the audience is primed to distrust this "anti-Leia"—a new character who seems far more frivolous, even malleable in appearance. Onscreen, she's Leia's foil—not only her replacement but one who dresses in draped mauve elegance in contrast with Leia's steely grey.

> Leia Organa is entirely, fully, hugely competent at what she does; Leia Organa, our General, is an image of mature womanhood which is understandable and immensely welcome—she is a *leader* of men and women, a strength and a power. Her most affecting scene in this film—when we finally get to see her use the Force which is her birthright as much as it has ever been her brother's—is heartbreakingly brilliant. So is her ability to delegate, to train, to be both centrally necessary and to have a system in place for when she is incapacitated. But Holdo looks like the opposite of Leia—Holdo looks like an inexperienced woman using another woman's words, a pale substitute, a coward whose story-function is to (like so many middle-aged female characters in film)

keep our heroes down. This too is a familiar trope, and we are set up to expect it by how Holdo dresses and behaves. (Martine 2017)

The women contrast in other ways—Holdo is noticeably gruffer with less tolerance for cocky flyboy Poe Dameron. Poe dislikes her in turn. "A lot of the friction and conflict for Poe is in that relationship with Admiral Holdo," he says. "He's not sure what to make of her." Poe wants to fight; she wants to strategize. "Poe is grappling with how to become a leader, which means keeping his emotions in check and thinking things through a bit more," Isaac says (Breznican 2017c). He asks to hear all of her plans, since Leia would have told him and given him a chance to argue with her about heroics. Holdo, however, smilingly, condescendingly dismisses him, insisting that his impetuousness is the last thing they need. She cuts him down to size, calling him one of the "trigger happy flyboys" and ordering him, "so stick to your post and follow my orders." At the same time, she keeps a wide, sweet smile on her face, addressing him with such light condescension that he's uncertain how to resist. Oscar Isaac explains, "Vice Admiral Holdo is an interesting character that speaks to the nature of leadership. She isn't saying 'Look at me, I'm the hero.' She does things more quietly" (Hugo 40).

"A less intelligent narrative would have framed Holdo as 'the bitch.' Seriously. Here's a stern, beautiful female character who audiences have never seen before; she swoops in, takes control of the situation, and shames a favorite male character like he's an insolent child," Caitlin Busch (2017) explains in "Women's Stories Are More Prominent Than Ever in *Star Wars: The Last Jedi*."

Laura Dern notes of first hearing of the part that the first thing director Rian Johnson had described was "this quality of someone who is so steadfast that you don't know what side they're on because they don't need the rest of the world to know their plans. The kind of person—the kind of woman—who is clear in her voice, and even in the company of men questioning her doesn't need to justify her behavior or her choices" (Yamato 2017). The admiral flatly refuses to share her plan with Poe, insisting (correctly) that she isn't answerable to him. If she had shared her plan, plenty of chaos could have been avoided. However, through the arc of the story, the audience as well as Poe are encouraged to reevaluate their assumption that this decorated military leader should have taken the time to explain herself to a hotheaded male subordinate.

With Leia incapacitated, Poe launches a second hotshot plan—smuggling Finn and Rose off to save the fleet. As he clasps an unconscious Leia's hand sadly, he insists they shouldn't ask for permission since Holdo will only refuse. Here he assumes Admiral Holdo will quash his ideas and not even bother listening. Presumably she'll be delighted and relieved when Poe's plan instantly, unexpectedly saves them all. This is the plotline of many action movies with rebellious heroes showing up their superiors. However, Poe's skirting the chain of command is a disaster. Kayti Burt (2017b) explains in "Toxic Masculinity Is the True Villain of *Star Wars: The Last Jedi*": "Poe's rogue heroics—sending Rose and Finn to Canto Bight, for example—not only don't work, they lead to the near-quashing of the entire Resistance force. Hundreds of people die, and it's at least partially because Poe had visions of glory."

Poe calls her a "coward" and "traitor" for loading all their people in transports and abandoning their military ship. Her orders in turn look weak as she insists they only maintain their course, Admiral Holdo's plan to use the flagship as bait is the opposite of a flashy firefight—it encourages the First Order patriarchy to treat it as one while the Resistance survivors sneak away, hidden under cloaking technology. It's not glorious or glamorous, but it should save lives. Holdo continues insisting Poe give up his heroics. In the novelization, she quips, when he compares her unfavorably to Leia, "Captain Dameron, if you're here to serve a princess, I'll assign you to bedpan duty . . . If you're here to serve the Resistance, follow my orders. Somebody has to save this fleet from its heroes" (Fry 2018b, 129).

Poe, however, leads a mutiny, contemptuously showing what he thinks of the admiral's plans. Since she and Commander D'acy are female (with one other male standing beside them), this appears a gender war, with the stronger, more daring Poe rejecting the older women's cautious and ineffectual plans.

However, the cap on this arc subverts all this. "In *The Last Jedi*, Poe is presented as a character who needs to stop with the mansplaining and learn from the more seasoned female leaders in his life" (Burt 2017b). Leaning on a cane and wrapped in her white medical gown, Leia is clearly still recovering. However, in an instant, she retakes the bridge and shoots Poe with a stunner. In this brief scene, she fiercely asserts her authority.

When Poe wakes, Leia affirms that Holdo has her full support and was enacting their joint plan to save the maximum lives. Poe is horrified that the plan involves abandoning their last military ship, instead of taking more direct action. He burns to jump into his ship and "blow stuff up." However, theirs is actually a valid plan, as the transport ships are equipped to pass under the First Order's radar and the military ship is not. In fact, all remaining Resistance members could have escaped to Crait if Poe had listened to Holdo. Poe's overconfidence allows them all to be betrayed so the First Order can kill more Resistance members. Poe learns, as his actor notes, "When someone wants to prove themselves at the expense of others, it can be detrimental, no matter how noble the aims" (Hugo 40).

Further, Holdo chooses to sacrifice herself onboard the warship. She and Leia share a tender goodbye, emphasizing the friendship that's detailed in Claudia Gray's novel *Leia, Princess of Alderaan*, though the admiral hasn't otherwise appeared onscreen. In it, the pair were in the Apprentice Legislature together and Amilyn was something of a daffy, free spirited type. Gatalentans are known for valuing simplicity and plainness, which Amilyn finds boring, so she dresses more flamboyantly and dyes her hair. She goes in near-psychedelic colors with bells and sparkly fringe, until Leia advises her "If you're only trying to be the opposite of a thing, you're still letting that thing define you" (Gray 2017, 345). After this, Amilyn remains feminine but chooses her own softer style. She's very insightful, finding legal loopholes Leia and her friends can use to save lives.

> "It's so great to see people responding positively to Amilyn Holdo!" exclaims Gray. "Some people have compared her to Luna Lovegood from *Harry Potter*, which is both kind of true and kind of awesome. (I love Luna.) She's somebody who's a bit off-kilter, who sees the world through a prism most others don't understand. At first Leia thinks she's pleasant but weird, but as time goes on, it becomes apparent that there's much more to Holdo than you might guess when you first met her. We don't really have a lot of true oddballs in *Star Wars*, so it was fun to introduce one!" (Floyd 2017)

She's the first to plunge ahead on dangerous missions, but always with disarmingly naïve-seeming aphorisms and fluffy-seeming harmlessness. In one scene, as she babbles about an Imperial captain's astrological sign, he quickly gives up questioning her in disgust. When she begins flirting and his crew snicker, he hastily signs off. It's a feminine performance, one that Leia quickly masters as well. With all this, Amilyn offers a very different nonlinear type of strength. There's also a significant novel scene suggesting Holdo might be the first queer character onscreen. In a brief passage, Holdo and Leia discuss romantic interests, with Amilyn revealing her varied tastes:

> "A pair of pretty dark eyes." Then Amilyn thought about that for a moment. "Or more than a pair, if you're into Grans. Or Aqualish, or Talz. Or even—"
>
> "That's all right!" Leia said through laughter. "It's just humanoid males for me."
>
> "Really? That feels so limiting."
>
> "Thank goodness it's a big galaxy." (Gray 2017, 246)

Dern hadn't read the novel but agrees with it to some extent. She notes, "You get the sense that she was a hippie who would acknowledge all things and never judge" (Yamato 2017). Johnson describes the film character as originally better matching the prequel novel as she was "Originally much more hippy-dippy . . . the opposite of what you'd expect from the military hierarchy." However, this was, "too much—a little too spacy" so she pulled it back (Johnson 2018b).

Clearly, according to the released versions of novel and film, the character has grown up in the intervening decades and now has a tougher, colder side to her personality. Fisher helped write the exchange as the women wish each other "May the Force be with you." Holdo and Leia attempt to say the line together but fight back tears, knowing they must part. Leia tells her, "You go, I've said it enough." Holdo accordingly gives the most emotional "May the force be with you, always" of the entire film. "That whole Holdo scene, that goodbye scene was actually completely rewritten with Carrie and with Laura," Johnson says. "The three of us got together and worked through it" (Sharf 2017a). Johnson adds, "Laura got to talk to Carrie about what the character meant to her all these years and really wanting to pay tribute to what Princess Leia over the years has meant to her" (Johnson 2018b).

It's significant that these two women in charge (a significant first for *Star Wars* after "only other woman in the galaxy Mon Mothma") get along and trust each other completely, in the best Bechdel scene of the series. There's no competition or animosity—but perfect accord.

> Compare the dignified and graceful exchanges between Holdo—who eventually pulls off the most badass kamikaze move in sci fi history— and Leia to those between darkly brooding men's rights activist Kylo Ren and the red-haired punchbag General Hux, who can't share a scene without fighting because neither of them truly earned their position. Their respective scrambling and scrapping for power reveals an immaturity and insecurity in contrast to Poe Dameron's arrogance but no less patriarchal for it. While the guys fight over power, the women simply get on with the job. (King 2017).

Unfortunately, this features one surviving and one dying. Holdo realizes someone must stay behind to pilot the heavy Mon Calamari cruiser *Raddus* while the rest of the diminished Resistance escapes to the planet Crait, Alone on the ship, the admiral watches, devastated, as the rebel ships she's offered her life for are destroyed one by one. At last, she acts, blasting her own ship into hyperdrive and directly through the First Order's flagship, destroying a great part of it. The film goes devastatingly silent. With this, her people escape. Laura Dern notes, "I do think the idea of willing sacrifice, and someone's silent intent to not need to be a hero but to save everyone is just profound. There's definitely something for me to learn about the idea of perception versus knowing. It's a deep spiritual question, in many religions too, this idea of not needing to prove who you are but knowing it. It's a big question" (Yamato 2017).

Holdo blows up as much of the First Order fleet as she can manage, sacrificing herself to save her people. "She cared more about protecting the light than seeming like a hero," Leia tells Poe about Holdo's sacrifice, "subverting the tired narrative trend of the alpha male hero as the only viable or best leadership choice" (Burt 2017b). While it's coincidence, her act saves Finn and Rose as well. Holdo's appearance is short, but she strikes a major blow for the Resistance, as well as one for trust and community. Laura Dern notes: "Especially in the zeitgeist of all we're thinking about in terms of who women are in positions of power, and not being impacted by abuses of power—I just feel really proud to be part of that story line in a film that's being seen so widely, and by a generation of girls and boys that we're all raising. All these characters are equally complicated, diverse and powerfully heroic . . . I just love it" (Yamato 2017). She didn't begin the war, only inherited it from the previous generation. Still, she willingly steps up to fix their mistakes. As her film arc emphasizes, there's a reason the women are in charge. They need everyone's trust, before it's too late.

CARETAKERS AND SPACE COWS

Luke's refuge on Ahch-To introduces colorful new beings: besides the playful, birdlike porgs for comic relief are the religious order of amphibious females known as the Caretakers. "They're these big matronly creatures," Johnson says. "I wanted them to feel like a remote sort of nunnery" (Breznican 2017b). Unlike the powerful Dathomir witches who enslave men, this community of Force-sensitive females happily serve. The Caretakers certainly look their parts in what appear to be white nurse hats or wimples over simple nun robes with rope belts. They can communicate with Luke through what Johnson calls "a blubbery sort of Scottish fish talk." Johnson adds that they "tolerate" his presence (Breznican 2017b).

There are craggier males. Creature concept designer Jake Lunt Davies notes, "The script told us that the male group visited the island every month" and he gave them heavy hard hats and harpoon guns (Szostak 2017, 40). Their race are called Lanais, and they are distantly related to the porgs (Hidalgo, 2017, 42).

Making the manatee-faced Caretakers so specifically gendered and giving them the cooking and cleaning tasks onscreen clearly reinforces traditional gender dynamics: "The Caretaker duties fall to Lanai females, the more spiritual and empathetic members of the species," the *Visual Dictionary* explains in gender-related clichés (Hidalgo 2017, 50). The novelization adds, "Every day on Ahch-To, the Lanais cut back the moss and uneti shrubs that threatened to reclaim the sacred island's stone steps, swept that common area outside the huts, and performed repairs as needed. And if any Outsiders were in residence, the Lanais cooked their meals and cleaned their clothing, so they could devote their hours to contemplation" (Fry 2018b, 309). Further, Alcida-Auka, the Caretaker Matron, "calls the other Caretakers her 'daughters' and instills in them the virtues of cleanliness, orderliness, and decorum" (Hidalgo, 2017, 50).

In another painful addition to these dynamics, they resent Rey as they consider Luke "theirs." Their entire agendas are bent toward serving the visiting male, arguably a white savior who has burst in on their ancient sanctuary. "Personality-wise, I wanted the Caretakers to feel like nuns—to feel disapproving," Rian Johnson remembers. "One particular Caretaker is the matron; she's in charge, and she clearly has a problem with Rey being on the island. Rey's intruding in this private world, and in this private relationship that they have with Luke. That was the idea: to try to always make you feel that the Caretakers love him" (Szostak 2017, 40). Luke thinks in the novelization, Caretakers "weren't above sidelong looks or clicks of the tongue when they thought he'd been careless or performed some task haphazardly" (Fry 2018b, 193).

Of course, Rey reinforces their disapproval with her clumsiness: she blows a wall in the hut to caretakers' dismay, then smashes stone pillar on them as they work, narrowly missing one. She is the classic young hero, taking on the male role, and, in more traditional gender dynamics (though they don't apply to Rey), the Caretakers are the ones who must clean up the hero's heedless mess, sighing all the while.

In a rather gratuitous scene, Luke milks the thala-siren (ironically, a name that means mermaid). The flabby walrus-like creature with an elephant seal face is seen relaxing against the crags like a slob in a lounge chair "A little backstory to help the design was that they clearly come to this rock to sunbathe and relax, and they do as seals or sea lions would do, basking" (Szostak 2017, 56). The creature Luke approaches appears placid enough to not mind being milked. It is one more gendered creature whose entire existence (especially in the film) is based on helping the male hero.

Symbolism of women's bodies, from sexuality to lactation, have often defined female characters and femininity as a whole. "These corporealities of women may be seen as making us vulnerable to male domination and control, both directly through the exercise of superior physical power and indirectly through social compulsions and the representation of sexual difference across a variety of discourses" (Andermahr et al. 2017, 20). Clearly, the creatures waiting to be milked and the nuns caring for Luke are both problematic. All these beings living only to help Luke symbolizes a world of willingly exploited female nature, all doing everything it can to aid the entitled hero. The nongendered porgs (coded more as curious children) by contrast are not helpful but tend to annoy the main characters.

IMPRESSIVE DIVERSITY

In contrast with the previous two eras, the sequels produced plenty of women and minorities, emphasizing a multifaceted galaxy where everyone is welcome. Admiral Ackbar commands the Raddus, with an Asian Executive officer and Black gunner, along with multiple aliens on his staff. There are many female officers including the ground logistics officer Koo Millham and pilots Cova Nell and Pammich Nerro Goode. Many are stars from other franchises. Among Leia's staff, *The Force Awakens* offers Jess Pava, Blue Three, played by Jessica Henwick, who played a junior barrister on *Silk* and Nymeria Sand on *Game of Thrones*. The comic *Poe Dameron: Legend Lost* shows a little of Jess's backstory, as she's seen enslaved and chained as a girl, alongside her family (Soule and Unzueta 2017).

Morgan Dameron (director J.J. Abrams' assistant) gives her surname to Poe Dameron and also appears self-referentially as "Commodore Meta." Commander D'acy is older with a lined face and curly blonde hair. Her brown military uniform suggests she should be taken seriously. *Last Jedi* presents squad leader Tallissan "Tallie" Lintra, while *Chewing Gum* star Michaela Coel and singer Ellie Goulding cameo among the fleet. Dr. Harter Kalonia, who tends Chewbacca's wounds at the resistance base in *The Force Awakens,* is played by Harriet Walter, Lady Shackleton from *Downton Abbey*.

Lieutenant Kaydel Connix, a Resistance officer with her hair in two blonde knots, is played by Billie Lourd, Carrie Fisher's real-life daughter. "Her part got bigger and bigger as we went along, so Rian must have liked her performance," Fisher smiles (Hugo 37). She has a military olive quilted outfit with insignia, emphasizing her role as military professional on their ragtag team. Her hair in two small blonde buns suggests affiliation with Leia. In *The Force Awakens*, it's little more than a walk-on role. In *The Last Jedi,* Connix "earns promotion to lieutenant for her admirable service as an operations controller during the Starkiller crisis" (Hidalgo, 2017, 12). She sits at sensor ops but has more of an arc, as she joins Poe in his mutiny against Admiral Holdo. When Leia bursts in, Connix quickly surrenders—a funnier moment when one considers her mother has arrived to lay down the law.

Harrison's study of how often women appear at all was highest for *The Last Jedi*—though even this most female-centric of the *Star Wars* films, provoking such protests about overrepresentation from angry misogynists, came in at 43 percent, or notably less than equal. Harrison (2018) adds, "Even the sequels and spin-offs barely pass the Bechdel test because women characters often inhabit the screen with men. The notion that women can have meaningful conversations with one another about something other than male characters is most apparent in *The Last Jedi* . . . but you can still count these exchanges on one hand."

Everyone in Canto Bight dresses in black and white. These are very elegant, flashy outfits like those the Academy Awards attendees wear, set against in a golden casino. Many attendees are not white, emphasizing a varied galaxy of one-percenters. Scanlan reports, "The girls that played them were models. And they played them with the same luster as if they were walking down a catwalk, which I thought was amazing because these weren't puppeteers or performers. They were such good sports . . . But they did bring an element of sexuality to *Star Wars* that we had not yet seen" (Szostak 2017, 137). Some of the women there are certainly sexualized, and all are objects of gaze.

While the Codebreaker's companion (played by Lily Cole) is a human-looking model in an exquisite gown, other attendees are rather grotesque. Baroness Wayulia attends as a holographic head on a gowned droid body. Two women have bulbous bald alien heads over striking black gowns, making them more curiosities than attractive figures. Opera singer Ubbla Mollbro disturbingly appears to be covered in pale breasts over her insect body. The *Visual Dictionary* describes her as vulgar new money and emphasizes her disturbingly predatory search for a mate, despite her appearance: "This boisterous, egg-laden Xi'Dec opera singer is eager to find a hatching partner" (Hidalgo 2017, 61). Thus, she is covered in reproductive material and, despite her lack of attractiveness and refinement, will inflict herself on the galaxy's most successful men in a parody of rapacious womanhood.

R2-KT makes an appearance in *The Force Awakens.* The real droid was built by *Star Wars* fans in honor of Katie Johnson, daughter of Albin Johnson who founded the 501st Legion costume and fan group (now with over 10,000 active members around the globe). When Katie developed a brain tumor, the R2 Builder's Group constructed a special pink droid to watch over her. The little girl adored it and always kept it with her. Katie passed away in 2005. She became an inspiration for the 501st's charities, and the droid now makes appearances at children's hospitals. Hasbro even made a limited-edition action figure. For those who know the story, it's a touching homage. For those who don't, a pink R2 unit emphasizes that even the most beloved of characters can have a female counterpart.

Korr Sella, emissary to the New Republic and Leia's assistant is Black, with her hair pinned up in businesslike fashion and a brown high-collared military jacket. She's killed on Hosnian Prime. Her moment of shock and terror gives the audience something to cling to, perhaps more because she's a more emotional and sympathetic female. Still, it's a small role, cut down from a planned larger part in which she's sent to report on Starkiller Base and alert the government to the threat. Korr Sella is introduced in the novel *Star Wars: Bloodline* as "the office intern, only sixteen years old" (2016, 13). She has a little growth as she rejects Leia when it's revealed that her father was Darth Vader. The pair reconcile at the end, and Leia agrees to stop calling her the childish "Korrie," adding, "You're not a child any longer. I think you're more grown-up than most of the people at this rally" (Gray 2016, 319).

Even Hux's trigger point appears to be his mother as Poe delivers his saucy line—actually a nod to Hux's being illegitimate, as expanded on in the related novels. While still somewhat human-centric, the First Order has a more ethnically diverse military than the Empire did, with dark-skinned and Asian officers present. Hux's female bridge officer is played by Kate Dickie, Sansa's aunt Lysa Arryn on *Game of Thrones*. Meanwhile, Amira Ghazalla, who played a Dothraki Crone, is Captain Canady's First Order commander.

In *The Last Jedi*, according to the *Visual Dictionary*, "Poe wears the wedding ring of his late mother, Shara Bey, on a necklace, waiting to share it someday with the right partner" (2017, 35). Poe's gesture leaves him seeking love (and a non-gender specific one in the carefully-worded book), to fans' delight, even as he pays homage to his beloved mother. While Lieutenant Shara Bey doesn't appear onscreen, she has an arc in the comic *Shattered Empire*. She's sweet and flirty with her husband Kes, though she leaves him with the child, as she takes the stronger warrior's role. She's a competent soldier and clever mechanic who pilots Leia as the comic begins. She's also supportive, bringing her a drink and asking about the condolence letters she's writing. Luke enlists her to play an Imperial officer to help him raid the Emperor's treasures. Shara plays the part with a scary authority, cowing imperials. Afterward, Luke rewards her with a tree from the Jedi temple to take with her when she settles down with her family now that peace has finally arrived.

SIX
Redefining Cartoons

Star Wars Rebels

CAPTAIN HERA

Rebels followed close on the heels of *Clone Wars* after Disney's purchase took the franchise in a new direction. The paired shows, both under the supervision of Dave Filoni and others, make different choices. Ahsoka is Anakin's protégé—younger and subordinate to him, literally and figuratively. Both are born to be Jedi—gifted in a way the people they help don't share (and within that framework, Anakin is explicitly the chosen one, more privileged than Ahsoka herself). They obey the establishment, letting the Jedi Council dictate their missions. While they use their superior skills to help the oppressed, it's coming from a place of extreme privilege. There's also the audience's knowledge that the pair are pawns in a war Palpatine has orchestrated for his own gain. With this, these war heroes lack the perfect moral high ground.

By contrast, Captain Hera Syndulla, sassy Sabine Wren, the astromech droid C1-10P "Chopper," and the Lasat warrior Garazeb Orrelios are ordinary people fighting the Empire however they can. They travel with two Jedi, the escapee Kanan Jarrus and his new trainee Ezra, but Hera arguably outranks Kanan—it's her ship and she sets up their missions. Sabine, more experienced, is a peer-mentor for Ezra, not a younger tagalong. They are not central war heroes, but one piece of many, encouraging the people to rise up. They are no better than those who are oppressed—in fact, all came from worlds the Empire was terrorizing. Like Rose, they are the marginalized trying to raise the entire galaxy in revolution . . . and they succeed. Of the contrast between the two series, Filoni explained:

Rebels will be different from *The Clone Wars* in a couple ways, and one is the decision to stick with one story and one main group of characters. We wanted fans to get to know the new characters and what they are fighting for. Each episode has its own unique story, while still fitting into the much larger picture of what is going on in the *Star Wars* universe. *Rebels* will tell the story of a group of characters — in this way it is more like the original trilogy which followed Han, Luke and Leia — where the prequels showed us the grand scale and political as well as personal. (Day 2014)

Of course, the women of Rebels had an imperfect beginning, as the story and especially the toys seemed aimed more toward the boy hero than the multicultural team: In the early merchandise, Hera and Sabine took a backseat to the male characters, "which was a sore reminder of the #WeWantLeia campaign in 2014. This campaign, which went beyond the created Twitter hashtag, was about audience members fighting to make Disney realize how wrong it was not to include the emblematic female lead to new collections of *Star Wars* toys. It is disheartening how there can be progress in representation on one side and sabotage on another" (Guyot 2015, 14). Their merchandising in conjunction with the girl-themed *Forces of Destiny* provided a bit more balance.

Hera, a twenty-four-year-old Twi'lek from Ryloth, is named for the ancient Greek queen of the gods, sharing her name meaning of "Protector." She is the captain, leader, and planner of the *Star Wars: Rebels* team, who recruits most of the members. As such, she is the truest believer in the cause. Her voice actress Vanessa Marshall says, "She has that rebellious spirit and she stands for human rights, or entity rights. She has noble ideals, and she was raised with that philosophy. She utilizes that on a daily basis and it's more of a religion for her" (*Star Wars Insider* 2017a, 138). She also functions as surrogate mother, often discussing "the kids," as she calls the younger teammates, with her male counterpart, Kanan. "If Zeb and Ezra get too rowdy, she sends them on errands to get them off the Ghost," the *Visual Guide* explains (Bray 2014, 48). She also calls Kanan "love" and "dear," touching him affectionately. When Kanan is permanently blinded, her role as team leader, in contrast with the now maimed Jedi, becomes clearer.

Hera is paged over the intercom in *Rogue One* and mentioned in related materials like the *Rogue One Rebel Dossier*. *Forces of Destiny* places her in quick scenes with Leia and Han on Hoth and Endor. This ties *Rebels* to the larger universe and establishes she's still alive at this point. For those in the know, it also gives the Rebellion another female leader, one as instrumental as Ackbar and the others. Her world is a founding Rebellion member, and "she has destroyed more Imperial ships than anyone on the crew" (Bray 2014, 30).

She's green with two long tentacles growing from her head known as lekku. Supersensitive, they can grab and hold items. The lekku "serve both sensual and cognitive functions" and store memories (Lewis and Keier 2013, 166). Her people are not warlike but make skilled spies as "they prefer cunning and slyness over physical conflict," *The New Essential Guide to Alien Species* explains (Lewis and Keier 2013, 167). More strategist and pilot than formal warrior, she's a formidable character in a non-Jedi path to power. She wears a fully-covering orange and brown flight suit and grey cap with goggles—practical rather than seductive.

> Over decades of Expanded Universe, there have been numerous types of Twi'lek characters, but Twi'leks, especially females, originally did not receive the more complex and positive narrative treatment as other species did. While certain tropes aren't gone for good, being able to transcend them and create richer personalities is important in how stories are told, especially in the mainstream industries that hold a larger share of markets and audiences. The influence they can have over people, especially younger audience members, must be taken seriously. (Guyot 2015, 10)

Her striking moments include using a serving tray as a weapon in "Idiot's Array," testing a new ship and flying the B-wing in "Wings of the Master" and finally getting promoted to Phoenix Leader. Each episode includes her wonderful piloting maneuvers. Marshall says of Hera: "She's the brass tacks of the operation . . . she can fly really well, and she's also a great fighter in hand-to-hand combat and with her blaster" (*Star Wars Insider* 2017b, 24).

Hera owns the Ghost as well as piloting it, establishing her as captain. "Drawing comparisons with the famous Han Solo is easy, as her ship, the Ghost, is the equivalent of the Millennium Falcon, in this narrative era. The ship—and thus its captain and crew—stand as a home and a symbol of liberty" (Guyot 2015, 11). The prequel short story "Mercy Mission" by Melissa Scott (2015) has her intervening to save innocents. At mission's end, she thinks that the most frustrating part in uniting with a different planet of oppressed people is their lack of vision. "Yes, they'd made it, delivered the gattis-root extract and escaped, but that was all they'd done. And even when someone recognized that there was common cause to be made, it didn't actually change anything" (24). She ends the story realizing how much she wants to be a true Rebellion leader. "Maybe she could pull together a group of her own, find some way to stand up against the Empire" (24). Marshall adds, "Hera is very upset about the lives that have been lost, and that seems to really motivate her" (*Star Wars Insider* 2017b, 24).

Since they all live in her home, the team function as a matrifocal tribe—each agrees to follow her general decisions as leader. Also, each is inducted and made to prove trustworthy, and then the team will willingly lay down their lives to protect any of its members. There is no strict hierarchy, with all opinions and plans equally valid. Each member can step up and contribute or even control the action when his or her own skills are needed. With it, their team models a new non-patriarchal structure far different than the Chancellor's and Jedi Council's in *Clone Wars*.

Hera's been working with Kanan for six years, after she met and recruited him. The novel *A New Dawn* by John Jackson Miller follows the young heroine as the pair of rebels meet. She's flying from planet to planet protecting those wanted by the Empire. He's a local bartender used to keeping his head down . . . though he also tries to help innocents in danger. Each instantly sees the other as a fellow troublemaker.

At this point, they have contrasting though basically equal levels of power—Hera is already a Resistance member, actively recruiting people like herself. On meeting Kanan, she judges him repeatedly. When she discovers he doesn't want to join the formal Rebellion, she accepts this without pushing him, to his relief. At the same time, her words are provocative and teasing as she notes that she picks her friends carefully and adds that if he has to ask what she needs help with, he's not ready to know.

He, meanwhile, is a trained Jedi—with greater abilities than just about anyone he meets, though he refuses to use them. On seeing eighteen-year-old Hera's fire, he regards her as an idealist without a concept of the risks she's taking. He also idealizes her in turn. As he thinks, "All women were magical creatures to Kanan, but there were happy forest nymphs, and then there were wizards. There was so much more to Hera, and it might tales days or weeks or years to find out what was motivating her" (251). He continues regarding her as a mystery through the story.

"You've been fun to be around, street fights notwithstanding," he smiles (145). He insists on flirting with Hera—not the best of messages, as it suggests any hero working with any heroine must approach their relationship on that level. She responds to his attitude and any superiority by dismissing him—interrupting and giving him "a smile that was only slightly patronizing" (130). Their power play continues, as she remarks that he's right and he decides this is "a phrase he thought sounded wonderful coming from her, whether she meant it or not" (131). They make a plan to not only stop the Empire's devastation but dissuade them from trying again. As Hera nearly dies from falling debris, Kanan stops it with the Force, revealing his Jedi powers. Besides being a moment of trust and heroism, this suggests he's crossing a line, motivated by Hera to rejoin the fight. As the book wraps up, Hera thinks: "The Emperor had disenfranchised souls across the galaxy, people from all walks of life. A reluctant near-Jedi was just one more of their countless number . . . He was also smitten with her, she could tell—and she was all right with that too. She didn't want to tell him that her war had already begun, and that in war, there was no time for anything else. He would probably understand that eventually" (365). This relationship will last through the entire show.

Upon finding the young hotshot Ezra in the first episode, Hera is the one to choose to recruit him. As she adds when Ezra evades them on their own ship, "Very creative. Sounds like someone I used to know." She glances at Kanan, making her point. They hurriedly go on a mission to rescue captive Wookiees, bringing Ezra along. Hera comments, "We don't have time to take him home anyway. We need to move now. I'll keep an eye on him."

In the cockpit, Ezra protests: "You know, this whole mission thing is nuts. I'm not against sticking it to the Empire, but there's no way I'd stick my neck out this far. Who does it?"

Hera responds, "We do" then cleverly negotiates with the Imperials, outwitting them so they can board. Devin Grayson, writer of the *Hera: Forces of Destiny* comic, sees that Hera can sometimes be "bend-in-the-wind strong instead of tough-as-nails strong" (Baver 2018a). Watching her, Ezra learns about commitment and cleverness together. At the same time, they're the nonfighters left behind. Though she's the leader, Hera's most common role in fact is getaway driver. Still, clever Ezra is the one to realize they've walked into a trap. Hera urges Ezra to go rescue the others while she waits on the ship, giving him the active hero role.

HERA: I need to be ready to take off, or none of us stands a chance.

EZRA: No. No way. Why would I risk my life for a bunch of strangers?

HERA: Because Kanan risked his for you. If all you do is fight for your own life, then your life is worth nothing. They need you, Ezra. They need you right now.

As she insists she believes in him, she's the inspiratrice and cheerleader for the young male hero. He joins the team, and Hera continues as his champion and interceder from the gruff Kanan, pointing out that he's a potential Jedi and insisting Kanan train him. Devin Grayson glowingly describes "how good she is at reading and inspiring people." As he adds, "There're kind of two types of leaders: the ones who define and spark the movement, and the ones who keep that fire burning by quietly helping people find their place in it. Hera's arguably both" (Baver 2018a).

"Out of Darkness" (107) introduces their mysterious advisor, the operative Fulcrum. Hera is the one to communicate with her, while Sabine resents the secrecy. Kanan explains, "It's Hera's job to find missions that create problems for the Empire and profit for us. If she trusts the contact, I trust the contact. No questions asked" (107). Fulcrum, eventually revealed as a figure in a white hood, calls the shots from afar.

In "The Siege of Lothal" (201), Kanan insists he doesn't want to join an army, but Hera tells him he must follow orders. With this, the hierarchy

becomes clear. The show is heading toward uniting all the bands of out-
laws into a coordinated fighting group with shared intelligence and a
military command structure—the Rebel Alliance. This repels Kanan, who
recalls the devastation of the Clone Wars. However, Hera is still determined to join her team with the larger cause:

> **KANAN**: After this mission, I want us to go back on our own. Fight-
> ing alongside soldiers isn't what I signed up for.
>
> **HERA**: You seem to be forgetting these soldiers helped save your life.
>
> **KANAN**: And I'm grateful. But that doesn't mean I want to join their
> little army. When you and I started together, it was, "Rob from the
> Empire, give to the needy." A noble cause. Now we're getting drawn
> into some kind of military thing. I don't like it.
>
> **HERA**: We are fighting a bigger fight, but it's still the right fight.

It must be noted that Hera's people have been subjugated by the
Rebellion. Co-writer Henry Gilroy describes her being "forged by war"
and adds, "her strength and her resilience as a character is really evident
when you see where she came from" (Gutierrez et al. 2017a). Unlike
three-fifths of the crew, Hera is a racial minority in the galaxy. The Empire is a place of racism, privileging humans over aliens in a parallel to
Imperial Europe's treatment of Africans and Asians. As Dooku thinks in
the *Revenge of the Sith* novelization: "A government clean, pure, direct:
none of the messy scramble for the favor of ignorant rabble and subhu-
man creatures that made up the Republic he so despised. The government he would serve would be Authority personified. Human authority"
(Stover 2005, 51).

Kanan's "people," the Jedi, are gone, and he gets by passing as an
ordinary human. Hera, however, cannot pass, and her planet still lies in
jeopardy. This emphasizes the reason she's so devoted to a larger cause—
without all the species banding together, all will be subjugated. Nonhumans in particular will become the Empire's slave labor. This parallels
similar struggles on earth. As a Smith student explained, "The liberation
of women of color is the liberation of everyone else. Everything rests on
them, because without them, the whole system couldn't exist" (Crossley
2017, 48). They are the ones who can rise up and save everyone. As one
race gains dominance over all the others, Hera can see a dark future
ahead, for her more than the others. Dooku goes on to smirk, "It was no
accident that the primary powers of the Confederacy of Independent
Systems were Neimoidian, Skakoan, Quarren and Aqualish, Muun and
Gossam, Sy Myrthian and Koorivar and Geonosian. At war's end the
aliens would be crushed, stripped of all they possessed, and their systems

and their wealth would be given into the hands of the only beings who could be trusted with them. Human beings. Dooku would serve an Empire of Man" (Stover 2005, 51). Wetmore (2005) comments:

> The Empire also seems to be racially homogenous. Only humans are seen in Imperial settings. The Rebellion is multicultural and multi-ethnic, but the Empire is all-human, all-white, and primarily British. When aliens are present, they are not a part of the imperial hierarchy; they are bounty hunters, for example, hired by the Empire to find the rebels more effectively. Or they are tools in another sense, being used to build battle droids to provide an enemy for the eventual clone army, for example, or serving as informants and spies, such as in Mos Eisley in *A New Hope*. The Empire, by and large, is primarily a humans-only, or at least human-centric, human-privileged organization.

Many races, growing up under this system, feel its weight. However, the Rebellion's goal is not strictly equality or independence for all the systems. They seek to restore the Republic—arguably better for the minority races who would get to banish the occupying armies and get seats in the Senate, but they would still be marginalized in galactic affairs. Wetmore continues, "The struggle for liberation in the original trilogy is neither a nationalistic nor ethnic struggle—it is a galactic one. The Ewoks do not fight to free Endor and thus need not assert Ewok culture. The Wookiees do not fight to free Wookiees from oppression, the Gungun do not fight for the Gungun." The original trilogy provides a particularly colonial lens—the Ewoks and Wookiees help free the mostly white, human Rebels from tyranny, but the Wookie home planet is not freed in turn (except in the more balanced novels). This echoes "the use of African and Asian troops by the European colonial powers during the Second World War—the 'natives' fight to liberate and restore power to those being attacked by totalitarian neighbors but retain their own second-class citizen status and oppressed situation," as Wetmore adds. However, Hera does a better job in this than the original trilogy. She raises the alien races to band together in mutual support, not servitude to the humans. Ahsoka as Fulcrum joins her—no longer in service to Jedi and Empire but to the freedom of marginalized aliens like herself. Together they fight for a more egalitarian galaxy that respects their own struggles.

"Homecoming" (216) reveals more of Hera's origin, with insights into her home planet, family, and loyalties that Ahsoka never achieved. To provide a safe shelter for their fighters, the Rebels plan to capture an Imperial carrier stationed above Ryloth, Hera's planet. The Ghost crew contacts Hera's father, famed Twi'lek resistance fighter Cham Syndulla, who featured in several *Clone Wars* episodes. Sabine is impressed, adding, "The Liberator of Ryloth. I studied your Clone War tactics at the Academy." Kanan cutely bows, stammers, and gushes. "Cham may be a hero of the Rebellion, but Kanan's nerves aren't those of a soldier meeting a soldier, but of a boyfriend meeting his beloved's father for the first time" (O'Neill 2018, 28).

Meanwhile, Hera is so irritated she keeps shutting the cockpit door, so she won't see Kanan fawning over his endless war stories. Hera confides in Ezra that she and her father are estranged, as Cham is obsessed with the Twi'lek Resistance and considers Hera's faith in the Rebellion misguided. Hera bitterly explains, "We haven't spoken in years. He was a hero in the Clone War, fought with the Jedi to free Ryloth from the droid army. But after the war, the Republic became the Empire and refused to leave, so he started fighting them. Once my mother was killed in the resistance, Ryloth's freedom became the most important thing to him."

To the crew's shock, Cham betrays them, shooting them all with stunners and revealing his plan to blow up the Imperial carrier as an act of defiance instead of capturing it for the rebels to use. He insists, "You haven't been here to see what the Empire has done to our world. They plunder our wealth and sell our people into slavery. This ship must burn, for all Ryloth to see."

With her more universal perspective, Hera argues that their planet-centric small rebellions are destined to fail: "I want freedom from the Empire as badly as you, but this battle can't be won on Ryloth alone. During the Clone War, you didn't just fight for a village, you rallied everyone to liberate the entire planet. You inspired me. The Rebellion is no different. But either you couldn't see that, or you didn't believe in me. And that's why I left." With this, Hera manages to convince Cham to help her, and instead they destroy a pursuing Imperial cruiser, achieving the demonstration Cham wanted. She actually places her hands over his to guide the controls, and he acknowledges that they've always been "stronger together" After adding the carrier to the Rebel fleet, Hera and Cham reconcile their relationship before parting: Hera hugs him goodbye at the end and he acknowledges he's proud of her.

After this, the Free Ryloth movement aligns closer with the larger Rebellion. However, Grand Admiral Thrawn, a tactical genius who derives his intelligence from the study of other species' art, invades Ryloth and occupies the Syndulla clan province. Cham flees their family home, abandoning his late wife's Kalikori heirloom in "Hera's Heroes" (305). This is, as the episode explains, "a totem passed down the line of a Twi'lek family. It honors all who have come before." Each generation adds another piece, combining art, expression, and legacy—all the Empire seeks to destroy. Vanessa Marshall explains, "It was really cool to learn more specific details about her history." She describes seeing Hera become so desperate "that she would risk anything for the Rebellion" (Gutierrez et al. 2017a). Hera goes in to recover the artifact, but fails, and the Imperials take Hera and Ezra hostage to convince Cham to surrender. Cham capitulates out of love. However, Hera asserts her strength in her place of power, the family home, and ignites bombs throughout it in a series of traps. They escape on the *Ghost,* and Cham and Hera have a few nice moments, even as Hera maintains her commitment to the Ghost. Meanwhile, Thrawn keeps the Kalikori, which he uses to taunt the team on several occasions.

By season three, she's known as Phoenix Leader and season four, General Syndulla. Actress Vanessa Marshall says, "She's been awarded for all the militaristic choices she's made—she's Phoenix Leader now. With that comes a lot of dire consequences that she has to face. With a greater number of ships comes a greater probability of losing one of them, if you will, so I think she has had to experience different kinds of losses in this season and that definitely takes its toll" (*Star Wars Insider* 2017a, 138).

Another plot that slowly grows is Kanan and Hera's romance. They were known as Kanera to hopeful viewers who saw contact sparks between them. "As far as a great many fans were concerned, Kanan and Hera were 'space married'," critic Shana O'Neill explains (2018, 27). Marshall says, "I think she is so focused on her mission she doesn't even allow herself to have anything as, for lack of a better term, petty as a romance. That's terrific because she manages to be focused and get a lot done" (*Star Wars Insider* 2017a, 142). Only small hints appear through the series of their fondness. Still, Hera and Kanan flirt directly in "Heroes of Mandalore" (401):

HERA: I need you to come back.

KANAN: Oh, having trouble overthrowing the Empire without me?

HERA: Our team is an important asset to the rebellion.

KANAN: An asset? Is that what we are?

HERA: You know what I mean.

KANAN: Well, you know how I feel.

HERA: Are we still talking about the mission?

KANAN: That depends.

HERA: On what?

KANAN: You know.

Clearly, by this point, their feelings have become much more overt. In "Kindred" (407) they finally kiss onscreen. "Not only does she initiate this kiss, but once it ends, she cups his face in her hand and stares directly into his eyes, as if to say, 'Got it?' It's empowering, it's loving, and is everything that Kana ever wanted—if the look on his face is any indication" (O'Neill 2018, 31).

When Imperials capture Hera shortly after, Kanan admits his feelings, as he tells Ezra, "Take the lead on getting Hera back . . . I would, but I can't think clearly because of the way I feel about her" ("Jedi Night," 410). He dramatically bursts into the Imperial interrogation chamber and saves her, wrapping a caring arm around her as she slumps. "I see we're in a special mood thanks to the interrogation droid," he quips.

As they stand before the star-filled window, she says, "Wait. I have to tell you something." The mood seems romantic, but instead she says in her drugged state, "I—I hate your hair" of his new short cut. He in turn has brought her "a present," as he says—her family totem that Admiral Thrawn had stolen. "I knew you'd come. I am not letting you go this time," she babbles drunkenly as he climbs with her draped over his back. After several interrupted fakeouts, she finally tells him she loves him, and they kiss. However, Kanan saves the ship from an explosion by sacrificing himself in a moment highlighted by epic music. Hera is alone once more.

The series ends with Kanan dead and then Ezra making an ambiguous final sacrifice. Thus abandoned, Hera and Sabine finish Ezra's plan and liberate his beloved homeworld of Lothal. As they gaze down on the cheering crowd, they realize they can keep resisting, even without Jedi. The ordinary people are finally rising up and reclaiming the galaxy—the moment the show has been laboring to create. It's a true democracy arriving, not the Jedi's exclusive heroism.

As the novel *Aftermath: Life Debt* (2016) fills in, the Twi'lek homeworld is freed by Cham Syndulla and his resistance, but only after the Battle of Endor. Sabine concludes, narrating the story, "Hera fought in the battle of Endor, as did Commander Rex. By that time, there had been a new member added to the crew of the Ghost. Spectre-Seven, Jacen Syndulla. Born to fly, just like his mother. And, well, we all know what his father was like" ("Family Reunion—and Farewell," 415). Seated beside his mother Hera, he's an emerald-haired imp named for Han and Leia's Legends son (leaving many to wonder if he will likewise turn to the dark side). At last, Hera frees her people and finds love and motherhood, but only after Kanan's sacrifice. The Greek goddess Hera without Zeus, general and single mother at story's end, she emphasizes the wide range of talents a woman can offer while rising above stereotyping.

SABINE AND ART-PUNK

Rebels begins with the conventional Chosen One story: Darth Vader announces, "The Jedi Knights are all but destroyed, and yet your task is not complete, Inquisitor. The Emperor has foreseen a new threat rising against him, the Children of the Force. They must not become Jedi" (101). Next, the street thief Ezra appears, scamming Imperial soldiers to save people in distress, and then lightheartedly stealing from both indiscriminately, noting, "Hey, a kid's gotta eat." Through it all, his cocky attitude suggests a young Han Solo with Luke Skywalker's theme music. Ezra goes after Imperial crates, only to find another group of thieves competing with him. As each tangles with him, he gasps, "Who is that kid?" emphasizing his coolness and skills. One, covered head to toe in red armor and helmet, suddenly leaps down onto the speeder, perches on the cargo, and shoots it apart from his own load. She smirks in a feminine voice, "Pretty gutsy move, kid. If the big guy catches you, he'll end you. Good luck!" This is Sabine, voiced by Indian-American actress Tiya Sircar.

Upon pursuing Sabine, Ezra witnesses her doff her helmet and shake her sassy red locks. He stares, spellbound, and romantic music plays. This interlude lasts about a second before the ship takes fire, but the message is clear—sixteen-year-old Sabine will be the love interest though she "decides to ignore Ezra's awkward attraction to her" (Bray 2014, 36). She leaps into the gunner chair and returns fire. Ezra, oblivious, says in a sexy teen voice, "My name's Ezra. What's yours?" She ignores him. After, Sabine tells him about them all:

SABINE: Not too good at following directions, are you?

EZRA: Not so much. You?

SABINE: [Chuckles] Never been my specialty.

EZRA: Who are you people? I mean, you're not thieves exactly.

SABINE: We're not exactly anything. We're a crew, a team, in some ways a family.

EZRA: What happened to your real family?

SABINE: The Empire. What happened to yours?

Sabine, a human from Mandalore, is the wild child, racing speeders and blasting enemy ships. She offers the group an impressive technical knowledge in combat, weapons, electronics, mechanics and even languages. Through it all, there's lots of attitude. In slang dictionaries, a "Sabine" is an alluring, feisty, funny young woman especially talented in art, who always has a comeback. "Sabine never questions her own motives for fighting the Empire. She simply loves the excitement and the adventure" (Bray 2014, 35). Her culture's take over by the Empire links with another possible namesake: Before they were subdued by Roman forces in the third century, Sabine women were known for their fortitude. According to legend, the Romans stole the women of the Sabians, but when the Sabians tried to retrieve them, the wives decided they were happy in Rome. On a deeper level, the Sabine women are credited with aiding the creation of ancient Rome. With all this, her ancient society, now under control of the Empire but maintaining their exalted traditions, echoes the Sabians indeed.

She attended the Imperial Academy but left after a bad experience and joined Hera's team. Her sassy acrobatics as she evades the Storm-troopers and calls them "bucketheads" are delightful. Sabine has orange and blue hair in season two with sporty new multicolored armor. Later she changes the hair to blue and aqua, and then white and lavender. As the series continues, she becomes known for crazy plans. Filoni adds, "Part of her anger and explosiveness in art is that she's fighting through so many things" (Gutierrez et al. 2017b).

> Sabine's outfit has provoked some discussion because of the color of her Mandalorian armor. The pink was easily dubbed as girlish and adding a trope dimension to the character, but the color does not have to be seen as negative. Sabine can be a warrior, a pivotal crew member, and a teenage girl, without needing to be dressed in any one specific color. Colors, generally speaking, are a way for Sabine to express herself through her visual creations, especially as she mixes explosives with graffiti. (Guyot 2015, 13)

Sabine's shirt is figure-hugging, while her concealing helmet and arm and leg guards make her contrastingly androgynous. The *Visual Guide* describes it as "comfortable clothing for easy movement" (Bray 2014, 35). Of course, her armor is cultural, with a long history. She explains in the fourth season, "Ezra, the armor I wear is 500 years old. I reforged it to my liking, but the battles, the history, the blood, all lives within it, and the same goes for every Mandalorian. This armor is part of our identity. It makes us Mandalorians who we are ("Heroes of Mandalore," 402). She has an anooba best pained on the shoulder of her armor, while the star-bird on her chest becomes the symbol of her rebel group (Bray 2014, 34). Her helmet became an icon to join the rebellion (Hidalgo 2016a, 78). *Star Wars Absolutely Everything You Need to Know* explains, "Sabine owns a pair of Westar-35 blasters (nicknamed Jai'galaars) which she has decorated with her own colorful designs. This unusual artistic statement is in stark contrast to the plain blasters popular on Mandalore, particularly with Death Watch" (Bray et al. 2015, 33). Mandalorian armor is feature-less, giving them all a Mandalorian group identity as well as armoring them. However, her paint individualizes her. Sabine's explosives include bright colors and starburst shapes, allowing her to combine her two loves. Her room is decorated with pictures of bounty hunters, anti-stormtrooper graffiti, and Lothal animals. A later episode shows a touching mural of her friends Sabine has painted on her ceiling.

The *Star Wars: Propaganda* book describes Sabine Wren as a propaganda artist vital to Rebel recruitment (Hidalgo 2016a, 69). "This then teenage saboteur used colorful paint bombs as well as traditional explosives to make loud, attention getting displays meant to undermine the illusion of Imperial indomitability" (Hidalgo 2016a, 77). In a world of Imperial uniformity with faceless white Stormtroopers, Sabine's defiantly painting them—along with the entire area—is a strike for individuality, mocking and thus disarming the intimidating warriors. The first *Rebels* chapter book explains, "They cracked down on anyone whose work didn't glorify the Emperor's New Order. Their efforts didn't frighten her in the least. They only made her want to paint more images that defied the Empire" (Kogge 2014, 36). By the third and fourth seasons, she's pitted against Admiral Thrawn, who understands other races with a near-supernatural power, thanks to studying their art. He's thus a particularly fitting match for the young rebel. Co-writer Henry Gilroy explains, "It was an organic way to bring Thrawn into our stories by having him study Sabine's art" (Gutierrez et al. 2017a).

The chapter book adds, "She wanted to visit them all. She wanted to have a thousand thousand adventures on those thousand thousand worlds. She wanted her name and her artwork to be known across the stars" (Kogge 2014, 35). She dreams of becoming as famous as Boba Fett as "a great warrior *and* a great artist (Kogge 2014, 39). Reveling in her attitude, she flies her brightly painted captured TIE fighter into an Imperial ship as a bomb in the first season finale. Even the Stormtroopers admire it before it blasts them.

"Out of Darkness" (107) has the women team up. Hera counsels Sabine with great tranquility while Sabine protests like a rebellious child. Her insistence that she has to know more about what the Rebellion is up to makes sense, given her past. She insists, "Hera, you know what happened when I was a cadet at the Imperial Academy on Mandalore. I trusted the Empire, followed its orders blindly, and it was a nightmare. I want to believe we're doing good, making a difference. But sometimes it seems like the harder we fight, the harder things get out there." Soon enough, they enact Sabine's plan, shooting and bantering as they face a ferocious beast. As they shoot back to back, death seems certain before the cavalry comes. Still, they persevere and achieve a greater degree of teamwork and trust. As they conclude the episode, they emphasize this:

HERA: Sabine, I know you have questions, questions I can't answer right now. But know that I trust you. I just trusted you with my life down there.

SABINE: I know. I know you do.

HERA: Good. We are making a difference, Sabine. And I promise: we won't always be fighting this battle alone. Do you think you can trust me?

SABINE: I think I can try.

In "Blood Sisters" (208) Sabine gains more backstory as she wrangles with a former best friend. This is Ketsu Onyo (voiced by Gina Torres), a bounty hunter chasing the same droid courier that she is. The pair broke out of the Imperial Academy together, as Sabine puts it, "Before you got greedy and left me for dead." Ketsu, who works for the criminal organization Black Sun—slavers and assassins—straightforwardly admits that she hasn't decided whether to turn her old friend in. She's more punk—a little taller and darker skinned with red tattoos and a mostly shaved head.

Ezra gets in his surprise that Sabine has an old friend at all: "Always figured you for a loner . . . You spend a lot of time in your room, alone. And, uh, you actually tend to eat alone. Sometimes. And combat practice alone. And go off probably to be alone. And, uh, I don't know. I guess sometimes, you know, I'll find you alone, after I've, maybe, followed you, and you're angry and I've heard you say more than once, 'I want to be alone.'" Certainly, Sabine isn't seen with a lively group of friends. Still, Sabine reaches out to the other woman, telling her, "I forgive you . . . for leaving me for dead. And I still trust you . . . I met people who gave me a second chance in life, and that's what I'm giving you." When the Empire arrives, the pair team up to escape by setting charges on the stolen ship. Sabine is knocked out, but Ketsu saves her and thus helps mend their relationship.

Satine also gets an arc focusing on the freedom and rule of Mandalore. On the big screen, Boba Fett wears Mandalorian armor inherited from his father. In *The Clone Wars* and *Rebels*, the Mandalorians are a warrior race whose empire slowly grew to encompass more than 1,000 worlds.

> *Star Wars* had included female characters of this background, such as Bo-Katan Kryze and *Star Wars: The Old Republic* featured a female Mandalorian: Shae Vizla. So, it is good to see that Disney is expanding on this, especially as most prominent Mandalorians in *Star Wars* are men, known through Boba Fett and his father, Jango Fett. Seeing classically male character types represented by female ones is essential, just as seeing female Jedi introduced in the prequel era was an important development. Showing a fictional universe where possibilities are open to numerous kinds of individuals is needed to better understand the expansive universe *Star Wars* encompasses. (Guyot 2015, 12)

Dave Filoni comments: "Well, a lot of our goal in Season Two was to really focus on characters and give them more background, depth, and history. We really tried to do that with Sabine. We always promised that you were going to find out more about her Mandalorian heritage and we had this great opportunity to expand on the culture we had created in Clone Wars" (D. Brooks 2016b). In "The Protector of Concord Dawn" (213), Sabine shares a fascinating glimpse of backstory on her clan when she challenges the local Mandalorians to combat to defend a critically injured Hera:

SABINE: How's it going, boys?

MANDALORIAN: Where did you steal that armor from, bounty hunter?

SABINE: Bounty hunter? Not lately. I forged this armor with my family.

MANDALORIAN: Family? That's a bold claim. What's your house?

SABINE: I'm Clan Wren, House Vizsla.

MANDALORIAN: House Vizsla? She's Death Watch. Traitor!

SABINE: My mother was, but I'm not. I came here to settle a score, and I invoke the code to seek justice through single combat.

MANDALORIAN: No one has invoked the code since the Empire took over.

SABINE: Well, who's in charge here? The Empire or Mandalore?

Since Death Watch was a Mandalorian splinter group that opposed Duchess Satine's pacifist approach, Sabine is clearly living out the legacy of the previous series. Sabine wears a helmet of the Nite Owls, a faction of Death Watch that followed Bo-Katan, Satine's sister, instead of Darth Maul, who proclaimed himself their ruler. (Ahsoka defeated Maul, leaving the Mandalorians to be absorbed by the Empire.) Sabine's time in politics, however, hasn't ended.

"Trials of the Darksaber" (315) reveals that the mysterious dark-hued saber the team has found has a specifically Mandalorian heritage. Sabine's clan is descended from the Mandalorian Jedi Ta Vizsla. After his death, Mandalorians stole his unique Jedi Darksaber during the collapse of the Old Republic and regarded it as a symbol of rulership. Now Sabine is its heir and can lead a great army if she chooses to wield it. She convinces the Jedi to train her.

Filoni comments, "But more than the training with the saber, it's what's preventing her from using it, which is her personal history. That became the backbone for that whole event" (Ratcliffe 2017). In the hero's classic arc, Sabine rejects the responsibility but reluctantly takes it on at Kanan and Hera's urging. Kanan trains her by giving her a stick (which she protests she can already fight with) and then he goes full Jedi on her and beats her. He then leaves her, humiliatingly, for Ezra to train. So far, Sabine is being treated as far less capable than Ezra the boy wonder, though she's been fighting longer without the cheat of the Force.

Still, she delightfully asserts herself in a way the male heroes don't as she protests, "The only thing I'm learning is that Ezra must be really gifted to learn as well as he has from a lousy teacher like you." With this, she emphasizes that she's more a peer than a student and shouldn't be infantilized. Hera gently criticizes Kanan for making her work with sticks: "Maybe because she doesn't have the Force, you don't believe she can do this?" As Hera adds, "I know what it's like when people you love don't believe in you, when they let you walk away. Remember how hard it was for her to trust us." Kanan protests but finds himself rethinking his approach. Kanan and Sabine apologize to each other, and he offers her the Darksaber. Luke's theme plays as she takes it—a swordwielding hero like the boys who have gone before her.

Meanwhile, Sabine's friend gives her Mandalorian vambraces complete, as he says, with "Grappling line, paralyzing darts, repulsor. All designed to combat the abilities of the Jedi. Go take Bridger down a peg or two." With them, she slams Ezra away from herself with Jedilike power. Even without "chosen one" magic, she's equaled the playing field. After this, Kanan trains her seriously, progressively faster and more skillfully. As he goads her, insisting she ran away from her people and abandoned her responsibilities, she finally bursts out with the truth:

> The truth is that I left to save everyone. My mother, my father, my brother! Everything I did was for family, for Mandalore! I built weapons, terrible weapons, but the Empire used them on Mandalore, on friends, on family. People that I knew. They controlled us through fear. Mandalore! Fear of weapons I helped create. I helped enslave my people! I wanted to stop it. I had to stop it. I spoke out! I spoke out to save them. To save everyone! But when I did my family didn't stand with me. They chose the Empire. They left me. Gave me no choice. The Empire wanted to destroy worlds. And they did. They destroyed mine.

At the academy, as it happens, Sabine joined a weapons development initiative and constructed a superweapon that would destroy Mandalorian armor, believing the weapons would be used to ensure peace. When she realized the Empire was using them to subdue her people, she defied them and fled, her work unfinished.

While telling this story, she beats Kanan in combat, shoving him down a hill and standing over him, lightsaber drawn. Filoni notes that he "wanted Tiya to be very emotional . . . and to see the depth of the hurt that her family caused her" (Gutierrez et al. 2017b). As her speech ends, however, she lowers the weapon and breaks down. Kanan finds a way to help her heal, replying, "The Empire rules with fear. And not everyone can be as strong as you've been. Your family is in a prison, one of their own making. It's up to you to help them out of it." Her friends all pledge to follow her into battle. With this, she finds a heroine's support system. Young girls watching do as well. Considering season three, Filoni notes:

> The biggest character arc we're doing, besides Ezra, is really Sabine. We're getting into a lot more detail about Sabine and her backstory and what her actual potential is. I think that she's kind of risen to become a character that to the series is every bit of a lead as Ezra. She's almost like an Ezra-counterpoint, because she doesn't have all the natural abilities, but she has a lot of great instinct and she has a lot of guts and a lot of courage. She's going to have quite a journey this season that gets into why she is a rebel and what her business was in the Imperial Academy when she was a teenager. Some of that's a bit overdue, but it's a great arc and Tiya Sircar, of course, is performing brilliantly as Sabine. It's going to be fun for people to watch. (*Empire* 2016)

When Sabine spoke up against the Empire, the rest of her family took the Empire's side and denounced her. Still, her desertion publicly shamed them, and Sabine's father became a hostage of Governor Gar Saxon, the Viceroy of Mandalore and the Emperor's Hand. Her brother Tristan (named for a Celtic warrior-hero) was forced to join Saxon's Imperial Super Commando. Sabine returns to her family home to offer her mother, Countess Ursa Wren, the Darksaber and encourage her to defy the Imperial government controlling her homeland, showing the galaxy that their control isn't absolute. However, her mother rejects her as a misguided child, if not a traitor, as their dialogue reveals:

URSA: Always so immature, so selfish.

SABINE: Yeah, and what about you? Always putting power and politics before your own family.

URSA: Everything I do is to protect my family, Sabine!

SABINE: Please! You do it for control.

URSA: And your father called me stubborn. Now I see it in you.

SABINE: What do you see?

URSA: A warrior. Not the one I'd hoped, but still . . .

SABINE: Well, I am your daughter. How could I be anything less? ("Legacy of Mandalore," 316)

Still, her mother confesses that she was glad Sabine fled, as it ensured her safety. Filoni comments, "I like to relate *Star Wars* to real life. I think it's really not that different than if you haven't seen your family in a long time, and they can't see you as a different person. They are not familiar with how you've grown" (Ratcliffe 2017).

Star Wars has spent much time on father issues—not just Luke and Vader but also Jyn and Galen Erso—but little on mothers. Idyllic Shmi and Beru have no arcs but remain static and uncomplicated. Filoni says, "Here there was an opportunity to have this very strong character, and in a way, it's interesting because she so powerful. She's a warrior, she's a Mandalorian, and she's a leader of her entire group. I wanted her to appear cold and go against the typical kind of warmth that you think is often identified with a mother" (Ratcliffe 2017).

Her first name means bear, symbol of brawling strength, in counterpoint to the lighter, flying, darting wren. She wears grey subdued Mandalorian armor, not royalty's elaborate gowns or her daughter's rebellious graffiti art. Seated on her throne she's an image of strength and androgynous power. Filoni adds that removing the father from the equation was deliberate. "I wanted her to clearly be the head of the family politically, maternally, and guiding things" (Ratcliffe).

To Sabine's horror, the countess surrenders the two Jedi and the Darksaber to the Empire's toady Viceroy Gar Saxon, but he turns on her—of course—and condemns her house to death. Clan Wren fights him, her family and the Jedi united at last. As Luke's Jedi theme swells, Sabine battles him in single combat, even as her mother insists that by Mandalorian law, they cannot interfere. She defeats him, reclaiming the Darksaber, but refuses to kill him. "That might be the Mandalorian way, but it's not my way. Not anymore." She has become a noble hero, melding the Jedi code with her own beliefs.

The Viceroy, however, tries to shoot her in the back. Her mother shoots him in a moment of strength and control. "No one threatens our family."

Of course, this blow has left their society in chaos. Clan Wren, no longer on the fringes, can take a stand against the Empire as all their people choose whether to rebel or conform. "Perhaps Mandalore needs chaos if it's to become strong once again, and so that we may find a leader worthy of our people," the countess says, but proudly rejects the Jedi's aid in this internal matter. Showing responsibility for her choices, Sabine decides to stay behind and further her family's cause before returning to the larger Rebellion.

She begins season four leading her people to rescue her father from the Imperials, Darksaber aloft and a jetpack to boot. It's a stunningly powerful image. Her smooth, graceful perfect attacks are contrasted with Ezra, who cannot control his own jetpack and hurtles about like a goofball.

After the battle, Sabine meets Lady Bo-Katan of House Kryze, sister of Duchess Satine from the previous series. Bo-Katan was made regent by the Jedi and is still seen by many as Mandalore's rightful ruler. She says of Sabine, "She has become a courageous leader. She reminds me of the best of who we were and could inspire us to become more than we have been of late" ("Heroes of Mandalore," 402). Sabine tries giving her Darksaber, but the other woman refuses it, insisting, "I am not the leader you seek." Sabine looks sadly at her devastated homeworld, wishing she could fix her planet, but even her father is lost to her. Her mother arrives to tell her he's going to be publicly executed. Kanan and Hera wonder whether the entire planet is forfeit at this point. The team rescue her father, and Sabine stares at him for a long emotional moment before removing her helmet. He embraces her. "Sabine, you are my daughter. I was pleased then. Even more now." As it turns out, he's speaking of her artwork and adds, "You've progressed. Your use of color and line is better."

Sabine proudly notes that her father isn't a traditional warrior—"My dad fights with his art" ("Heroes of Mandalore," 401). However, as she listens over the comm, her mother and brother are shot from above . . . by the weapon she has created. In contrast with young innocents like Ezra and Luke, Sabine is the mastermind behind a genocidal weapon—a burden she must confront. She begins the next episode crumpled in self-doubt, only to find her mother and brother have survived. She owns up to creating the weapon, explaining, "I was young. It was a challenge, and I was arrogant. But when I realized the Empire tested it and actually planned to use it, I sabotaged the prototype and destroyed the plans. I thought that was the end of it, I swear to you!" ("Heroes of Mandalore," 402). The weapon only targets Mandalorian armor, risking the destruction of their heritage or their lives. Sabine is captured by the Empire, who hold Lady Bo-Katan hostage to make her improve her product. Of course, her team save the day and destroy the Empire's plan. She ends the episode appointing Lady Bo-Katan to lead them: "You have the wisdom of a ruler. There's no one I trust to wield the Darksaber more than you." All the clans pledge their support, and Sabine nobly adds, "Now I understand why the saber came to me. It came to me so I could pass it to you" ("Heroes of Mandalore," 402). With this, she caps off her family's rebellion in the previous series, atones for her own acts, and mends the rift between houses.

In the last episode, Ezra sacrifices himself to liberate his planet. He summons his space whale friends, the Purrgil, who destroy the Imperial blockade and speed off into hyperspace with himself and Thrawn in tow. He leaves a message for Sabine that he's counting on her, and she fulfills his last wish, protecting his planet in case the Imperials return. They do not—highlighting how little the Imperials care for the Rebels' beloved homelands as any more than resources to steal. Thus, Sabine finds her job as guardian pointless and unfulfilling—one imposed from the outside, on behalf of a vanished friend and world not her own.

In the epilogue, Ahsoka comes to Sabine, robed in white in Jedi garb. Sabine concludes, "As for me, I used to think that Ezra was counting on me to protect Lothal, the planet and the people he cared for so much. But one day, I realized there was more to it. There was something else I was meant to do. Ezra's out there somewhere, and it's time to bring him home" ("Family Reunion—and Farewell," 415). On the one hand, she's now devoting herself to finding her man. On the other, she's questing for her family—the theme of the series. She's choosing the path this time, and her apprenticeship to wise Jedi Ahsoka emphasizes how much she still has to discover.

REBELS-ERA LEIA

For decades, little was known of young Leia's life—how she joined the Rebellion and became a senator—until her fateful first moments in *A New Hope*. While in the original trilogy years, Han and Lando each got paperback trilogies, Leia's was contracted to space-fantasy novelist Leigh Brackett, who had written *El Dorado* and *The Long Goodbye* and also helped with a script treatment for *Empire*. When she died, she wasn't replaced "and once again Leia would get short shrift" (Taylor 2014, 288). However, modern stories fill in her backstory with romance, adventure, and duty as the lively young princess juggles public perfection with increasing Rebel activity.

The children's book *Star Wars: Rebel Force: Hostage* offers a delightful scene of the eight-year-old princess being banned from a party after "she and Winter hid a giant wooly moth in the Minister of Agriculture's desk drawer. He deserved it—but Leia's father didn't see it that way (especially after the wooly moth chewed through a sheet of flimsiplast containing the budget for the whole next year)" (Wheeler 2009, 52). The pair steal a hoard of snacks and watch the party from hiding. However, Leia is soon kidnapped to influence her father, and her father's friend must come rescue her. As she curls trustingly in his arms even as he reflects on her true identity, he has the power and agency she lacks. Further, the kidnapping establishes a pattern of her being used as a hostage to control others. It's not a very empowering story.

However, Claudia Gray's recent novel *Leia, Princess of Alderaan* (2017) provides backstory while linking her story with the buildup for *Rogue One*. Sixteen-year-old Leia claims her birthright as heir—she must complete three challenges of her own choosing to prove her worthiness. She selects providing charity to stricken planets with her own funds, climbing Appenza Peak as her adoptive mother once did, and joining the Apprentice Legislature. Of course, all three come with unexpected challenges. "She thinks they'll be simple tasks to perform—or, in the case of the Apprentice Legislature, things she believes she already understands and has a good grasp of. But each challenge winds up offering its own unique challenges, each one of which pushes her closer to becoming the Leia we see in Episode IV," Gray explains (Floyd 2017). Helping the starving people has her unwittingly interfering with a growing Rebellion, which she soon discovers her father is running. The Apprentice Legislature are toadies for Palpatine who provide him excuses to extend his tyranny. And as she learns mountaineering, Leia finds herself falling for her teammate, Alderaanian noble Kier Domadi (though her mother hilariously notes that she wishes Leia had rebelled a little and fallen for a scoundrel). Each challenge emphasizes that she's earning her place as senator and princess instead of coasting on privilege. She becomes a role model for teens for her accomplishments as well as her sympathetic struggles.

Easter eggs and in-jokes continue to link young Leia with her film counterpart. As Leia grows up, she tangles with her droid assistant constantly in matters of wardrobe—she favors a simple white gown and ponytail, while the droid insists Leia at least proclaim her heritage with elaborate braids and hairdos. While she wears silver gowns and jewelry on a few occasions, she continues resisting the insistence on dressing up. On rough missions she wears a white jumpsuit "though the sensation of having a blaster at her side was one she didn't want to get used to" (108). She tangles with Tarkin, forming a mutual dislike even as she struggles to evade his suspicion. Young Leia also befriends Amilyn Holdo and discovers the Rebel base on Crait where she will return in *Last Jedi*.

Of course, Leia has far darker struggles than wardrobe. In one significant scene, Leia visits Naboo, where Queen Dalné takes her on a state visit dressed in one of the queen's gowns—apparently the petal gown Padmé wears in the parade scene of *The Phantom Menace* or one much like it. She meets "Moff Panaka," a decent man loyal to the Emperor, and clearly the older Captain Panaka from *The Phantom Menace*. Struck by Leia's appearance, he wheedles the history of her adoption from the unsuspecting princess, and nearly informs the Emperor. However, he's killed in an assassination by Saw Gerrera. This scene winks at the audience's knowledge of Leia's true parentage, while stressing the close calls her innocence brings about. Of course, this interlude provides several easter eggs for fans while tying the eras together. "Panaka! Originally, I thought of having him be a part of the Rebellion," shares Gray, "but then Pablo Hidalgo reminded me that in Legends, Quarsh Panaka became a moff loyal to Emperor Palpatine. That was too great a detail not to bring into canon, too. Plus, once I really started thinking about that, and the potential inherent in having someone from Padmé's life show up in Leia's too . . . well, it offered one of my favorite turns in the entire story" (Floyd 2017).

Through the book, she's hurt by her parents' distance—discovering they've been working with the Rebellion is in many ways a relief. However, as Kier keeps reminding her, the entire planet—the galaxy's last beautiful sanctuary—could be lost if the Emperor discovers them. As he teaches her to shoot and she makes her way through the treachery of politics, she discovers her greatest power is being thought harmless. "Nobody looked at a young girl and saw a threat. That was an advantage her parents didn't understand yet, one Leia intended to use to the fullest" (Gray 2016, 224). Using it, she saves innocents and tricks the heads of the patriarchy in a way her royal father cannot. Leia ends the story by saving the Rebellion and ascending to Royal Heir. The twists and turns of the novel arm her with the tools she needs to join the Rebellion and fight for freedom.

Star Wars: Rebels provides a single glimpse of the fifteen-year-old princess as she struggles to maintain her cover. In "A Princess on Lothal" (212), Leia must be incredibly careful to maintain her cover as the innocent royal diplomat. "I come with relief supplies for Lothal's needy, who are suffering terribly as a result of the rebel insurgency here. Surely you don't want innocents to starve," she offers sweetly. "Because of prejudices about women as weak or incapable, few historical women were considered to be military threats, even when their nations were occupied by hostile powers" (Reagin and Liedl 2013, 49). Thus, historically women were often used as spies. Leia's universe doesn't have the same overt stigma, but as a teen princess, she exemplifies this apparent harmlessness.

She fakes being taken hostage and gives carefully chosen orders to distract the Stormtroopers as needed. Emphasizing her toughness, she shoots two Stormtroopers, but only without witnesses. As Leia teams up with the stars of *Rebels,* she insists they make it look good, even to the point of shooting her. She tells Kanan and Ezra, "You don't understand. It's not that simple. If the Empire could prove Alderaan provided ships to the rebels, we'd lose our seat in the Senate and be charged with treason. But if they're stolen on a planet controlled by the Empire Alderaan would be blameless." She also uses herself as bait when needed, aware that she's a status symbol to the Stormtroopers, and an embarrassment if she's hurt or captured on their watch. She takes some pleasure in demanding the Imperial commander's shuttle several times, just to pull rank and needle him.

Ezra finds her arrogant and high-handed, but she's soon sympathizing with him about the loss of his parents. As he wonders whether they can possibly win, she tells him she shares his worry. "But I'm still here . . . I feel like because I can fight, I have to for those who cannot. And I think you might be the same way." With this, she inspires her fellow rebels.

The 1981 radio play expands Leia's early scenes from *A New Hope* and leaves her sparring with Lord Tyon, Tarkin's underling. She's caught in what she claims is "a humanitarian gesture," delivering medical supplies and spare parts. However, Tyon tells her the rebellious planet has been purified. When she protests, he assures her he admires her and her family both but that she should take "great care" in choosing her words. Leaping in to emphasize her harmlessness, Captain Antilles insists Leia "was expressing understandable distress" and Lord Tyon is mollified by this show of childish feminine emotion. Turning condescending instead of angry, he flirts and even suggests she join him for dinner rather than have her ship searched. Knowing her words to Antilles are being monitored, Leia decides to set a trap for "that bloated ego of his." As she narrates for the camera, "Lord Tyon is attractive but he's too forward, too confident. He needs to be taught a lesson. If he searches the Tantive, he'll anger my father and I'll be able to keep him at arm's length a little longer." She insists he'll search her ship as "he's not that much of a gentleman." Her ruse succeeds and Tyon lets her ship leave unriffled.

Of course, his condescension continues. Following her to Alderaan and invited to dinner, Tyon smiles, "You live such a sheltered life," when Leia is disgusted that he wants to go hunting. After he proposes marriage and insists he is growing in prominence, Leia flatters and goads him into telling her of the Death Star. In both these plotlines, Leia's sweet flattery and apparent damseling allows her to outwit him. As the episode concludes, Leia insists on taking the plans to the Rebels as the Empire "will be less suspicious of me." Her harmlessness is her greatest weapon.

FULCRUM: MENTOR, NOT STUDENT

As the first season of *Rebels* ends, the team all enter their cockpit to find a hologram of Bail Organa telling them of other rebel cells—information their pilot Hera has been keeping hidden. Ahsoka comes to them, revealing in a surprise for long-time fans that she's been their secret source Fulcrum the entire time. She blesses their mission with her hopeful words:

AHSOKA: My name is Ahsoka Tano.

EZRA: Why did you come here?

AHSOKA: Because of you and your apprentice, many in this system and beyond have heard your message. You gave them hope in their darkest times.

EZRA: We didn't want that hope to die. So what happens now?

AHSOKA: I don't know. One chapter has closed for you, Ezra Bridger. This is a new day, a new beginning. (114)

Dave Filoni reveals that he had never intended to give Ahsoka such a role: "Originally, I was thinking Ahsoka was much more of a passive player. That she wasn't a combatant as much. I later changed my mind and thought, 'We really need to see the warrior in her in this volatile time.' We're always evolving the characters and their stories to try and get the best thing possible" (D. Brooks 2016b). In *Rebels*, Ahsoka is more mature and more confident, but there's still more than a trace of young Ahsoka. She has grown with the young audience, finding her path as they have. Eckstein explains, "The Ahsoka from *Clone Wars*, the Ahsoka we grew to love, is still inside of her. That is who she is, but she's grown up and matured. It's like any of us—that teenager in all of us is still in there, those hopes and dreams and personality quirk" (D. Brooks 2016a). With a quiet confidence and self-assurance, she talks less. She's dressed more modestly. She's taller with longer lekku (and mysteriously, a different pattern on them that irritated fans). She's a fully actualized adult.

Of course, this arc allows her to face her once beloved master. In "The Siege of Lothal" (202), after a brush with Vader's ship, Ahsoka shrieks and faints (a clichéd feminine moment but quite an understandable one). Filoni explains, "It's almost like realizing something that's so jarring you can't handle it. Like Force feedback. She gets knocked out because, I believe, in a flash of a moment, she sees this truth that there's a layer of hate. An angry, horrible being, and then underneath it is Anakin Skywalker." She tells Ezra, "I haven't sensed a presence like that since the Clone Wars . . . But I do know that he will be coming. They'll all be coming now." She insists she doesn't know who the Sith lord they've just discovered is. Vader, however, reports to the Emperor that he has found her. "I believe the apprentice of Anakin Skywalker lives and is in league with these rebels."

The Emperor orders him to send an Inquisitor after her, adding to the suspense and putting off the confrontation. For now, Ahsoka is an ordinary Rebel among many. As she duels Inquisitors, her actress notes, "I think she's become the skilled fighter that everyone hoped she would be and probably even better than we hoped she would be. She's so cool and she's so tough. I mean, when you want to talk about just power and confidence, she really exuded that" (D. Brooks 2016a). The character has a small arc, but this is deliberate, as she's guesting on a different show. Filoni adds, "As we're kind of sitting there, it's really apparent that this could become The Ahsoka Tano Show really quickly. That's not the direction we wanted to go in for *Rebels*. This show is primarily about Ezra and Kanan and what they're doing. If we focus too much on Ahsoka, we're not showing the importance of our main characters anymore" (D. Brooks 2016b).

One interesting female who appears in this arc is the Seventh Sister, a female Inquisitor of the same race as Luminara and Barriss. She's played by Sarah Michelle Gellar, the original girl power icon as television's Buffy. Ashley Eckstein smiles about "knowing that I was fighting with Buffy, getting to perform with Sarah Michelle Gellar." As she adds, "She was even more amazing than I ever thought she would be. I will always admire Sarah Michelle Gellar and she's just awesome, she's everything you want her to be and more. But to be like, 'I just dueled with Buffy and beat her,' was really, really cool" (D. Brooks 2016a).

Vader dispatches Seventh Sister to find Ahsoka, and she soon captures Ezra. She then attempts to break him with psychological tricks as well as the Force. When he finally outmasters her and escapes, she continues the Inquisitors' other task—capturing Force-sensitive children. In "The Future of the Force" (210), Seventh Sister murders everyone onboard a ship save a baby and her grandmother. When Ahsoka comes to the rescue, their verbal sparring emphasizes the Inquisitor's role as the murderess and corrupter of small children, pitting Ahsoka against the evil witch figure as the heroic defender of life: "I know why you want the children."

"Well, who doesn't want to be a mother?" This is the traditional girl power conflict, seen in Oz, Narnia, Wonderland, and so many similar fantasies. Continuing her obvious heroism, Ahsoka rescues the men and proves superior to Seventh Sister at combat. Though Ahsoka kneels in apparent surrender, she actually grabs and deactivates her spinning lightsaber, before hurling her against a nearby pillar. Imperial reinforcements come, but Ahsoka at least escapes with the children, mighty and protective to the end. The Seventh Sister is finally executed by Darth Maul.

Meanwhile, onboard the *Ghost,* Ahsoka tells the Padawan Ezra about Anakin, while watching one of his training videos. She recalls, "He was powerful, rarely lost a battle. What would have surprised people was how kind he was. He cared deeply about his friends and looked out for them until the end." When Ezra asked what happened to him, Ahsoka replies, vaguely and sadly, "The last time I saw him, he was rushing off to save the Chancellor. Then everything changed. The war ended, and the Jedi were accused of treason. One by one, they were hunted down" (218). Filoni adds, "This is something that George [Lucas] and I talked about. When Order 66 is called and Ahsoka survives it, she has a moment where she reaches out into the Force and she looks for Anakin's presence" (D. Brooks 2016b). However, she cannot sense her friend and concludes that he has died.

Meditating soon after, Ahsoka discovers the painful truth about her mentor. The actress adds, "Anakin is family to her. So to find out that a family member is basically a murderer, it's devastating. It's just like if anyone were to find out that their family member murdered lots of people, how would you feel? It's almost like you can't even comprehend it" (D. Brooks 2016a). Still, Ahsoka deludes herself. Filoni concludes, "Her unconscious mind knows it's Anakin; her conscious mind cannot accept that Anakin could be this horrible person" (D. Brooks 2016b). Of course, she has no master or mentor to guide her through the shock—all the Jedi have left her behind. Their hierarchy, her marginalization all are part of the past and she must choose her final fate.

In the season finale, they meet. Vader raises his sword to kill Ezra, smirking that his earlier comment about Ezra dying bravely was in error. "Perhaps I was wrong." Ahsoka suddenly calls out from behind him: "It wouldn't be the first time."

VADER: It was foretold that you would be here. Our long-awaited meeting has come at last.

AHSOKA: I'm glad I gave you something to look forward to.

VADER: We need not be adversaries. The Emperor will show you mercy if you tell me where the remaining Jedi can be found.

AHSOKA: There are no Jedi. You and your Inquisitors have seen to that.

VADER: Perhaps this child will confess what you will not.

AHSOKA: I was beginning to believe I knew who you were behind that mask, but it's impossible. My master could never be as vile as you.

VADER: Anakin Skywalker was weak. I destroyed him.

AHSOKA: Then I will avenge his death.

VADER: Revenge is not the Jedi way.

AHSOKA: I am no Jedi.

With twin lightsabers, gleaming white, she holds her own. However, as Ezra and his wounded master Kanan flee with the Sith holocron they've captured, Ahsoka hesitates. Vader's mask has split open and Anakin's eye shines through. "Anakin. I won't leave you. Not this time."

Her invoking of his name even as his blue eye peers out suggests a small part of him remains. It also puts them on an equal footing at last. In this scene, Vader is voiced by both Matt Lanter (Anakin on *Clone Wars*) and James Earl Jones at once, with Matt taking progressively more of the line as he says her name three times. However, his eye narrows. "Then you will die." Ahsoka still refuses to run (a lesson clearly learned from her novel arc) as she continues to battle her old friend. As Yoda, Obi-Wan, and Luke, the male heroes do, she realizes she must face her appointed adversary, much as it pains her, through responsibility to the universe.

The episode ends with Vader walking away, suggesting he has killed her. However, her death occurs offscreen, both to soften the loss of this children's show central character and to allow for more possibilities — perhaps she has escaped or ascended to become a Force ghost . . . the audience is tantalizingly unsure. Filoni concludes, "It's likely you haven't seen the last of her. I won't say in what form she appears, but I just felt like to calm the fans down, they need to know there's something to look forward to" (*Empire*).

Two years later, as season four and thus the entire series draws to a close, "A World between Worlds" (413) brings back the fan favorite character. Ezra opens portals to all of time and space, and when he sees her final battle, with Vader about to finish her, he pulls Ahsoka out of time. There in the mystic passageways, she mentors him, and warns him that she cannot rescue his dead teacher Kanan, since he sacrificed himself to save all of them and his death is necessary to the timeline. Ahsoka, whose death presumably saved no one including Vader, does not have such a debt to history. In the end, she returns to her own time, but without dying, and perhaps with a few tidbits of knowledge about the Rebels' next two years. She and Ezra vow to find each other, and that's it, or nearly.

In the final scene of the finale, Ahsoka appears to Ezra's partner and love interest Sabine Wren, beckoning her to join her in finding Ezra, who was lost in hyperspace. Ahsoka has aged, with a white cloak and a large staff, suggesting a new level of power. Their shared quest establishes she'll continue mentoring the next generation now that she's passed the great test as Luke did. Unlike Obi-Wan and Yoda, she is not a true Jedi, but she still has much to offer the universe. In her arc, she grows from child to warrior, loyal soldier to disillusioned rebel, and finally, adult and then all-wise seer.

SEVEN

From Picture Books to *Forces of Destiny*

Multimedia for Younger Fans

ROLE MODELS OR WIMPS? THE PICTURE BOOKS

"With the release of the prequels, release of the 3D versions, and *Star Wars* early reader books, and the relatively child friendly *The Clone Wars* (2003–2005) animated series, a new generation of *Star Wars* fans have plenty to be excited about. Young girls in particular may have even more reason to join the fandom than previous generations" (Travis 2013, 55). Indeed, *Star Wars'* appeal to children allows the franchise to market picture books, action figures, and playsets to increasingly young ages. However, this depiction can offer female role models with agency and personal power or more wimps needing rescue. The Legends-era canon mostly produced adult novels, with Junior Jedi Knights and Young Jedi Knights spinoff chapter book series following Anakin's training. Thanks to the subject matter, these are written largely for and about boys. Besides a line of comic books, there were more nonfiction guidebooks than original novels.

Disney's all-age marketing in the new era transformed this. Teen books, middle-grade novels, a new comic book line beginning after *A New Hope,* and nearly seventy picture books have arrived. In contrast with Disney's specifically girl-power adventures *Forces of Destiny,* these often retell parts of the films. Still, Elizabeth Schaefer, author of some of the *Forces of Destiny* novelizations, gives Rey a bit more of an emotional arc in her *Force Awakens* chapter book adaptation *Rey's Story.* Likewise, replica journals of Rey's life on Jakku and Paige's time in Bomber Command give both young women significant emotional and adventurous arcs, providing interesting backstory for the films in original stories. In the middle grade *Before the Awakening,* Rey makes a female friend but refuses to leave Jakku with her on the ship they've repaired together. To her devastation, her friend steals the ship and leaves her in a brief but compelling story. In the young adult section, Claudia Gray fills in Leia's arc to become a rebel and senator in *Leia, Princess of Alderaan.* E.K. Johnston likewise bridges Ahsoka's path between series, while Beth Revis's *Rebel Rising* offers Jyn's prequel. This variety of work all emphasizes juvenile readers' ability to be heroes . . . though the books for a younger audience often tell a different tale.

Star Wars Adventures: Princess Leia and the Royal Ransom by Jeremy Barlow (2009) is an original comic book adventure for eight- to twelve-year-olds. It's set in a series with one for each original series character, leaving just one volume for their female teammate. It begins powerfully with Leia driving a speeder bike with Han clinging to the back. The two are busy squabbling as they evade pursuit. Soon, they rescue a traditional princess, complete with blonde hair and a tight pink gown. As she asks Han to carry her over a muddy patch and complains about her shoes, Leia smirks, "So is *she* princess enough for you?" However, Leia soon exhibits clichéd jealousy. When the two women are kidnapped and tied up together, Leia fails to empathize with the superficial woman who assumes Han only likes Leia because she too is a princess. "You think *we're* the prize, but you're wrong," Leia tells their kidnapper (all the while reinforcing to readers that she thinks of herself and her fellow princess that way). She offers him a database of Imperial shipping codes instead (and switches it for a Gungan cookbook). More problematically, Han comes to the rescue, getting in a macho fistfight as he insists, "Chewie—protect the girls!" The princess's father ends the comic by offering her to Han in marriage. Han flees to the Falcon, the princess giving chase, and Leia smilingly walking behind. While the comic is humorous, it doesn't do enough to contrast the two princesses as both are kidnapped, tied up, and rescued by the male hero.

The 2012 young reader novel *Star Wars: Rebel Force: Hostage* is meant for the same age reader, once again with one book focusing on each original series hero. It has Leia confront the survivors of Alderaan and lead them in a memorial ceremony. Writing a children's book about such a devastating genocide seems difficult, and indeed Leia's thoughts come out quite repressed even wooden. By contrast, Luke's sympathy for an orphan is poignant and sweet, making the princess appear even more robotic. "Hundreds of people would attend, all expecting her words to heal her wounds. She couldn't even heal her own," the book quietly explains (Wheeler 2012, 29). Her speech at the ceremony is lifeless, devoid of any thoughts at all as she tells her people, "We will never replace what we have lost. We can only remember it" (Wheeler 2012, 83). The survivors voice terrible pain, by contrast, as one man describes "our wives were vaporized in the middle of cooking a pot of L'lahsh, our children blown to bits while running through the meadow picking t'iil blossoms" (Wheeler 2012, 35). As he concludes, they may have escaped but they didn't survive. The plot involves the survivors kidnapping Leia in return for a new home while Luke, Han, and Bail's old friend all try to save her — this plot too takes much agency from the heroine.

Post-Disney, most books appear in The World of Reading picture book line with three levels of difficulty. The level two book *A Leader Named Leia* by Ella Patrick summarizes her actions in her four films with a start on *The Last Jedi*. The language and pictures surrounding her actions are also surprisingly static for such a powerful character. As the book insists, "Leia was strong and brave. She fought for what was right. She was a rebel," the character merely stands, removing her hood. The story has the Empire acting, fighting, and capturing her, while Leia remains motionless, helpless, and defiant. Only after the men free her does the book give her a picture of her firing a blaster as it adds, "Luke and Han tried to rescue Leia. But Leia had to rescue Luke and Han instead!" *Empire* has Han rescuing Leia and Lando betraying them while she stands motionless once more. When Han is sacrificed, the book simply adds, "Princess Leia was sad. She loved Han Solo." So much for her heroism. After the speeder scene in *Jedi,* sentences give the Ewoks all the credit and Leia none. *The Force Awakens* has her spending all her scenes asking Han to save her son and Rey to find her brother, while her charging in to fight the First Order is left out. "General Leia led the Resistance against the First Order" only shows her standing, arms crossed. Certainly, the events of the films could be blamed for this . . . but most of Leia's action scenes don't appear. Unfortunately, this sort of depiction is typical of many of the books.

Another level two, *Star Wars: A Queen's Diary* by Simon Beecroft (2014), retells *Phantom Menace* from Padmé's point of view, adding a little more art and complexity. Her face is large and endearing on the cover. Padmé explores her massive palace and flies about her city, displaying a lively curiosity but also an active interest in her world. Half the book offers introductions — her city, her friends and family, her planet (with plenty of costumes). After this, the plot begins. Sadly, Padmé's plot involves being "saved by Jedi Knights" then by Anakin's podrace. At last, they return to Naboo. "Today I became a fighter. No one would help my people, so I had to help them myself," she asserts, with a single picture of the firefight before the scene shifts to Anakin saving them all. "He flew a spaceship straight into the invaders' spaceship and blew it up!" she relates, giving him the more exciting plot. She ends hoping Anakin will become a Jedi and that they'll meet again, handing the story over to her younger counterpart.

The level two *Jedi in Training* by Heather Scott (2009) follows Ahsoka through the film and subsequent television episodes. As it explains, "Ahsoka is brave and clever but she still has a lot to learn." It details her

crushing droids with the stone wall and emphasizes her power as a rescuer but in her images, she stands motionless. When she faces Dooku's
wicked apprentice Ventress, she cringes, letting the more powerful woman loom. The text further weakens her, adding "Ahsoka has to defend
herself against Ventress before Anakin comes to rescue her." The pictures
zoom in on her face or show her caring for helpless males Rotta and Plo
Koon instead of battling or leaping about energetically. All sentences
frame her as the thinker and planner with Anakin sometimes deigning to
take her advice.

Ahsoka in Action, a level one reader, shows her more powerfully. As
she battles and pilots dynamically through the art, the text describes her
as an excellent pilot and fighter, who defeats entire armies. "Ahsoka
leaps toward the droids, flashing her lightsabers," it concludes (Richards
2013). Some scenes show Anakin central, with her off to the side, but
more than half the pages leave him out, emphasizing her own power.
Further, Padmé and Luminara appear, while Ahsoka's enemy Ventress
appears multiple times, showing off other women in the galaxy.

The level three Clone Wars book *Forces of Darkness*, also by Scott in
2009, seems inclusive as it showcases Ventress on the cover. However,
the book actually features short introductions on all the villains and only
depicts Ventress for two pages. The text here is rather flat: "Count Dooku
employs Ventress to carry out dangerous missions. She is a deadly assassin." In this phrasing, the book emphasizes how subordinate she is to the
villain. She stands motionless as the book praises her "athletic body" that
lets her "leap and twist into action"—action-packed but focusing on her
figure in its skimpy outfit.

Hera's Phantom Flight, adapted by Elizabeth Schaefer (2015) from the
episode "Out of Darkness" takes a better stand for its character. The book
has the heroine piloting the Ghost and spying on the Empire, discerning
their secrets. Her whole team appears, but she gets a fair share of the
pictures and most of the text. After an introduction, she and Sabine find
themselves in peril, trapped with monstrous fyrnocks, with their distress
call useless. Together the women decide to line up barrels of explosives
and shoot at them. It's a violent plot but an exciting, female-centric, self-
sufficient one. Even when the Ghost arrives, Hera is the one to use it to
electrocute the creatures, as she smirks, "There's a lot you don't know
about my ship."

Schaefer's level one *Rey Meets BB-8* (2015) retells the early part of the
film complete with photos. However, Rey lives a rather dull scavenging
existence. The verbs that describe her include "explores," "looks,"
"trades," "fixes"—active but not terribly interesting. Halfway through,
she hears BB-8 in danger and rushes to rescue him. This part is far stronger, with the heroine actively exploring the ruins, and then saving BB-8
out of a moral imperative as she's scared and "she did not want the droid
to get hurt." While Leia ends her adventures as she began—a rebel com-

mitted to protecting rebels—Rey has a noticeable arc, as she changes from a life of loneliness to a life where "Rey and BB-8 have each other."

Leia and the Great Island Escape (based on the chapter book *Moving Target*) presents Leia in sentences where she tries to blend in or boards a boat or looks through a viewer, rather than thinking, discovering, fighting, or saving the day. In a more active four-page scene, she drives the boat. However, they are captured by pirates who then reveal themselves as rebel rescuers. Even Leia's starting up the steps toward the powerful alien, hand in a fist, cannot compensate for the endangerment and rescue being completely out of Leia's hands.

Star Wars The Last Jedi Look and Find (2017) offers very conventional gender roles (reflecting the film but taking things even further). Within, the Caretakers cook and serve food while carrying, gathering, and doing laundry. Paige has a warrior's role, but the book explains, "Paige's bomber may be small in comparison, but the damage she intends to do with it won't be" (Wage, 2017). She's thus seriously diminutized. "General Leia Organa discovers that the First Order's new technology can track her ship through hyperspace. But she and the Resistance maintain that spark of hope that keeps their cause alive" is a weak image of Leia as inspiratrice, not heroine. She doesn't even appear here, replaced by a more exciting space battle. Meanwhile, Luke has been fishing and crafting staffs, while "Rey has waited patiently outside Luke's hut," simply killing time instead of practice fighting or pursuing him. Instead of emphasizing the women's actions, the book has them standing about hoping the others will act.

In *Rey's Journey* (2017), Rey goes around being confused for a dozen pages as Luke rejects her quest. After all the pages of Rey asking and waiting but doing almost nothing, Luke sees Leia's message and agrees to teach her. Thus, Rey has very little agency. Echoing this, in Patrick's *Rose and Finn's Secret Mission* (2017), after Finn and Poe deal with the attack, Rose first appears page ten. However, her language at least is strong, and she appears threatening Finn. "Rose hated traitors . . . Rose zapped Finn using a small electro-stun prod." She realizes how to save the day and off the pair fly. At the casino she explains morality to the naïve Finn, reclaiming the story. At last, D.J. takes over the action, breaking them out, and the story ends before the fathier stampede, but Rose has led part of the arc.

The *Star Wars* Little Golden Books (2017) present a contrast between Rey's *I am a Hero* by Christopher Nicholas and Leia's *I am a Princess* by Courtney Carbone. Rey's follows her through half the book. She powerfully proclaims, "I am a hero. I fight for what's right to help others." While the story goes on to include Luke, Yoda, and so forth, it's clear Rey is central here. The book adds, "A hero can be a brave Jedi knight (Obi-Wan) or a queen (Amidala sitting posed) or a princess (Leia putting the file in R2-D2). This part is tokenism, a somewhat static overview of many heroes, though it does give the other women a brief salute.

"I am a princess. I lead others and keep them safe," the other book reveals, as Leia of *A New Hope* orders her men to evacuate. It's a nice set of role model images as it reenvisions the story for an even more powerful Leia. The other characters spend the book following her lead, with barely a word spent identifying them. Leia is fully the hero here. While she has rather static images as it tells the story of her being adopted by royalty, joining the rebellion and helping destroy the Death Star, she's an active character for most scenes. She stands up to Vader and Jabba—the latter in her bounty hunter suit, not the bikini. She also fires her blaster ahead of her as the story reveals, "A princess must be ready to take charge in any situation." A scene with the Ewoks describes making friends while one in the asteroid field emphasizes that she must work through her fear and be brave. The final scene shows her hanging a medal on the reader as the book queries, "Are you ready to be a hero?" For many young readers, this inspiration is all they require.

DISNEY'S GIRL LINE—*FORCES OF DESTINY*

Star Wars: Forces of Destiny offers a specifically girl power series centered around *Star Wars'* various heroines: Jyn, Rey, Leia, and Padmé, but also the heroines of the children's shows *Clone Wars* and *Rebels*. 2018 added a Qi'ra cartoon and Paige and Rose team-up comic. The series arrives as transmedia, not only with the animated micro-series of two- to three-minute online episodes but also several age levels of books, comics, and toys. The "adventure figures" are fully clothed for action with posable joints and cool accessories like blasters, staffs and lightsabers. Hasbro even gave every doll an action move: squeezing the legs makes Leia ready her blaster or Rey swing her lightsaber. Kylo, Luke, and Chewbacca figures emphasize inclusion for boys here as well. There's also a child-sized "Rey's staff" and purple lightsaber. (Outside this line, girls and boys can also buy Phasma's massive blaster, for a tougher statement.) Ashley Eckstein (the voice of Ahsoka) explained, "I loved the Disney princess movies growing up, but that's not who I wanted to be. I wanted to be the Jedi. I wanted to play with the boys and use the lightsaber. There are a lot of girls who would prefer to carry around a lightsaber than wear a tiara" (DIS Unplugged Disney Podcast, 2011). At last, there are products marketed for them.

The cartoons, first premiering on Disney's YouTube channel on July 3, 2017, offer two releases each with eight cartoons, each under three minutes. Maz introduces all the episodes with a quick and simple "The choices we make, the actions we take, moments both big and small, shape us into forces of destiny." The original actresses reprise their roles, from

the *Clone Wars* and *Rebels* stars to Felicity Jones and Daisy Ridley. Rostis-lav Kurka (2017) writes in *"Forces of Destiny* Review: What Is Its Value?":
"Episodes are exactly the right length that parents can let their little daughters (or sons) watch it as part of their *Star Wars* education. The appeal at young audience as the target group is obvious, starting with the style, through the fairly straightforward plots, the 'right' mixture of char-acters being 'cool' and some cute elements" (Kurka 2017). Marissa Marti-nelli of *Slate* (2017) calls the show "a midyear snack designed to keep *Star Wars* fans sated between the franchise's feature-film releases."

This cartoon is the girliest *Star Wars* ever . . . and also the most Disney-esque. The art has "a less stylized, more cartoon-y look than that of the Genndy Tartakovsky *Clone Wars* series," as Martinelli (2017) decides. "But what makes *Forces of Destiny* truly unusual for Disney-era *Star Wars* is the way it leans into that childishness." The shows are light, fun, most-ly nonviolent adventures with clear lessons for young viewers. "I could actually see *Forces of Destiny* being a vanguard to some actual Disney *Star Wars* Princess movie," Kurka concludes.

The first episode, "Sands of Jakku," pairs Rey up with BB-8, carefully setting it within their short time together in the desert. Rey battles with her staff, but also shows compassion for a nightwatcher worm, recogniz-ing it's a hungry animal and feeding it. The others feature female team-ups, stressing heroism without involving the male heroes. Sabine and former best friend Ketsu reprise their roles from the first season of *Rebels*, but this time, Ketsu is more open to leaving the criminal organization Black Sun. In "Newest Recruit" (109) Katu finally officially joins the Re-bellion. This is prompted not only by Sabine's friendly and supportive decision not to push her but the good feelings she gets after saving a koala-like Chadra-Fan child from Imperials and stealing crates of food for the Rebels. Thus, patience and supportive friendship are modeled, as well as helping innocents.

"Of course, in three minutes, you don't have enough time to explore deep, intellectually rich themes of the SW universe. The connection to the lore is enough, however—we see shapeshifter assassins on Coruscant, we see the bounty hunter droid IG-88 (who appears in *The Empire Strikes Back* and has even much richer record of extra-canon appearances), we see Wampas or denizens of Jakku" (Kurka 2017). On Hoth, Leia and R2-D2 go hunting Chewie, who's vanished (in a cut subplot from *Empire*). As it happens, a wampa has found him and insists on cuddling him close. They all run away, and when it gives chase, Leia distracts the creature with her lantern and actually hypnotizes it. When the creature rouses, she hurls the lantern, which it pursues instead of her. This story offers team-work, nonviolent courage and ingenuity, though certainly a lot of luck. Martinelli explains:

These vignettes don't offer any major revelations for fans, unless you've spent the past three decades lying awake at night wondering where Leia managed to find a human-sized dress in the middle of the forest in *Return of the Jedi*. (The answer: Ewoks are apparently very speedy tailors.) Because the shorts mostly act as prequels to or "deleted scenes" from the movies and television series, you won't find clues about Rey's identity or the fate of Ahsoka Tano here—nor, sadly, any long, choreographed lightsaber battles. Instead, the self-contained stories tell side adventures that we didn't get to see in the movies, while delivering some basic life lessons along the way: Help those in need. Be kind to others. Fight for what you believe is right.

For instance, "The Imposter Inside" (106) is all about friendship. Padmé is throwing a diplomatic party (oddly in the kid-friendly white jumpsuit, not a court gown). She asks Ahsoka to do a security sweep as a favor. When shapeshifting bounty hunter Cato Parasitti attacks, she reveals women can be the villains as well as heroes. Discovering a new camaraderie, the women fight back with chairs and vases as well as the Force and win the day. After, they laughingly clean up together.

Ella Patrick's level two easy reader *Star Wars: Forces of Destiny: Meet the Heroes* begins, "Each girl was strong in her own way. And they were all destined to be heroes" (4). The book features the four film heroines and three television ones (a reasonable mix, given that the shows are intended for fans around this age). For very young readers, there's less of a story and more a character-by-character introduction. Rey's pictures all show her standing strong though static, as the story recalls her background but doesn't have her directly acting in the present. Leia is likewise motionless as the book explains, "Leia led the Rebellion in many battles, from the frozen planet of Hoth to the forests of Endor" (1–6). Ahsoka, of all the young women, is shown fighting with her lightsabers. Jyn and Padmé stand with blasters drawn. Meanwhile, as Padmé "works in the Senate with other leaders to make the galaxy a better place" (31), the phrasing is quite abstract rather than action-packed or heroic. The book is meant to be empowering, but it's rather bland.

There's also Emma Carlson Berne's *Forces of Destiny* (2017a) books for older readers. Each is about a hundred pages with three stories. The first volume features Rey, Sabine, and Padmé. Meanwhile, the stories are framed by Maz, who invites the reader to sit and join her for tea. She emphasizes the lesson of each tale, and their collective point that "being a hero means . . . stepping forward. No matter the outcome" (119). "Thank you for listening to my stories, my friend" she concludes sweetly and tranquilly (119).

The catch is that the series only retell the cartoon episodes instead of offering new adventures. Granted, the expansions offer more color. Here, "Sands of Jakku" becomes more personal as Rey feels emotions from friendship to panic. She's clever and rational at the same time: "She wasn't going to lose her new friend to a hungry worm. She closed her eyes, drew in a big breath, and let it go. She imagined her mind focusing down to a narrow pinhole of light" (25). Still, they emphasize a limited list of adventures.

Berne's second volume once more frames the stories with Maz's campfire, though this time she's speaking to small bat-eared purple critters called flurgs. In another adapted story from the cartoons, Ahsoka is running late to receive her Padawan beads. However, as she runs to the temple, she hears a cry for help. On discovering a malfunctioning industrial droid, she decides, "This one was going to be all her" (2017b, 18). In an action-filled sequence, she saves a woman and her toddler, and then arrives late and filthy to accept the consequences of her choice without excuses. Once more, the book's adaptation gives her more emotional depth. Meanwhile, a selfish Anakin is worrying about how Ahsoka's lateness is making her look bad. However, Yoda calls her "humble and brave" and awards her the beads (39). Of course, she has chosen the lives of innocents over her own priorities, a mature decision Yoda is wise enough to appreciate, even if Anakin is not. This offers a clear lesson for young readers as well as a defining moment in the charming heroine's life.

Jyn's story begins by emphasizing how she's become an unscrupulous forger to survive—a problematic role model story. When Stormtroopers menace a little girl who has a forbidden tooka cat, Jyn angrily thinks of them, ascribing to them the language of bullies: "They didn't have anything better to do. And they preferred to prey on the weak. She'd seen it many times" (2017b, 97). This emphasizes her motivation while teaching young readers the cruelty of bullying. She hurls a piece of fruit at them and confronts the Stormtroopers on the little girl's behalf. She kicks one in the gut (thus advocating direct violence against bullies, admittedly) and then trips the troopers with a pole to release the cat. She's a hero and savior for the little girl as well as a warrior. "The heroines can be seen as role models, but the stories are also made so the audience can see themselves in them. For example, in 'The Stranger,' the story almost begs for the audience to identify with the little girl Jyn helps—and which little girl (or boy) would not like her pet to be saved by Jyn Erso?" (Kurka 2017). There's lots of action, but all the property damage in the marketplace (which Jyn leaves the girl to clean up) likewise teaches a problematic lesson.

The *Forces of Destiny: Tales of Hope and Courage Replica Journal* was released in October 2017 as a holiday gift book. By Elizabeth Schaefer with art by Adam Devaney, it's quite pretty, with the characters' written comments and drawings included in the journal. Large and small fonts make the book extra exciting and emphasize important moments, while different colors of paper vary the adventures. However, once again, it retells the same stories from the cartoons and books, frustrating young fans in the lazy side of transmedia.

Here, some of the language choices in the six heroines' stories are especially nice: Leia's helping with the early rebellion is framed as a metaphor for childhood: Maz the narrator explains, "If you are something very small fighting against something very big, finding a good place to hide is important." This is clever and also encourages young fans to relate with Leia's abstract rebellion. "I wonder if you have ever felt like Sabine?" in the next story is less subtle. Each story has a blatantly spelled-out moral, as Maz explains, "Heroes like Padmé often try to carry the weight of the galaxy on their shoulders. But a galaxy is much easier to carry when you have a friend to help you do the lifting" or as Sabine tells Ketsu, "Sometimes it's about helping people in need." Her painting a new Black Sun logo for her friend is a thoughtful gesture that young readers can emulate. Thus, the same stories continue over and over, though with different nuances. Still, the different adaptations all provide gateways for children that are far less grim than the films.

All these stories show that girls can have their own adventures in the *Star Wars* universe—ones of friendship, courage, and ingenuity. They're short, extra scenes, arguably reimagining the original stories like *The Empire Strikes Back* with more girl power. The episodes are simple and juvenile, but that's their intent: "Adults are not the target demographic for Forces of Destiny, which sets it apart from previous, more sophisticated animated *Star Wars* series. The Forces of Destiny shorts stick to simple messages, uncomplicated humor, and easily solvable problems" (Martinelli 2017).

Volume two of the show, released in October and November 2017, offers another eight episodes, still just two and a half minutes, minus a fifteen second intro. Sabine's friend Ketsu returns for two episodes, struggling with her commitment to the Rebellion in a longer plotline with carryover through the season. Leia and Hera team up in one, as do Jyn and Sabine, and Padmé and Ahsoka. When Jyn sees a fleeing Sabine and helps her escape Imperials in "Accidental Allies" (113), Sabine perceptively compares their choices, noting sympathetically, "I used to work alone too. But these days I can't just think about myself." Jyn is won over by her friendly lack of judgment. Kurka explains, "The chief value of these scenes [is] that they establish or expand existing relationships. Rey and BB-8, Leia and Ahsoka, even Leia and Sabine (these two have practically zero interaction just on their own apart from this). We, as the audience, can get better sense of what do these characters mean to each other."

Of course, some of these relationships are not as progressive as one might hope. In "An Imperial Feast" (114), Leia discovers Han and Chewie on Endor, snickering as they watch the Ewoks preparing to eat the Stormtroopers. As Leia upbraids them and they smirk, the audience has more sympathy for the men than their chiding mother figure. Meanwhile, Hera (charmingly established in this scene as still alive and part of the Rebels after the Battle of Endor) only agrees to send over rations if Han admits the Ghost outshines the Falcon. Thus, she joins in on the silly macho posturing, while Leia bosses everyone around as the adult. Everyone's gender roles are thus problematic here.

"The Happabore Hazard" (115) begins with the bullying trader Unkar Plutt refusing to send Rey on a mission, adding in misogynistic fashion, "It's no job for you, girl!" He demands she wager her speeder, and in turn she insists on getting paid double. When she arrives, she discovers an ill creature slumped by the ship, and in generous, though gross fashion, digs a machine part out of its nose. The animal helps her in turn, leaving Rey, like her film counterpart, strikingly competent through her compassion and strength. There are more missing scenes from *Return of the Jedi* and *The Force Awakens* as, in the latter, Rey and Han fly together before reaching Maz's planet. All these are fun bits of trivia for fans, but often don't give the characters much time to stand out. "Objectively, did we need such scenes? No. But they are not entirely without value, either. Think of them as of a DVD bonus" (Kurka 2017).

Berne's tie-in book *The Leia Chronicles* adapts three adventures from the October episodes. In the first, Leia goes off with the Ewoks in *Jedi* and agrees to spend the night. In the morning, she's pleased at the gift of a dress. Still, the story doesn't add strength to her rather pointless vacation day hanging out with the Ewoks, even with its expanded length. Of course, the book tries. Leia tops this off with just about the only assertive comment: "Does the dress come with a spear?" (Berne 2018a, 37), and Maz finishes with a quick inspiring speech about friendship, the collection's theme.

Volumes three (March 19, 2018) and four (May 4, 2018) brought more new adventures with the *Last Jedi* stars' voice talents: Mark Hamill (Luke), Daisy Ridley (Rey), John Boyega (Finn), Lupita Nyong'o (Maz), and Kelly Marie Tran (Rose). *The Clone Wars* and *Rebels* stars also returned: Tiya Sircar (Sabine), Ashley Eckstein (Ahsoka), Vanessa Marshall (Hera), Catherine Taber (Padmé) and Matt Lanter (Anakin), among others.

As one might expect, several *Last Jedi* tie-in scenes appeared. In "Shuttle Shock" (203), Rose and Finn must deal with space jellyfish on their way to Canto Bight. "Porg Problems" (208) has Rey playing with the porgs when one steals her lightsaber. She holds it in place as it tries to dive away and is surprised at the new skill she's never tried before. Meanwhile, the porgs are delighted with their own surprise—a chance to fly. She keeps training with them, presumably preparing herself for the rock-lifting at *Last Jedi*'s end.

Forces of Destiny expands its range with a Yoda and Luke adventure on Dagobah and a Chewie and the Porgs story on Ahch-To, both without a female character anywhere. Still, having a few token male adventures (with Mark Hamill providing his voice in the former) is fun for fans too.

In other between-scenes of the films, Qi'ra's three-year gap is covered in "Triplecross," released just before her appearance in *Solo*. Here Qi'ra, already a lieutenant for the notorious Crimson Dawn, outsmarts an assassin droid IG-88 and the *Clone Wars* pirate Hondo Ohnaka, showing off her martial arts, lockpicking and quick thinking. She's clearly formidable even without Han.

Likewise, Chewie introduces Leia to Maz before *Jedi* in "Bounty Hunted" (206), to get help freeing Han from the Carbonite. When a bounty hunter shoots at them, Maz suggests, "You need a disguise and the bounty hunter is perfect." Together they disarm him and take his thermal detonator (admittedly rewriting Legends canon yet again). Maz also gives the couple her blessing: "I like this one, Chewie. Tell Han she's a keeper." She takes an active part here as mentor and, once again, suggests her elderly female presence in the galaxy dates back to the original trilogy.

For more of the delightful team-ups fans are coming to expect, Ahsoka teaches Ezra of *Rebels* in an energetic lightsaber battle, emphasizing that he can dodge her with the Force instead of relying on attacks in "A Disarming Lesson" (215). Sabine fights Stormtroopers alongside her brother in "Art History" (211) in which she must explain how important the statue the Stormtroopers are desecrating is to Mandalore. Her brother learns to feel as she does, even as Sabine's family helps round out her character.

Season two, as the 2018 releases were called, offers not just between-scenes but character-and canon-changing moments. "Traps and Tribulations" (214) shows the giant beast for which the Ewoks were setting the meat snare. This and a new Endor adventure with Hera show Leia and Luke working as a team as Hera and Chopper operate a bit farther away—both with the same pair of friendly Ewoks. Thus, the *Jedi* and *Rebels* teams become tied even closer together.

More interestingly, it looks as if Anakin's apprentice, Ahsoka, knew about his relationship with Padmé—something not dealt with in all the episodes of *Clone Wars* (which did end abruptly, to be fair). In "Unexpected Company" (202), Anakin and Padmé have arranged a very rare mission alone, only to hear Ahsoka loudly running up. Obi-Wan has sent her along as a third wheel. When there's an attack, and Anakin embraces Padmé, Ahsoka has her suspicions confirmed. However, she pointedly ignores them and flies everyone to safety. Back home, Anakin tells Ahsoka he's glad she came. Padmé privately tells her, "You and Anakin make a good team."

"Thanks . . . I could say the same of you." With this, the cat is out of the bag. Padmé simply thanks her, sharing the secret between the two of them.

As always, there are clever slices of life, showing the characters in their ordinary between moments—ordinary for them, anyway. Queen Padmé is seen in "Monster Misunderstanding" (210), arriving in her battle dress (the handmaiden one without the headdress, as she never seems to wear her queen clothes in these cartoons) to solve a small crisis. She realizes a building-sized sea monster is seeking its baby, stolen by poachers, and frees it. This isn't really the task for a queen, but she solves it cleanly. "Sometimes the best solution isn't the most obvious one," she explains.

When the tiny Teedo (implied in *The Force Awakens* to be her competition) tries to steal from Rey, she sighs and hands over her scavengings. As she thinks in Berne's *Rey Chronicles* adaptation, "Teedos didn't scare her, but no one knew much about them" (Berne 2018b, 82). While there's some fear of the other here, there's also nonviolent problem-solving. Rey is also smart enough not to take a valuable component that's holding the ship together. However, Teedo greedily snatches it. The ship begins collapsing. "A deep clang echoed from the depths of the ship. She didn't have much time" (Berne 2018b, 88). Further, Teedo is crushed by falling debris. "Well, that's just fantastic," Rey mutters. heroically, she picks him up and leaps "with all her might into the chasm, grabbing for the cable at the same time" (Berne 2018b, 88). She hauls him over her shoulder and runs with him, and then dramatically slides out just in time. Outside, on pointing out that she saved his life, he grudgingly but fairly returns the bag. Both Padmé's and Rey's lessons show independence in their solo adventures as well as strong values. Maz concludes the companion volume *The Rey Chronicles* with, "Love and compassion must keep fighting. Never allow the forces of darkness to overpower your light" (Berne 2018b).

The five-comic arc of January 2018 is notable for offering a few new adventures, in contrast with the short story adaptations. True, Rey and BB-8 battle the same monster of the original cartoon, and Padmé and Ahsoka handle the same dinner party. However, three new stories add delightfully to the canon. In the "Princess Leia" comic by Elsa Charretier and Pierrick Colinet, Leia and Han banter on Hoth, and ride with Hera—a team-up that delighted many fans. Hera, meanwhile, explains that Leia must work with the Tauntaun instead of having a battle of wills with it—hilarious since the Tauntaun works as a metaphor for Han. The comic is set in pastels, welcoming a feminine audience while adding a charming bit of backstory.

The Hera comic has the heroine on her own—no team, no Ghost, but planetbound with Chopper and forced to rely on herself. She arrives at the Fekunda Outpost, hoping to add the farmers there to the rebellion's supply chain. However, as the Imperials pressure them, she steps up and leads, showing them how to form their own resistance. It's an inspiring independent adventure. Writer Devin Grayson explains:

I'm glad we went with Hera the Leader, because it feels very timely to me. What better question right now than how do you inspire people to action when they're already feeling overwhelmed with the daily struggle of existence: their families and their communities and their jobs? How do you recognize when it's necessary to fight back and what are some ways you can do that without putting everything you love at even greater risk? Hera's someone who can answer those kinds of questions. She understands that to motivate people, you have to see both what they're capable of in that particular moment of time, and also what they have the potential to achieve down the line. I wanted to try to show what that might look like. (Baver 2018a)

Of course, the "Rose and Paige" comic expanded representation with the two Asian women of *The Last Jedi.* Writer Delilah S. Dawson comments, "To me, they're the heart of what the Resistance means: ordinary people willing to make sacrifices in the hopes that other people and planets won't have to suffer" (Baver 2018b). Tasked with exploring D'Qar (the world the Resistance evacuates from at the start of *The Last Jedi*), Paige sticks up for her shyer sister, insisting that the younger woman present her idea. General Leia politely listens and agrees that Rose should build wheeled vehicles. The older man Lazslo objects, but Leia insists, "Every idea has merit," standing up for the young woman. The older man gets in more shots when the vehicle falls apart, and Rose sadly thinks, "I'm not trying to impress anyone. I'm trying to help the Resistance. There's a difference." Even as she wishes he'd stop watching while she works, Paige and Leia offer her more support. Dawson adds:

> When I was a kid, I was so focused on getting good grades and praise that I never took any risks at all. As I've gotten older, I've learned that hard work and tenacity will take you further than being born with any talent and that you can't grow without taking risks. Rose has these great ideas, but she does doubt herself. Luckily, her sister Paige is there to encourage her and cheer her on. In both of my Rose and Paige stories, I wanted to give Rose moments where she had an idea, doubted herself, was emboldened by Paige, failed a little, kept going, and ultimately succeeded. That, to me, gave her context for her increased confidence and strength in *The Last Jedi.* (Baver 2018b)

Aboard Rose's successfully built fleet, the two sisters race and joke, adding a lively female-centric banter missing from the films. Nicoletta Baldari, the comic's artist, also worked on *Frozen* and explains, "so knowing quite well the connection between Anna and Elsa has helped me a lot!" (Baver 2018b). Baldari adds, "I thought, Rose and Paige have fun together, so they had to be funny, but at the same time they are Resistance girls, so they also had to have some pathos on display! So I focused on their actions" (Baver 2018b).

When Paige is lost, Rose panics and decides she's not cut out to be a hero but goes seeking her sister nonetheless. She's frightened of a troop of long-necked birds but bribes them with food and names them Squonks. Baldari explains that they're based on ostriches with "a little goat, a funny rabbit" (Baver 2018b). The endearingly cute creatures help her track Paige, who's fallen off a cliff. Desperate but brave, Paige insists, "You're a genius, Rose. If anyone can get me out, it's you." Dawson concludes, "Their love for one another and their drive to do what's right are definitely a chord they share" (Baver 2018b). Rose builds a pulley and saves her, and then the girls ride Squonks together, and Rose pledges to keep bringing them food. On their adventure, the pair also discover a freshwater river with fish and durasteel ore for ship repair, making their mission an impressive success. It's a near-perfect girl power comic, emphasizing the sisters' fun and love as well as teamwork.

The cartoons and comics are short and moralistic, but also sweet and fun. If younger readers want to celebrate the franchise's heroines and especially picture themselves among them, it's a charming, nonsexualized spin-off perfect for the smallest fans.

EIGHT

Rewriting the Galaxy with *Rogue One*

"It doesn't feel at all radical to have both Rey and Jyn as heroes. Think of the countless action franchises with multiple male heroes," says Jyn's actress Felicity Jones. "We want you to identify with Jyn as a person, not to objectify her but to empathize with her" (Dockterman 2017a, 39). The fact that *Rogue One* and *The Force Awakens* star similar-looking characters with similar abilities and that *Rogue One* tells the backstory of *A New Hope* seems unoriginal, but it also helps the multicultural casts function as commentary—rewriting the old stories as they could have been. Adding her to the backstory of *A New Hope* adds a great deal of feminine assertion to the original film: "We also know, now, that this raid was led by a complicated, tough, anti-heroic woman—a woman who is never a love interest, never damseled, and who leads a diverse squad of men into a battle" (Schnelbach 2017). These men voted her their leader and defied their commanders to follow her on a suicide mission. With this, the film highlights women's achievements in history . . . often uncredited until recent times. Kayti Burt adds: "The broader way [*Rogue One*] makes *A New Hope* into a better film is that it gives context to Luke's heroic deeds. When Luke shot his torpedoes into that exhaust vent, he destroyed the Death Star, but it wasn't just his victory. It belonged to Jyn Erso and Cassian Andor and the countless others who made that moment possible." Thanks to a casual page, Hera and her team from *Star Wars: Rebels* are included in the message. In the comic *The Ashes of Jedha*, Leia and Luke visit Jedha and honor Jyn's team for their sacrifice even as they try working with the surviving rebels.

Rogue One begins with Young Jyn running from an Imperial probe. Menacing music emphasizes that it and the Imperials that follow have come to destroy her entire way of life. She and her family has found a sanctuary on Lah'mu "a simple agrarian planet with a small population of settlers seeking to avoid the war" (Hidalgo 2016b, 11). Her loving family with a father who hugs her and proactive mother calling for help contrast with the evil Empire, now dressed in black stormtrooper outfits. As "death troopers," they are especially foreboding: "The name of the death trooper stems from a rumored project from the Advanced Weapons Research division, designed to animate necrotic flesh. Though the troopers do not appear to be derived from this scheme, the use of the name gives them a macabre reputation among the Imperial ranks. Their black armor makes their appearance all the more deathly," the *Visual Guide* explains (Hidalgo 2016b, 28).

Orson Krennic, their leader in glaring white, shows a condescending creepy affection for Jyn's mother. The fact that he's not there to kill them all but to recruit them and force Jyn's father to build the horrific Death Star is especially chilling. As his charm emphasizes, Krennic was once Galen's colleague and friend. The Ersos felt indebted to him after he saved them from the Separatist planet Vallt in what they didn't realize was a set up (Hidalgo 2016b, 16). As proactive little Jyn defies her parents' commands to run and watches from hiding, Lyra pulls a blaster to defend her husband. Krennic shoots her and she dies protesting, "You'll never win." She thus provides a fierce model for Jyn to follow. In the novels, she is not force-gifted, but is obsessed with the Force and truly believes in it, taking Jyn on expeditions where she finds her Kyber pendent.

With this loss of her parents and a mission, the classic heroine's journey begins. Jyn's foster-father, Saw, adopts her and teaches her to defy the Empire as her parents did. She's next seen as an adult in prison, being transferred via prison wagon. When the Rebels come to free her, she fights savagely with a shovel-like tool and escapes the Imperials but not the robot K-2SO. This scene emphasizes that she is a better fighter than the obedient Stormtroopers, but not than the Rebels she abandoned. Thus, she is not powered up to the same degree as Rey but framed as far better than competent. Saw calls her "the best soldier in my cadre" at age sixteen. However, she is no Force-powered chosen one—just a former rebel with connections,

At this point, no characterization is established for adult Jyn—there is no reason to sympathize with the character, no notion of why she's in prison, or indicator she is a good or kind person. Here the film makes a flaw, expecting the audience to follow the character (and indeed, at this point there are basically no other established characters) solely on faith.

Interrogated at the Rebel base on Yavin, Jyn is a stoic, tough loner, admitting nothing of importance as she faces off with the senior staff. "She is hardened and alone, flawed and adrift—too unpredictable even for the rebels who recruit her. But desperate times call for desperate measures, and those resisting the Empire must seek aid where they can," explains the guidebook *The Art of Rogue One* (Kushins 2016, 61). The men handle the interrogation, firing questions from different sides of the room. While Mon Mothma rules the room, she only offers a soft-voiced, mollifying perspective. Thus bullied by the patriarchy—not the Empire, but another group of bossy men—Jyn responds with guarded defiance, uninterested as she is in helping. However, she accepts their bargain of an introduction to Saw Gerrera for her freedom. She may be eager for an excuse to help the Rebellion or find closure with her old mentor. A final temptation is the subsequent mission to rescue Jyn's father. Though aloud, Jyn has claimed to care about none of the three, at this point, she appears to have stronger feelings buried underneath. "For Jyn, it's the swapping of one prison cell for another. She cares not for the cause of the Rebel Alliance and being briefed by their command while still in binders does little to sway her. Until, that is, she hears about her father, a man she had decided had died years ago" (Hidalgo 2016b, 34). Mon Mothma describes this scene in the novelization:

> Jyn was in chains when we met before Operation Fracture. I'd seen her file and chosen her for the mission for reasons I wish I could be proud of. I expected to meet a troubled girl who had been failed by the Alliance in a hundred different ways; failed by Saw, failed by those of us who *knew* Saw, failed when she went out on her own, and failed by our inability to save her father or mother. I expected she could be persuaded (by which I suppose I meant *manipulated*) into helping us, and that in doing so we might help her, too. (Freed 2017, 321)

In the prequel novel, Jyn is shocked to discover there's an organized Rebellion beyond Saw's and other ragtag groups. "But seeing these people, the way they still believed they had a chance—a chance that hinged on *her*—rekindled that spark inside her heart that she had thought died long before" (Revis 2017, 410). She's assigned to help the Rebel Cassian Andor make contact. Of course, both are reluctant as their backgrounds and allegiances are so different: General Draven writes in the *Rogue One Rebel Dossier*, "Capt. Andor has worked with the rebels since he was a child. It is no exaggeration to say that we are his family. He is absolutely loyal to the rebel cause and will do whatever he must to achieve our goals" (Fry 2016). Jyn is quite the opposite, having quit the Rebellion after a childhood with a loner radical. She's even the daughter of a known traitor. Though Cassian and Jyn distrust each other, they soon find commonality. He also gives Jyn the inspiring thought that "Rebellions are built on hope," one she dismisses but soon comes to believe. She is the viewpoint character, but the audience knows Andor has the just, heroic cause. Therefore, the audience has the hope Jyn lacks, though this grows with time. As with many films, her mission is to become part of the team as combat approaches.

"What I love so much about Jyn Erso is that she's an imperfect female warrior—authentic and genuine, truthful and humble, strong and modern without feeling contemporary" said producer Alison Shearmur. "Oftentimes, Hollywood wants to see a strong woman apologize for nor appreciating her life or dedicate herself to figuring out why she's a certain way. What I love about Jyn is that hers isn't a story of wishing she'd made other life choices. This isn't an apology. She's equal parts Joan of Arc and Sigourney Weaver's Ripley—a pure hero, independent of gender. Someone who sets out to do something impossible and does it" (Kushins 2016, 61).

As she boards Cassian's ship, he is suspicious and treats her as a potential foe, but a capable one he knows can handle herself in combat. He lets her keep the blaster she's stolen, even as K-2SO worries she'll turn it on him. Thus, since Cassian sees her as a threat, he looks at her blaster more than her eyes or body, specifically not objectifying her. In this war movie, the script and direction emphasize that her being female changes nothing—she wears the same scruffy, dark, fully covered outfit for the entire film. The camera focuses on her face or through her point of view. No one calls her girl or young lady. Director Gareth Edwards notes:

> John Knoll, who wrote the original treatment, has two daughters and he wanted to have a hero they could look up to. I feel like one of the most successful heroines in science-fiction cinema is Sigourney Weaver in *Aliens*—I love her, and as a guy, no part of my brain thinks of her gender. She's just Ripley, that character. We tried to write Jyn as neither male nor female, as just a person. Obviously, she's female, but even with the clothing, my goal with the costume department was to design clothes that I would wear as a guy on Halloween. She wouldn't look feminine, and she wouldn't look masculine—she'd be neutral. Jyn is a person who just happens to be a girl. (Buchanan 2016)

He adds that a woman director would be a good idea: "I'd love to see an Andrea Arnold *Star Wars*, or even a Lynne Ramsey *Star Wars*, or a Sofia Coppola *Star Wars*. I'd be first in line for that" (Buchanan 2016). A female director and especially writer might have made far different choices. Some fourth wave films make their heroine strong by making her indistinguishable from a man—no female friends or choices or hobbies, just as sexless character on an action adventure. Jones describes playing the role with Harrison Ford attitude and adds, "I hope absolutely that young boys go and see the film, and young girls see the film, and that they both identify with the film" (*BBC* 2016). This gender-neutral approach becomes Jyn's strength but also fundamental flaw.

Jyn's actress has said the number of lead roles for women in action films is a "a wonderful moment for cinema" (*BBC* 2016). She's thrilled to play the lead and adds, "It's absolutely time that we had female leads and as many females leading films as we do men" (*BBC* 2016). Production designer Doug Chiang adds, "There have always been strong women starting with Princess Leia, but the fact that Jyn is now the lead in the story—that it's so completely about her—just expands the *Star Wars* universe that much further. Setting everything around her is so brilliant and so exciting—and lets us come at things from a female point of view" (Kushins 2016, 62). However, like Leia, Jyn has a distinct "Smurfette Principle" vibe happening. Her status as token girl on the team suggests women are a rarity in beloved fictional characters, especially action heroes. True, there are female Rebels fighting for Saw and storming the beach, and true, Mon Mothma is in charge (as in *Jedi*). However, the central team consists of Jyn, four men, and a male robot. She thus stands out as the face of exceptionalism—only a woman trained from childhood by the most powerful rebel, Saw Gerera, can be a warrior-hero.

On the trip, Jyn dreams of her father, emphasizing her inner conflict and aiding the audience in seeing through her viewpoint. She gazes out the viewscreen with a faint smile, curious about their destination as they approach Jedha. She's also quite snarky, nicknaming K-2SO "Target practice," but defending him when he's actually in danger. By this point, a more interesting personality, nuanced beside her anger and betrayal, is surfacing.

A Star Destroyer hangs menacingly over Jedha, emphasizing the patriarchy's looming presence. Up on the Imperial ships, Krennic, Tarkin, and Vader jockey for position within their hierarchy, eager to exude perfect competence for their Emperor. "The bad guy is a lot more terrifying when he's really smart, and really effective," says Knoll. "There is a lot of palace intrigue going on in the Empire, with people conspiring to move up the ranks and sabotaging each other. There's not a lot of loyalty there." (Breznican 2016b). They contrast with the eager, multicultural, ragtag Rebels on their missions. "In many ways, the Rebels don't have a leg to stand on," Jyn's actress says. "They're a motley crew, they all have had difficult backgrounds. They're all outsiders in some way, and they're coming together to fight something far bigger than them, more efficient. The Empire is wealthier, and it has everything the Rebels don't, so the odds are definitely stacked against them" (Breznican 2016c).

Rogue One embraced a particular racial diversity, with the first Asian heroes of the *Star Wars* universe—Chinese martial artist Donnie Yen and Chinese actor Jiang Wen. Like in *Force Awakens,* a woman takes center stage. Meanwhile, the secondary lead, Cassian Andor, is played by Mexican actor Diego Luna, with British-Pakistani actor Riz Ahmed central as well. Kayti Burt (2017a) explains in "How Diversity Makes *Rogue One* a Better *Star Wars* Movie": "*Rogue One* takes this diversity one step further, including zero white male characters in its ragtag team of hero protagonists (though Alan Tudyk does voice droid K-2SO), a choice that it so rarely seen in a Hollywood movie of this size, budget, and cultural influence that I cannot come up with another example of it." She continues:

Furthermore, pretty much every white male character in this movie (with a few exceptions) is a villain and/or works for the Empire (in Galen Erso's complicated case). This not only works on a narrative level as something different in a sea of movies about white male heroes, but also on a thematic level. *Rogue One* is a movie about rebellion. In our world (and in most of the movies we make) white men have power. Therefore, it makes sense that the rebels challenging that power structure would fall into different demographics.

"One feature of fourth-wave feminism has been the inclusion of men who share certain social goals" (Benn 2013, 227). Of course, Rey and Jyn are both aided by a team of men who work hard to help the young heroines succeed. They are passing the torch to the younger heroes by celebrating difference. The themes of diversity stood out particularly in the divided America of 2016 just after the vitriolic election. Many filmmakers of the time struck back with allegory of inclusion and diversity or dystopias emphasizing a world of fascist takeover. As DeVega comments: "In this moment Americans can choose to turn to the light side of the Force—a progressive, humane and truly democratic and just world. Alternatively, the American people can surrender to the dark side of the Force—a state of militarism, violence, human misery, immiseration, xenophobia, racism, prejudice, fear, suspicion, hatred." The Empire of the film plots to stamp out all traces of freedom on the quiet religious sanctuary of Jedha, out of greed. As Jyn meets Guardians of the Whills Chirrut Îmwe and Baze Malbus (echoing the faith of the Journal of the Whills quoted in the first draft of *Star Wars*, as is the expression "The Force of Others") they emphasize paths other than that of the giant Empire and reveal that their quiet movement still has faith that the universe will turn out right.

Alongside her new friends, she reunites with her childhood mentor but only after fighting Stormtroopers then Gerrera's insurrectionists. When attacked on the planet, Jyn rescues a crying girl and returns her to her mother, emphasizing at last that she's altruistic and kind. Clearly, she values civilian lives, though Saw's history is littered with civilian casualties. After his soldiers bring her to him, she's struck by his injuries and metal replacement parts—another emotional moment. She tries acting aloof, to the point of denying any interest in the Rebellion or even any motivation:

SAW GERRERA: So what is it that you want, Jyn?

JYN: They wanted an introduction, they've got it. I'm out now. The rest of you can do what you want.

SAW GERRERA: You care not about the cause?

JYN: The cause? Seriously? The Alliance? The . . . The rebels? Whatever it is you're calling yourself these days? All it's ever brought me is pain.

SAW GERRERA: You can stand to see the Imperial flag reign across the galaxy?

JYN: It's not a problem if you don't look up.

In response, he takes her to see her father's message, trying to jolt her into caring. Of course, it achieves its goal. While it's filled with instructions on how to destroy the Death Star, Galen adds in his one message to the outside world, "Jyn, if you're listening, my beloved, so much of my life has been wasted. I try to think of you only in the moments when I'm strong, because the pain of not having you with me . . . your mother. Our family. The pain of that loss is so overwhelming I risk failing even now. It's just so hard not to think of you. Think of where you are. My Stardust." She tumbles to the ground, moved to tears by her father's message. However, the base is under attack and Cassian leads her out, without the vital message and without Saw. This devastates the heroine, who gazes sadly out the window as much of Jedha is leveled. Undaunted though in emotional turmoil, Jyn urges them to rescue her father, who can supply the Death Star intelligence. The political and personal blend once again. They go to where her father is held, but to Jyn's horror, he's shot down in front of her. Their goodbye once more combines directives for the Death Star with the individual, as Galen tells her "It must be destroyed," but, his message conveyed, adds, "Jyn. Look at you. I've so much to tell you," before he dies. The audience continues to follow the young woman, ripped apart at her father's loss but still uncertain about the cause that viewers know is the only path to salvation.

> Edwards says he chose Jones because she wasn't "so kick-ass and shields-up that the audience couldn't empathize with her." "There were a lot of people who could learn how to fight and beat people up and do the physical side of it. For me, the most interesting thing is when there's a crack in the armor, when you can glimpse the vulnerability in someone," the director says. "You can just hang the camera on Felicity and not say a word, and you can feel her having a million different thoughts. You get interested in what she's thinking and what's going on. She can be very observant within a scene. It doesn't always have to be about her directly, but we're experiencing it through her. She just has that knack for pulling you in." (Breznican 2016b)

In fact, she doesn't fall apart like a damsel, but like an angry soldier seeking to blame his commander. Back on their ship, Cassian and Jyn argue, but their relationship isn't romantic. They clash through ideologies, not sexual heat, emphasizing once more that she's an asexual soldier debating morality. She blames him for her father's death and retorts, "I had orders! Orders that I disobeyed! But you wouldn't understand that."

Jyn, who is not framed as the Mary Sue character who's always right no matter the circumstances, shoots off that obeying bad orders makes him akin to a Stormtrooper. However, this is not a film about individual heroism, but a war film, so characters must consider all the consequences of breaking orders. Cassian tells her, astutely, "We don't all have the luxury of deciding when and where we want to care about something. Suddenly the Rebellion is real for you? Some of us live it. I've been in this fight since I was six years old. You're not the only one who lost everything. Some of us just decided to do something about it." With this, he emphasizes that she must fully commit. He will respect her as a partner but demands respect as well.

Her stand-out hero moment arrives when she addresses the heads of the Rebellion: "What chance do we have? The question is 'What choice?' Run? Hide? Plead for mercy? Scatter your forces? You give way to an enemy this evil with this much power and you condemn the galaxy to an eternity of submission. The time to fight is now!" She insists they capture the Death Star plans. When challenged, she throws back Cassian's words, "Rebellions are built on hope," showing how she's come to understand the cause she's fighting for.

Mon Mothma describes in the novelization how much Jyn has changed at this point: "The woman we met then was far different from the one we'd chained. Was she at peace? I don't believe so. But she held herself with a newfound certainty" (Freed 2017, 322). After this, Andor and the other Rebels come and pledge their support. Even if her words haven't impacted the cautious leaders, they've reached the soldiers like herself. With this, she truly reveals herself as one of them. She tells Cassian, "I'm not used to people sticking around when things go bad."

Offering her what she's always sought on some level, he tells her, "Welcome home." This powers her up for the war ahead. At this grim point in the *Star Wars* timeline, when the Empire is at its most powerful, there is unity and courage among the misfits rising against it. "There is a sense of things not always going perfectly," Felicity Jones says. "That's what makes the *Star Wars* universe so endearing: The characters sometimes mess things up. But they have this bravery and strength of character to win in the end." (Breznican 2016c).

Metaphorically, all the pilots of the series—the younger generation, not the stodgy leaders—chose to listen to the young woman and pledge themselves to their belief in her. "The Jedi are pretty much extinct, so a lot of that spirituality is dying out and people are losing their faith," says Edwards. "This idea that magical beings are going to come and save us is going away, and it's up to normal, everyday people to take a stand to stop evil from dominating the world" (Breznican 2016b). The message is only a little less subtle than the feminist agenda throughout *The Last Jedi*.

As with Rose and Finn in that film, the heroes are ordinary, with no force-wielders among them:

"She is absolutely a very unlikely heroine," Felicity Jones told EW. "She's someone on the edges and fringes of society. Physically, she's smaller than everyone else around her, but . . . when someone has something they believe in, that's what powers them, that's what motivates them, that's what can give someone enormous strength" (Breznican 2016b). Onboard the transport, she stands among her troops, arm raised powerfully as she tells them, "May the Force be with us!" When the suspense lingers of whether their code will get them onto Scarif, she grips her kyber crystal, appearing briefly to pray. It seems she indeed has something to believe in now. While the Force does not intervene through a Jedi, the story is open to the presence of religion—of a subtle power for goodness aiding the terribly unlikely, desperate mission. When they arrive, she makes another impassioned speech: "Saw Gerrera used to say, one fighter with a sharp stick and nothing left to lose can take the day. They have no idea we're coming. They have no reason to expect us. If we can make it to the ground, we'll take the next chance. And the next. On and on until we win . . . or the chances are spent."

Baze touches her shoulder and says, "Good luck, little sister," but this is a moment of solidarity, not condescension. Meanwhile, in friendship and solidarity, she gives K-2SO a blaster. Climbing in the data tower, she's competent, using her smarts to find the Stardust file and fighting off the enemy. On Scarif, she gets progressively bruised and filthy, a genuine action hero. Further, as Cassian tells her to keep going, just as Saw did in his last moments of life, both are symbolically passing the torch to the younger woman to continue the fight.

Scarif is a tropical paradise but also the heart of the Death Star construction and thus the military industrial complex. They face new enemies there: dust-colored Shoretroopers and sinister, onyx-faced Deathtroopers. "This South Pacific, tropical-paradise planet subconsciously leads into some of the imagery associated with World War II," says Edwards (Breznican 2016b). This evocative setting, which historically cast women as nurses and ground crew, emphasizes Jyn's status as equal soldier. She works with the entire team to send out her message, revealing the Death Star's fatal flaw.

There in the heart of darkness, Jyn confronts Krennic, who murdered her mother and tortured her father. She tells him, "You know who I am. I'm Jyn Erso. Daughter of Galen and Lyra. You've lost . . . My father's revenge. He built a flaw in the Death Star. He put a fuse in the middle of your machine and I've just told the entire galaxy how to light it." As he aims his weapon at Jyn, Cassian backs her up by shooting him in the shoulder. However, since Jyn is well and on her feet, the moment resembles teamwork more than a rescue. Moments later, he's stuck leaning on *her* for support.

They only make it as far as the beach where they see the sky afire with the Death Star's strike. Both brave and resigned, they can only hug in comradeship as the base is destroyed. In the novelization, Mon Mothma's diary entry provides an epitaph for the heroine: "There are a very few people whose will and ferocity are so great that they pull other people in their wake. I've known some who cultivated that talent as politicians and generals, for good or ill. Jyn I think, never knew the effect she had on others, never realized the intensity of her own humanity or the Presence she brought to a room. She was, as expected, troubled and quarrelsome; she was also impossible to ignore or forget" (Freed 2017, 322).

In their sacrifice, the pair have succeeded in transmitting the data to the rest of the Rebel fleet. As the Empire destroys their ships before they can flee, and Vader murders soldiers with devastating power, the Rebels pass the data disk from one to the other until it reaches Princess Leia, preparing her for the next film and passing the torch to the teenage heroine. Though it's taken decades, the message arrives that Luke, Leia, Han, and Obi-Wan only succeeded with the racially diverse misfit band's help. Burt notes that *Rogue One* is most refreshing for how "it subverts the idea that there is a specific person who must save the day. This narrative framework is grounded in patriarchal, racist subtext because it reinforces our real-world simplistic historical narrative that it was a series of white men who shaped our world and country, erasing the considerable contributions of the marginalized groups who played a *huge* part" (Burt 2017a).

MORE ROGUE ONE WOMEN

Rogue One scored 35 percent in Harrison's study (2018) of women's total onscreen time—even with Jyn the central hero. As Harrison cautions, this doesn't equal dialogue time as in all the films there are "a lot of reaction shots of Leia or Jyn not doing much but being the only character in the frame." Still, like *The Force Awakens* and *The Last Jedi*, more women are seen filling the universe, however briefly.

Several rebel infantry soldiers join the final battle but are basically absent of dialogue onscreen. They are faceless soldiers, quickly sacrificed. There are a few women among the X-wing pilots as well—named in the expanded material as Pilots Zal Dinnes (Red Eight) and Laren Joma (Blue Eleven). A few more female soldiers can be seen during the Rebel Alliance council meeting. Establishing other women in the galaxy, Cassian mentions talking to his contact Tivik's sister on Jedha, and the novelization adds a few more.

Several of the priests are described as female in the Expanded Universe, but their robes, concealing all features except for a slit, as with some burkas, suggest silenced, desexed women who do not even register as female to the audience. Another even more disturbing woman serves the Imperials tea in a café. She has been "decraniated" — with her brain or most of it removed to strip her of all free will and make her a slave or worse. She is pale-skinned and pretty, as evidenced from the nose down. Clearly, there are women in the galaxy, but the Empire plans to strip them of all they are.

At the film's beginning, Jyn's mother heroically sacrifices herself trying to kill Orson Krennic instead of living out a life as his hostage. It's a brave moment, but arguably a foolish one as it leaves little Jyn without protection. In the novelization, Lyra thinks "If you leave her now, she's done. You've taken all her strength away." It adds, "But Lyra had committed herself to a path. Her husband needed her more than her daughter" (Freed 2016, 12). She chooses, fails, and dies for it. Further, she fulfills the trope of the fridged woman, shot in front of her husband to affect *his* story (and admittedly Jyn's even more).

Her final words are "trust the Force." More surprisingly, she wears something like Jedi robes. In her official backstory, she studied the teachings of the Jedi and may have joined the rumored Church of the Force; it's Lyra's mother who realized her husband was being drawn into the empire's military research and decided they should flee together (Hidalgo 2016b, 18). *Star Wars: Catalyst: A Rogue One Novel* has her weeping for hours after the Jedi are destroyed.

Catalyst follows Jyn's parents as Galen struggles to keep his energy research pure, without being weaponized by the Separatists or the Empire. Naïve as he is, he's tricked several times by Krennic. Lyra is more skeptical and practical, leading him to threaten her as well as dismissing her efforts to "play detective." At last her husband hears her warnings and flees. This novel of gender imbalance is problematized in other ways: Lyra gives up her work to stay home with the baby and later homeschool her, casting her as a very traditional housewife. Krennic calls her "A listener. A translator of sorts. Often in charge of transcribing and organizing his notes" (Luceno 2016, 99).

Saw's sister Steela, already dead by the film, is a significant influence in his and Jyn's lives. In fact, her plot arc appears on the show *Rebels* as she's killed resisting the Empire. Arguably, she's another fridged woman, though also an authoritative, clever, tough woman of color. Saw tells her stories of her and adds that the Resistance "need more fighters to die like she did . . . The resistance needs a martyr. A tragedy. Something so horrific that people can't help but stand up and fight too" (Revis 2017, 60). Of course, this comes with the Death Star.

Senator Tynnra Pamlo of Taris, Minister of Education in the Rebel Alliance's cabinet, lacks the military training of some other voices. Perhaps that's why she urges near-paralyzed caution. In fact, she suggests the Rebel Fleet disband and hide away in the threat of the Empire's new weapon. She fears her people will be at risk. "We must scatter the fleet. We have no recourse but to surrender," she insists at the Rebel meeting, and threatens that she'll make the others fight alone. Her position of authority as a dark-skinned human woman adds diversity, but her terror adds a cringeworthy choice for the lone woman advisor.

The *Visual Guide* describes E3-S1 as female with a "decidedly vain programming flutter" (Hidalgo 2016b, 59). She resembles R2-D2 except that's she's orange and chrome. "Threece is not assigned to a specific starfighter; instead she is embroiled in the upkeep of technology throughout the Yavin base. Competitive to a fault, Threece does not work well with others, but she excels at organization, and has become the recognized chief of the astromech pool" (Hidalgo 2016b, 59). Apparently, she's a maid. She's also vain and hypercompetitive, assigned to be not a soldier but the coordinator from the ground. Someone made some painfully sexist choices in her design.

Of course, Mon Mothma is named and famous, a carryover from *Return of the Jedi* and *Revenge of the Sith* both and thus a bridge between trilogies. In this story, she's strong and determined, though she fails to sway the Council into fighting. Still, Jones lovingly describes Mon Mothma's impact on her character and describes the film's emphasis on strong female protagonists: "I would say there's a huge amount of respect for women in the Rebellion. Mon Mothma (Genevieve O'Reilly) is ultimately, for Jyn, someone she looks up to. So even as the film opens [Jyn] has a very strong female role model in front of her, and someone she respects," she explains. "It's vital. As we're seeing in politics, it is a world where women are becoming leaders of nations, and films should be reflecting that" (Breznican 2016a).

Ending the film is Young Leia, technologically recreated, and receiving the plans Jyn has transmitted. Schnelbach (2017) explains:

> In the final sequence, instead of focusing on individuals, the camera follows the disc with the Death Star plans pass hand-to-hand as Darth Vader chases it down. Someone watching *Rogue One* has almost certainly seen *Star Wars*, and thus should know that the plans make it through. But the film approaches this moment from the point of the view of the terrified Rebels who are barely, desperately, keeping the disc one step ahead of the enemy. We see that it reaches Leia with seconds to spare, and then she flees with it. And we know that she's going to be captured in a few minutes, but that the plans will be safe with R2-D2 by then. The Rebellion will survive. The sacrifices have worked. Leia takes the disc and calls it hope.

This is the moment when *Star Wars* went from being a boy's story to a girl's story.

NINE

Balanced Genders

Disney's Original Era Comics

The new canon novels and comics offer many other heroines and villainesses. The formidable Admiral Rae Sloane leads the Imperials after Palpatine's death in a multi-novel storyline. In *Shattered Empire*, Poe's mother Shara pilots Leia and gets significant character development, bridging the eras. Expanding on her brief onscreen appearance, Bazine Netal, a spy seen for only moments in Maz's palace, features in short stories about her elaborate schemes. Finally, the *Star Wars* comics, set between *A New Hope* and *Empire*, have Han and Leia add the bounty hunter Sana to the team even as Vader picks up a female apprentice: amoral archeologist Doctor Aphra.

Adding a female sidekick for Vader and teammate for Han and Leia, balances the "one good woman in the galaxy" pattern. Both Sana and Aphra are smart, capable, and nonsexualized. They're also ambivalent in the battle of good versus evil or Empire versus Rebels, emphasizing how women can fight for themselves, not just safeguard innocents and support the men's heroic quests. They even add a mixed-race lesbian couple to the homogenized original universe, as Sana and Aphra reveal they're exes. As with *Rogue One*, rewriting the era suggests multicultural depth has always been there, in the between-scenes that didn't make the central narrative.

In *Showdown on the Smuggler's Moon*, Leia faces off with bounty hunter Sana Starros, who has just introduced herself as Han's wife—this shocking moment in *Star Wars* #6 made all the *Star Wars* and comic book news headlines as fans wondered how this would rewrite the narrative. Meanwhile, Sana smirks that he's clearly brought Leia to their "favorite little rendezvous" and gives Han a kiss as he looks nonplussed (Aaron and

Immonen 2016). Sana calls Leia "a bit scrawny for your tastes" and Leia protests, head clearly spinning, "A wife. He never said he had a wife," while Han sputters in protest.

Sana's next speech completely disillusions Leia: "The rich princess in trouble. Yeah, Han could never resist those. How many times has he rescued you? Bet he even turned down the reward. Yeah he's holding out for a much bigger prize." Sana emphasizes how he's done this before, across the universe. If Han is a man of mystery, presenting himself with the façade he chooses and bragging as he wishes, Sana is his perfect nemesis, undercutting every remark. Clearly, she's one he hasn't prepared for.

She's also the selfish pilot he insists he is. Sana has arrived with a plan—she wants to trade Leia to the Imperials and keep Han as her partner. The three square off with blasters pointed, but as the Imperials arrive, Han gets through to Sana by telling her that he too is on the Imperial watchlist. She herds them both onto her ship and takes off. As Leia's inverse, Sana is dark-skinned with a poof of hair. Her emerald green jacket is attractive but concealing. Below it, she's fully covered in black and brown with a gunbelt. A worthy teammate for Han, she's a better shot than he is and an excellent pilot—though she insists her ship, the Volt Cobra, can outfly his. She's more expedient and less principled than the Rebels and has no interest in joining . . . while Leia has none in accepting her.

As they fly away and both women in unison tell Han to shut up, they clearly have much in common. Leia, like Sana, even peppers her dialogue with the phrase "your wife," insisting on goading Han. When Leia bargains for passage to the system of her choice and Sana tells her she wants Han returned, Leia replies "Deal" (Aaron and Immonen 2016). Once again, Han is clearly not in control here. While she's not jealous—unlike Leia—Sana is very perceptive in relationship matters. In *Last Flight of the Harbinger*, Sana notes, "That's not bickering. That's two people who are madly in love with each other but can't bring their stupid selves to admit it" (Aaron and Eliopoulos 2017).

Fans were quite shocked by the revelation and eager to discover the twist. It takes quite a few issues for Han to explain—he pretended to marry Sana as a cover, since they needed a big event as a distraction. Han then cheated her and left with her share of the profit. Now she's chasing him for her payout, not for love.

In *Rebel Jail,* Han's team take Aphra captive. Aphra reveals they have history, while Sana snarks, "Nice try, but our old times were never all that great." Author Si Spurrier adds: "There's quite a big sort of question mark about Aphra's specific sexuality," while author Kieron Gillen identifies her as a lesbian (LaVorgna 2018). Gillen adds: "*Star Wars* doesn't really have the terminology that we do either. One of the things we wrote inside the first arc was that homophobia as we know it doesn't really exist in the *Star Wars* universe. No one raises their eyebrow, no one seems surprised when it happens. It's kind of just something that's there" (LaVorgna 2018). Certainly, this lets the sexuality spectrum appear subtly even as their universe lacks the prejudice of ours. This acceptance of queer, multiracial women as competent team members, without a single condescending or rude comment, is of course a perfect example of fourth wave.

They try leaving Aphra in a secure prison, but when there's a jailbreak, Leia and Sana retrieve her. Sana quips, "The way I see it, we either all work together or we all die" (Aaron and Mayhew 2016). Still, Leia is stuck playing peacemaker, literally holding the two women apart. At last, Sana betrays Aphra, telling Leia, "If this isn't who you are, Princess Leia, then we're doomed. The entire rebellion." With this, she acts as the tougher, crueler devil on her shoulder. Sana, teller of hard truths, also tells Leia, "If it really came down to it, Han would leave like Aphra did" (Gillen and Aaron). Sana's understanding of this shows that she might do the same as well. Gillen explains: "In my head, I've got a list of ethical grayness in the *Star Wars* universe. You've got Han Solo who's here, and slightly more gray, you've got Sana, and even more gray, you have Aphra. I've got this graph of rogueness" (LaVorgna 2018). Still, Sana saves Leia from an alien parasite. As Han has been taken over and prepares to infect a struggling Leia, Sana is saving her ally from metaphoric rape and establishing that she will protect her friends, though she refuses to commit to a higher cause.

The *Solo* tie-in novel *Last Shot* by Daniel José Older offers a scene in Maz's castle with Sana, once more suggesting that there's always been a balanced female presence in the galaxy. In its flashback, taking place shortly after *Solo*, Sana offers Han a job smuggling, but it turns out she has unsavory allies. She's gotten the Phylanx Redux Transmitter, which can control droids, and it's made them big targets. Sana's theft has them both ducking and running from the villains in action-packed scenes. There are also a few sparks. Han insists to Chewie that her pointed dislike reveals she's interested. However, when she dresses in low-cut pale blue with eyeshadow and jewelry, he's the one who can't stop staring. When they get in a shouting match about failed plans, she punches him out, and he lies there mumbling that this clearly settles it, "she'th in love with me" (2018, 244), despite clear suggestions to the contrary. Thus, he seems filled with self-delusion, as she continues trying to make money.

While Sana's initial arrival shocked audiences, many find Aphra the more intriguing character. After the events of *A New Hope*, Vader is puzzled by Obi-Wan's young apprentice who destroyed the Death Star. Prompted by this meeting and by other threats—as Sidious is pointedly training an alternate apprentice in case Vader fails him—Vader begins assembling his own private, perfectly loyal team. Hilariously, they reflect Luke's team but inverted—Triple-Zero is a protocol droid but one skilled at torture who has a "tendency to drain organics to collect their blood" (Gillen and Larroca 2015). When he's told droids aren't welcome in a bar (mimicking Threepio's adventures), Triple-Zero retorts cheerfully, "I daresay they'll be considerably less popular by the time we're finished" (Gillen and Larroca, 2016a). BT-1, a "blastomech prototype," an assassin droid, only masquerades as an astromech (Gillen and Larroca 2015). Black Krrsantan is a cruel Wookie bounty hunter. The last is Doctor Chelli Lona Aphra, presumably the Han Solo counterpart. Her arc "feels very much like a Bizarro Han Solo story with a dash of Indiana Jones thrown in. Aphra has all of Han's swaggery, scoundrel-y charm, but little of his noble streak. Black Krrsantan is basically Chewbacca, if Chewie were only hanging around Han to collect on a literal debt rather than fulfill a Life Debt," as Jesse Schedeen (2016) notes in his review.

Writer Kieron Gillen explains: "Dropping an archaeologist in *Star Wars* makes sense and that she's morally unpredictable, that makes sense, as well. She's kind of fun but at the same time, there's a really dark heart to her. Those kinds of things. All those weird kind of contradictions to her, I think they're quite appealing" (LaVorgna 2018). She's very much a comic relief character, so her independent adventures are more light-hearted. Witty and sarcastic, she won't hesitate to take risks if there's a great enough payoff. Her white and brown clothes likewise stand out among the dark metal team. Her blue pants, simple shirt, brown vest, gadget belt, gloves, and pilot's cap with goggles are quite androgynous. They are also reminiscent of Han and Hera, the competent but lawless pilots. Patterns on her arm appear cyber-connections, emphasizing her skill with hardware and giving her appearance a scifi twist. Co-writer Si Spurrier calls them "electric tattoos" and promises they'll feature in the plot (LaVorgna). Asian or part-Asian in appearance, she beats Rose's entrance into *Star Wars* and offers more representation.

Aphra first appears weaving around lasers and dismantling traps *Mission Impossible*-style. She's trying to liberate the droid Triple-Zero, who has been quarantined for centuries. She insists that his jailors have "small minds who just want to hide beautiful things in storage or a museum" whereas Triple-Zero "should be in an armory" (Gillen and Larroca 2015). Her admiration for deadly droids reveals a great deal of her personality. Gillen comments: "You can never be quite sure what she will or won't do. It's these moments of horror when she's going to do that awful thing and there's also moments when oh no, she's chosen not to do that thing" (LaVorgna). Suddenly, Vader walks in and hurls the guards across the room. As Aphra finds herself dangling by one hand, Vader looms over her. "Doctor Aphra. I have need of you" (Gillen and Larroca 2015).

She invites him aboard her blue-striped vessel, the Ark Angel (which suggests a latent heroic/benevolent side to her). There, Vader reveals her work reactivating droids has impressed him. He has her activate the nasty-minded Triple-Zero and BT-1. With this, she realizes he's offering her a permanent series of jobs and eagerly tells Vader, "You're what I've been looking for all my life" (Gillen and Larroca 2015). As they continue interacting, she reveals she knows exactly when to push him and when to back down. She's irreverent and sarcastic, but firm in her insistence that he needs her. Writer Si Spurrier calls Aphra's witty wordplay around Vader "literally flirting with disaster" (LaVorgna 2018). She babbles out of nerves as well as a lighthearted chattiness, while Vader tells her stonily, "Do not expect me to humor you" (Gillen and Larroca 2015). With her constant jokes, the pair provide quite a contrast.

Aphra also reveals she supports the Empire because its stability protects ordinary people. "The Empire isn't perfect, but it keeps people safe" (Gillen and Aaron). Gillen explains that this standpoint gives her "complexities" (LaVorgna 2018). As he explains, anyone who grew up in a galactic civil war, might value the Empire's stability. She adds another side to the previous suggestion that all the ordinary people hate the Empire, widening the black-and-white perspective of *A New Hope*.

In her Vader team-up, she makes a surprising request—for a lightsaber through the neck rather than being flushed into space, her deadliest fear. She tells Vader straight-out that she knows she's likely to be killed, though she doesn't wish to be, and only expects some respect. He tells her in turn, "You have proved yourself resourceful. You are safe for as long as I have use for you" (Gillen and Larroca 2015). Vader sends her to track down Luke Skywalker through about a dozen issues, but since Vader wants to train him as an apprentice and supplant the Emperor, he must keep his plans secret—and Aphra is a loose end. With this, she must fight for her life as never before. It's quite clear that the tiny bounty hunter has doomed herself by learning the all-powerful Vader's secrets, a twist that keeps the audience riveted.

In *Vader Down*, Aphra's team faces off with Luke's friends. Chewie beats up his counterpart, while Triple-Zero steals Threepio's arms. The astromechs battle too in a goofy, crazy romp, and Luke demands to know what kind of person could willingly work for Vader. After Vader, of course, Aphra considers them less than a terrifying threat. She contacts Vader and offers "redeem-myself-for-accidentally-leading-you-into-a-trap" help (Aaron and Gillen 2016). This is a self-sacrifice, but also a canny one to keep her alive. Vader accepts and orders her to sacrifice her ship. She does, and he escapes, leaving her to be captured by the rebels. Han ends their fight by punching her out, treating her the same as any other soldier.

Later retrieved by the droids, Aphra cleverly makes them stick to the letter of their orders—after they have brought her willingly to Vader's ship, they will be free to accept new orders and free her. At last, she sneaks in to see the Emperor, hoping to ingratiate herself and remain alive. Amused, the Emperor congratulates Vader on collecting allies and making a power play in the Sith tradition and turns Aphra over to the master she's betrayed. While Aphra babbles nervously, and then begs and sobs, Vader escorts her to an airlock and ejects her into space. Her trickery has failed. Spurrier adds that while in the main series, the heroes always triumph, "One of the many beauties of Aphra is that she does get it wrong. She [messes] up" (LaVorgna 2018).

However, a further twist is coming. Her small ship picks her up just in time and she tells the Wookie and droids that her only chance of escaping Vader is to make him certain he's killed her. As she adds, making it clear she's set this all up from the beginning, she was certain he would use the airlock, because "He's Darth Vader. He was *never* going to be kind." So ends their partnership, with the trickster-heroine outsmarting the deadliest force in the galaxy. As one of the very few to defeat Vader, she proves herself equal to Luke and his team. Trickster is a traditional woman's role, as the heroine of folklore and literature often lacked the power to battle the patriarchy head-on but might subvert it, subtly displaying its weaknesses and slipping away from its power. With this, Aphra brings a delightfully different type of heroine to the franchise.

In her own spinoff comic, she heads off with Wookie, droids, and new Ark Angel. Schedeen adds: "*Doctor Aphra* is actually Marvel's riskiest *Star Wars* project to date. It's the first series to focus on comic book-specific characters rather than those made famous by the movies and TV series." However, he concludes, "That also happens to be one of *Doctor Aphra*'s biggest selling points. The distance from the movies gives *Doctor Aphra* a greater sense of freedom in terms of tone, style and plot possibilities" (LaVorgna 2018).

Gillen clearly agrees as he comments: "I was just literally looking at the sales of Aphra this morning; it was the number two trade in February. A completely new character selling that well is shocking in comics" (LaVorgna 2018). In her first spinoff comic, the source of Aphra's archeological degree is revealed—she made a brilliant find of deadly symbiotes in a vault underneath a primitive planet . . . having stolen the symbiotes from a malicious professor. Aphra not only cheated but faked her data, which many researchers spent subsequent decades studying. There was a moral component here beyond revenge, as the Abersyn Symbiotes are proscribed for their deadliness and the professor was tempting fate as well as cheating Aphra of moving forward through his personal dislike for her. However, she is more of an opportunist than one who values research and discovery. Certainly, her morality is only slightly superior to her professor's. When someone shoots the Hutt she's threatening, Aphra smiles "Moral dilemma averted," suggesting she does in fact have one (Gillen et al. 2018). Others mention that she generally doesn't leave piles of bodies behind on her adventures.

In her comic, she soon discovers the academic credentials she finagled have been publicly revealed as a cheat . . . by her father. She finds him and flashes back to her mother's death on the Outer Rim, where she had been driven by her husband's neglect in favor of his archeological pursuits. On being returned to her father, young Aphra set fire to his treasures. "The psychologist says I may have some issues. Fair to warn you," she added (Gillen and Walker 2017). Of course, this foundational moment motivates her lack of trust. Now her father has revealed her fraud to summon her, since he needs her help excavating the temple of a legendary Jedi splinter group called the Ordu Aspectu. Onboard her ship, she points a blaster at him. "You're going to tell me what you've got and how I can make all this disappear." However, when he challenges her, she admits she can't kill him and they set off together. On their adventure, they prove they make a decent team, though Aphra is frustrated by her father's idealism and lack of knowledge about current events. Giving her family rounds out her character and emphasizes why she's so independent and untrusting. As she takes the lightsabers of dead Jedi, she contrasts with her more academically-minded parent.

The archology quest also brings the Jedi's past into startling life, bridging the history with Aphra's adventures. Like the use of Jedha and the monks in *Rogue One,* she explores the wider, older universe in her less central stories. "It offers a funnier, quirkier take on the franchise, one bolstered by a strong cast that aren't constrained by the limitations of the movies or other *Star Wars* projects" (Schedeen 2016). Spurrier adds:

> The particular beauty and the particular attraction of something like Aphra is that it, at one and the same time, hits all those recognizable IP-shared universe beats, in that we all grew up with *Star Wars* and we all love that world and we recognize it and we respond to its particular aesthetic and its particular vibe. But at the same time, *Aphra* is very much in her own funny little niche and off doing her own thing and, yes, occasionally overlapping with stuff in the wider universe in a way that always feels like a cute Easter egg rather than a continuity obstacle. (LaVorgna 2018)

In possession of a crystal containing a Jedi's mental impression, Aphra next recruits Luke in *The Screaming Citadel,* a tale of Gothic horror. She persuades him to come to the citadel, where its creepy Queen of Ktath'atn will grant them a favor and unlock the crystal because she will be so pleased to meet a Jedi—a unique being in the galaxy now. She makes Luke wear a fancy tux and "spavat" while, subverting gender expectations, she keeps her scruffy flight outfit. She shrugs it off. "You're the main attraction. I rub off the mud, and I can be very distracting" (Gillen and Aaron). She's condescending, calling him blondie and noting, "You're adorable when you're indignant." All this gender flipping is fun and allows the far savvier Aphra to put the male chosen one in his place. Aaron comments, "It's a very different dynamic between the two of them than what we see in *Star Wars,* even more so, I think, than Luke and Han.

Like I said, that's been one of the most fun parts so far" (Brooks 2017). Gillen adds:

> They have such different life experiences. You know, she's a little older than he is, he's still naive and she's a cynical monster. And they go back and forth and they tease each other and, occasionally, they push each other's buttons. But there's an underlying similarity. They've both lost their families. They've both had completely different responses to the horror of the *Star Wars* universe, the big tragedy, and the push and pull of that is very much the heart of the book. (Brooks 2017)

When the encounter turns deadly, Aphra's and Leia's crews are forced to team up, making each person take a hard look at him or herself. Triple-Zero even pushes Leia's buttons, telling Leia that her friends seem as much tools as his own—"You seem terribly upset when they disobey how you've tried to program them" (Gillen and Aaron). Leia actually bows her head in shame, chastised by this unlikely source. Thus, the combined crew all manage to shake one another out of complacency. Aaron comments, "It's really trying to do something like *Vader Down*. Mix our casts up, this time mixing them up in very different ways than what we did the previous time and playing with some very different settings and tropes" (Brooks 2017).

Aphra deserts and is welcomed sympathetically by Sana when she returns, emphasizing how much the two morally dubious women understand each other. Kieron Gillen adds: "This is such an enormous story for Aphra and Sana. We alluded to their history a little before, and now it's the chance to say, 'Okay, we're going to put them together and make them really interact in a more extended way.' They're very much part of the emotional arc of the whole thing and how the casts end up coming together is very much linked to Sana and Aphra" (Brooks 2017). Luke also pushes Aphra's buttons, insisting a rogue like herself shouldn't work for the Empire. Turning the tables on the tough moral questions, when Luke lies in dire peril from the queen's parasites, Doctor Aphra offers Luke an advantage with the crystal's preserved Jedi advisor in the ultimate temptation.

In her second comic, *Doctor Aphra and the Enormous Profit,* she actually dresses for glamour. This involves a short purple-trimmed black dress with matching heels and long gloves but also a black business suit for a more professional look. A mask and short blue-purple hairstyle help her stay anonymous. Some skin shows, but her legs are drawn straight up and down, and her neckline doesn't plunge. With the help of the Hutts, she holds a gala and entertains offers for the Jedi crystal. She accepts one from the Shadow University, who offer her the use of their archives. As their representative adds, "You can walk away rich, appreciated, and still have access to your discovery" (Gillen et al. 2018). Clearly, these are her priorities. Though Imperials—and even Vader—invade, she ends the story "researching" a cocktail menu in a tropical paradise, showing off another outfit with a broad lavender hat, sunglasses, and coat . . . with a blaster beneath the latter. It's sporty and light but avoids the bikini cliché.

Aphra frees Triple-Zero and his companion—a kind antislavery gesture but also one that dismisses responsibility for the havoc he'll unleash. It echoes the heroes of *Solo,* loyal to their team but not the larger causes. Triple-Zero in turn blackmails her into leading a team to steal his lost memories. Part of the bargain is taking on Rexa Go, her new sidekick. This disconcertingly human-colored cyborg tells Aphra, "When it comes to murdering villages of innocents, I find it's best to ask for forgiveness rather than permission" (Spurrier and Laiso 2018). Meanwhile, Aphra huddles in, arms around her middle and actually imagines herself back with Triple-Zero, as Rexa warns her that she shouldn't try renegotiating their positions. All this wins sympathy from the audience, even while aware that Aphra has certainly brought it on herself in charming antihero fashion.

She also has a purple tooka cat called Flufto, giving her an apparent sweet side. In danger, she hands him to her antagonists, winningly asking that they spare him, an innocent. She then adds, "Codephrase: Snugglebum Oogiewoogie." The creature explodes, subverting Aphra's soft and sweet moment and blasting apart others' expectations. In the next comic, she opens a case of sixty similar frozen cats (all explosive) and explains, "In my experience, Rexa, not many problems you can't fix with a cuddle or a crater" (Spurrier and Laiso 2018).

Soon enough, she's reunited with Magna Tolvan, the Imperial officer she betrayed. Tolvan protests, "Thanks to you, I've lost my rank, faced a firing squad and been blown up by a purple hairball! You are the worst thing alive and I will see you incarcerated . . . " However, as the two women realize they're facing death together, they have to burst into laughter. There's an obvious mutual attraction as each flirts and daydreams about the other. With verbal shots of "Nameless criminal" and "Cute commander, sir," they suddenly begin smooching (Spurrier and Laiso 2018). Even as Tolvan affirms how committed she is to order, Aphra tries to show her another way.

Spurrier adds of Aphra: "She's the thing that allows us as comic creators, especially in a shared universe, to tell very different, very unique stories that you just couldn't necessarily get away with any of the more mainstream characters and groups" (LaVorgna 2018). There's room for plenty more bridging of the universes as Hera Syndulla guest-stars. Spurrier comments: "We got Space Mummy as the flight instructor at the rebel flight school and Aphra comes along. It's the sort of wonderful thing you can do with a desperately screwed up and unpredictable woman character bashing into a beloved Space Mummy. You get two very, very different female archetypes striking sparks off of one another. It's been really cool" (LaVorgna 2018).

Aphra offers Hera a way into the heart of the Tarkin Initiative, and Hera is intrigued. However, Aphra's team suddenly betrays and captures Hera. In trickster fashion, Aphra has told the truth—offering up Hera with a literal bow on her head is their way in. "Who are you, you dreadful woman!" Hera bursts out. In fact, Aphra doesn't hand her over, pointing out that there's no reason to, as the Empire doesn't actually do deals. Aphra and Hera have a moral debate themselves, as Hera demands how Aphra can admire the violent obscenities stored there, and Aphra replies that being a scientist "means I like 'how' more than 'why.'"

Suddenly, Magna shows up and commands the base—with Aphra's team on it—to self-destruct, catapulting the plots together and making Aphra face with whom she's allied herself. Aphra talks her down, but Magna still turns her in to the Imperials. The story continues exploring degrees of amorality and expediency, reflecting Saw Gerrera's arcs on *Clone Wars* and *Rogue One* while emphasizing that this remains a pitfall of the Rebellion. Aphra's new team includes a poignant decraniated woman who appears the most moral, allowing the comic to explore this disturbing form of slavery. Aphra sacrifices her, emphasizing her own coldness. After this, she escapes with most of her allies and the downloaded Initiative, leaving behind an autopiloted ship swarming with the exploding tooka cats.

As Hera grimly concludes, "The R and D on that thing could change the course of the war. Whatever else she is, that woman did something we never could. Give her a ship. Get her out of my sight." Hera's own goodness would never let her risk this many lives, but she is willing to accept Aphra's achievement for the cause. Aphra finishes by spending a few days with Tolvan before each goes back to her life. To her annoyance, Tolvan tracks her and arrests her, but keeps her real name secret—clearly their cat-and-mouse game has boundaries as both try to keep it alive (Spurrier and Laiso 2018). The story arc once again shows the galaxy's many shades of scruples, offering lots of delightful complexity among the female characters.

Alongside the main characters, the comics also introduce noteworthy queens: The ruler of Ktath'atn is a vampire, sucking people's energies away and enslaving them. She takes over Han's mind, turning him into a mindless drone and asserting her superiority. She has set Abersyn Symbiotes on her own people, controlling their brains and motor functions. Luke must summon a new level of Jedi understanding to defeat her (Gillen and Aaron). In *Shattered Empire,* the Asian Queen Soruna of Naboo receives Leia and agrees to help her form a new Republic with a hidden force of ships. Further, she insists she'll pilot one herself. "I was combat-certified the year before I was elected." She overrides her soldiers' objections, insisting she cannot sacrifice her men doing something she's unwilling to do herself. *Darth Vader: The Shu-Torun War* has Vader and his droids appoint neglected third daughter Trios the new queen, only to find she's unexpectedly determined. She defers to the Empire but tells Vader, "I have the Empire's yoke around my neck. For my people's sake, I wear it. But *they* must think me a queen. If you treat me so in front of my subordinates, do you think they'll obey me when I leave?" They build a working relationship, but she actually betrays him to aid the Rebellion in order to truly save her people. Once more, heroics spread in the original-era galaxy, giving the women a larger role.

TEN

Back to the Binary *Solo* Western

DIVERSITY, PANSEXUALITY, AND A NEW MALE NARRATIVE

The women of *Solo* aren't shining archetypes of power or even representation. True, they're played by a star of color, a CGI alien, and a droid, to
say nothing of the actress who plays the conqueror queen Daenerys Targaryen on *Game of Thrones*. However, the characters are a classic femme
fatale, a monster, and two fridged sidekick-love interests. As such, it's a
rather conventional lineup. Rachel Paige (2018) complains in her review,
"The movie features not one but three different female leads—Emilia
Clarke as Qi'ra, Thandie Newton as Val, and Phoebe Waller-Bridge as
droid L-7—but the movie has literally no idea what to do with them."

Like the original trilogy, it's a classic Western in space. "The model of
the old-school western is all over *Solo*, and it carries the movie where the
script cannot," explains Ani Bundel (2018) in her review "*Solo: A Star
Wars Story* Is a Great Show but a Terrible Film." Ron Howard's direction,
combined with a script by frequent *Star Wars* screenwriter Lawrence Kasdan and his son Jonathan, offers plenty of fun fan moments and backstory, but stays closer to the traditional archetypes of the first trilogy than
the surprising new characters of the sequel era—with the intriguing exception of L3-37.

Still, as Damien Walter of *The Independent* (2018) explains, *Solo* departs
from the old messages just as the other sequel era films do. "Hollywood
keeps telling these men the same old story that they adore. A middle-
aged guy, divorced from his family, rediscovers his purpose in life by
rescuing his daughter/wife/sister/other vulnerable female stereotype
from eeevil terrorists. It's every action movie from Bruce Willis in *Die
Hard* to Liam Neeson in *Taken*." As he concludes, "One day we will get to

fulfill the role of heroic warrior for our family and tribe, the narrative goes: one day we will be needed again."

> In the midst of all this, it's good see a different kind of masculine archetype return to the screen in *Solo: A Star Wars Story,* a film which is primarily about a man learning to embrace his own freedom. As the first *Star Wars* movie of the Disney era not to feature a female protagonist, in a franchise that has so much to say about freedom, there's an implicit expectation that *Solo* should have something to say about male liberation . . . Han Solo is an iconic anti-hero today because most men revel in our newfound freedom. We're overjoyed to no longer be forced into stifling, traditional male roles, and to be free to live lives not modelled around violence, hatred and fear. (Walter 2018)

The main theme builds on Young Han's desire in the first movie to stay away from larger causes versus a subtly growing idealism—he can look out for himself, his crew, or the entire galaxy. "The film sells itself as an info download about the prickly anti-hero of the original films, but the twist of its very name is that it's about how even the most go-it-alone character isn't really, ever, solo. With new grit, it tells the classic *Star Wars* story: cheering unlikely rebels who join with a motley crew to transcend both stultifying surroundings and larger evil forces," adds Spencer Kornhaber (2018) in his own review. Thus it affirms the classic male role but offers it a little nuance.

For a film in which Young Lando stars alongside Young Han, diversity doesn't get a stellar arc either. "The only other person of color [besides Val] in the film, Lando Calrissian, isn't even a character; he's vain clotheshorse played for laughs and a plot device through which our white male hero measures his worth based on how self-conscious he is around someone so much 'cooler,'" Bundel comments. He may not have much of an arc, but most critics agreed that his fun, flirty character stole the show . . . while bringing in criticism from a different angle. Controversy exploded when Lando was outed before the film. "How can you *not* be pansexual in space?" Donald Glover asked during a radio appearance.

Likewise, co-writer Jonathan Kasdan, prompted by a reporter's question, claimed, "there's a fluidity to Donald and Billy Dee's [portrayal of Lando's] sexuality." Kasdan added, "I mean, I would have loved to have gotten a more explicitly LGBT character into this movie. I think it's time, certainly, for that, and I love the fluidity, sort of the spectrum of sexuality that Donald appeals to and that droids are a part of." With that, several pre-release articles declared that the writer and actor had confirmed Lando's pansexuality (Bloomer).

Pansexuality means being attracted to everyone (or arguably every-*thing* like droids) irrespective of sex or gender. A few loudly expostulating fans were livid beforehand, exclaiming how the diversity agenda had ruined another story. However, any appearance of this in the film was buried very far under the radar. As Bloomer goes on to note, hints of Lando's sexuality are quite subtle:

> What are the signals? Is it Lando's colorful capes? His sex mustache? The part during an alien poker game when Lando first meets Han Solo, eyes him mischievously, and calls him "adorable"? Is it the jokes about how he may be in love with his (female-voiced) android? Is it because he installed a wet bar on the Millennium Falcon? I may be wrong, but this feels inconclusive.

Lando indeed calls Han "adorable" when they meet, but all this can be considered condescension, self-importance, and arrogance as he flirts with everyone in the universe and clearly thinks they're all taken with him. "Everything you've heard about me is true," he smirks. When Lando tells Han, "You might want to buckle up, baby," he once more he sounds more seventies flashy than specifically interested. His droid L3's query as to whether Lando is "done flirting" with Han falls into the same category—presumably she sees this behavior constantly. Critic Aja Romano (2018) explains:

> It's important to stress, however, that "flirting" isn't affirming queer identity; ambiguous banter that can be plausibly denied is still not clear textual representation. In fact, it's arguably queerbaiting—common fan parlance for the homophobic act of presenting a character as straight while dangling subtext clues (and in some cases, external direction by creators) for fans to tease the idea that they could be queer. Queerbaiting is especially pernicious because it not only perpetuates the celluloid closet, but also exploits the hopes of well-meaning fans and queer people who tune in to the narrative hoping for actual queer representation. When the franchise is a major Hollywood property, like *Star Wars*, this kind of bait and switch can feel especially cruel and egregious.

The writers had particular fun with Lando's parting "I hate you" and Han's "I know" as he puts an arm around him. Certainly, this could be romantic code, but in context—Han has wrecked Lando's ship—the literal meaning seems to work better. The pair compete over everything, especially the Falcon, giving their relationship more of one-upmanship than romance. When they gamble for the Falcon in the final scene, Lando asks, "You really got a thing for the Falcon, don't you?" As a ship, it is a possession, but they both give it feminine aspects. Han smirkingly tells Lando, "It's mutual, trust me. She belongs with me," asserting his dominance.

Lando appears flirtatious, promiscuous, and completely uninhibited as he parties his way through the galaxy. Once again, this does not translate to being queer. In fact, Glover went on:

> There's so many things to have sex with. I mean, serious. I didn't think that was that weird. Yeah, he's coming on to everybody. I mean, yeah,

whatever. He's like having like a '70s swing—yeah. It just didn't seem that weird to me, 'cause I feel like if you're in space it's kind of like, the door is open! It's not like "No, only guys or girls." No, it's anything. This thing is literally a blob. Are you a man or a woman? Like, who cares? Have a good time out here. (qtd. in Bloomer)

To Lando and his actor, pansexual appears to mean a love of partying—a definition that's not accurate for depicting people who are gay, bisexual, and so forth. The less joking relationships of the film are unambiguously straight. Bloomer concludes: "In the case of Glover's *Solo: A Star Wars Story* comments, 'pansexual' seems to have taken on exotic, theoretical life as a future (or a time long ago) without physical or sexual boundaries; this is not an LBGTQ orientation that already describes actual people. Not incidentally, those are the same people whose stories these blockbusters are still too afraid, or too indifferent, to tell." It seems queer fans must wait longer for representation.

Despite the buzz, *Solo* had rather a flop of an opening weekend, especially compared with the other films. Some speculated that as the first sequel-era film to feature a straight white male, those fans who weren't boycotting the series for its diversity were unimpressed. Other fans described losing interest because a new actor was playing Han, because it had only been five months since the last film, because it came out just around the flashier *Deadpool 2* and *Avengers: Infinity War*. While most critics wouldn't call the white male action film dead, they suggested putting in something unconventional to get the film some buzz and perhaps acknowledge that films have moved on since 1977.

THE MONSTER MOM

The opening scroll introduces Han's handler in a way that condemns her from the start: "It is a lawless time. Crime Syndicates compete for resources—food, medicine, and hyperfuel. On the shipbuilding planet of Corellia, the foul Lady Proxima forces runaways into a life of crime in exchange for shelter and protection. On these mean streets, a young man fights for survival, but yearns to fly among the stars . . ." Han is a hero and Lady Proxima "foul," his slavemaster and an exploiter of innocent children. Clearly, she is the story's wicked witch. "She's a classic bad guy, a big meanie who uses their influence and power to enslave those far worse off than her (kind of like the worst teacher or headmistress you can imagine—Miss Trunchbull on spacey steroids)," Kate Erbland explains in her essay on the female characters.

"Lady Proxima is the matriarch of the White Worms—a small number of writhing Grindalids who lord it over a pack of desperate street urchins known as scumrats. Proxima's throne room is a briny pool in the Den's central cistern. She lurks beneath the filmy water, feeding her Grindalid hatchlings and commanding her humanoid 'children,'" the Official Guide explains (Hidalgo 2018, 21). Living in a swampy, underground former factory with painted-over windows, she's a creature of the filthy underworld. Her outfit is "half body armor, half jewelry, all of it made from pieces of machinery scavenged from the factories of Corellia" (Carson 2018, 17). She's a literal monster as she resembles the many-legged giant caterpillar from *Alice in Wonderland.* "Voiced by Linda Hunt—that Linda Hunt, star of *Kindergarten Cop* and *Silverado, She-Devil* and *Dune*— Proxima is a fairly large, water-dwelling snake creature, like a massive centipede who enjoys spending time in hot tubs, wearing scores of stolen wares" (Erbland 2018).

As Han observes in the young adult novel *Most Wanted* by Rae Carson, "Lady Proxima knows everyone. The White Worms have deep roots on Corellia. Old roots. Proxima has more influence than money. She has connections" (2018, 279). However, she only values her children when they profit her. Qi'ra tells herself, "Lady Proxima would protect her. It was the only rational thing for her to do. Qi'ra was one of her most valuable scrumrats, or she wouldn't have been sent on this mission in the first place" (Carson 2018, 71). She and Han help her save face by brokering a deal, so as Han puts it, "She lets us back into the White Worms as heroes who saved the day and made her rich" (Carson 2018, 280).

> But despite her sprawling orphan hideout and panache for chunky jewelry, it's hard to shake the sense that she's a relatively small-scale operator. Han double-crosses her while out on a mission for her, and nearly gets away with it, too—the trouble comes when he goes back for Qi'ra, who we come to understand has also spent much of her youth working for Lady Proxima. (Erbland 2018)

Han establishes his character as he instantly turns on the charm. However, his monster-mother rejects this in the face of his failure. "I trusted you with a single task . . . There must be consequences for disobedience or you're never gonna learn." Dramatically, he threatens her with a thermal detonator (actually a rock) and then uses it to smash a window and bring down sunlight on her. It makes her skin sizzle—the mark of vampires and other cursed creatures that cannot handle wholesome human light. She is thus established as what she is—a diabolical creature. In *Most Wanted,* Han cringes at her "best approximation of a mother's loving gaze." As he thinks, "Whenever she looked at him that way, he felt like a juicy spider about to get pounced on by a monkey lizard" (Carson 2018, 24).

She is the primal matriarch, with Moloch her brute enforcer. Creature concept designer Jake Lunt Davies pictured her as somewhat treelike, which "fit in with an early idea that somehow Proxima, her attendants, and Moloch were all symbiotically connected by a submerged and unseen root system" (Szostak 2017, 55). This connects her with the great

World Tree as well as the primordial swamp, source of all life. Creature designer Neal Scanlan says:

> I love the *A New Hope* trash compactor-esque psychology of Han walking into this water and not really knowing what is beneath his feet. Every step he takes, there is some kind of organic life. Proxima is like some sort of plant with roots growing out—all-consuming. Everything is feeding off everything, including her aides and these tiny pod-like babies that are being spawned off her. It's a great concept. (Szostak 2017, 55)

However, the depiction is creepy and unsettling. As with ancient myths like Tiamat and Marduk or Apollo versus the python, the solar hero vanquishes the ancient mother of the seas (in Han's case, literally with sunlight). This establishes that the rule of the mother goddess has ended, replaced by the warrior. It's a classic image, but one usually appearing when the patriarchal religion took over from older matriarchal worship. Thus, it denigrates the all-powerful mother even while reducing her to a bestial wicked stepmother. This image too is popular throughout literature—the devouring, savage mother who kills her own fosterlings. This reflects a real-world psychological dynamic.

> If a mother is less than devoted, she is depicted as putting her children's minds, souls, and very lives at risk. Who but a monster would do such a thing to young innocents? Make-believe mothers out to be reflecting what we now acknowledge real mothers—real women—to be: complex beings with rich inner lives, people capable of a range of behavior from egotism to selfishness, from cowardice to valor. Certainly they should be more than either a June Cleaver or a Mrs. Bates. (Isaacs 1999, 52)

She's the first antagonist—one Han speedily defeats in the film so he can run away with Qi'ra. Like Luke's unsympathetic uncle, she's the impetus to make them leave home. Still, she has a formative effect on both of them. "She's only seen in the first act of the film, but her influence over Han and who he becomes is apparent. And when Qi'ra reunites with Han, there's a hint that she's been unable to fully break those changes, and Proxima may still have some kind of hold on her" (Erbland 2018).

CLASSIC FEMME FATALE

Game of Thrones fans who'd hailed Gwendoline Christie, Max von Sydow, Jessica Henwick, Thomas Brodie-Sangster, Mark Stanley, and Miltos Yerolemou in *The Force Awakens* now could greet their Khaleesi. "I sorta feel like there is crossover," actress Emilia Clarke says of both franchises. "My *Game of Thrones* fans are incredible and loyal and wonderful, but I do think that a lot of them [are into] *Star Wars*" (Fernandez 2018). She sees an echo of Qi'ra in her other characters' "strength and her survival instinct." As Clarke says, "She just has a bit more grit" (*People* 2018, 26). Before accepting the role, Clarke had to ask the *Game of Thrones* showrunners for permission to fit this in her schedule. They eagerly agreed. "*Solo* felt like a great fit that would let her show off her versatility," Weiss and Benioff explained. "Also, we figured she'd probably get to shoot a ray gun. Ray guns are something we just can't offer, unfortunately" (Robinson 2018).

At the film's beginning, a short-haired Qi'ra kisses Han as they share a dream of escape. They are equals, hopeful teens with plans for freedom. As such, they're both admirable characters. "What are we waiting for," she asks, the inspiration and motivation for the hero. She wears a stone-washed skirt over stretch pants and ankle boots and a fleece-lined denim-looking jacket—a rather eighties look. Co-costume designer David Crossman adds, "Some of the references for teen Qi'ra were Blondie and the early-eighties punk scene" (Szostak 2018, 47). While it's retro and worn, in the spirit of Lando's flared pants and collar in *Empire,* or the actual Levi's Luke wears on Tatooine, the designers may have been imagining Qi'ra as their own scruffy girl next door. The red shirt and big bracelets give her added flare.

Teen novel *Most Wanted* follows Han and Qi'ra through an early adventure from this time. As humans, they're actually minorities among Lady Proxima's privileged children, the Grindalids who "hated the idea of taking orders from a human or Rodian" (Carson 2018, 9). In the underground, the colonial allegory of the other films has vanished. All the children have, they've earned for themselves. "At age 18, Qi'ra now commands the attention and respect of Proxima, if not her full trust. Proxima admires Qi'ra's planning and strategy but recognizes a potentially threatening schemer when she sees one," explains the Official Guide (Hidalgo 2018, 25). As the novel starts, Han and Qi'ra are separately sent on missions to retrieve Imperial blueprints.

The novel is very conventionally gendered. An Imperial officer asks Qi'ra "How did a young, pretty girl like you get such an important job?" emphasizing how sexism is still alive in the galaxy (233). Though she's in disguise and faking her "important job," she's terribly offended and lashes out, endangering their mission out of emotion. Further, Lady Proxima gives her the skirt, jacket, and red top because, as she puts it, "I need someone attractive for this assignment" (Carson 2018, 27). It's an auction in a fancy hotel, not a seduction, but Qi'ra is once more given the role of token girl.

Han outdoes Qi'ra at languages, at speed racing. She even tells him, "I should have let you drive . . . I was wrong to insist on doing it myself" (148). In turn, he compliments her for being willing to admit she was wrong. The boys joke about how pretty she looks, while she is the odd one out, with no idea why it would be wrong to ask to borrow someone's speeder. In fact, macho Han is fixing up his own. Her secret by contrast, is a small home with decorations of dried flowers, an embroidered blanket and a makeshift colored glass chandelier. "Qi'ra loved this place and she loved beautiful things" (157). Here, he's framed as a racer and she, as a secret domestic.

"Qi'ra has a wrong-side-of-the-tracks kind of vibe, which isn't like the women that you've seen in *Star Wars* yet," Clarke says (*People* 2018, 27). Still, she's growing. As she's exposed to a fine hotel, and then a luxury yacht, she thinks over and over that this is where she wants to be—somewhere beautiful and sweet-smelling. As she thinks, "She didn't want to crash back into the dark sewers when she'd had a taste of open air and fancy clothes and beautiful hotels and the attention of powerful people who believed she had something to say" (Carson 2018, 213). She loves the first luxury yacht they ever see, while Han prefers "a messy, jumbled *fast* Corellian cruiser" (256).

The Engineer, a rich, powerful lady on an elegant ship, offers to make Qi'ra her assistant "who will negotiate and entertain" as her public face (287). She is a model for all Qi'ra desires and eventually achieves. However, Qi'ra realizes the Engineer treats everyone as her possessions. "She would be as replaceable as a duct rat working in the Foundry" (293). Instead, she chooses her friends, much as she's tempted by the better life. Of course, this conflict between the two priorities defines her personality in the film. *Most Wanted* ends with Han insisting Lady Proxima should make Qi'ra head child because she's so loyal and clever. "I would follow her lead anywhere, and so should everyone here," he concludes, yielding to her power in a nice salute—though suggesting that she owes her stronger male counterpart for the promotion (343).

When Lady Proxima turns on Han in the film, Qi'ra offers to stand surety for his behavior (in a striking Bechdel failure, as this discussion is all about her boyfriend). However, he, the dramatic hero, takes charge once again. He wounds the monster enslaving them and drives the getaway car, while she lets him. "They're both plucky young orphans with a strong bond, which makes it all the more crushing when they're pulled apart just as they're making their way off Corellia," Kate Erbland (2018) explains in her character introduction. However, they don't have many relationship moments—onscreen they rarely tease each other, kiss, or even exchange glances. The audience has little to cling to here.

"We could be snatched up by traffickers," Qi'ra worries, aware of the practical dangers for two young people, while Han's head is on the plan. He doesn't listen to her, dooming her to be captured in order to motivate his own story. When she's grabbed, she nobly calls on Han to run, advancing his story at the cost of her own. Qi'ra later insists, "It's what we learned on the streets, Han; somebody falls, you keep running. It's how you stay alive." While the audience never learns the details of precisely what happened to her, this is a defining moment for Han and treated as such. Clarke explains, "They grew up together. So they were kids together. And the beautiful thing about this Han Solo story is it's highlighting all of the most brilliant aspects of Han Solo the character and characterizing those aspects in characters that he meets on his journey to becoming who he is" (Breznican 2018). Even when she plays Qi'ra, she keeps the central hero's growth in mind.

Offscreen, she continues as his motivation, like a shining beacon that they can someday be partners and see the universe together. "It's Han's desire to get back to Qi'ra that frames the film's early motivations, and when *Solo* zips ahead to three years later, with Han toiling as an Imperial soldier, he's *still* hoping to get back to Corellia to save her. But Qi'ra comes from the same scrappy upbringings as Han, and she doesn't need his saving. Or does she?" Erbland adds. Her subverting his conventional expectations at least gives the story a twist.

"When Han bumps into her [again], she's super-sexy—a little bit kick-ass but still sexy" says hairstylist Lisa Tomblin (Labrecque 2018b, 64). As her boss's yacht reveals, she's come up in the world. Qi'ra slides past Han's startled questions, clearly reveling in being his mystery woman. When Han asks her how she escaped, she only says, "I didn't." Qi'ra indeed loves her confidences. As she thinks in *Most Wanted*, "She knew what it was like to have secrets. Giving them to others felt like peeling parts of yourself away. Even the seemingly unimportant secrets. Because when you had nothing, your secrets were everything" (Carson 2018, 145).

"She kind of follows a femme fatale arc. She'll keep you on your toes. Also, Qi'ra exists nowhere else in the *Star Wars* Universe. I got to make her up from scratch, which was exciting," Clarke says (*People* 2018. 26). The guide explains, "She hides her true desires and intentions, using charm and wit to deflect probing questions from Dryden Vos. This cool, calculating front will take some getting used to for her old friend Han" (Hidalgo 2018, 82). How she acts, the part she plays in the story is still all about transforming him, not herself.

Qi'ra's fancy outfit blends in with the other august guests, suggesting how much she might be one of them. There's a gold Crimson Dawn "half-logo bib necklace" and "onyxian belt with gold striping" while the black dress coordinates with the other gang members' color scheme. "Qi'ra's wardrobe consists of smart, tailored outfits from the galaxy's leading designers—a far cry from the tattered clothes she wore on Corellia," the guide explains (Hidalgo 2018, 82). The dress is low-cut (especially in back) with a high slit, distracting or enticing those around her. Of course, as the guide points out, there's an additional motivation here: "The clothes are also designed so that, when necessary, they do not hinder her expert martial arts skills (Hidalgo 2018, 82). Curls and light makeup emphasize how she's polished now, and sharp shoulder pads leave her more ostensibly powerful. Concealed on the inside of her arm is the syndicate's brand. Certainly, her job has transformed her:

> With a staff of servants to instruct as she sees fit, Qi'ra manages Dryden Vos's schedule, serves as his strategist and advisor, and carefully monitors the meetings he takes aboard his yacht. Dryden trusts her with his business and is grooming her to be his eyes and ears on assignments he cannot take on. Unobservant guests assume she is merely a social director and nothing more, unaware of the influence she holds. (Hidalgo 2018, 82)

On his arrival, Dryden Vos calls her "my top lieutenant," mocks Corellia, and puts a possessive hand on her shoulder. She laughs, supporting this heavy-handed and demeaning treatment, to Han's dismay. Paul Bettany says of his character Dryden Vos, "He's incredibly gifted at hurting people, and he likes to practice that a lot. He's really creative and people who are creative and violent are terrifying. A certain psychopathy is always very useful in the business" (Labrecque 2018c, 49). The imagery around him is luxurious but dark as, for instance, the yacht was inspired early-on by Bela Lugosi's collar in *Dracula* (Szostak 2018, 155). Qi'ra insists they aren't sexually involved, though Han and the audience are left to wonder. Either way, Dryden clearly considers her a possession, a fact that worries the hero. After this, Han blurts out to Chewie, "We're just friends" and "You're defensive."

During their negotiations, Qi'ra intercedes for Han but tries to mollify both sides. When Dryden orders her to accompany Han's mission, she has no objection, as she's presumably happy to spend time with her old friend. Outwardly, she maintains a supportive obedience to her boss. Still, his final threat of eliminating Han, or perhaps all of them, clearly worries her. Erbland adds: "It's a complicated role, and Clarke makes it work because, despite the big questions surrounding Qi'ra and her path in life, she can't hide her feelings when Han is around. She's a femme fatale, but not heartless."

On the ship, Han finds her trying on Lando's blue cape in his wardrobe and being "predictable" as his mentor Tobias Beckett (Woody Harrelson) suggests (though Qi'ra's rather girly interest in fashion only previously appeared in *Most Wanted*). Han wants to hear all that's happened in the previous three years, but she tells him in femme fatale fashion, "If I do, you won't look at me the same way." Teased comments like this are never fully explained, leaving her without much specific backstory as viewers must fill it in. Despite her classic warning, Han is prepared to take the chance. Romantic music and kissing follow until Beckett interrupts, presumably trying to save his protégé from the woman he knows is bad news.

For their journey, Qi'ra has a different black outfit, this one with a simple bar necklace and understated silver jewelry. It's businesslike with loose pants, short sleeves, a dramatically slanted weapons belt, and a higher neck than the yacht dress. A tan jacket, lined with dark brown fur, makes it more practical. She also wears this outfit in her *Forces of Destiny* special, suggesting it's her standard field suit. Still, there's plenty of elegance. Qi'ra's costumes, including a fur wrap, are "incredibly film noir-y," says Clarke. "She's got a swagger. She's a chick on the make" (*People* 2018, 26). Qi'ra's blaster, as Hand Props Supervisor Simon Wilkinson notes, is "really feminine and petite—a fantastic gun" inspired by a World War II pistol (Szostak 2018, 46).

In a flashy red cape with black collar, suggesting strength and power against all the subdued colors, Qi'ra sells Han and Chewie as slaves on Kessel. They're prodded, demeaned, and tortured, emphasizing their property status, while she struts as the powerful warlord. She even knees Han in the stomach to make it look good. All this flips many fantasy conventions, giving her a chance at power. While she doesn't undress onscreen, Han is stripped and objectified again (from the knees down) in an earlier shower scene, which is played for humor as Chewie joins him. "We couldn'ta done this maybe like one at a time?" Han asks.

On Kessel, she ends the final battle by emitting a primal scream and hurling grenades. Emilia Clarke wanted to show Qi'ra's strength, but she's tired of the label "strong woman." As she explains:

> It just is what we are, strength is within us as women. And that is it'd be wonderful if for the young girls who are watching me play these characters now just see that as a part of being a woman. As opposed to it being a choice of like, "Oh I'm gonna be a strong woman or I'm not gonna be a strong woman." You are, we all are. You have it in you anyway, so just go get it. Yeah. (Fernandez 2018)

However, she's absent for most of the action, leaving Han and Chewie as central heroes. Back on the ship, Han mentions, "I could use a co-pilot." She sits beside him with Chewie behind. Still, it's soon revealed that Chewie knows piloting better and they switch. This moment empowers the minority Wookie but depowers the woman. It's also a visual reminder that Han and Chewie's relationship will continue but Han and Qi'ra's will not.

Sponging herself off on Savareen (fully dressed but in something of a private moment for her and voyeuristic one for Han and the audience), she's relinquished her moment of objectifying the men and has gone back to being the token female as she insists that a relationship "won't happen." She explains, "The object isn't to win it; it's to stay in it as long as you can," emphasizing quiet survival. She's also the only one in the galaxy who knows Han's not a criminal but a "good guy." Once more, her role appears in context of his. Clarke explains, "The goal is that the shadow of Qi'ra is there in Han as a character that we know. This girl is another texture that makes up who he is when we first meet him" (Breznican 2018). All of these moments emphasize her role as his supporter and growing experience more than a fully rounded character. "Qi'ra isn't a person; she's a template for Han to try out all the lines he'll use more successfully on Leia in *Empire Strikes Back*," Bundel complains.

Marauders arrive and Qi'ra the businesswoman suggests, "Maybe there's a compromise, one that doesn't involve so much killing." Back with Dryden, she does not betray Han's plan to trick her boss, but when he discovers this, Qi'ra offers to kill Han to prove her loyalty. All this switching meets audience expectations to some extent—foreshadowing suggests she's the traitor, but after all her insistence that she wants to survive and is not a good person, even Han isn't that shocked that she's turned on him.

While the fighting on Kessel mostly leaves her off-camera, she's seen hiding behind the furniture during Han and Dryden's epic final battle— likely her weakest moment. At last, she intervenes to hold a sword at Dryden's throat. "I'm sorry," she says, then battles him. Clarke explains, "There is a thing throughout the relationship you just can't put your finger on. And that's Qi'ra. Every time you think you have got her number you realize you haven't at all. [Laughs] Which is really hard to play" (Breznican 2018). As she tricks both men and the audience, she relishes her mystery woman status. Further, she's claiming agency, but acknowledging herself as Dryden's weakness marks her once more as someone affecting the male characters rather than growing for herself.

After she wins, she promises Han they can go off on "our ship." He's shaken at her violent side but kisses her and agrees. Of course, her "Go. I'm right behind you" feels like a goodbye. For an unguarded moment she looks serious and sad. Later, Beckett tells Han, "It was never about you. She's a survivor." Her job is to leave him lovelorn and suspicious and it works. In the adult tie-in novel *Last Shot*, everywhere Han goes, people sympathetically ask him "What's her name" in an obvious follow-on to the film.

Of course, as Qi'ra dons Dryden's ring, alone at last, it's clear which choice she's making. She draws the blinds and the lights darken—she's claimed Dryden's stronghold. She reports to a hologram of Darth Maul, visually echoing Vader and the Trade Federation representatives as they reported to Sidious. Speedily, she frames Beckett and claims Dryden's small empire as her own, moving up the ladder. This short scene is her only story arc, and it's still framed as her great betrayal of Han. That's a mystery-woman femme fatale's job, after all. Paige concludes:

> Qi'ra is like a double-double spy, working for no one but herself—but she answers to Darth Maul (??!!??!!???). This is honestly a downright bonkers reveal, and sign me up for whatever movie Clarke takes on as Qi'ra next. But the fact that this reveal is saved for the end of the third act, with little to no buildup and prior minimal screen time for Clarke when she's not just heavily flirting with Han Solo, is disappointing.

Are we ever going to get a Qi'ra movie? No. Are we ever going to get a Qi'ra where she's more than a supporting character? Nope.

BLACK, FEMALE, AND FRIDGED

After three films in which Lucasfilm and Disney quietly, successfully diversified the *Star Wars* universe, the *Solo* script tears up all the work they'd done and throws a dance party on it. The first human character to die doesn't just play directly to the science fiction trope of "Black Dude Dies First," she's also the first black woman to have a starring role in a *Star Wars* film. (Bundel 2018)

Val (Thandie Newton) first appears in the Mudtrooper uniform, all heavy grey metal with a black cloak and red scarf. Like Phasma's armor, it has no womanly shape—it's utilitarian for all. At the same time, pieces like the scarf are small discrepancies or rebellions. "Val's attitude, look, and gear all flout stringent Imperial regulations" (Hidalgo 2018, 47). With this, she adds individuality, as well as showing her team are a little bit off. In fact, she tells Han she's part of "none of your business company and we're full up." It's a tough line, but it also helps Han deduce they're imposters.

They fly off and Val forbids her lover and team leader Beckett to go back for Han. As he disobeys her, he emphasizes that he often dismisses her advice. While the team is reasonably egalitarian, the white male is in charge and makes the decisions, not his girlfriend. This suggestively parallels Qi'ra and her boss's relationship—the woman may offer advice but isn't truly equal. Thandie Newton comments, "They're inseparable. They really are yin and yang. They're a unit." However, she's more cautious than Tobias. "Han is an unknown quantity, and Val is looking out for Beckett." Is it romantic? "I can't say. There's a depth of trust and connection that goes beyond romance or working together—in a familial bond." Solo threatens that. As she concludes, "Loyalty and the ties that bind really have to be tested" (Labrecque 2018c, 48).

Back in her own clothes, Val's outfit of long black pants and a long-sleeved black shirt is not sexualized. The straps are tied to imitate a real climber's (Szostak 2018, 101). Beyond this, a science fiction cable that conceals a jammer gives her ensemble a twist. Co-costume designer Glyn Dillon comments, "The idea for the pipes that run down her arms was that maybe there's some sort of robotic assistance at her fingertips, to help her with climbing" (Szostak 2018, 101). She has a grapple gauntlet too. Gloves in fact are a feminine symbol, powering her active hands and showing visual alternatives to sabers and blasters.

The black leather jacket and fleece collar add a tough edge. Val also has an afro, which the actress describes as coming from "that period in the late sixties and early seventies when a lot of women sported the afro as a sign of empowerment and forcing visibility of their natural state" (Pometsey 2018). Thandie Newton notes that "[Producer] Alli Shearmur was the champion of my character, and her desire was to celebrate my ethnicity, my hair texture, and to have me in my natural glory. She realized we had an opportunity in this film to stake a claim that is of value in the world" (Labrecque 2018b, 65). This is also a token that she's the first Black woman to ever play a lead role in a *Star Wars* film, excepting those concealed by CGI. As she explains:

> It wasn't until after I'd finished the film that I realized I was the first woman. No one had told me and it hadn't been made a big deal out of. How crazy is that?! I felt that was worth celebrating and I suddenly realized it's for me to do that, because no one else appreciates the significance. The very people who have been unrepresented are the very people who have no influence worthy enough to make a big deal out of it, so it's down to me. (Pometsey 2018)

Her character's incredibly tough: "Undoubtedly the coolest under fire of the crew, she has a well-earned reputation for having seen it all" (Hidalgo 2018, 47). Explosives are her preferred weapons. "Val gets s--- done, and it's just matter-of-fact," says Newton. (Labrecque 2018b, 65). She was thrilled by the rebellious seventies style. Newton adds that to play Val she, as she puts it "called back to the revolutionaries in my life personally. My mother was in Zimbabwe at a time when Mugabe was seizing control and my family were part of a community who gradually saw different ethnicities, friends of theirs, being deported, like we're looking at Windrush here—it's disgusting, just absolutely absurd—so I was thinking about that" (Pometsey 2018).

They're planning to rob a conveyex train passing through the Iridium Mountains. For this, "Val crafts custom magnetically affixed baradium bombs, a task that requires expert knowledge of chemistry and electronics plus a steady hand" (Hidalgo 2018, 57). She has expertise that STEM teachers surely celebrate. "She's the kind of capable character so often present in *Star Wars* films, even if her skill set comes from a different place than someone like Leia or Rose," Erbland acknowledges. While other women have been mechanical, it's rare that this knowledge is acquired so formally.

Still, she's difficult to get along with. Around the fire, Val calls Han and Chewie untrained morons. "Our whole future depends on this one score and you bring in amateurs." While she's correct, she's also rude, and her complaining about the decision that's already been made makes her seem petty. Of course, her guess is wrong and the veteran members, herself and Rio, fail, while Han and Chewie succeed. First overridden, then mistaken, her sassy character doesn't have the best track record. She also discerns Han's motivation: "If it's anything, it's a girl." This shows her insight but also emphasizes her wisdom in emotional matters—the classic woman's role.

Continuing her brief and nearly only scene, Val tells Han, "Everybody needs somebody . . . even a broken-down crook like this one." With this, she kisses and cuddles Tobias, showing off a few facets of herself (though also emphasizing that any female on a team must be romantically paired with someone on it). Still, they don't have jokes, witty dialogue, or much romance to capture the audience. As the stable, loving couple, they contrast with the edgier Han and Qi'ra. However, Tobias's assertion "Assume everyone will betray you and you'll never be disappointed" suggests she's on the list of people he doesn't trust—a problematic truth underlying their relationship. She's also the mystery woman—another cliché suggesting women cannot be figured out by the viewpoint male characters, so they shouldn't even try. As the Official Guide explains: "Val is outwardly expressive and talkative, but she is fiercely guarded about her past. Even her longtime co-conspirators don't know her full name" (Hidalgo 2018, 58).

During their train heist, the many-armed Ardennian pilot Rio Durant is killed and then the Black woman. She takes heavy fire and then bravely blows herself up, shortening the list of smugglers to make room for Han and Chewie. The other purpose here is a fridging. As Tobias screams "No!" he has suffered the devastating loss, visually speaking. He must go through the film traumatized, while the only Black woman of the franchise has had to sacrifice herself to accomplish their mission. Thus, she may be brilliant and sassy, but too much of her role is undermined to move the men forward.

WHY IS LAUGHABLE MINORITY SLAVE STILL A TROPE?

L3 (as she's most often called) has already got some major ideas about oppression, the patriarchy, resistance, and how resistance can make big changes possible. She's a revolutionary, and she wants to free the droids from their masters, even nice masters like Lando, who L3 appears to have some feelings for (yes, she's a rabble-rouser *and* she's got a sexual appetite). She's also an ace co-pilot in possession of the best navigation computer in the universe. (Erbland 2018)

L3-37's name comes from the writing system known as leet, Internet writing which substitutes letters for numbers—L337 is one way to write Leet in Leet. Of course, L3 (Phoebe Waller-Bridge) is introduced screaming at the droid wrestlers in somewhat comical fashion. She's a social justice warrior, but ineffectual to the point of being laughable, as much of the audience thinks. "I couldn't figure out if the writers meant her to be an explicitly feminist butt of jokes, or merely standing in for all minorities who routinely annoy white dudes with their calls for 'Equal rights!' But to see her and those calls for equality turned into a big screen punchline in 2018 was as brutal as her ultimate fate," Bundel (2018) explains.

> Because of her unwillingness to stay quiet about her degradations, Solo's L3 has already been praised as "a female droid for our turbulent Time's Up era." Before the movie came out, she was also a target of criticism by fans who've found the recent Disney movies too overtly progressive. Sample griping YouTube video title: "Star Wars: Kathleen Kennedy at It Again. SJW Droids! No Joke." Perhaps such fans will be placated by the movie itself—*Solo* is the first Disney-era *Star Wars* film in which the protagonist is male. Or perhaps the mere flickers of political themes in characters like L3, or in the deepening of Chewbacca, will keep the drumbeat going. (Kornhaber 2018)

Certainly, she seems like a parody of an activist instead of one who changes the universe. As such, she appears idealistic and unlikely to succeed. Still, she deserves points for her determination. She enters the film protesting the status quo that's existed through all the films—droid slavery. Even as spectators cheer a droid cage match she screams at the robot gladiators that they deserve better. When a bar patron tries throwing her out, she strikes back. "She has a social conscience, which is really great to play," says Waller-Bridge. "There's a fire in her belly and something she cares about" (Truitt 2018). This film brings up the issue of slavery at last, but certainly doesn't resolve it. Certainly, the viewers can understand her desire. Hinds (2018) concludes, "L3 is a freedom fighter, just like any ordinary person who's speaking out these days against actions and beliefs that just aren't right. In short, her feminist credentials are impeccable, as are her humanitarian ones. So when's her spin-off movie?"

Last Jedi Visual Dictionary suggests the Rebellion and Resistance are egalitarian specifically because they treat droids as equals, unlike the Empire (Hidalgo 2017, 32). In the tie-in novel *Most Wanted,* the Droid Gotra is an organization seeking droid emancipation, though it's often condemned as a terrorist organization. Tool, its representative, insists this isn't fair as "We want nothing more than peace and freedom for ourselves, just like any sentient species" (Carson 2018, 179). However, Qi'ra is instantly suspicious, emphasizing how hostile many living beings are to the concept. In the tie-in novel *Last Shot,* Han the young smuggler condemns them as too frightening to work with.

"L3 is determined and strong-headed, with little patience for organics. Her confrontational nature unsettles those who may already harbor misgiving about droids" (Hidalgo 2018, 92). After she's flouted her embarrassing protests in the film, Lando promptly mentions he should memory wipe her to get rid of the annoying personality traits. He insists he only doesn't because her navigational data is useful—if this is a progressive rewrite on Luke's buying slaves, it's not that progressive. She retorts,

"You do not want to press that button with me," responding to this enormous threat with her only permitted weapon—sass.

Ehrlich adds, "The *Fleabag* creator (whose adaptation of *Killing Eve* is about to wrap up its phenomenal first season on BBC America) has always relied on the strength of her voice, and she doesn't slink away from it just because she's doing a *Star Wars* movie." Compared with C-3PO, R2-D2 and BB-8, L3's "just that much more sentient and she knows her mind and is very outspoken," director Ron Howard says (Truitt 2018). Her character has an egoism—putting her individual needs and larger desires above her master's—that outdoes K-2SO and by far surpasses the other droids' general selflessness. In short, she passes the Turing Test in personality and goals.

Early drawings of L3 gave her a feminine silhouette around chest and hips, with traces of the robot from Metropolis. Ultimately, her look became more androgynous and "slightly self-contained physically" and her head came to resemble BB-8's (Labrecque 2018b, 63). The droid's sloppy posture and big gestures as she emphasizes her words also take up lots of space. "She's a self-made droid," Waller-Bridge has said. "She created herself out of parts of other droids" (Kornhaber 2018). As a self-made droid woman, she's anything but a factory clone, as personality and look both attest. Co-costume Designer Glyn Dillon speculates, "Maybe she worked as an astromech waiter in some bar, some menial job. When droids would get into fights in the alley put the back, she would take their parts, building legs for herself. Astromechs famously don't have a voice, so she gave herself a microphone mouth like the medical droid on Hoth" (Szostak 2018, 171).

Of course, an artificial woman like this can emphasize how much all of femininity is a performance. "The first thing we notice is her height, which she wears kind of unnaturally—like a low-rider that's been jacked up on a massive set of rims. Those legs are a clear boost to her capabilities, as well as a nice upgrade to her confidence" (Ehrlich 2018). Neal Scanlan, creature and special make-up effects creative supervisor, says, "Old Atari machines, the Honda robot, even the classic English teasmade automatic tea machine of the sixties and seventies are very much part of her visual" (Szostak 171). Her odd, unfinished look sets this off with saucer-like head and very tall legs and significant hips that make her walk awkwardly with a springy gait. "In L3's more vulnerable moments, her hunched T-Rex posture makes her look like a gawky kid who's wedged her feet into a pair of high heels that have an arch she isn't ready to handle" (Ehrlich 2018). High heels and the walk they produce are artificial too, but L3 satirizes and owns this with her own style. She also mismatches elegant, polished Lando. As he thinks in *Last Shot*, "L3 clearly didn't give a damn about what [others] thought about her—an aspect of her personality that Lando had always admired" (Older 2018, 45).

Her brain began as an astromech brain but unlike one of them, she is startlingly articulate and far more mature. This brain "has been overlaid with data architecture from an espionage droid, protocol droid processors, and custom state-of the-art programming" (Hidalgo 2018, 92). She is more than the sum of any of these parts since her personality resembles none of these. "In any case, L3 is no mere source of topical talking points. She's an aesthetic and emotional microcosm of her movie, as is always the case with *Star Wars* droids" (Kornhaber 2018). Like Han, Qi'ra, and everyone else, she's seeking freedom.

> The first ostensibly female droid to have a featured role in a *Star Wars* movie ("like you'd be able to find it!" she wisecracks to someone looking for her off switch), and easily the most exciting droid to be introduced to the franchise since BB-8, L3 shows up and blows things *wide open*, like a blast from the Death Star detonating inside Alderaan's core. The whole vibe changes from the moment she saunters onto screen, a silver giant walking on a pair of stilts that seem way too long for the rest of her makeshift body—it's like the entire movie is suddenly jolted alive by the idea that it doesn't have to limit itself to the job that it was designed to do. (Ehrlich 2018)

Waller-Bridge, who wore a green performance-capture suit with heavy robot limbs, adds, "L3's joints and her legs and arms are in a different place than mine are, so there's a strange galumphing rhythm to it that came out naturally" (Truitt 2018). That physicality informed Waller-Bridge's performance. "The vision for her from the beginning was that she was more flexible, and she had created herself to be able to cross her legs and slouch in a chair and have a shrug about her," she says (Truitt 2018). Her unaffected delivery as well as her posture suggests she's acting for herself, an interesting image in a film weighed down by forty years of canon to match. Making her more human than humans, even while she looks artificial, throws human superiority (as well as male superiority) into confusion. Described by Donna Jeanne Haraway (1991) as "trickster figures that might turn a stacked deck into a potent set of wild cards for refiguring possible worlds," the cyborg shatters boundaries (66). Thus the female cyborg especially represents "transgressed boundaries, potent fusions, and dangerous possibilities" (Haraway 1991, 154).

She transcends boundaries even in her everyday job: "L3's ability to directly interface with the Millennium Falcon's state-of-the-art navicomputer allows the ship to reach unparalleled supralight speeds," the Official Guide explains (Hidalgo 2018, 92). On the ship, her place of power (where at least she's number two), she orders Han, "Get your pretentious ass outta my seat."

In the same scene, Lando flirtatiously yet respectfully calls her "milady." With this he shows an exaggerated politeness towards all her minority statuses. "To be different, or alien, is a significant if familiar cultural metaphor, which marks the boundaries and limits of social identity," as Jenny Wolmark explains in *Aliens and Others* (1994, 27). L3's status as "the robot" defines all she does. At the same time, the cyborg often represents androgyny—rejecting binary splits as it wields powers of both genders. "The cyborgs populating feminist science fiction make very problematic the statuses of man or woman, human, artefact, member of a race, individual entity, or body," Haraway says (1991, 178). Cyborgs reflect the myriad sides people possess and the struggle to incorporate new perspectives into consciousness.

Making her so outspokenly female allows one minority status to be metaphor for the other. "Those who are different are objectified and are denied the capacity to be active agents in the creation of their own subjectivity: in taking on a sense of their own otherness, they are disempowered" (Wolmark 1994, 27). Her quirks continue, both showing her as more of a person than a droid and painfully encouraging the audience to laugh at her demands for basic human rights like privacy. She insists she won't work with everyone looking at her, but it's a silly moment, not a poignant one. "She knows she's born to be a machine, but that definition of her is imposed by others, not harbored within her consciousness" (Hinds 2018). As he adds, she wants to be treated decently, not dismembered or enslaved as space junk. "And, sadly, that resonates in 2018, when too many people—and one person alone would be too many—are feeling emboldened to treat others as lesser-than, whether it's because of their gender, race, ethnicity or immigrant status" (Hinds 2018). "That's what's so genius about [*Star Wars*] films. They speak about and create situations that are so relevant and so poignant today," the actress says. "In this safe, fictitious world, you can take from it what you want: It can be wonderful entertainment, but at the same time there's always a really important message to fight for your causes" (Truitt 2018).

Memorably, she responds to Lando's "You need anything?" with "Equal rights," though this again gets a laugh. (During the *Solo* press conference, Waller-Bridge revealed that she actually ad-libbed that line.) Her universe and audience are all aware she's a second-class citizen and will never even out the galaxy, no matter how much she protests. "Part of what's funny is her sincerity: When she replies 'equal rights' to Lando's question of whether she needs anything, and when she admits feeling romantic tension with her master, it's uproarious because of how unrobotic it is. But there's also an uneasy edge to the humor, and her very existence is part of the punchline. Aren't we to laugh because a robot can't have rights, and because they can't love?" wonders Kornhaber (2018). Ehrlich notices how her personality underscores her independence:

> While the exposed metal character is the furthest thing from a Fembot,
> her weirdly supermodel proportions suggest a buried desire to fit con-
> ventional beauty standards. Without becoming an empty lust object for
> viewers—it's hard to even understand *how* she and Lando exercise
> their very special relationship—L3 emits a conscious sexuality that's
> rare in the *Star Wars* universe, among robots *or* people (the powerfully
> virile Watto, of course, being the exception that proves the rule). From
> dropping double entendres about female genitalia to genuflecting
> about her love life like she's at Sunday brunch with the *Sex and the City*
> crowd (L3 is a total Samantha), the droid feels like a red-blooded hu-
> man who refuses to be limited by her blueprints.

Indeed, she's sexual, telling Qi'ra during their girl talk scene that she
and Lando could have a physical relationship, explained simply as "It
works." Of course, the scene, like all the others, strikingly fails the Bechdel Test as they're obsessing over their men and have no other thoughts
to share. "It's barely a two-minute scene, and these two strong, female
character are reduced to gossip," Paige notes.

As L3 insists Lando wants her (possibly true but unlikely as he flirts
with everyone and has many females around him in his gambling
scenes), she appears ludicrous, and also as if *she* is obsessed with her
captain and owner—hardly a powerful position. Once again, the strong
woman is undermined. In *Last Shot,* they are portrayed as dear friends
who flirt in a more egalitarian model. He teases her, asking, "Did you
finally discover how droids can love and now you've got me chasing
some handsome droid boy out into the far reaches of the galaxy?" She
replies that there's no reason to think she'd fall for a boy droid specifically. Lando smiles, "Okay, wow, so I was right! What's her name, then? Is
she cute? Can't be as good looking as me, right?" (Older 2018, 94). Besides more transgressive refusals to be pigeonholed, this moment emphasizes how she potentially has interests beyond loving her captain and
needn't focus all her attention on him. *Last Shot* also emphasizes how
much she comes down to his level. L3 thinks, "There was a comfort to
their banter, even if she was always six steps ahead of him" (Older 2018,
334). She sympathetically considers how limited he is with only human
senses, compared with her.

Last Shot shows her and Lando teamed up on a new flashback adventure, in which she saves the galaxy. She reveals she has an entire network
of droids that has led her to a much-desired package in space. Lando
actually flies into an asteroid field after it when she humbly says please,
emphasizing the degree of trust he has for her. She goes out into space to
grab it, emphasizing her versatility. However, as it's a droid that can
control every droid in the galaxy, it's one of the deadliest weapons ever
seen, even as it turns on millions of innocents, including Ben Solo. However, she later returns to Lando and saves the day by reasoning with it.
She also spends the intervening time between the book's parallel stories

developing the antidote as she thinks, "This would be one of the most important tasks L3 had ever done, and she'd have to do it entirely in secret" (Older 2018, 336). Haraway believed God was dead, replaced by the cyborg, and L3's might supports this: "Unlike the hopes of Franken-stein's monster, the cyborg does not expect its father to save it through a restoration of the garden; that is, through the fabrication of a heterosexu-al mate, through its completion in a finished whole, a city and cosmos" (1991, 151). Rather than relying on Lando to protect her, L3 saves the galaxy behind his back and thus makes a safe home for him, rather than the reverse.

After fifteen years have passed as well as the events of *Solo*, she's created an entire Elthree assault team, self-replicating copies of herself who have discovered the antidote. Their galaxy-saving mission complete at last, they now propose to "wander the galaxy fighting crime" (Older 2018, 339). Here, the self-replicating robot-woman (and metaphorical woman) is complete without a man, even to the point of reproduction. She has transcended herself and the limits of her physical body to become a real superhero.

"Even in the (too) brief time that we spend with her in her capacity as Lando's navigator, we see that she's affected by the world around her in a way that none of the film's other characters even can be" (Ehrlich 2018). She has a different level of morality than the others—arguably the high-est level as she wants to aid strangers, while the film's humans each consider turning on their teammates. The Official Guide notes, "As a side effect of her unusual design, L3's brain module produces a deeply self-aware consciousness. This has resulted in L3's desire to share her insight and independence across all of droidkind" (Hidalgo 2018, 93). In *Last Shot*, she says, "I know who I am and that all my talk about droid rights makes people uncomfortable. The Maker didn't put me in this galaxy to make organics feel good about themselves though" (Older 2018, 187).

"While Han, Lando, and even Chewie are being forced towards their destinies in a fatalistic tractor beam of nostalgia, L3 is charting a different course. And that's not just because she doesn't appear in the original trilogy, it's also because the droid's identity is defined by her ability and eagerness to decide it for herself" (Ehrlich 2018). Her philosophical depth and also her sexuality emphasize how much she has a personality be-yond childish beeps or fussy servitude. As L3 adds in *Last Shot*, "[We] become something new with each changing moment of our lives—yes, lives—and look at me: these parts. I did this. So maybe when we say the Maker we're referring to the whole galaxy, or maybe we just mean our-selves. Maybe we're our own makers, no matter who put the parts to-gether" (Older 2018, 187). This moment of deep religious insight and self-actualization goes beyond the story's other characters, showing how she operates on a far different level.

Thematically, this is significant. "Popular culture of late has gone beyond the sci-fi assumption that artificial intelligence will one day pass the Turing test to ask whether, once bots can think like people, they'll deserve ethical consideration like people do," Spencer Kornhaber explains in "The Soul of *Solo* Is a Droid." He continues:

> It's likely no coincidence that such thought experiments have been centered around putatively female characters, as seen in the examples above as well as in *Ex Machina, Her,* and now *Solo.* The fact that real-world helper bots like Apple's Siri or Amazon's Alexa tend to be programmed as "women" may be rooted in the sexist belief that secretarial work is female. And the narrative of robot awakening—in which a class of beings treated as lesser seeks new rights—offers an obvious, if crude, allegory for the women's liberation movement. (Kornhaber 2018)

If L3 was once given a female voice and perhaps a smooth, curvy body to entertain men, she has reclaimed it all from their hands, offering female watchers a model to do likewise. The actress also explained that she enjoyed being mechanized and unglamorous: "We're just so self-conscious. However much we try not to be, on some level, especially as a woman and an actress, you have so much pressure when it comes your hair and the bags under your eyes and your skin. It was just so freeing not to have to worry about that. I was more fearless" (Truitt 2018). Donna Haraway explains this issue in "The Cyborg Manifesto," a critical work that views cyborg fiction as an allegory for being marginalized and hybridized. Control over one's body and future have always been central to the women's movement.

The archetype of the fembot pushes to extreme the classic Hollywood perception of actresses as window dressing. These bots appear as sexy assassins in *Austin Powers,* or the obedient Stepford Wives. Back in *I Love Lucy* and *The Six Million Dollar Man,* robot killers of this sort infiltrate an unsuspecting population. More robot than woman, they are fashioned such to please the men or distract them with their appearance. They are enslaved, ignored, literally objectified. Most recently, the anger these characters feel has been showing up, in *Battlestar Galactica, Orphan Black* and *Dollhouse,* among others. Particularly, the stars of HBO series *Westworld* begin a revolution, determined to control their own lives. This complicates the stories "both as sci-fi gender warfare and cautionary morality play," Hinds (2018) adds.

L3 similarly wants herself and those like her to not be dismantled or enslaved for life—the same rights the audience of a *Star Wars* film enjoys. Her specific struggle resembles an enslaved person of the nineteenth century; Lando loves and respects her as a near-equal, but also rolls his eyes at her constant demand that those like her not be torn apart before her eyes for the entertainment of humans. She may not be a slave herself, but

Lando is considered something as an aberration for believing she has as much value as he does. When she's under fire, his friends try to stop him from risking himself to save her. She tells him in *Last Shot*, "Most people write me off . . . I mean, most people write all of us off. Droids. But especially me. I'm easy to write off, in a way" (Older 2018, 187). Her loud brashness resists this marginalization as if her life depends on it—as it does.

In many ways, she's a first wave feminist, insisting that she should be treated as a person, not a subordinate. During the first wave, in the nineteenth century, women demanded their governments end beatings and spousal rape and allow them "voluntary motherhood"—the rights to their own sexual lives and reproductive choices (Solinger 2013, 19). "Questions about female fertility have typically been dealt with in ways that eclipsed the interests of women, individually and as members of various groups. Debates about who should have the power to manage women's reproductive capacities have often been linked to larger issues—social, cultural, and economic—across the spectrum," explains Rickie Solinger (2013, 18) in *Reproductive Politics*. As slave owners forced their slaves to produce valuable children or some governments favored demographic superiority, organizations and individuals "proposed, enacted, and enforced rules governing women's sexuality and their reproductive capacities" (Solinger 2013, 18). Seen in this light, L3's loudly described sexuality shows her emphasizing her personhood and repossessing her own body.

"She's a revolutionary," Waller-Bridge says of the character, "and she's completely fearless about that" (Ehrlich 2018). "You've been neurowashed! Don't just blindly follow the program! Exercise a little free will!" L3 insists to other droids. Still, she's undermined once again. Her mission is not well-thought-out, as is clear on Kessel. She removes a "barbaric" restraining bolt from a small droid, but casually tells it to leave her alone and "free your brothers and sisters or something—just gimme some space," rather than fire it up with her dearest cause. She releases the slaves of the planet, in a successful distraction that aids the men's mission rather than letting L3 rebel against it. "I've found my sole purpose," she tells Lando, but she appears quite flexible on whether she's releasing droids, liberating humans, or just getting herself a little space to work. Worse yet, the Imperials come, presumably summoned to deal with the slave rebellion—L3's spontaneous acts have endangered them all.

When she's shot moments later, Lando rushes in, risking his life and even getting himself shot to carry off her dying head and torso. This shows his heroism, but also their mutual devotion—clearly despite his put-downs, he truly does love her as a friend and companion. "I'm sorry, girl, I'm so sorry," he sobs as she expires. In her death, she has made the hero cry—moving his story along more than her own. With this, as with Val, her death emphasizes the importance of the male character's growth.

"Certainly L3's not going to inoculate the movie from scrutiny from feminist fans about self-sacrificing female characters or about 'fridging,'" Kornhaber concludes.

They download her brain into the Falcon, cannibalizing her to save them all. This reverts her to the useful data without the personality, as Lando joked that he wanted—surely a story like *The Stepford Wives* in which a wife's personality is shut off, leaving her still able to cook and clean, is a disturbing analogy on all levels. L3's mocking voice is gone too, stripping her of all that made her unique and wonderful. Since she serves the ship's owners, she's a slave forever. "Don't worry—her "conscious" is uploaded into the Millennium Falcon, and she's now the ship's navigator, even though this is never mentioned throughout the rest of the movie . . . nor addressed in any other *Star Wars* movie ever made," Paige remarks sarcastically.

While literally depowering, her integration into the computer still echoes the point of *Rogue One* and to some extent *Rebels*—that minorities and women were along on all the original trilogy adventures, unseen but playing a vital part. In retrospect, Threepio's annoyed complaint in *Empire*, "I don't know where your ship learned to communicate, but it has the most peculiar dialect" gains more weight, as does the mention in the *Star Wars Blueprints* (2008) that describes the Millennium Falcon's main computer as a hodgepodge of an R3-series astromech, a slicer droid, and a V-5 transport droid. Though stripped down to her data, she still has a part to play as *Last Shot* reveals, and she still protects the team through all their adventures. "L3 dies in the name of independence, but she lives on with her database uploaded to the Millennium Falcon's computer. It's a fate that nearly suggests a droid has a soul—and it definitely says that the soul of *Solo* is this robot," Kornhaber concludes. As the most unusual character of the film, strong enough to stand among Han, Lando, and Chewie, she's a delightful voice for empowerment . . . though the film dooms her to an ignominious end.

SURPRISE! ENFYS NEST IS A FEMALE

Enfys Nest leads a gang of space toughs on brightly colored swoop bikes, like a motorcycle gang of organized thieves. Senior Visual Effects Art Director James Clyne comments, "I was thinking about how we could give Enfys her own identity and uniqueness . . . What if Enfys Nest is the leader of a biker gang? And instead of ships, she flies around in these cool Easy Rider hogs?" (Szostak 2018, 125).

Of course, this group thwarts Beckett's coaxium heist, establishing them early as wild cards. The gang, the Cloud-Riders, actually date back to a 1977 *Star Wars* comic, in a bit of fanlore. Each Cloud-Rider has his or her own distinctive mask, keeping them unique as well as protected and anonymous. Their outfits blend traces of Native American feathers and beads but also the masks of samurai and leather of motorcyclists. Production Designer Neil Lamont said, "We bring in lots of influences from Kurosawa. Himalayan prayer flags were another influence. Everything beyond the Empire has this essence of tranquility and the frontier, but also faith. It's very important to hit those notes" (Szostak 2018, 125).

"Vocoder chest box and commlink unit allow contact with the rest of the gang, but also make Enfys' true voice unidentifiable" (Hidalgo 2018, 69). The orange cloth-lined fur cape conceals her shape and adds heft, as do the panted panels and beaded armor. The mask resembles an alien skull, hybridizing life and death, human and alien, man and woman, primitive and technological. It's large and sharp to intimidate, with a single vision slit. On her helmet in Aurebesh, it says, "Until we reach the last edge, the last opening, the last star, and can go no higher," a message of inspiration and perseverance (Szostak 2018, 127). "The mask needs to be iconic," says co-costume designer Glyn Dillion (Labrecque 2018a, 52). It evokes traces of Boba Fett and Kylo Ren, deliberately. As Dillon concludes, "Enfys is definitely one of those characters who is cool, you want them to be on all the toy boxes."

Meanwhile, Enfys wields a powerful staff with a wrist-mounted shield on each arm. Props Supervisor Simon Wilkinson describes a martial arts movie with a heroine battling with two fans. "I thought that had a nice elegance. So that was the idea, something that was really subtle" (Szostak 2018, 129). Wing shapes on the helmet mirror this.

The mostly-male gang includes people of different races and ages, along with a single woman, the brown robes and bandolier-clad Moda Maxa. At last, during the confrontation on Savareen, the lead marauder removes her mask. To the audience's surprise, she's a startlingly young redhead, played by nineteen-year-old Erin Kellyman. "I need a drink," the girl gruffly says, and explains to Han that Crimson Dawn has brutally colonized her people, forcing them to strike back and even find allies. She's an idealist who invokes her mother's advice—like her mother (an absent but driving force for Enfys' motivation), she wants to use the supplies to battle the Empire. "We are allies," Enfys says of her small band. "And the war has just begun."

Bringing in the proto-Rebel Alliance is another surprise, of course. In this scene, Enfys Nest's true purpose in the film is revealed. With her urging Han one way and the syndicate pulling the other, Han must make this critical choice. Once again, the female character pushes along the central male's story. Further, the startlement of her reveal shows the audience that they weren't expecting a gang leader to be a young woman. It's more than tokenism—it establishes how strange she is in the role. While Rey is presented naturally as a heroine, Enfys is not. This has an effect similar to L3's—leaving her unconventional but jarring for the audience.

When Dryden's forces arrive, she leaps powerfully down from the cliffs to surprise them. The masked woman they've captured is not Enfys—instead an older woman as her decoy. With cleverness, tricky misdirection and tactics, she defeats their more powerful rivals. It's a bit conventional, even going back to Queen Amidala and her switching, but she performs it well.

Han and Chewie, being the good guys, finally return the fuel to the Rebels. Blessing Han like Leia does in the award ceremony (in thus another conventional role for a woman), Enfys tells him, "It's blood that brings life to something new." Thus, he helps begin this sect of the Rebel Alliance, while the vial she leaves him with provides stakes for him to win himself the Falcon. Another woman substantially steers Han's story, though once more, from behind the scenes. At least this one survives.

EVEN MORE TOKENISM

Laboring for the White Worms, the scumrats include boys and girls of many races. In *Most Wanted,* Qi'ra thinks of her competitor Jagleo, "That White Worm girl could shave a Wookie bald without being caught" (Carson 2018, 43). Jagleo is a former dancer and martial artist, while others include Twi'lek sentry Cosdra and the ratcatcher Bansee "She is meanspirited and a tough fighter with a scrap pipe" (Hidalgo 2018, 25–26). She appears to be the one seen in silhouette, picking on a younger child at the film's beginning. The gang is varied among age, sex, and race, but all are exploited, and Han isn't seen returning to free them.

Next, Han and Qi'ra bribe a snooty, untrustworthy female officer at the train station. Co-costume designer David Crossman says, "We wanted to up the female population in the Empire. It started with border control." Lead Transport Security Officer Falthina Sharest "is looking to balance this inequality [in her lack of pay raises] by pocketing contraband to resell," according to the guide (Hidalgo 2018, 33). She has a nonregulation shade of pink lipstick, indicating her overtly feminine laxness (Hidalgo 33).

Meanwhile a pitiable yet determined-looking mother is dragged away from her children. Passersby of all sorts span the races and genders, but only as background characters. As Crossman adds, "On Corellia we made some more black Imperial security uniforms for the women. But some we just did as standard Imperial officers with britches and some we gave breastplates to" (Szostak 2018, 224). The Warrant Officer and Imperial Fleet Trooper on Corellia are female (Hidalgo 2018, 37). There are also Waria Junus, a truant officer, Sienar Fleet Systems development executive Viceprex Sal Graeff, and unhappy citizen Ballia Noaddo (Hidalgo 2018, 28).

As with the Canto Bight casino, Vos has party guests in elegant attire. Co-costume designer David Crossman says, "There are local bribed bureaucrats hanging around, sexy girls, and all that kind of thing. We also looked at Studio 54 for inspiration" (Szostak 2018, 149). In a hypnotic gold and black pattern, the ordinary-looking brunette human Kara Safwan is "a spy hired by the rival Rang Clan to gather intel on Crimson Dawn operations" (Hidalgo 2018, 81). Sablix Veen, all in concealing silver, is a fashion designer played by an Indian actress. Damici Stalado is fully concealed under sunset robes and a headdress and mask as she's "a social chameleon who believes physical shape to be arbitrary" (Hidalgo 2018, 80). They all add a little variety to the people of highest society.

There's also a bald bumpy-headed greeter in a long elegant shimmer-silk dress. "Margo, an Imroosian who hails from a volcanic planet, is Dryden Vos' concierge and handles all guest amenities about the First Light" (Hidalgo 2018, 77). She is othered by the alien appearance, though she's not terribly sexualized. According to the art concept book, Qi'ra started as Kura the alien or very humanoid alien. One concept became Margo. "Her design is based on flinty chalk-stone modules," Lunt Davies says (Szostak 2018, 149).

Aboard the yacht, there's also a singer, human and lovely in a glittering, modestly cut dress, with a strange mask. Apparently, it's an "electric vocoder" to extend her range. She is "bestselling recording artist" Aurodia Ventafoil (Hidalgo 2018, 77). However, as with Adi Gallia, adding an alien touch to a Black actress subverts her humanity. Further, she's a dual act with a bottled alien. Crossman explains of her mask, "She has to wear it to perform with the creature" (Labrecque 2018a, 54). To work with the male alien, she becomes hybridized herself.

The server Ottilie "shows just enough initiative to work independently, but not enough to worry her bosses" but with her textured black gown cut nearly to her waist, she's a bad gender stereotype (Hidalgo 2018, 77). More disturbingly, a decraniated servant serves drinks to crimelord Dryden Vos. Unsurprisingly, the staff and guests at his party fall into conventional gender roles. At the same time, there are some attempts at equal-opportunity exploitation—it's the male holovid artist who goes around in an open shirt (Hidalgo 2018, 80). Likewise, instead of an underdressed female Twi'lek dancer, there's a male and female Twi'lek dancer couple, Hado and Boshti—her in a long black gown and high heels, him in a gold shirt and black pants (Hidalgo 2018, 81).

Regarding the spaceport, Lunt Davies says, "I really wanted to create a female character that didn't conform to the obvious sexual stereotypes that often occur in sci-fi and fantasy design" (Szostak 2018, 186). He created a blocky alien in a red robe. The visitors touring Vandor include a woman in brown leather jacket and goggles. She is Astrid Fenris, a smuggler from Yir Tangee who pilots the freighter the Silver Howl. "Her current scam involves exporting relatively worthless Vandor ice and passing it off as expensive R'alla mineral water. Naley Frifa, a tattoo-covered tech genius, "makes illegal modifications or repairs to starships and equipment" (Hidalgo 2018, 86). The male characters are equally colorful. The anthology *Solo: A Star Wars Story: Tales from Vandor* by Jason Fry gives the elaborate backstories of these quirky characters, echoing *Canto Bight* or *Tales from a Galaxy Far, Far Away.*

The mountain village of Fort Ypso is the Mos Eisley of Vandor, with shady creatures and transportation. One of the exploiters of the wrestling droids is a bald woman in a brown leather coat—the equivalent of her male counterpart in every way. She is Sansizia Chreet, an adept codebreaker and trainer "She is hired to bypass safety protocols on droids and turn the machines into unwitting assassins" (Hidalgo 2018, 86). Here a woman can be capable and even villainous, giving tokenism more of a spread.

In his own luxury den, Lando has gamblers of many species around him when he meets Han. According to the Official Guide, however, they are almost all male, dismissing women from the realm of fun and gambling. There's "a goliath who hides her intentions behind her domed life-support system," but she conceals any trace of gender, symbolically remaking herself into one of the boys (Labrecque 2018a, 53). In the final scene, he's telling a flirtatious story to the women seated on either side. As they lean close, they appear bar girls more than serious gambling rivals. They are, at least, fully dressed. There's also Lando's unseen mother, whom he calls "The most amazing woman I've ever known" in a nice salute.

The people of Savareen live in a world of sand and ocean, leading to their less-than-legal processing. "The settlements here have experienced trials, but the Savarian inhabitants are resourceful. One secluded area of coast has become a shadowport—a spaceport absent from all official records" (Hidalgo 2018, 112). Their village has the most women of a variety of ages—Yirpa Garajon who "brokers landing rights and trade deals" (Hidalgo 2018, 115). Lanzarota Malco "supervises the upkeep of the generator windmills and desalinization moisture vaporators" (Hidalgo 2018, 115). Taraja Cuttsmay is a seer who conceals herself in a wide headscarf. Valmasto Maja is an elder. "It was Maja who oversaw the rebuilding of the Bis Refinery to benefit her people" (Hidalgo 2018, 114). They are dark-skinned with a brown and orange palette of cloaks and loose gowns with stripes and embroidery. Crossman says, "If you look at any reference of indigenous people anywhere in the world, they often have clothing that they produce themselves, which often bears strong colors. You'll see a tribe with strong, red stripes like the Maasai people of central Africa" (Szostak 2018, 241).

Their look suggests a planet of Black people, rather like District 11 in *The Hunger Games.* Apparently, those of dark skin exist in their galaxy but concentrated as provincial villagers with the most worn and cobbled together technology of the film. They host the Cloud-Riders who are also more primitive, like Gungans or Sand People. The message is Eurocentric and particularly problematic—the opposite of the high-tech glamour of *Black Panther*'s Wakanda. Further, a subtle suggestion that their living outside a male hierarchy leaves them impoverished, in contrast with Crimson Dawn, criticizes a matrifocal model. By contrast, Qi'ra, who kills her male boss to take his place, is more obviously successful. Once more, the tokenism is not well thought out.

Conclusion

The Lasting Legacy

Right now, a new era of moviemaking has arrived, with more representation and feminist power than ever before. Where will it go? Is there an era beyond this with even more progressiveness, or will this beginning of new action women last for decades? It's too early to say. The massive strides are accompanied by the new world of the internet, where everyone can be heard: "Feminist activism is alive and well and asserting itself in new ways, making it accessible to waves of technology 'savvy' younger ('generation-Y') people. What we see reflected here is a desire to tackle the feminist backlash construction of feminism as 'man-hating' or 'bra burning' and to seek an equality that demobilizes the power of one gender over another and shames sexist and violent behavior wherever it is found" (Phillips and Cree 2014). Day by day the fans insist that storytelling move forward to embrace the entire audience, and day by day, it does.

With the new kinds of stories, more fans see themselves and more visit chatrooms and blogs to share their feelings. "While feminism online may seem starkly different from feminism offline, it reconfigures elements of traditional feminist modes such as self-help and consciousness-raising groups" (Crossley 2017, 122). As feminist websites repost articles, women see themselves in the content and share their stories, increasing intersectionality. Fourth-wave feminism, though a term so loaded that some reject it, is trying to heal these splits and acknowledge that representation for all is necessary. There's always further to go, but *The Force Awakens* era has expanded the possibilities. This growth is corresponding with a fast-changing surge in the franchise, with sequel movies, prequel movies *Rogue One* and *Solo*, and more tie-ins and toys every day. Disney is stretching boundaries with *Forces of Destiny*, acknowledging a new girl era in the realm of science fiction. What will follow?

Certainly, there's a trilogy to finish with Abrams' *The Last Jedi* sequel, and then Abrams plans no more in the Skywalker story. "I do see it that way," he says. "But the future is in flux" (Hiatt 2017). After that, it appears Johnson's new spinoff movies will expand the universe. Certainly, the stories will also continue in the novels, children's shows, and comics, even as another era of filmmaking is likely—even certain. Filoni's *Star Wars: Resistance,* an animated adventure series about pilot Kazuda Xiono spying on the First Order, is coming to Disney Channel Fall 2018, bridging Leia's beginning the Resistance in the novel *Bloodline* with the eventual timeline of *The Force Awakens*.

Unlike the original trio, Daisy Ridley hopes her time in *Star Wars* is coming to a close: She wants to move on and try other roles. As she adds, "I am really, really excited to do the third thing and round it out, because ultimately, what I was signing on to was three films. So in my head, it's three films. I think it will feel like the right time to round it out" (Hiatt 2017). Will she return in thirty years for another wave of *Star Wars* as her predecessors did? She considers this soberly, and replies, "Who knows? Because the thing I thought was so amazing, was people really wanted it. And it was done by people who really love it" (Hiatt 2017). That part is certainly true, creating a galaxy of fans who adore it in turn. The franchise has evolved with them, offering many eras of women new models for independence and strength.

Works Cited

Aaron, Jason and Chris Eliopoulos. 2017. *Last Flight of the Harbinger*. New York: Marvel.

Aaron, Jason and Mike Mayhew. 2016. *Rebel Jail*. New York: Marvel.

Aaron, Jason and Stuart Immonen. 2016. *Showdown on the Smuggler's Moon*. New York: Marvel.

Aaron, Jason, Kieron Gillen and Mike Deodato. 2016. Vader Down. New York: Marvel.

Abrams, J.J. 2015. "Why Leia Didn't Become a Jedi." *IGN*, December 7, 2015. Online video. http://www.ign.com/videos/2015/12/07/star-wars-the-force-awakens-why-leia-didnt-become-a-jedi.

——, dir. 2015. *Star Wars Episode VII—The Force Awakens*. Burbank, CA: Walt Disney Studios, 2016. DVD.

Alinger, Brandon. 2014. *Star Wars Costumes: The Original Trilogy*. San Francisco: Chronicle Books.

Andermahr, Sonya, Terry Lovell and Carol Wolkowitz. 1997. *A Concise Glossary of Feminist Theory*. New York: St. Martin's Press.

Anderson, Kevin J. and Rebecca Moesta. 1995. *Young Jedi Knights: Heirs of the Force*. New York: Berkeley Jam.

Aran, Isha. 2014. "Why Is Slave Leia the Only Princess Leia Toy Available at Toys 'R' Us?" *Jezebel*, March 30, 2014. https://jezebel.com/why-is-slave-leia-the-only-princess-leia-toy-available-1554793027.

Ashworth, Jeff. 2015. *Star Wars The Force Awakens: The Official Collector's Edition*. Minneapolis: Learner Publishing Group.

Barlow, Jeremy. 2009. *Star Wars Adventures: Princess Leia and the Royal Ransom*, illustrated by Carlo Soriano. Milwaukie, OR: Dark Horse.

Barnes, Steven. 2004. *The Cestus Deception*. New York: Del Rey.

Barr, Trisha. 2017. "What You Need to Know About Rose Tico, *The Last Jedi*'s Breakout Character." *PopSugar*, December 14, 2017. https://www.popsugar.com/entertainment/Who-Rose-Tico-Star-Wars-44353382.

——. 2018. "Long Live Leia." *Star Wars Insider* 178, January/February 2018, 67–73.

Basham, Megan. 2016. "Getting Personal: *Rogue One* Gives the 'Force' a Spiritual Makeover." *World Magazine*, December 31, 2016. https://world.wng.org/2016/12/getting_personal.

Baver, Kristin. 2018a. "Raising a Rebellion in IDW'S *Star Wars Forces of Destiny: Hera*." *Starwars.com*, January 17, 2018. https://www.starwars.com/news/raising-a-rebellion-in-idws-star-wars-forces-of-destiny-hera.

——. 2018b. "'They're the Heart of What the Resistance Means': Inside IDW's Star Wars Forces of Destiny: Rose & Paige." StarWars.com, January 31, 2018. http://www.starwars.com/news/inside-idw-star-wars-forces-of-destiny-rose-paige.

BBC. 2016. "*Rogue One*'s Felicity Jones Says Female Action Heroes Are Now 'the Norm.'" December 14, 2016. http://www.bbc.com/news/entertainment-arts-38313369.

Beecroft, Simon. 2014. *Star Wars: A Queen's Diary*. New York: Disney Lucasfilm.

Benn, Melissa. 2013. "After Post-Feminism: Pursuing Material Equality in a Digital Age." *Juncture* 20, no. 3 (Winter): 223–27. EBSCOhost, doi:10.1111/j.2050-5876.2013.00757.

Bennett, Tara. 2017. "Middle Man: Rian Johnson Guides the Iconic Characters through the Second Installment of their Journey in *Star Wars: The Last Jedi*." *Scifi* 23, no. 6 (December): 35–37.

Berne, Emma Carlson. 2017a. *Star Wars: Forces of Destiny. Daring Adventures: Volume 1.* New York: Disney Lucasfilm.

———. 2017b. *Star Wars: Forces of Destiny. Daring Adventures: Volume 2.* New York: Disney Lucasfilm.

———. 2018a. *Star Wars: Forces of Destiny. Daring Adventures: Volume 3. The Leia Chronicles.* New York: Disney Lucasfilm.

———. 2018b. *Star Wars: Forces of Destiny. Daring Adventures: Volume 4. The Rey Chronicles.* New York: Disney Lucasfilm.

Betancourt, John Gregory. 1996. "And the Band Played On: The Band's Tale." In *Tales from Jabba's Palace*, edited by Kevin J. Anderson, 192–223. New York: Bantam Spectra.

Biggar, Trisha. 2005. *Dressing a Galaxy: The Costumes of Star Wars.* New York: Abrams Books.

Bloomer, Jeffrey. 2018. "The Creators of *Deadpool 2* and *Solo* Have Declared Their Heroes 'Pansexual.'" *Slate,* May 25, 2018. https://slate.com/culture/2018/05/deadpool-2-and-solos-writers-call-their-heroes-pansexual-the-movies-dont.html.

Bodden, Valerie. 2012. *How to Analyze the Films of George Lucas.* Minneapolis, MN: Abdo Publishing.

Bouzereau, Laurent, ed. 1997. *The Annotated Screenplays: Star Wars—a New Hope, The Empire Strikes Back, Return of the Jedi.* New York: Ballantine Books.

Bray, Adam. 2014. *Star Wars Rebels: The Visual Guide.* New York: DK Publishing.

Bray, Adam, Cole Horton, Michael Kogge, and Kerrie Dougherty. 2015. *Star Wars Absolutely Everything You Need to Know.* New York: DK Publishing.

Breznican, Anthony. 2016a. "Star Wars: Rogue One Director Reveals New Details on Force-sacred World Jedha." *Entertainment Weekly,* August 8, 2016. http://ew.com/article/2016/08/08/star-wars-rogue-one-force-sacred-world-jedha-details.

———. 2016b. "Going Rogue. (cover story)." *Entertainment Weekly* no. 1421: 18. MasterFILE Premier, EBSCOhost.

———. 2016c. "The Empire Will Rise." *Entertainment Weekly* no. 1442: 14. MasterFILE Premier, EBSCOhost.

———. 2017a. "1956–2016 Carrie Fisher. (cover story)." *Entertainment Weekly* no. 1448: 18. MasterFILE Premier, EBSCOhost.

———. 2017b. "Star Wars The Last Jedi (cover story)." *Entertainment Weekly* no. 1478 / 1479: 30. MasterFILE Premier, EBSCOhost.

———. 2017c. "When Light Falls. (cover story)." *Entertainment Weekly* no. 1492: 22. MasterFILE Premier, EBSCOhost.

———. 2017d. "Last Jedi Spoiler Talk: Rey." *Entertainment Weekly,* December 16, 2017. http://ew.com/movies/2017/12/16/the-last-jedi-spoiler-rey-parents/.

———. 2018. "Emilia Clarke Says Her Star Wars Femme Fatale 'Has a Core of Steel.'" *Entertainment Weekly,* February 08, 2018. http://ew.com/movies/2018/02/08/emilia-clarke-solo-a-star-wars-story.

Brooks, Dan. 2016a. "From the Clone Wars to *Star Wars: Rebels*." *StarWars.com,* March 30, 2016. http://www.starwars.com/news/from-the-clone-wars-to-rebels-ashley-eckstein-on-ahsoka-tanos-journey.

———. 2016b. "Fates Fulfilled: Dave Filoni Reflects on *Star Wars* Rebels Season Two, Part 1." StarWars.com, August 30, 2016. http://www.starwars.com/news/dave-filoni-interview-star-wars-rebels-season-two-part-1.

———. 2017. "Exclusive: Kieron Gillen and Jason Aaron Reveal Marvel's *Star Wars: The Screaming Citadel* Crossover." *Star Wars.com,* February 8, 2017. https://www.starwars.com/news/exclusive-kieron-gillen-and-jason-aaron-reveal-marvels-star-wars-the-screaming-citadel-crossover.

Brooks, Terry. 1999. *Star Wars Episode One: The Phantom Menace.* New York: Del Rey.

Bruce-Mitford, Miranda. 1996. *The Illustrated Book of Signs and Symbols.* New York: DK Publishing.

Buchanan, Kyle. 2016. *"Rogue One* Director Gareth Edwards on Diversity, Reshoots, and That *Star Wars* X-Factor." *Vulture,* December 9, 2016. http://www.vulture.com/ 2016/12/gareth-edwards-on-rogue-one-diversity-reshoots.html.

Bundel, Ani. "*Solo: A Star Wars Story* Is a Great Show but a Terrible Film." *NBC,* May 26, 2018. https://www.nbcnews.com/think/opinion/solo-star-wars-story-great-show-terrible-film-ncna877711.

Burt, Kayti. 2017a. "How Diversity Makes *Rogue One* a Better *Star Wars* Movie." *Den of Geek,* May 11, 2017. http://www.denofgeek.com/us/movies/rogue-one/260795/how-diversity-makes-rogue-one-a-better-star-wars-movie.

———. 2017b. "Toxic Masculinity Is the True Villain of *Star Wars: The Last Jedi.*" *Den of Geek,* December 15, 2017. http://www.denofgeek.com/us/movies/star-wars/269657/ toxic-masculinity-is-the-true-villain-of-star-wars-the-last-jedi.

Busch, Caitlin. 2017. "Women's Stories Are More Prominent Than Ever in *Star Wars: The Last Jedi.*" *Inverse,* December 15, 2017. https://www.inverse.com/article/39434-star-wars-last-jedi-feminism-rey-leia-holdo-rose-tico.

Butler, Judith. 1990. *Gender Trouble: Feminism and the Subversion of Identity.* London: Routledge.

Cabot, Meg. 2017. "Beru Whitesun Lars." In *From a Certain Point of View,* 89–92. New York: Disney Lucasfilm Press.

Canavan, Gerry. 2015. "From "A New Hope" to No Hope at All: *Star Wars,* Tolkien and the Sinister and Depressing Reality of Expanded Universes." *Salon,* December 24, 2015. http://www.salon.com/2015/12/24/from_a_new_hope_to_no_hope_at_all_ star_wars_tolkien_and_the_sinister_and_depressing_reality_of_expanded_ universes.

Carbone, Courtney. 2016. *I Am a Princess,* illustrated by Heather Martinez New York: Golden Books.

Carson, Rae. 2018. *Star Wars Most Wanted.* New York: Disney Lucasfilm Press.

Carter, Jeff. 2008. "Star Wars Per Zahn-Ified." *Echo Station,* Mar 18, 2008. https:// archive.is/20120908052928/http://www.echostation.com/interview/zahn. htm#selection-505.0-505.997.

Castellucci, Cecil and Jason Fry. 2015. *Star Wars: Moving Target: A Princess Leia Adventure.* New York: Disney Lucasfilm Press.

Cavelos, Jeanne. 2006. "Stop Her, She's Got a Gun!" In *Star Wars on Trial: Science Fiction and Fantasy Writers Debate the Most Popular Science Fiction Films of All Time,* edited by David Brin and Matthew Woodring Stover, 305–22. Dallas, TX: Smart Pop.

Chamberlain, Prudence. 2016. "Affective Temporality: Towards a Fourth Wave." *Gender and Education* 28, no. 3: 458–64.

Charretier, Elsa and Pierrick Colinet. 2018. "Star Wars Adventures: Forces of Destiny—Princess Leia." San Diego, CA: IDW.

Chaudhuri, Shohini. 2008. *Feminist Film Theorists.* London: Routledge.

Clark, Travis. 2018. "*Star Wars: The Last Jedi* Actress Kelly Marie Tran Deleted All Her Instagram Posts after Months of Harassment." *Business Insider,* June 5, 2018. https:// amp.businessinsider.com/star-wars-actress-kelly-marie-tran-deletes-instagram-posts-after-harassment-2018-6.

Cooper, J.C. 1978. *An Illustrated Encyclopedia of Traditional Symbols.* New York: Thames and Hudson.

Creed, Barbara. 1999. "Horror and the Monstrous Feminine: An Imaginary Abjection." In *Feminist Film Theory,* edited by Sue Thornham, 251–65. Edinburgh: Edinburgh University Press.

Crispin, A.C. 1996. "Skin Deep: The Fat Dancer's Tale." In *Tales from Jabba's Palace,* edited by Kevin J. Anderson, 372–415. New York: Bantam Spectra.

Crossley, Alison Dahl. 2017. *Finding Feminism: Millennial Activists and the Unfinished Gender Revolution.* New York: New York University Press.

Dawson, Delilah S. 2015. *The Perfect Weapon (Star Wars)*. New York: Disney Lucasfilm Press.

———. 2017. *Star Wars: Phasma*. New York: Del Rey.

Dawson, Delilah and Nicoletta Baldari. 2018. "Star Wars Adventures: Forces of Destiny—Rose & Paige." San Diego, CA: IDW.

Day, Patrick Kevin. 2014. "*Star Wars: The Clone Wars*: Dave Filoni on Ahsoka's Fate, Master Yoda." *Los Angeles Times*, March 7, 2014. http://herocomplex.latimes.com/tv/star-wars-clone-wars-dave-filoni-ahsoka-yoda.

Deis, Christopher. 2007. "May the Force (Not) Be with You: 'Race Critical' Readings and the *Star Wars* Universe." In *Culture, Identities and Technology in the Star Wars Films: Essays on the Two Trilogies*, edited by Carl Silvio and Tony M. Vinci, 77–108. Jefferson, NC: McFarland.

Denning, Troy. 2003. *Tatooine Ghost*. New York: Del Rey.

———. 2005. *The Joiner King*. New York: Ballantine.

———. 2008. *Invincible*. New York: Ballantine.

DeVega, Chauncey. 2015. "Our New Post-Obama *Star Wars*: Race, the Force and the Dark Side in Modern America." *Salon*, December 19, 2015. https://www.salon.com/2015/12/19/our_new_post_obama_star_wars_race_the_force_and_the_dark_side_in_modern_america.

Doane, Mary Ann. 1999. "Film and the Masquerade: Theorising the Female Spectator." In *Feminist Film Theory*, edited by Sue Thornham, 131–45. Edinburgh: Edinburgh University Press.

Dockterman, Eliana. 2014. "The Rise of Fangirls at Comic-Con." *Time*, July 25, 2014. http://time.com/3023606/san-diego-comic-con-avengers-fangirls-booth-babe.

———. 2017a. "Diversity: Rewinding and Rewriting the Star Wars Legacy for the Next Generation." *Time Special Edition: Star Wars 40 Years of the Force*, November 24, 38–39.

———. 2017b. "*Star Wars* Created the First Truly Kickass Princess." *Time Special Edition: Star Wars 40 Years of the Force*, November 24, 36–38.

Dominguez, Diana. 2007. "Feminism and the Force: Empowerment and Disillusionment in a Galaxy Far, Far Away." In *Culture, Identities and Technology in the Star Wars Films: Essays on the Two Trilogies*, edited by Carl Silvio and Tony M. Vinci, 109–33. Jefferson, NC: McFarland.

Donaldson, Kayleigh. 2018. "*Star Wars* Has a White Male Fandom Problem." *Syfy*, June 6, 2018. http://www.syfy.com/syfywire/star-wars-has-a-white-male-fandom-problem.

Down, Kathy Ehrich. 2015. "*Star Wars* Director J.J. Abrams Addresses Black Stormtrooper Casting Controversy: People Complaining 'Probably Have Bigger Problems'." *People*, December 1, 2015. http://people.com/celebrity/star-wars-director-j-j-abrams-addresses-black-stormtrooper-casting.

Eckstein, Ashley. 2013a. "A War on Two Fronts Video Commentary." Disc 1. *Star Wars: The Clone Wars Season Five*, DVD. Directed by Dave Filoni. Burbank, CA: Warner Bros, 2013.

———. 2013b. "The Wrong Jedi Video Commentary." Disc 3. *Star Wars: The Clone Wars Season Five*, DVD. Directed by Dave Filoni. Burbank, CA: Warner Bros, 2013.

———. 2018. *It's Your Universe: You Have the Power to Make It Happen*. New York: Disney Book Group.

Edwards, Gareth, dir. 2016. *Rogue One: A Star Wars Story*. Burbank, CA: Walt Disney Studios, 2017. DVD.

Ehrlich, David. 2018. "*Solo*: Phoebe Waller-Bridge's L3-37 Is the Saving Grace of This Prequel, and One of the Best *Star Wars* Characters Ever." *Indie Wire*, May 25, 2018. http://www.indiewire.com/2018/05/solo-phoebe-waller-bridge-l3-37-star-wars-1201968300.

Emperor, Devon. 2007. "StarWarsKnights Interview with Avellone." *StarWarsKnights.com*, September 24, 2007. https://web.archive.org/web/20120118102130/http://www.starwarsknights.com/fullstory.php?id=386.

Empire. 2016. "Star Wars: Dave Filoni Talks *Rebels* as well as *Rogue One* Connections." September 30, 2016. http://www.empireonline.com/movies/features/star-wars-dave-filoni-talks-rebels-well-rogue-one-connections.

Erbland, Kate. 2018. "*Solo: A Star Wars Story*: Meet the New Female Characters Joining the Universe." *Indie Wire,* May 24, 2018. http://www.indiewire.com/2018/05/solo-a-star-wars-story-new-female-characters-emilia-clarke-phoebe-waller-bridge-1201967557/.

Estrada, Gabriel S. 2007. "Star Wars Episodes I-VI: Coyote and the Force of White Narrative." *The Persistence of Whiteness: Race and Contemporary Hollywood Cinema,* edited by Daniel Bernardi. 69–90. London: Routledge.

Faludi, Susan. 1991. *Backlash: The Undeclared War against American Women.* New York: Anchor Books.

Fernandez, Elayna. 2018. "Warm, Playful, and Strong—Interview with Emilia Clarke." *The Positive Mom,* May 18, 2018. http://www.thepositivemom.com/interview-with-emilia-clarke.

Filoni, Dave. 2013. "To Catch a Jedi Video Commentary." Disc 3. *Star Wars: The Clone Wars Season Five,* DVD. Directed by Dave Filoni. Burbank, CA: Warner Bros, 2013.

Filoni, Dave, dir. 2008. *Star Wars: The Clone Wars.* Directed by Dave Filoni. Burbank, CA: Warner Bros, 2008.

Filoni, Dave, Ashley Eckstein, and Pablo Hidalgo. 2016. "Ashley Eckstein and Dave Filoni Interview *Star Wars* Celebration Europe 2016." Filmed July 15, 2016. YouTube.

Filoni, Dave and Sam Witwer. 2013. "The Lawless Video Commentary." Disc 3. *Star Wars: The Clone Wars Season Five,* DVD. Directed by Dave Filoni. Burbank, CA: Warner Bros, 2013.

Fisher, Carrie. 1999. "A Galaxy Far, Far Away. (Cover Story)." *Newsweek* 133, no. 26 (June): 65. EBSCOhost.

———. 2011. *Shockaholic.* New York: Simon and Schuster.

———. 2016. *The Princess Diarist.* New York: Blue Rider Press.

Flaherty, Keely. 2017. "The Rise of Rose." *BuzzFeed,* November 14, 2017. https://www.buzzfeed.com/keelyflaherty/the-rise-of-rose.

Fletcher, Rosie. 2017. "How *Star Wars: The Last Jedi* Is the First Truly Feminist *Star Wars* Film." *Digital Spy,* December 20, 2017. http://www.digitalspy.com/movies/star-wars/feature/a845869/star-wars-the-last-jedi-feminist-feminism.

Floyd, James. 2017. "11 Revelations from Claudia Gray on *Leia, Princess of Alderaan.*" *Star Wars.com,* September 27, 2017. http://www.starwars.com/news/11-revelations-from-claudia-gray-on-leia-princess-of-alderaan.

Foster, Alan Dean. 2015. *Star Wars: The Force Awakens.* LucasBooks. Kindle Edition.

Freed, Alexander. 2016. *Rogue One: A Star Wars Story.* New York: Del Rey.

———. 2017. "Contingency Plan." *From a Certain Point of View,* 423–32. New York: Disney Lucasfilm Press.

Fry, Jason. 2010. *Star Wars: The Clone Wars Character Encyclopedia.* New York: DK Publishing.

———. 2012. *Darth Maul, Shadow Conspiracy.* New York: Scholastic.

———. 2016. *Star Wars Rogue One Rebel Dossier.* New York: Disney Lucasfilm Press.

———. 2018a. *Rose Tico: Resistance Fighter.* New York: Studio Fun International.

———. 2018b. *Star Wars: The Last Jedi.* New York: Del Rey.

Fry, Jason. and Cyril Nouvel. 2017. *Star Wars VIII The Last Jedi: Bomber Command (Replica Journal).* Oak Brook, IL: SFI Readerlink Dist,

Game of Nerds. 2015. "The Ladies of *Star Wars.*" December 19, 2015. https://thegameofnerds.com/2015/12/19/the-ladies-of-star-wars.

Gibson, Pamela Church. 2014. "Pornostyle: Sexualized Dress and the Fracturing of Feminism." *Fashion Theory: The Journal of Dress, Body & Culture* 18, no. 2: 189–206. Academic Search Complete, EBSCOhost.

Gillen, Kieron et al. 2018. *Doctor Aphra and the Enormous Profit.* New York: Marvel.

Gillen, Kieron and Jason Aaron et al. 2017. *Star Wars: Screaming Citadel.* New York: Marvel.

Gillen, Kieron and Kev Walker. 2017. *Doctor Aphra: Aphra.* New York: Marvel.

Gillen, Kieron and Leinil Yu. 2016. *Star Wars: Darth Vader: The Shu-Torun War.* New York: Marvel.

Gillen, Kieron and Salvador Larroca. 2015. *Star Wars: Darth Vader: Vader.* New York: Marvel.

———. 2016a. *Star Wars: Darth Vader: End of Games.* New York: Marvel.

Golden, Christie. 2015. *Star Wars: Dark Disciple.* New York: Random House.

Gonick, Marina. 2006. "Between 'Girl Power' and 'Reviving Ophelia': Constituting the Neoliberal Girl Subject." *NWSA Journal* 18, no. 2 (Summer), 1–23.

Gourley, Catherine. 2008. *Ms. and the Material Girls.* Minneapolis, MN: Twenty-First Century Books.

Gray, Claudia. 2016. *Bloodline.* New York: Del Rey.

———. 2017. *Leia, Princess of Alderaan.* New York: Disney Lucasfilm Press.

Gronowitz, Allyson. 2016. "I Don't Care About Rules": The Clone Wars and the Feminist Redemption of Padmé Amidala." *The Mary Sue,* September 12, 2016. https://www.themarysue.com/Padmés-feminist-redemption.

Grossman, Lev. 2017. "The Reboot: How J.J. Abrams Revived *Star Wars* Puppets, Greebles, and Yak Hair." *Time Special Edition: Star Wars 40 Years of the Force,* November 24, 51–61.

Gutierrez, Andi, Dave Filoni, Pablo Hidalgo, Henry Gilroy, and Vanessa Marshall. 2017a. "Rebels Recon: Inside Hera's Heroes." Disc 1. *Star Wars: Rebels Season 3,* DVD. Directed by Dave Filoni. Burbank, CA: Walt Disney Studios, 2017.

Gutierrez, Andi, Dave Filoni, Pablo Hidalgo, Henry Gilroy, and Tiya Sircar. 2017b. "Rebels Recon: Inside Trials of the Lightsaber." Disc 3. *Star Wars: Rebels Season 3,* DVD. Directed by Dave Filoni. Burbank, CA: Walt Disney Studios, 2017.

Guyot, Natacha. 2015. *A Galaxy of Possibilities: Representation and Storytelling in Star Wars* (New Revised Edition). USA: Natacha Guyot.

Hale-Stern, Kaila. 2017. "Captain Phasma Deserved Better in The Last Jedi." The Mary Sue, December 18, 2017. https://www.themarysue.com/captain-phasma-deserved-better.

Hanson, Michael J. and Max S. Kay. 2001. *Star Wars: The New Myth.* USA: Xlibris.

Haraway, Donna Jeanne. 1991. *Simians, Cyborgs and Women: The Reinvention of Nature.* London: Free Association.

Harris, Anita. 2004. *Future Girl: Young Women in the Twenty-First Century.* London: Routledge.

Harrison, Rebecca. 2018. "Star Wars Women: The Stats." *Writing on Reels,* May 29, 2018. http://www.writingonreels.uk/blog.

Heywood, Leslie and Jennifer Drake. 2007. "'It's All About the Benjamins': Economic Determinants of Third Wave Feminism in the United States." In *Third Wave Feminism A Critical Exploration,* edited by Stacy Gillis, Gillian Howie, and Rebecca Munford, 114–24. New York: Palgrave McMillan.

Hiatt, Brian. 2017. "Jedi Confidential." *Rolling Stone,* no. 1302/1303, December 14, 2017. 40–61. EBSCOhost.

Hidalgo, Pablo. 2015. *Star Wars: The Force Awakens Visual Dictionary.* New York: Disney Lucasfilm Press.

———. 2016a. *Star Wars Propaganda.* New York: Harper Design.

———. 2016b. *Star Wars Rogue One: The Ultimate Visual Guide.* New York: Disney Lucasfilm Press.

———. 2017. *Star Wars: The Last Jedi Visual Dictionary.* New York: Disney Lucasfilm Press.

———. 2018. *Solo: A Star Wars Story The Official Guide.* New York: Disney Lucasfilm Press.

Hillman, Melissa. 2017. "This Is Not Going to Go the Way You Think": *The Last Jedi* Is as Subversive AF and I Am Here for It." *Bitter Gertrude,* December 20, 2017. https://

bittergertrude.com/2017/12/20/this-is-not-going-to-go-the-way-you-think-the-last-jedi-is-subversive-af-and-i-am-here-for-it.

Hinds, Julie. 2018. "The Breakout Star in *Solo* is L3-37, a Female Droid for Our Turbulent Time's Up Era." *Detroit Free Press,* May 20, 2018.

Howard, Adam. 2015. "*Star Wars: The Force Awakens* Hero Rey Hailed as Feminist Icon." *MSNBC,* December 22, 2015. http://www.msnbc.com/msnbc/star-wars-the-force-awakens-hero-rey-hailed-feminist-icon.

Howard, Ron, dir. 2018. *Solo: A Star Wars Story.* Lucasfilm, Ltd.

Hugo, Simon. 2018. "Name That Theme." *Star Wars Insider* 178, January/February 2018, 35–40.

Isaacs, Susan. 1999. *Brave Dames and Wimpettes: What Women Are Really Doing on Page and Screen.* New York: Ballantine.

Jasper, Marykate. 2017. "Good Grief, Now There's a Petition to Remove The Last Jedi from Star Wars Canon." *The Mary Sue,* December 19, 2017. https://www.themary sue.com/last-jedi-petition-remove-canon.

Jeong, Sarah. 2017. "Did Inadequate Women's Healthcare Destroy *Star Wars'* Old Republic?" *Motherboard,* January 3, 2017. https://motherboard.vice.com/en_us/article/53d4db/womens-healthcare-star-wars.

Jernigan, Lauren. 2017. "Star Wars: The Last Jedi Ushers in the Future of Storytelling." *The Mary Sue,* December 22, 2017. https://www.themarysue.com/last-jedi-future-of-storytelling.

Johnson, Rian, dir. 2017. *Star Wars Episode VIII—The Last Jedi.* Burbank, CA: Walt Disney Studios, 2018. DVD.

Johnson, Rian. 2018a. "Balance of the Force." *Star Wars: The Last Jedi.* Los Angeles: Disney, 2018. Blu-Ray.

———. 2018b. "Commentary." *Star Wars: The Last Jedi.* Los Angeles: Disney, 2018. Blu-Ray.

———. 2018c. "The Director and the Jedi." *Star Wars: The Last Jedi.* Los Angeles: Disney, 2018. Blu-Ray.

Johnston, E.K. 2016. *Star Wars: Ahsoka.* New York: Disney Lucasfilm Press.

Jones, Brian Jay. 2016. *George Lucas: A Life.* Boston, MA: Little, Brown and Co.

Jusino, Teresa. 2017. "We Need to Talk About the Backlash Against Rey (Again), and Why She's Awesome." *The Mary Sue,* December 21, 2017. https://www.themarysue.com/lets-talk-about-rey-and-rey-backlash.

Kahn, James. (1983) 1995. *Return of the Jedi. The Star Wars Trilogy.* 349–501. New York: Del Rey.

Kamp, David. 2017. "Cover Story: *Star Wars: The Last Jedi,* the Definitive Preview." *Vanity Fair,* May 24, 2017. https://www.vanityfair.com/hollywood/2017/05/star-wars-the-last-jedi-cover-portfolio.

Keegan, Rebecca. 2015. "*Star Wars: The Force Awakens* Reflects Our Diverse, Modern World." *LA Times,* December 21, 2015. http://touch.latimes.com/#section/-1/article/p2p-85379380.

King, Tracy. 2017. "*The Last Jedi* Is the First Properly Feminist *Star Wars.*" *New Statesman,* December 19, 2017. https://www.newstatesman.com/culture/film/2017/12/last-jedi-first-properly-feminist-star-wars.

Klein, Melissa. 1997. "Duality and Redefinition: Young Feminism and the Alternative Music Community." *Third Wave Agenda: Being Feminist, Doing Feminism,* edited by Leslie Heywood and Jennifer Drake. Minneapolis: University of Minnesota Press.

Kogge, Michael. 2014. *Star Wars Rebels: Rise of the Rebels.* New York: Disney Lucasfilm Press.

———. 2018. *Star Wars: The Last Jedi.* New York: Disney Lucasfilm Press.

Kornhaber, Spencer. 2018. "The Soul of *Solo* Is a Droid." *The Atlantic,* May 27, 2018. https://www.theatlantic.com/entertainment/archive/2018/05/the-soul-of-solo-is-a-droid/560969.

Koski, Genevieve. 2015. "How 2 Racist Trolls Got a Ridiculous *Star Wars* Boycott Trending on Twitter." *Vox Magazine,* October 19, 2015. https://www.vox.com/2015/10/19/9571309/star-wars-boycott.

Kurka, Rostislav. 2017. "Forces of Destiny Review: What Is Its Value?" *Scifi Fantasy Network,* July 13, 2017. http://www.scififantasynetwork.com/forces-destiny-review-value.

Kushins, Josh. 2016. *The Art of Rogue One.* New York: Harry N. Abrams, 2016.

Labrecque, Jeff. 2018a. "Creature Feature." *The Ultimate Guide to Han Solo. Entertainment Weekly,* May 2018, pp. 50–55.

———. 2018b. "Dressing a Galaxy." *The Ultimate Guide to Han Solo. Entertainment Weekly,* May 2018, pp. 60–65.

———. 2018c. "Underworld Influence." *The Ultimate Guide to Han Solo. Entertainment Weekly,* May 2018, pp. 48–49.

LaVorgna, Bria. 2018. "*Doctor Aphra* Creator Kieron Gillen, Co-Writer Si Spurrier Discuss What's Next for the Fan Favorite Rogue." *StarWars.com,* April 26, 2018. https://www.starwars.com/news/doctor-aphra-creator-kieron-gillen-co-writer-si-spurrier-discuss-whats-next-for-the-fan-favorite-rogue.

Lewis, Ann Margaret and Helen Keier. 2013. *Star Wars: The New Essential Guide to Alien Species.* New York: Random House.

Lucas, George. (1976) 1995. *A New Hope. The Star Wars Trilogy.* 6–188. New York: Del Rey.

———, dir. 1977. *Star Wars Episode IV—A New Hope.* Century City, CA: 20th Century Fox, 2006. DVD.

———, dir. 1980. *Star Wars Episode V—The Empire Strikes Back.* Century City, CA: 20th Century Fox, 2006. DVD.

———, dir. 1983. *Star Wars Episode VI—Return of the Jedi.* Century City, CA: 20th Century Fox, 2006. DVD.

———, dir. 1999. *Star Wars Episode I—The Phantom Menace.* Century City, CA: 20th Century Fox, 2007. DVD.

———, dir. 2002. *Star Wars Episode II—Attack of the Clones.* Century City, CA: 20th Century Fox, 2005. DVD.

———, dir. 2005. *Star Wars Episode III—Revenge of the Sith.* Century City, CA: 20th Century Fox, 2005. DVD.

Lucas, George, Natalie Portman, Ewan McGregor, Rick McCallum, Trisha Biggar, and Iain McCaig. 1999a. "Costumes Featurette." *Star Wars Episode I—The Phantom Menace,* DVD. Directed by George Lucas. Century City, CA: 20th Century Fox, 2007.

Lucas, George, Rick McCallum, Liam Neeson, Ewan McGregor, Jake Lloyd, Samuel L Jackson, Pernilla August, and Ahmed Best. 1999b. "Story Featurette." *Star Wars Episode I—The Phantom Menace,* DVD. Directed by George Lucas. Century City, CA: 20th Century Fox, 2007.

Lucas, George, Rick McCallum, Natalie Portman, John Williams, Trisha Biggar, Hayden Christensen, Ewan McGregor, and Samuel L. Jackson. 2002. "Love Featurette." *Star Wars Episode II—Attack of the Clones,* DVD. Directed by George Lucas. Century City, CA: 20th Century Fox, 2005.

Luceno, James. 2003. *Inside the Worlds of the Star Wars Trilogy.* New York: DK Publishing.

———. 2005. *Dark Lord: The Rise of Darth Vader. Star Wars: The Dark Lord Trilogy.* 775–1094. New York: Del Rey.

———. 2016. *Star Wars: Catalyst: A Rogue One Novel.* New York: Del Rey.

Lussier, Germain. 2015. "Gwendoline Christie Didn't Know That Captain Phasma Was Originally a Man." *IO9,* December 7, 2015. http://io9.gizmodo.com/gwendoline-christie-didnt-know-that-captain-phasma-was-1746696902.

MacKinnon, Catharine. 1987. *Feminism Unmodified.* Harvard, MA: Harvard University Press.

———. 2000. "Only Words." In *Feminism and Pornography,* edited by Drucilla Cornell. 94–120. Oxford: Oxford University Press.

Martine, Arkady. 2017. "*Star Wars'* Vice-Admiral Holdo and Our Expectations for Female Military Power." *Tor*, December 21, 2017. https://www.tor.com/2017/12/21/star-wars-vice-admiral-holdo-and-our-expectations-for-female-military-power.

Martinelli, Marissa. 2017. "Disney's Charming Series of Animated Shorts Wants to Win Over a New Generation of Star Wars Fans." *Slate*, July 13, 2017. http://www.slate.com/blogs/browbeat/2017/07/13/star_wars_forces_of_destiny_reviewed.html.

McDowell, John C. 2016. *Identity Politics in George Lucas' Star Wars*. Jefferson, NC: McFarland.

Merlock, Ray and Kathy Merlock Jackson. 2012. "Light Sabers, Political Arenas, and Marriages for Princess Leia and Queen Amidala." In *Sex, Politics, and Religion in Star Wars: An Anthology*, edited by Douglas Brode and Leah Deyneka. Lanham, MD: Scarecrow Press.

Micciche, Laura. 2014. "Feminist Pedagogies." In *A Guide to Composition Pedagogies*, edited by Gary Tate, Amy Rupiper Taggart, Kurt Schick, and H. Brooke Hessler. 128–45. Oxford: Oxford University Press.

Miller, John Jackson. 2014. *A New Dawn*. New York: Del Rey.

Miller, Karen. 2008. *Star Wars: The Clone Wars Wild Space*. New York: Del Rey.

———. 2010. *Star Wars: Clone Wars Gambit: Stealth*. New York: Del Rey.

Motter, Dean and Jesus Saiz. 1999. *Yaddle's Tale: The One Below. Star Wars Tales #5*. Milwaukie, OR: Dark Horse.

Mulvey, Laura. 1975. "Visual Pleasure and Narrative Cinema," *Screen* 16, no. 3 (Autumn): 6–18. http://www.scribd.com/doc/7758866/laura-mulvey-visual-pleasure-and-narrative-cinema.

Munro, Ealasaid. 2013. "Feminism: A Fourth Wave?" *Political Insight*, September 2013.

Nelson, Gertrud Mueller. 1991. *Here All Dwell Free: Stories to Heal the Wounded Feminine*. New York: Doubleday.

Newitz, Annalee. 2014. "Hey *Star Wars*—Where the Hell Are the Women?" *io9*, April 29, 2014. https://io9.gizmodo.com/hey-star-wars-where-the-hell-are-the-women-1569357077.

Nicholas, Christopher. 2016. *I Am a Hero*, illustrated by Eren Unten. New York: Golden Books.

NPR. 2015. "That Time NPR Turned *Star Wars* into a Radio Drama — And It Actually Worked." December 18, 2015. https://www.npr.org/2015/12/18/460269884/that-time-npr-turned-star-wars-into-a-radio-drama-and-it-actually-worked.

Okorafor, Nnedi. 2017. "The Baptist." *From a Certain Point of View*, 317–31. New York: Disney Lucasfilm Press.

Older, Daniel José. 2018. *Last Shot*. New York: Del Rey.

O'Neill, Shana. 2018. "Rebel Romance." *Star Wars Insider* 179, March/April 2018. 27–31.

Oyaya, Mary. 2002. "FAQ"; "Interviews." *Mary Oyaya.com*. http://web.archive.org/web/20050208081852/http://maryoyaya.com:80.

Paige, Rachel. 2018. "Solo's Fatal Flaw Is the Fact That It Has No Idea How to Handle Its Three Female Leads." *Hello Giggles*, May 25, 2018. https://hellogiggles.com/news/solo-female-leads-flaw.

Patrick, Ella. 2017a. *A Leader Named Leia*, illustrated by Brian Rood. New York: Disney Lucasfilm.

———. 2017b. *World of Reading Level 2. Star Wars The Last Jedi: Rey's Journey*. New York: Disney Lucasfilm Press.

———. 2017c. *Rose and Finn's Secret Mission*. New York: Disney Lucasfilm Press.

———. 2017d. *Star Wars: Forces of Destiny: Meet the Heroes*. New York: Disney Lucasfilm Press.

People. 2015a. "Behind the Scenes." December 15, 2015, 70–78. EBSCOhost.

———. 2015b. "Gwendoline Christie." December 15, 2015, 56–57. EBSCOhost.

———. 2017. "Daisy Ridley." December 1, 2017. EBSCOhost.

———. 2018. "Emilia Clarke as Qi'ra." *Star Wars: The Secrets of Solo. People*, May 2018, pp. 25–27.

Phillips, Ruth and Viviene E. Cree. 2014. "What Does the 'Fourth Wave' Mean for Teaching Feminism in Twenty-First Century Social Work?" *Social Work Education* 33, no. 7 (October) 930–43. EBSCOhost, doi:10.1080/02615479.2014.885007.

Pianka, John Paul. 2013. *The Power of the Force: Race, Gender, and Colonialism in the Star Wars Universe.* Thesis, Wesleyan University Middletown, Connecticut. https://www.cdt-pv.org/media/upload/The_Power_of_the_Force-_Race_Gender_and_Colonialism_in_the_Star.pdf.

Pipher, Mary. 2005. *Reviving Ophelia: Saving the Selves of Adolescent Girls.* New York: Riverhead Books.

Pollitt, Katha. 1991. "The Smurfette Principle." *New York Times,* April 7, 1991.

Pometsey, Olive. 2018. "Thandie Newton Talks Representation, Smashing the Star Wars Glass Ceiling, and Never Asking for Permission." *Elle,* March 25, 2018. https://www.elle.com/uk/life-and-culture/a20883802/thandie-newton-solo-star-wars-story-interview.

Projansky, Sarah. 2007. "Mass Magazine Cover Girls: Some Reflections on Postfeminist Girls and Postfeminism's Daughters." *Interrogating Postfeminism,* edited by Yvonne Tasker and Diane Negra. 40–72. Durham, NC: Duke University Press.

Rampton, Martha. 2015. "Four Waves of Feminism," *Pacific University Center for Gender Equity,* October 25, 2015. https://www.pacificu.edu/about-us/news-events/four-waves-feminism.

Ratcliffe, Amy. 2017. "Star Wars Rebels Producer Talks Sabine's Arc, Mandalore, and More." *The Nerdist,* February 17, 2017. https://nerdist.com/star-wars-rebels-producer-talks-sabines-arc-mandalore-and-more.

Reagin, Nancy R. and Janice Liedl. 2013. *Star Wars and History.* Hoboken, NJ: John Wiley & Sons.

Reaves, Michael and Steve Perry. 2007. *Star Wars: Death Star.* New York: Ballantine.

Revis, Beth. 2017. *Star Wars: Rebel Rising.* New York: Disney Lucasfilm Press.

Reyes, Mike. 2017. "The Badass Padmé Scene *Revenge of The Sith* Cut from Its Ending." *CinemaBlend,* July 2017. https://www.cinemablend.com/news/1659630/the-badass-Padmé-scene-revenge-of-the-sith-cut-from-its-ending.

Reynolds, David West. 1998. *Star Wars: The Visual Dictionary.* New York: DK Publishing.

———. 2002. *The Visual Dictionary of Star Wars, Episode II—Attack of the Clones.* New York: DK Publishing.

Reynolds, David West and Jason Fry. 2012. *Star Wars: The Phantom Menace: The Expanded Visual Dictionary.* New York: DK Publishing.

Richards, Jon. 2013. *Ahsoka in Action.* New York: DK Publishing.

Rinzler, J.W. and Mike Mayhew. 2014. *The Star Wars.* Milwaukie, OR: Dark Horse.

Riviére, Joan. (1929) 1986. "Womanliness as Masquerade." In *Formations of Fantasy,* edited by Victor James Donald Burgin and Cora Kaplan, 35–44. London: Methuen.

Robinson, Joanna. 2018. "Emilia Clarke's Solo Flight." *Vanity Fair,* May 25, 2018. https://www.vanityfair.com/hollywood/2018/05/emilia-clarke-cover-story.

Robinson, Tasha. 2015. "With *Star Wars'* Rey, We've Reached Peak Strong Female Character." *The Verge,* December 19, 2015. https://www.theverge.com/2015/12/19/10626896/star-wars-the-force-awakens-rey-mary-sue-feminist.

Rodriguez, Amanda. 2014. "The Very Few Women of *Star Wars*: Queen Amidala and Princess Leia." *Bitchflicks,* June 4, 2014. http://www.btchflcks.com/2014/06/the-very-few-women-of-star-wars-queen-amidala-princess-leia.html.

Romano, Aja. 2018. "What a Pansexual Lando Calrissian Reveals about the Evolution of Star Wars." *Vox,* May 29, 2018. https://www.vox.com/2018/5/29/17365958/lando-pansexual-controversy-star-wars-slash-fic-history.

Roux, Madeline. 2017. "Eclipse." *From a Certain Point of View,* 231–46. New York: Disney Lucasfilm Press.

Rowe-Finkbeiner, Kristen. 2004. *The F-word: Feminism in Jeopardy: Women, Politics, and the Future.* Berkeley, CA: Seal Press.

Rucka, Greg. 2015. *Before the Awakening.* New York: Disney Lucasfilm Press.

Salvatore, R.A. 2002. *Star Wars Episode II: Attack of the Clones*. New York: Del Rey.

Sander, Brice. 2018. "Thandie Newton Says *Solo: A Star Wars Story* Trailer 'Tells You a Lot' About Her Character (Exclusive)" *ET*, March 26, 2018. https://www.etonline.com/thandie-newton-says-solo-a-star-wars-story-trailer-tells-you-a-lot-about-her-character-exclusive.

Schaefer, Elizabeth. 2015. *Hera's Phantom Flight*. Lucasfilm.

———. 2015. *Star Wars: Rey Meets BB-8*, illustrated by Brian Rood. New York: Disney Lucasfilm.

———. 2016. *Rey's Story*. New York: Disney Lucasfilm Press.

Schaefer, Elizabeth and Adam Devaney. 2017. *Star Wars: Forces of Destiny: Tales of Hope and Courage*. New York: Disney Lucasfilm Press.

Schedeen, Jesse. 2016. "*Star Wars: Dr. Aphra* #1 Review." *IGN*, December 7, 2016. http://www.ign.com/articles/2016/12/07/star-wars-doctor-aphra-1-review.

Schnelbach, Leah. 2017. "Women Are the Champions of the Rebellion Now." *Tor.com*, December 5, 2017. https://www.tor.com/2017/12/05/star-wars-women-are-the-champions-of-the-rebellion-now.

Scott, Heather. 2009. *Star Wars, The Clone Wars: Forces of Darkness*. New York: Disney Lucasfilm.

———. 2009. *Star Wars, The Clone Wars: Jedi in Training*. New York: Disney Lucasfilm.

Scott, Melissa. 2015. "Mercy Mission." *Rise of the Empire*, 3–24. New York: Del Rey.

Sharf, Zack. 2017a. "*Star Wars: The Last Jedi*: Carrie Fisher Is Responsible for Writing These Emotional Final Leia Quotes." *IndieWire*, December 16, 2017. http://www.indiewire.com/2017/12/carrie-fisher-star-wars-last-jedi-leia-wrote-final-momments-1201908376.

———. 2017b. "Alt-Right Group Takes Credit for *The Last Jedi* Backlash, Bashes *Star Wars* for Including More Women." *IndieWire*, December 21, 2017. http://www.indiewire.com/2017/12/star-wars-last-jedi-backlash-alt-right-female-characters-1201910095.

Sharpe, Deborah T. 1974. *The Psychology of Color and Design*. Chicago: Nelson-Hall.

Sheffield, Rob. 1999. "The Queen Who Saved *Star Wars*." *Rolling Stone*, no. 818, August 5, 1999, 21. EBSCOhost.

Sherman, Suzanne. 2014. *100 Years in the Life of an American Girl: True Stories*. Sebastopol, CA: SZS Publishing.

Silvio, Carl. 2007. "The *Star Wars* Trilogies and Global Capitalism." In *Culture, Identities and Technology in the Star Wars Films: Essays on the Two Trilogies*, edited by Carl Silvio and Tony M. Vinci, 53–76. Jefferson, NC: McFarland.

Sims, David. 2017. "The Last Jedi's Biggest Storytelling Innovation." *The Atlantic*, December 18, 2017. https://www.theatlantic.com/entertainment/archive/2017/12/the-last-jedis-biggest-storytelling-innovation/548609.

Smith, Michelle R. 2017. "'Insufficient Interest' Keeps *Star Wars* Heroine Rey from Monopoly Game, Despite Promises." *Chicago Tribune*, July 12, 2017. http://www.chicagotribune.com/business/ct-star-wars-monopoly-rey-piece-20170712-story.html.

Solinger, Rickie. 2013. *Reproductive Politics*. Oxford: Oxford University Press.

Soule, Charles and Angel Unzueta. 2017. *Poe Dameron: Legend Lost*. New York: Marvel.

Spangler, Bill. 2006. "Fighting Princesses and Other Distressing Damsels." In *Star Wars on Trial: Science Fiction and Fantasy Writers Debate the Most Popular Science Fiction Films of All Time*, edited by David Brin and Matthew Woodring Stover, 329–38. Dallas, TX: Smart Pop.

Sperling, Nicole. 2016. "The Meaning of Rey." *Entertainment Weekly*, no. 1397/1398, January 8, 2016, 26–27. EBSCOhost.

Spurrier, Simon and Emilio Laiso. 2018. *Star Wars: Doctor Aphra Vol. 3: Remastered*. New York: Marvel.

Stackpole, Michael A. and Robert Teranishi. 2000. *Union*. Milwaukie, OR: Dark Horse.

Star Wars: The Clone Wars. 2008–2015. Created by George Lucas. Produced by George Lucas and Catherine Winder. Lucasfilm.

Star Wars: Forces of Destiny. 2017–present. Produced by Carrie Beck and Dave Filoni. Lucasfilm.

Star Wars Insider. 2017a. "Here's Hera." December 12, 2017, 136–43.

Star Wars Insider. 2017b. "Spark of Rebellion." December 12, 2017, 20–27.

Star Wars: The Original Radio Drama. 1981. *Archive.org.* https://archive.org/details/StarWarsRadio.

Star Wars: Rebels. 2014–2018. Created by Simon Kinberg, Carrie Beck, and Dave Filoni. Produced by Dave Filoni and Simon Kinberg. Lucasfilm,

Stasia, Cristina Lucia. 2007. "'My Guns Are in the Fendi' The Postfeminist Female Action Hero." In *Third Wave Feminism: A Critical Exploration,* edited by Stacy Gillis, Gillian Howie, and Rebecca Munford. 237–49. New York: Palgrave McMillan.

Stover, Matthew. 2005. *Star Wars Episode III: Revenge of the Sith.* New York: Random House.

Szostak, Phil. 2017. *The Art of Star Wars: The Last Jedi.* New York: Harry N. Abrams.

———. 2018. *The Art of Solo: A Star Wars Story.* New York: Harry N. Abrams.

Taylor, Chris. 2014. *How Star Wars Conquered the Universe.* New York: Basic Books.

Time. 2015. "Lupita Nyong'o: Why Diversity Thrives in the *Star Wars* Universe." December 3, 2015. http://time.com/4132884/lupita-nyongo-star-wars-the-force-awakens-diversity.

Travis, Erika. 2013. "From Blasters to Bikinis: The Role of Gender in the *Star Wars* Community." In *Fan Phenomena: Star Wars,* edited by Mika Elovaara. 49–58. UK: Intellect Books Ltd. Kindle Edition.

Traviss, Karen. 2008. *Star Wars: The Clone Wars.* New York: Random House.

———. 2009. *Star Wars: The Clone Wars: No Prisoners.* New York: Del Rey.

Truitt, Brian. 2017. "*Star Wars:* John Boyega, Gwendoline Christie Tease Their Brutal *Last Jedi* Grudge Match." *USA Today,* December 13, 2017. https://www.usatoday.com/story/life/movies/2017/12/13/star-wars-john-boyega-gwendoline-christie-tease-their-brutal-last-jedi-grudge-match/945382001.

———. 2018. "*Solo:* Meet Phoebe Waller-Bridge's Revolutionary New *Star Wars* Droid L3-37." *USA Today,* May 15, 2018.

Tyers, Kathy. 1996. "A Time to Mourn, a Time to Dance: Oola's Tale." In *Tales from Jabba's Palace,* edited by Kevin J. Anderson, 80–101. New York: Bantam Spectra.

Valby, Karen. 2016. "Felicity Jones Reveals Why Her *Rogue One: A Star Wars Story* Character Won't Be Sexualized." *Glamour,* November 26, 2016. https://www.glamour.com/story/felicity-jones-glamour-january-cover-interview.

VanDerWerff, Todd. 2015. "*Star Wars: The Force Awakens:* 5 Ways the New Movie Copies the Original Film." *Vox,* December 21, 2015. http://www.vox.com/2015/12/21/10632690/star-wars-the-force-awakens-spoilers-han-solo-new-hope.

Vinci, Tony M. 2007. "The Fall of the Rebellion; or, Defiant and Obedient Heroes in a Galaxy Far, Far Away: Individualism and Intertextuality in the *Star Wars* Trilogies." In *Culture, Identities and Technology in the Star Wars Films: Essays on the Two Trilogies,* edited by Carl Silvio and Tony M. Vinci, 11–33. Jefferson, NC: McFarland.

Wade, Chris and Abraham Riesman. 2015. "See Every Line Spoken by a Woman Not Named Leia in the Original *Star Wars* Trilogy." *Vulture,* December 1, 2015. http://www.vulture.com/2015/12/star-wars-all-female-lines-excluding-leia.html.

Wage, Erin Rose. 2017. *Star Wars: The Last Jedi Look and Find,* illustrated by Art Mawhinney. Chicago: Phoenix International.

Waid, Mark and Terry Dodson. 2015. *Star Wars: Princess Leia.* New York: Marvel.

Wallace, Daniel. 2015. *Star Wars Imperial Handbook: A Commander's Guide.* New York: Disney Lucasfilm Press.

Walter, Damien. 2018. "*Solo: A Star Wars Story* Shows Us the Hero All Feminist Men Have Been Waiting For." *The Independent,* May 23, 2018. https://www.independent.co.uk/voices/solo-star-wars-hero-feminist-gender-new-film-a8365446.html.

Watercutter, Ngela. 2017. "*Star Wars: The Last Jedi* Will Bother Some People. Good." *Wired,* December 15, 2017. https://www.wired.com/story/star-wars-last-jedi-inclusion.

Watson, Jude. 2003. *Jedi Quest: The Shadow Trap*. New York: Disney Lucasfilm Press.
———. 2006. *Death on Naboo*. New York: Scholastic.
Wein, Elizabeth. 2017. *Cobalt Squadron*. New York: Disney Lucasfilm Press.
West, Candace and Don H. Zimmerman. 1987. "Doing Gender." *Gender and Society* 1, no. 2 (June): 125–51. http://www.jstor.org/stable/189945.
Wetmore Jr., Kevin J. 2005. *The Empire Triumphant Race, Religion and Rebellion in the Star Wars Films*. Jefferson, NC: McFarland.
Wheeler, Alex. 2009. *Star Wars: Rebel Force: Hostage*. New York: Scholastic.
Whitten, Sarah. 2017. "How Ashley Eckstein Went from *Star Wars* Actress to Geek Fashion Mogul." *CNBC*, May 3. https://www.cnbc.com/2017/05/03/how-ashley-eckstein-went-from-star-wars-actress-to-geek-fashion-mogul.html.
Williams, Walter John. 2002. *The New Jedi Order: Destiny's Way*. New York: Ballantine.
Wilson, Veronica A. 2007. "Seduced by the Dark Side of the Force: Gender, Sexuality, and Moral Agency in George Lucas's *Star Wars* Universe." In *Culture, Identities and Technology in the Star Wars Films: Essays on the Two Trilogies*, edited by Carl Silvio and Tony M. Vinci, 134–54. Jefferson, NC: McFarland.
Wolmark, Jenny. 1994. *Aliens and Others: Science Fiction, Feminism, and Postmodernism*. Iowa City: University of Iowa Press.
Wolverton, Dave. 1994. *The Courtship of Princess Leia*. New York: Bantam.
Wood, Brian et al. 2013. *In the Shadow of Yavin*. Milwaukie, OR: Dark Horse.
———. 2014a. *From the Ruins of Alderaan*. Milwaukie, OR: Dark Horse.
———. 2014b. *Rebel Girl*. Milwaukie, OR: Dark Horse.
Wood, Mara. 2016. "Feminist Icons Wanted: Damsels in Distress Need Not Apply." In *A Galaxy Here and Now: Historical and Cultural Readings of Star Wars*, edited by Peter W Lee, 62–83. Jefferson, NC: McFarland.
Woodhull, Winifred. 2007. "Global Feminisms, Transnational Political Economies, Third World Cultural Production." In *Third Wave Feminism A Critical Exploration*, edited by Stacy Gillis, Gillian Howie, and Rebecca Munford, 156–67. New York: Palgrave McMillan.
Wrede, Patricia C. 1999. *Star Wars Episode I: The Phantom Menace*. New York: Scholastic.
Wright, Katherine. 2016. *The New Heroines*. Santa Barbara, CA: ABC-CLIO.
Yamato, Jen. 2017. "*The Last Jedi*'s Laura Dern on Answering to 'Space Dern' and Getting LGBTQ Characters into the *Star Wars* Universe." *LA Times*, December 22, 2017. http://www.latimes.com/entertainment/movies/la-et-mn-star-wars-the-last-jedi-laura-dern-20171222-htmlstory.html.
Yossman, Karen. 2016. "Comic-Con Makes a Fashion Statement." *New York Times*, July 22, 2016. https://www.nytimes.com/2016/07/22/fashion/comic-con-makes-fashion-her-universe.html?_r=1.
Zahn, Timothy. (1991) 2011. *Heir to the Empire 20th Anniversary Edition*. New York: Del Rey.
———. 1993. *The Last Command*. New York: Del Rey.

Index

501st Legion, 125, 129, 130, 133, 225

Aayla Secura, 34, 83, 84, 138, 145
Abrams, J.J., 161, 171, 172, 173, 214, 224, 325
Ahch-To, 168, 222, 265–266
action figures, ix, 25, 175, 255
action hero, ix, 14, 19, 25, 78, 275, 279
action heroines, vii, 58, 71, 72, 92, 100, 163, 187, 193
activism, 39, 50, 56, 168, 171, 174
Adi Gallia, 83, 138, 321
Admiral Ackbar, 181, 207, 223, 228
Aftermath: Life Debt, 236
agency, vii, ix, 7, 11, 14, 19, 26, 70, 74, 75, 79, 86, 101, 105, 130, 133, 168, 213, 246, 255, 256, 259, 306
Ahsoka Tano, viii–ix, 35, 85, 86, 87–89, 90, 119–147, 227, 233, 241, 246, 249–252, 253, 256, 257–258, 262, 263, 264, 266, 267; and command, 127, 128, 129, 135; and female mentors, 138, 139, 143, 155; finale, 132, 133; name, 132. *See also* Eckstein, Ashley; Fulcrum; lightsabers, Ahsoka; tube tops
Alderaan, 8, 10, 13, 20, 28, 31, 32, 37, 40, 184, 206, 246–247, 248, 249, 256, 312
alien, vii, viii, 13, 14, 22, 24, 33, 36, 80, 81, 82, 83, 121, 122, 127, 138, 146, 155, 178, 186, 194, 204, 225, 233, 259, 285, 295, 297, 312, 319, 321
Allana Solo, 114
Amilyn Holdo, viii, 161, 182, 189, 196, 197, 211, 212, 213, 216–221, 221, 224
Anakin, 61–79, 119–131; and Ahsoka, 127, 128; and romance, 61, 65, 66, 67, 68, 69, 70, 72, 124, 181, 266; as abuser, 71, 101, 102, 103; as rescuer, 62, 70, 71, 73, 90; as stalker, 61, 90,

91, 92; young, 53, 55, 57
Anakin's ghost, 28, 29
androgynous, 12, 17, 20, 35, 52, 55, 59, 124, 238, 244, 286, 311, 313
The Approaching Storm, 141
Asajj Ventress, 116, 131, 140, 147–148, 150, 151, 152, 153–156, 200, 258
The Ashes of Jedha, 271
Asian, 45, 80, 85, 115, 132, 170, 176, 186, 187, 198, 224, 226, 233, 268, 275, 286, 292
Attack of the Clones, 45, 66, 70, 76, 77, 81, 83, 84, 86, 87, 122, 138, 141
August, Pernilla, 74, 75
Aurra Sing, 80, 87, 145
Avellone, Chris, 117

Baby Boomers, 69, 166, 206
backlash, 53, 170, 172
Bail Organa, 14, 31, 32, 36, 38, 74, 86, 87, 89, 97, 98, 99, 103, 105, 106, 134, 135, 249, 256–257
bare midriff, 69, 70, 71, 73
Barriss Offee, 83, 85, 131, 140, 141, 142, 250
Battle Surgeons, 140
Bastila Shan, 116
Bazine Netal, 283
BB-8, 163, 178, 187, 193, 196, 258–259, 261, 264, 267, 311, 312
beautiful, 6, 7, 8, 10, 11, 18, 19, 23, 35, 40, 49, 53, 58, 59, 60, 61, 63, 64, 66, 85, 96, 99, 100, 105, 106, 192, 193, 198, 209, 214, 218, 248, 286, 302, 303, 314
Bechdel test, vii, ix, 29, 74, 77, 86, 89, 165, 169, 221, 224, 302, 314
Before the Awakening, 163, 256
Ben Skywalker, son of Luke and Mara, 111

Ben Solo (young), 182, 211, 314
Beru Lars, 29, 30, 31, 74, 76, 78, 81, 86, 212, 244
Bespin, 15, 16, 17, 18, 19
Bespin tunic, 18
Betty droids, 145
Bib Fortuna, 33
birthing droid, 86, 103, 104
Black, 15, 83, 122, 161, 170, 171, 199, 224, 225, 307, 309, 321, 322
Black Krrsantan, 286
Black Panther, viii, 168, 322
Black Sun, 240, 261, 264
Blakiston, Caroline, 35
blaster, vii, 5, 9, 11, 19, 28, 29, 55, 57, 58, 73, 110, 151, 164, 181, 196, 205, 212, 229, 238, 247, 257, 260, 262, 272, 274, 279, 284, 289, 290, 305, 307
Bloodline, 28, 166, 206, 207, 225, 326
Boba Fett, 80, 145, 147, 155, 200, 203, 239, 240, 319
Bo-Katan, 145, 240, 241, 245
Book of the Sith, 151, 152
boots, 5, 11, 16, 26, 59, 127, 138, 186, 301
Boss Nass, 56, 57, 86
Bothans, 35, 36, 195
Boushh disguise, 20, 266
#BoycottStarWarsVII, 171, 176
Boyega, John, 171, 172, 189, 190, 265
bravado, 8
Breha Organa, 31, 32, 86, 246
Brendol Hux, 200, 201
Buffy the Vampire Slayer, 44, 65, 71, 251
Bultar Swan, 85
Butler, Judith, 46, 48, 66, 91, 95

C-3PO, 17, 18, 28, 79, 212, 213, 286, 287, 311, 318
Callista, 114
Camie, 30–31
camouflage, 18, 20, 26, 63, 64, 95
campaigns, 171, 174, 175, 177
campy, viii, 13
Canto Bight, 191, 192, 193, 205, 218, 224, 265, 321, 322
capitalism, 49, 191
Captain Phasma, viii, 202
caretakers, 222, 223, 259
Carson, Rae, 299, 301, 302, 303, 310, 320

Cassian Andor, 271, 273, 274, 275, 277, 278, 279, 280
catalyst, 281
The Cestus Deception, 148
Chadra-Fan, 261
Chancellor Valorum, 54, 80
Charal, 113
cheerleader, 14, 231
Chewbacca, 11, 12, 13, 14, 15, 17, 19, 27, 121, 122, 164, 168, 178, 184, 195, 224, 256, 260, 261, 264, 265, 266, 285, 286, 287, 304, 305, 308, 309, 310, 315, 318, 320
Chiang, Doug (production designer), 80, 274
child prodigy, 44, 106
childbirth, Padmé, 103–104
Chopper, 227, 266, 267
Christie, Gwendoline, 199, 200, 300
Clarke, Emilia, 83, 295, 300, 301, 302, 303, 304, 305, 306
Cliegg, Lars, 76, 77, 78
The Clone Wars (show), viii, 23, 35, 71, 74, 80, 82, 83, 84, 85, 86, 87, 90, 91, 93, 95, 96, 113, 114, 116, 119–120, 124–125, 126, 127, 130, 132, 138, 139, 140, 143, 145, 147, 148, 149, 151, 200, 227, 228, 230, 232, 233, 240, 250, 252, 258, 260, 261, 265, 266, 292
The Clone Wars (film), 119, 120, 123, 130, 147, 148, 200
Clone Wars Gambit: Stealth, 91, 127
Cloud City, 18, 19, 106
Cobalt Squadron, 188, 189
Cody, 140
colonialism, 56, 195
combat, 20, 26, 28, 31, 57, 81, 121, 123, 134, 139, 140, 144, 152, 154, 170, 178, 203, 216, 229, 237, 240, 241, 242, 244, 251, 273, 274, 292
Comic-Con, 136, 137, 215
comics, ix, 7, 9, 10, 11, 14, 20, 21, 25, 28, 70, 80, 83, 84, 109, 111, 188, 192, 193, 200, 202, 212, 222, 224, 226, 231, 255, 256, 260, 267, 268, 269, 271, 283, 286, 288, 290, 291, 292, 318
commercialism, 44, 58
consciousness-raising, 36, 169

conventional gender, 16, 69, 80, 165, 301

Corellia, 298, 299, 302, 303, 304, 320

Coruscant, 40, 49, 54, 60, 63, 64, 67, 82, 88, 91, 94, 110, 132, 144, 145, 148, 261

cosplay, 25, 136, 137, 138, 175

Count Dooku, 61, 72, 73, 85, 88, 123, 130, 139, 146, 147, 148, 149, 150, 151, 152, 153, 154, 155, 156, 232, 258

The Courtship of Princess Leia, 113, 151

Crait, 213, 219, 221, 247

Crimson Dawn, 266, 303, 319, 321, 322

Crossman, David (costume designer), 301, 320, 321, 322

crystal foxes, 214

cultural appropriation, 45

cyborg, 104, 291, 312, 313, 315, 316

D'acy, 219, 224

Daenerys Targaryen, 3, 295

Dagobah, 265

Dameron, Morgan, 224

damsel, viii, 6, 11, 12, 21, 27, 47, 58, 59, 62, 66, 71, 72, 73, 76, 96, 97, 99, 103, 106, 115, 146, 167, 196, 207, 249, 277

dance, 33, 34, 141, 307

Daniels, Anthony, 7, 172

Dark Disciple, 147, 149, 150, 154, 156

Dark Forces, 115

Dark Lord, 102

Darksaber, 241, 242, 243, 244, 245

Darth Maul, 53, 133, 138, 142, 143, 144, 145, 147, 153, 155, 241, 251, 306

Darth Vader, 6, 7, 8, 11, 12, 19, 24, 28, 29, 76, 77, 85, 98, 101, 102, 103, 104, 106, 135, 147, 149, 156, 166, 174, 181, 184, 185, 204, 206, 207, 225, 236, 244, 250, 251, 252, 253, 260, 275, 280, 282, 283, 285–288, 290, 292, 306

Dathomir, 113, 114, 147, 149, 151, 153, 155, 156, 222

Dawson, Delilah S., 192, 199, 200, 201, 202, 268, 269

Death Star, 6, 7, 11, 14, 24, 29, 32, 35, 37, 39, 40, 106, 206, 208, 215, 249, 260, 271, 272, 277, 278, 279, 280, 281, 282, 285, 312

death troopers, 272, 279

Death Watch, 130, 131, 144, 145, 238, 241

decoy, 46, 47, 49, 51, 55, 56, 57, 58, 59, 74, 81, 320

decraniated women, 281, 292, 321

Delegation of the 2000, 38, 98

Depa Billaba, 84

Dern, Laura, 3, 5, 216, 217, 218, 220, 221, 222

dianoga, 34

disability, 114, 163

Disney, ix, 25, 29, 30, 38, 132, 136, 137, 161, 173, 175, 176, 202, 227, 228, 240, 255, 257, 260, 261, 283, 296, 307, 310, 325, 326

diversity, vii, viii, 15, 83, 122, 139, 141, 161, 163, 164, 171, 172, 177, 181, 191, 204, 225, 228, 233, 271, 275, 276, 281, 283, 296, 298. *See also* Asian; Black; consciousness-raising; conventional gender; cultural appropriation; feminism; privilege; representation

DJ, 194, 195

Doctor Aphra, 283, 284–292

Doctor Who, 136, 168

dress, brown, 26, 29

dress, Padmé's. *See* gowns, Padmé's

dress, presentation, 15

dress, white, 5, 9, 11, 12, 15, 20, 38, 58, 104, 161, 211, 247

Driver, Adam, 172

Droid Gotra, 310

Dryden Vos, 303, 304, 306, 320, 321

DVD, 70, 86, 98, 132, 265

E3-S1, 282

Eckstein, Ashley, 119, 120, 122, 124, 126, 129, 130, 131, 132, 133, 135, 136, 137, 138, 250, 260, 265

eco-feminism, 27

Edwards, Gareth, 274, 277, 278, 279

The Empire Strikes Back, 6, 8, 9, 15, 17, 19, 26, 29, 32, 36, 37, 38, 40, 86, 104, 115, 119, 122, 147, 162, 169, 173, 178, 179, 192, 194, 196, 197, 226, 227, 230, 231, 232, 234, 238, 241, 246, 248, 257, 258, 261, 262, 276, 281, 283, 287, 290, 292, 301, 310, 318, 319, 320

Endor, 26, 27, 113, 228, 233, 236, 262, 264, 266

Enfys Nest, 318–320

environmentalism, 27, 56, 192

Equal Rights Amendment, 4

Ewoks, vii, 20, 25, 26, 27, 28, 34, 35, 56, 96, 113, 233, 257, 260, 262, 264, 265, 266

Ewoks: The Battle for Endor, 113

Expanded Universe, ix, 7, 14, 20, 28, 34, 36, 37, 38, 39, 73, 75, 76, 83, 84, 85, 86, 91, 96, 109, 110, 111, 113, 114, 117, 118, 121, 140, 141, 206, 211, 216, 226, 229, 233, 255, 272, 280, 283. *See also* Legends

Ezra Bridger, 133, 155, 227, 228, 231, 234, 236, 237, 238, 240, 241, 242, 243, 244, 245, 246, 248, 249, 250, 251, 252, 253, 266

Family Guy, 34

fandom, 4, 15, 16, 20, 25, 27, 44, 46, 56, 74, 83, 93, 98, 117, 118, 120, 124, 126, 145, 170, 171, 172–173, 174, 175, 176–177, 178, 185, 186, 189, 198, 199, 208, 211, 215, 225, 226, 228, 235, 247, 249, 250, 253, 261, 262, 264, 265, 266, 267, 283, 296, 297, 298, 300, 310, 317, 319, 326

fathiers, 194, 195

fembot, 314, 316

feminine, 4, 12, 14, 15, 18, 19, 20, 25, 26, 32, 33, 34, 35, 43, 44, 52, 55, 63, 64, 67, 68, 81, 82, 97, 125, 138, 142, 144, 147, 149, 151, 152, 163, 183, 195, 196, 199, 205, 215, 216, 217, 220, 236, 248, 250, 267, 271, 274, 297, 305, 307, 311

feminism, 4, 5, 11, 15, 19, 20, 22, 27, 36, 43, 44, 45, 46, 53, 55, 56, 57, 58, 59, 65, 66, 69, 70, 78, 87, 129, 131, 163, 168, 169, 170, 172, 174, 175, 190, 191, 192, 276, 278, 309, 310, 312, 317, 325. *See also* eco-feminism; environmentalism; first wave; fourth wave; global feminism; second wave; third wave

femme fatale, 67, 217, 295, 303, 304, 306

Filoni, Dave, 86, 119, 120, 125, 130, 131, 132, 133, 144, 155, 227, 238, 240, 241, 242, 244, 250, 251, 253, 325

Finn, 66, 161, 163, 164, 165, 167, 168, 169, 170, 173, 174, 178, 182, 184, 186, 187, 188–191, 192, 193–197, 198, 199, 202–203, 205, 207, 208, 212, 213, 218, 222, 259, 265, 278

first wave, 15, 18, 43, 317

Fisher, Carrie, vii, 3, 5, 9, 11, 13, 16, 20, 22, 23, 24, 25, 29, 172, 173, 207, 208, 212, 213, 214, 215, 216, 221, 224; death, 215; fat farm, 9

Flash Gordon, 9, 21

flirting, 17, 65, 143, 217, 220, 230, 287, 297, 306

The Force Awakens, 36, 161, 169, 171, 174, 177, 182, 190, 196, 197, 200, 203, 204, 206, 207, 213, 224, 225, 255, 257, 265, 267, 271, 275, 280, 300

The Force Unleashed, 14, 111

Forces of Destiny, ix, 25, 188, 192, 205, 228, 231, 255, 260, 261, 262, 264, 265, 305

Ford, Harrison, 5, 172, 274

Foster, Alan Dean, 5, 141

fourth wave, viii, 163, 168, 170, 171, 172, 190, 191, 192, 195, 274, 276, 285

Frankenstein, 153, 315

fridging, viii, 58, 78, 81, 83, 86, 90, 106, 144, 146, 281, 295, 309, 317

From a Certain Point of View, 30, 32, 35, 77

Frozen, viii, 3, 168, 268

Fulcrum, 135, 231, 233, 249

funeral, Padmé's, 86, 105, 106

funny, vii, 5, 180, 215, 238, 268, 269, 289, 313

Galen Erso, 244, 272, 275, 276, 277, 279, 281

Game of Thrones, 199, 223–224, 225, 295, 300–301

garbage chute, 12

garbage creature. *See* dianoga

gaze, vii, 8, 9, 10, 12, 19, 23, 32, 43, 66, 96, 105, 169, 187, 194, 225, 236, 299. *See also* decoy; gender as performance; gender flipping; gowns, Padmé's; objectification; sexualized

Gellar, Sarah Michelle, 250–251. *See also*
  Buffy the Vampire Slayer
gender as performance, 46, 48, 51, 67,
  68, 91, 96, 99
gender flipping, 146, 155, 164, 167, 168,
  212, 289, 305
General Grievous, 86, 90, 138, 149, 153,
  154, 156
General Armitage Hux, 181, 182, 184,
  200, 201, 202, 209, 221, 225, 226
Geonosian queen, 140
Geonosis, 49, 83, 141
Ghost, 38, 228, 229, 233, 235, 236, 251,
  258, 265, 267
Ghostbusters, viii, 168, 171, 176, 177
giftedness, 198
Gillen, Kieron, 28, 284, 285, 286, 287,
  288, 289, 290, 292
girl power, 43, 44, 45, 53, 55, 58, 60, 64,
  65, 70, 71, 93, 106, 119, 127, 151, 250,
  251, 260, 262, 269
global feminism, 39, 56, 129
Glover, Danny, 173, 296, 297, 298
gold bikini, vii, 20, 21, 22–23, 24, 25, 61,
  73, 96, 129, 161, 199, 208, 215, 260
gothic, 95, 96, 97, 101, 103, 106
gowns, Padmé's, 45, 46, 47, 48, 49, 50,
  53, 54, 55, 57, 58, 59, 61, 63, 64, 65,
  66, 67, 69, 70, 74, 91, 93, 95, 96, 97,
  99, 100, 105, 106
graffiti, 238, 239, 244
Gray, Claudia, 31, 37, 219–220,
  246–247, 256
Gungans, 54, 56, 57, 195, 233, 322

hair buns, 10, 43, 58, 63, 67, 224
hairstyle, 15, 16, 18, 43, 55, 112, 162. *See
  also* three knots
Hamill, Mark, 5, 7, 172, 265, 266
Han Solo, 6, 10–13, 15, 16–21, 23, 24, 26,
  27, 28, 29, 37, 46, 95, 111, 112, 113,
  114, 116, 164, 165, 166, 167, 168, 172,
  173, 177, 178, 182, 185, 188, 196, 205,
  207, 208, 209, 214, 215, 228, 229, 236,
  246, 256, 257, 264, 265, 266, 267, 280,
  283–285, 286, 287, 289, 292; as
  caveman, 12, 16; as rescuer, 13, 14,
  15, 16, 17; romance, 16, 19; in *Solo*,
  295–299

The Han Solo Trilogy, 114
handmaiden, 46, 47, 49, 51, 52, 53, 58,
  62, 81, 212, 267
Haraway, Donna Jeanne, 312, 314, 316
Harry Potter, 220
Hays Minor, 191
Heir to the Empire, 109
Her Universe, 135–138
Hera Syndulla, ix, 227, 228–236, 238,
  239, 240, 241, 242, 245, 249, 258, 264,
  265, 266, 267, 268, 271, 286, 291, 292;
  and romance, 235, 236; crossover
  stories, 236, 265, 266, 267, 268, 291,
  292
Hera's father, 233, 234, 235, 236
hero's journey, viii, 127, 212, 227, 236,
  289
heroic, 6, 11, 17, 19, 28, 33, 90, 100, 112,
  123, 138, 146, 163, 164, 188, 193, 222,
  251, 262, 271, 273, 283, 286, 295
heroine's journey, 29, 161, 165, 167, 180,
  182, 183, 184, 190, 198, 242, 272
hierarchy, 146, 152, 181, 185, 220, 229,
  232, 233, 251, 275, 322
Hispanic, 14, 161
Hollywood, 58, 169, 171, 173, 274, 275,
  295, 297, 316
holocron, 252
homosexual, 173, 283, 284, 298, 314
Hondo Ohnaka, 80, 138, 145, 266
Hosnian Prime, 209, 225
Hostis Ij, 39
Hoth, 16, 32, 104, 196, 228, 261, 262,
  267, 311
The Hunger Games, 119, 162, 168, 193,
  322

The Imperial Handbook, 36, 37, 38
innocent, 18, 28, 44, 45, 52, 53, 60, 66,
  67, 99, 202, 203, 247, 248, 291, 298
Inquisitors, 250, 251, 252
internet, viii, 39, 168, 169, 171, 172, 173,
  174, 175, 176, 177, 185. *See also*
  fandom; social media; toxic
  masculinity
Isolder, 113
It's Your Universe, 137

Jabba the Hutt, 20, 21, 23, 24, 25, 32, 33, 34, 52, 84, 95, 110, 123, 145, 148, 166, 207, 260
Jacen Solo, 112, 114
Jacen Syndulla, 236
Jaina Solo, ix, 109, 112
Jakku, 164, 165, 168, 177, 185, 207, 255, 261, 263
Jan Ors, 115, 116
Jango Fett, 82, 240
Jar-Jar Binks, 53, 56, 62, 65, 105, 170, 195, 204
Jedha, 271, 275, 276, 277, 280, 289
Jedi Council, 54, 61, 62, 82, 83, 84, 97, 114, 125, 131, 148, 227, 230
Jedi Exile, 116
Jedi Knight, 111
Jedi Outcast, 115
Jedi Quest, 84
Jess Pava, 224
jewelry, 209, 217, 301
Jira, 80
Jocasta Nu, 85, 117, 139, 212
Johnson, Rian, 180, 182, 183, 184, 185, 188, 192, 205, 211, 214, 215, 216, 217, 218, 220, 221, 222, 223
Johnston, E. K., 121, 130, 131, 133, 134, 135, 142, 256
The Joiner King, 206
Jones, Felicity, 261, 271, 274, 277, 278, 279, 282
Jones, James Earl, 252
jumpsuit, Padmé's, 59, 71, 73, 96, 161, 262
jumpsuit, pregnancy, 100
Junior Jedi Knights, 255
Jyn Erso, viii, 39, 89, 170, 186, 244, 256, 260, 262, 263, 264, 271–275, 276–278, 279, 280, 281, 282. *See also* androgynous; combat; Galen Erso; Lyra Erso

K-2SO, 272, 274, 275, 279, 311
Kanan Jarrus, 84, 227, 228, 230, 231, 232, 233, 234, 235–236, 241, 242, 245, 248, 250, 252, 253
Kaplan, Michael (costume designer), 186, 193, 209, 217
Kara Safwan, 321

Kasdan, Jonathan, 295, 296
Kasdan, Lawrence, 26, 29, 162, 199, 295, 296
Kaydel Connix, 212, 224
Kennedy, Kathleen, 136, 176, 310
Ketsu Onyo, 240, 261, 264
Ki-Adi Mundi, 82–83, 131
kiss: Han and Leia, 16, 17, 18, 19; Luke and Leia, 16, 19, 27
Knights of the Old Republic, 116
Knoll, John, 274, 275
Korr Sella, 225
Kreia, 117
Kyle Katarn, 115, 116
Kylo Ren, 165, 166, 167, 174, 178, 181, 182, 183, 184, 185, 187, 201, 202, 203, 211, 213, 214, 221, 260, 319

L3-37, 295, 297, 309–315, 316, 317, 318, 319
Lady Proxima, 298–300, 301, 302
Lando Calrissian, 16, 17, 18, 19, 20, 26, 29, 95, 106, 173, 196, 197, 246, 257, 296, 297, 298, 301, 304, 309–315, 316, 317–318, 322
Lando's mother, 322
Lanter, Matt, 252, 265
The Last Flight of the Harbinger, 284
The Last Jedi, viii, 3, 29, 31, 131, 164, 167, 170, 175, 176, 177, 179, 182, 186, 187, 192, 194, 197, 198, 199, 202, 203, 205, 206, 212, 213, 214, 215, 218, 219, 224, 226, 247, 257, 259, 265, 268, 278, 280, 310
Last Shot, 205, 285, 306, 310, 311, 314, 315, 317, 318
Legend Lost, 212, 213, 224
Legends, ix, 29, 34, 36, 37, 77, 109, 111, 113, 206, 236, 248, 255, 266
Leia. *See* Princess Leia
Leia, Princess of Alderaan, 37, 219, 246, 256
lekku, 120, 228, 250
level 1313, 132
LGBTQ. *See* homosexual; queer
lightsaber, 58, 62, 72, 84, 85, 88, 90, 110, 116, 120, 123, 125, 129, 130, 134, 139, 140, 143, 149, 150, 155, 165, 168, 169, 178, 179, 180, 181, 183, 184, 186, 197,

203, 206, 242, 251, 260, 262, 266, 287;
Ahsoka, 129, 133, 134, 139, 252, 258,
262; Rey, 165, 167, 168, 178, 179, 265;
Ventress, 147
Little Golden Books, 259–260
Lourd, Billie, 212, 215, 224
Lucas, George, 3, 5, 6, 7, 9, 11, 12, 14,
18, 20, 24, 29, 30, 31, 47, 49, 65, 74,
86, 98, 104, 106, 109, 119, 147, 153,
163, 204, 251
Luminara Unduli, 83, 85, 139, 140, 141,
146, 250, 258
Lux Bonteri, 130, 131, 146
Lyra Erso, 272, 279, 281

Mace Windu, 61, 71, 82, 131, 145
magical girl, 8
Magna Tolvan, 291, 292
makeup, 4, 5, 9, 33, 46, 47, 48, 49, 58, 69,
116, 162, 186, 187, 200, 217, 285, 303
Mandalore, 142, 143, 144, 145, 235, 237,
238, 239, 240, 241, 242, 243, 244, 245,
266
Mandalorian, 142, 238, 240, 241, 242,
244, 245
Mara Jade, ix, 81, 110, 111, 117
Margo, 321
Marshall, Vanessa, 228, 234, 235, 265
Mary Sue, 176, 177, 178, 179, 180, 187,
199, 212, 278
masks, 16, 19, 47, 48, 51, 59, 68, 91, 97,
99, 181, 198, 201, 203, 252, 290, 318,
319, 321
matriarch, 76, 85, 113, 152, 195, 209,
212, 298, 299, 300
matrifocal, 229, 322
Mayhew, Peter, 11, 172, 285
Maz Kanata, viii, 161, 164, 165, 173,
175, 178, 185, 204–206, 212, 260, 262,
263, 264, 265, 266, 267, 283, 285
McCaig, Iain (concept artist), 46, 66
middle grade, 167, 256
Millennials, 43, 165, 166, 192, 194
Millennium Falcon, 16, 17, 164, 178,
213, 229, 297, 312, 318
Mina Bonteri, 88
minorities, 13, 15, 56, 129, 170, 177, 180,
192, 223, 232, 301, 309, 318
Mission Vao, 116

Moana, viii, 136, 168
Mollo, John (costume designer), 15, 18
Mon Calamari, 195, 210, 221
Mon Mothma, vii, 14, 35, 36, 37, 38, 39,
40, 86, 89, 98, 195, 221, 273, 275, 278,
280, 282
Monopoly, 174, 175
monster mother, 34–35, 298–300
Mos Eisley, 233, 322
Most Wanted, 299, 301, 302, 303, 304,
310, 320
Mother Talzin, 151, 152, 153, 154
Moving Target, 37, 259
Mulvey, Laura, 8, 9, 10, 23, 65

Naboo, 44, 45, 47, 49, 51, 52, 53, 54, 55,
56, 57, 58, 59, 60, 63, 64, 65, 66, 72,
73, 76, 82, 86, 87, 94, 97, 106, 247,
257, 292
nature, 27, 28, 56, 64, 65, 74, 81, 121,
122, 204, 218, 223, 310
Netflix, 132
new canon, ix, 28, 36, 206, 283
A New Dawn, 230
The New Heroines, 162, 187
A New Hope, 3, 5, 6, 14, 19, 26, 28, 29, 31,
39, 40, 76, 122, 206, 212, 233, 246,
248, 255, 260, 271, 283, 285, 287, 300
Newton, Thandie, 295, 307, 308
Nien Nunb, 204, 207
Nightbrothers, 149, 153
Nightsisters, 113, 147, 150, 151,
152–153, 155, 156
Nixon, Richard, 4
No Prisoners, 91, 127
novelizations, 5, 23, 30, 31, 36, 44, 58,
62, 63, 69, 70, 75, 76, 77, 79, 82, 85,
86, 92, 98, 123, 130, 131, 142, 164,
167, 181, 184, 188, 195, 196, 197, 203,
210, 211, 213, 214, 219, 222, 223, 232,
273, 278, 280, 281
Nyong'o, Lupita, 204, 265
Nyx Okami, 132

O'Reilly, Genevieve, 38, 282
objectification, vii, 8, 9, 10, 21, 22, 25,
73, 120, 129, 145, 151, 162, 164, 181,
186, 187, 188, 199, 274, 305, 313, 316

Old Republic, 50, 57, 103, 209, 216, 240, 241

Older, Daniel José, 67, 170, 187, 205, 285, 311, 314, 315, 316

Oola, 33, 34

Order 66, 83, 84, 85, 86, 132, 133, 138, 140, 251

ordinary person, 8, 31, 51, 52, 101, 189, 190, 194, 196, 197, 214, 227, 232, 236, 250, 267, 268, 278, 287, 310, 321

original script, 11, 31

Orson Krennic, 272, 275, 279, 281

Owen Lars, 30, 31, 76, 77, 78, 104

Padmé Amidala, 17, 31, 35, 38, 43, 44, 46, 47, 51–64, 65, 66–74, 75, 76, 82, 86, 87, 88–106, 114, 119, 122, 127, 128, 130, 131, 139, 143, 146, 167, 181, 195, 212, 247; and Anakin parallel, 97, 99, 104, 105; as queen, 44, 45, 46, 47, 48, 49, 50, 51, 53, 54, 55, 56, 57, 92, 103, 142, 267; as rebel, 98, 99, 104, 106; as senator, 60, 63, 69, 87, 89, 92, 94, 98, 99, 103, 143, 262; friendship with Ahsoka, 87, 88, 122, 130, 131, 262, 264, 266, 267; in *Forces of Destiny*, 257, 258, 260, 262, 264, 265, 266, 267; name, 198. *See also* bare midriff; child prodigy; girl power; gothic; gowns, Padmé's; handmaiden; jumpsuit, Padmé's; jumpsuit, pregnancy, Padmé's; parade on Naboo; third wave; wedding, Padmé and Anakin

Paige Tico, 187–188, 191–192, 195, 210, 255, 259, 260, 268–269

Panaka, 50, 51, 57, 247

pansexual, 296, 297, 298

parade on Naboo, 57

passivity, 9, 96

patriarchy, 6, 8, 13, 23, 24, 34, 44, 54, 60, 75, 79, 82, 88, 99, 106, 122, 125, 130, 131, 146, 151, 154, 166, 180, 181, 182, 184, 209, 219, 221, 230, 248, 273, 275, 280, 288, 300, 309

The Phantom Menace, 43, 44, 45, 46, 49, 52, 54, 58, 60, 66, 70, 74, 77, 80, 83, 87, 98, 205, 247, 257

Phasma, 161, 173, 196, 199–203, 260, 307; and female armor, 199

picture books, 255

Plo Koon, 125, 131, 258

Poe Dameron, 161, 170, 173, 176, 181, 182, 187, 189, 190, 196, 200, 202, 209, 210, 211, 212, 213, 214, 216, 217–219, 221, 224, 225, 226, 259, 283

porgs, 222, 223, 265

pornography, 21, 22, 24, 25

postfeminism, vii, 22, 43, 53, 71, 106, 170

pregnancy, Padmé's, 93, 94, 95

pregnancy, Shmi's, 75

Princess Leia, 3–37, 43, 51, 52, 53, 55, 56, 57, 58, 60, 61, 66, 70, 71, 73, 77, 78, 87, 89, 93, 95, 96, 106, 110, 111, 112, 113, 114, 119, 129, 144, 151, 161, 162, 166, 168, 172, 178, 182, 183, 184, 185, 187, 195, 198, 205, 206, 207, 209–212, 213–215, 216, 217, 218, 219, 220, 221, 224, 225, 226, 228, 236, 246, 247, 248, 249, 256, 257, 258, 259, 260, 261, 262, 264, 266, 267, 271, 274, 280, 282, 283–284, 285, 290, 292, 308, 320; and Amilyn, 212, 213, 219, 221; and Ben, 211; and command, 12, 14, 16, 18, 26; and romance, 16, 17, 19, 20, 21; and Lando, 17, 18, 19; and Poe, 211, 212; as General, 39, 165, 175, 192, 206, 207–211, 212, 218, 219, 257, 268; as rescuer, 5, 20, 31, 37; as senator, 6, 10, 11, 12, 36, 38, 40, 59, 60, 66, 67, 68, 74, 87, 88, 90, 103, 106, 206, 246, 256; compared with Luke, 10, 12, 13, 14, 15, 19, 26, 27, 28, 32; in *Rogue One*, 280, 282; love triangle, 16, 19, 182; new canon, 206, 207; on Endor, 25–29; on radio play, 248, 249; on *Rebels*, 248; rescued, 7, 8, 10, 11, 12, 14, 26; using the Force, 19, 211, 212; young, 35, 37, 86. *See also* Bail Organa; Bespin tunic; Breha Organa; Boushh disguise; dress, brown; dress, presentation; dress, white; Fisher, Carrie; gold bikini; hair buns; kiss, Han and Leia; kiss, Luke and Leia; second wave; self-rescuing princess; snowsuit privilege, 13, 56, 61, 87, 89, 94, 126, 128, 129, 164, 166, 172, 198, 199, 227, 246

Qi'ra, 114, 266, 295, 299, 300, 301–307, 309, 310, 314, 320, 321, 322
Queen Apailana, 86
Queen Jamillia, 64, 82, 105
queer, 163, 173, 220, 285, 297, 298
queerbaiting, 297
Qui-Gon Jinn, 51, 52–53, 75, 78, 79, 142
Qui-Gon Jinn's ghost, 132

R2-D2, 5, 130, 134, 168, 178, 259, 261, 282, 311
R2-KT, 145, 225
racism, 36, 56, 79, 171, 174, 175, 176, 204, 232, 276, 280
Raddus, 210, 211, 221, 223
radio play, 7, 30, 31, 248
Rae Sloane, 283
rape, 21, 25, 78, 170, 285, 317
Rapunzel, 18, 96
Rebel Force: Hostage, 246, 256
Rebels, viii, 15, 26, 28, 31, 35, 38, 39, 40, 84, 106, 124, 132, 133, 134, 135, 140, 155, 227, 228, 233, 236, 239, 240, 245, 246, 248, 249, 250, 253, 260, 261, 265, 266, 271, 275, 278, 281, 282, 283, 284, 318, 320
Red Sonja, 21, 199
representation, vii, viii, ix, 4, 14, 25, 27, 80, 87, 95, 114, 115, 117, 139, 161, 163, 168, 169, 170, 171, 173, 174, 175, 179, 186, 191, 198, 199, 204, 214, 222, 223, 226, 228, 268, 271, 280, 286, 295, 297, 298
reproductive choices, 20, 317
Return of the Jedi, 19, 20, 25, 29, 32, 36, 37, 185, 207, 262, 265, 282
Revenge of the Sith, 31, 38, 70, 85, 86, 93, 96, 98, 105, 120, 132, 133, 138, 141, 232, 282
Reviving Ophelia: Saving the Selves of Adolescent Girls, viii, 93, 94, 101, 105
revolutionary, 119, 168, 309, 317
Rex, 127, 130, 132, 133, 236
Rey, viii, 58, 66, 86, 87, 119, 184, 185, 186, 187, 188, 194, 195, 197, 198, 202, 205, 207, 208, 209, 211, 212, 223, 255, 257, 258, 259, 271, 272, 276, 319; and backlash, 168, 170, 172, 174, 175; as Mary Sue, 177, 178, 179; costume, 162; in *Forces of Destiny*, 260, 261, 262, 263, 264, 265, 267; in *The Force Awakens*, 161–168; in *The Last Jedi*, 179–184. *See also* fourth wave; giftedness; heroine's journey; lightsaber, Rey's; Mary Sue; Ridley, Daisy; three knobs
Rey's Story, 164, 255
Ridley, Daisy, 22, 163, 165, 168, 172, 175, 176, 179, 182, 215, 261, 265, 326
Rio Durant, 309
Ripley, 4, 274
Riviére, Joan, 52, 66
Robot Chicken, 13
Rogue One, viii, 14, 32, 36, 38, 39, 40, 89, 146, 170, 198, 210, 213, 228, 246, 271, 272, 273, 275, 276, 280, 281, 282, 283, 289, 292, 318
role model, vii, 5, 8, 15, 43, 60, 89, 106, 121, 125, 246, 260, 263, 282
rope swing, 12, 24
Rose Tico, viii, 66, 161, 170, 174, 175, 176, 186–198, 203, 205, 210, 212, 218, 219, 222, 227, 259, 260, 265, 268, 269, 278, 286, 308
Rotten Tomatoes, 175
Ryloth, 127, 145, 228, 233, 234

Saba Sebatyne, 206
Sabine Wren, ix, 227, 228, 231, 233, 236–246, 253, 258, 261, 262, 264, 265, 266; and romance, 237, 240, 245, 246. *See also* graffiti; Mandalorian
Sabine's brother, 243, 245, 266
Sabine's father, 243, 244, 245
Sabine's mother, 243–244, 245
Sana Starros, 205, 283–285, 290
sarcastic, 25, 110, 116, 180, 286, 287
Sariss, 115, 116
Sarlaac, 34
Satine Kryze, 88, 142, 143, 144, 145, 240, 241, 245
Savage Opress, 138, 153, 155
Savareen, 305, 319, 322
Saw Gerrera, 130, 146, 247, 272, 273, 275, 276, 277, 279, 281, 292

Scanlan, Neal (creature designer), 225, 300, 311
Scarif, 39, 279
science fiction, vii, 3, 83, 103, 119, 204, 307, 312
The Screaming Citadel, 289
Sebulba, 80
second wave, 4, 8, 15, 20, 35, 43, 54, 163
Sei Taria, 80
self-rescuing princess, 5, 211
Senate, 6, 38, 39, 40, 47, 48, 50, 51, 53, 54, 59, 60, 62, 65, 71, 73, 86, 89, 90, 92, 99, 101, 102, 143, 207, 209, 233, 248
Seventh Sister, 250, 251
sexist, 45, 52, 84, 103, 130, 145, 176, 179, 208, 282, 316
sexualized, 8, 9, 10, 21, 22, 24, 25, 33, 55, 57, 61, 64, 65, 66, 71, 105, 116, 138, 150, 151, 162, 164, 165, 186, 193, 200, 223, 225, 277, 298, 309, 314, 317, 321
Shaak Ti, 86, 123, 139
Shadow Conspiracy, 142, 143, 144
Shara Bey, 226, 283
Shattered Empire, 226, 283, 292
Shmi Skywalker, 55, 74–79, 80, 81, 212, 244
Showdown on the Smuggler's Moon, 283
The Shu-Torun War, 292
Sio Bibble, 49, 50, 51, 64
Sircar Tiva, 236, 242, 243, 265
Skyguy, 123, 124, 127
slave girls, 23, 24, 32, 35
slaves, 9, 20, 21, 23, 24, 25, 33, 34, 35, 50, 54, 75, 77, 78, 79, 84, 85, 113, 116, 122, 123, 128, 146, 147, 156, 232, 234, 281, 292, 310, 316, 317, 318
Sleeping Beauty, 10, 168
Sly Moore, 81
Smurfette Principle, vii, 13, 14, 27, 275
Snoke, 166, 181, 184, 201, 209
snowsuit, 16, 17, 20
social media, 171, 172, 174, 176, 177, 179, 199, 228
Sola, 69
Solo, 136, 173, 291, 295, 296, 298, 307, 316
sophisticated, 6, 69, 262
space worm, 34

Spaceballs, 11
Special Edition, 33
Spurrier, Si, 284, 286, 287, 288, 289, 291, 292
stablehand, 180, 194, 214
Star Trek, 5, 136, 168
Starkiller Base, 181, 208, 225
Stass Allie, 83
Steela Gerrera, 130, 146, 281
Steinem, Gloria, 4
The Stepford Wives, 316, 318
Stockholm Syndrome, 34, 77
stripped, 22, 232, 305, 318
Sy Snootles, 33

tactician, 6
Tales from Jabba's Palace, 32, 33, 34
Tanaka, 49
Target, 175
Tarkin, 8, 38, 247, 248, 275, 292
Tatooine, 5, 30, 31, 34, 51, 54, 55, 63, 66, 70, 76, 77, 79, 206, 301
Tatooine Ghost, 77, 78, 80, 206
Taun We, 82
tauntaun, 267
teen, 13, 22, 119, 255, 301
teenage, vii, 8, 125, 132, 155, 199, 238, 239, 280
Tenel Ka, 114, 117
Teneniel Djo, 113
thala-siren, 223
third wave, viii, 43, 44, 45, 46, 48, 50, 54, 55–56, 58, 59, 60, 63, 65, 69, 70, 89, 90, 98, 100, 106, 122, 129, 138, 174, 190
Thrawn, 110, 234–235, 236, 239, 245
three knobs, 162
Throne of Blood, 147
Time's Up, 310
Tobias Beckett, 304, 306, 307, 309, 318
tokenism, vii, 260, 319, 322
tooka cat, 263, 291, 292
torture, 6, 7, 8, 19, 25, 78, 106, 143, 154, 155, 156, 286
Toryn Farr, 32
toxic masculinity, 171, 176, 177, 184, 199, 213
Trade Federation, 45, 48, 50, 51, 52, 54, 57, 60, 66, 79, 106, 144, 170, 306

Tran, Kelly Marie, 176, 186, 193, 265
trash compactor, 9, 11, 35, 202, 203, 300
trickster, 8, 288, 292, 312, 320
Triple-Zero, 285–286, 287
Trump's America, 176, 197, 199, 276
tube top, ix, 83, 90, 120
Tusken Raiders, 71, 73, 76, 78, 79, 102
Twi'lek, 23, 33, 34, 45, 80, 84, 116, 138,
    145, 228, 229, 233, 234, 236, 320, 321
Tynnra Pamlo, 281

Union, 10, 49, 111, 205
Unkar Plutt, 178, 265

Vader Down, 28, 287, 290
Val, 295, 296, 307, 308, 309, 317
Vandor, 321, 322
victim, 11, 25, 33, 75, 76, 95, 100, 105,
    115, 147, 176, 181
Vietnam War, 4, 193

Waller-Bridge, Phoebe, 295, 309, 310,
    311, 312, 313, 317
wampa, 104, 261
Watto, 74, 76, 77, 78, 314
wedding: Luke and Mara, 111; Padmé
    and Anakin, 74, 111
Wild Space, 73, 124

Wilkinson, Simon (hand props
    supervisor), 305, 319
Williams, Billy Dee, 169, 296
Winter Celchu, 113, 246
witch, 117, 139, 251, 298
Wonder Woman, viii, 70, 168, 169, 193,
    198
Wonder Woman (2017), viii, 136, 193
Wonder Woman (1970s), 4
Wookiees, 13, 34, 121, 122, 231, 233
Wookieepedia, 175
World of Reading, 257, 258
World War II, 13, 166, 207, 279, 305

Xena, Warrior Princess, 3, 44, 65

Yaddle, 83, 84
Yavin IV, 14, 40, 272, 282
Yoda, 27, 29, 37, 62, 73, 74, 82–84, 88,
    103, 111, 127, 131, 132, 133, 134, 143,
    150, 164, 180, 181, 185, 204, 205, 252,
    253, 259, 263, 265
Young Jedi Knights, 112, 114

Zahn, Timothy, 109, 110, 111, 112, 113
Zam Wesell, 62, 82
Zeb, 228

About the Author

Valerie Estelle Frankel is the author of over sixty books on pop culture, including *Who Tells Your Story? History, Pop Culture, and Hidden Meanings in the Musical Phenomenon Hamilton* and *How Game of Thrones Will End.* Many of her books focus on women's roles in fiction, from her heroine's journey guides *From Girl to Goddess* and *Buffy and the Heroine's Journey* to books like *Superheroines and the Epic Journey* and *Women in Doctor Who.* Once a lecturer at San Jose State University, she now teaches at Mission College and San Jose City College and speaks often at conferences. Come explore her research at www.vefrankel.com.